Open Scotland?

Journalists, Spin Doctors and Lobbyists

Philip Schlesinger
David Miller
William Dinan

POLYGON
AT EDINBURGH

To Ernest and Laraine
PS

In memory of Ena Miller (1926–2000) who lived
to see the implementation of her settled will.
DM

For Ciara, Carol, Kathleen and Mum.
WD

© Philip Schlesinger, David Miller and William Dinan, 2001

Polygon at Edinburgh
An imprint of Edinburgh University Press Ltd
22 George Square, Edinburgh

Typeset in Adobe Garamond
by Textype, Typesetters Cambridge, and
printed and bound in Great Britain by
MPG Books Ltd, Bodmin

A CIP Record for this book is available from the British Library

ISBN 1 902930 28 2 (paperback)

Contents

Part III

List of figures

Biographical information

Philip Schlesinger is Professor of Film and Media Studies at the University of Stirling and Director of Stirling Media Research Institute. He is also Visiting Professor of Media and Communication at the University of Oslo and held the Queen Victoria Eugenia Chair of Doctoral Studies at the Complutense University of Madrid in 2000–1. He is author of *Putting 'Reality' Together* (Methuen, 1987, 2nd edn) and *Media, State and Nation*, and co-author of *Televising 'Terrorism'* (Comedia, 1983), *Women Viewing Violence* (BFI Publishing, 1992) and *Reporting Crime* (The Clarendon Press, 1994). He is an editor of *Media, Culture and Society* journal and a member of the board of Scottish Screen. He is presently working on questions of identity, space and time.

David Miller is a member of the Stirling Media Research Institute. He is the author of *Don't Mention the War: Northern Ireland, Propaganda and the Media* (Pluto, 1994); co-author of *The Circuit of Mass Communication: Media Strategies, Representation and Audience Reception in the AIDS Crisis* (Sage, 1998); co-author of *Market Killing: What the Free Market does and what Social Scientists can do about it* (Longman, 2000); editor of *Rethinking Northern Ireland: Colonialism, Power and Ideology* (Longman, 1998); and co-editor of *War and Words: The Northern Ireland Media Reader* (Beyond the Pale, 1996).

William Dinan is currently working on an ESRC-funded project on 'Corporate Public Relations in British and Multinational Corporations'. He has previously worked on two other ESRC-funded studies based at the Stirling Media Research Institute: 'The Scottish Parliament and Political Communication' (1999) and 'Political Communication and Democracy' (1996–8). He has a BA (Hons) in Sociology and Economics from University College, Cork, and an MSc in Social Research Methods from the University of Surrey. He is currently undertaking a PhD on the role of public relations, market research and advertising in Scottish politics. His research interests include political communication and the promotional industries, public opinion, and research methods.

Preface

Back in 1995, we began research on 'Political Communication and Democracy', an investigation funded by the Economic and Social Research Council (ESRC). At the time, we were convinced that such a study meant analysing Scotland's public domain within the wider frameworks of the UK and the EU. We sensed that the Scottish dimension of political communication was going to become more important, and we were right. That hunch, and the evidence we then began to assemble to substantiate it, was the start of this book. Thus a good deal of the thinking and data-gathering that lies behind the research presented here preceded devolution.

But it was the known imminence of devolution that really gave us the spur, in 1997, to undertake some more intensive work. It was our good fortune, once again, to be funded by the ESRC, in 1999, for work on 'The Scottish Parliament and Political Communication'. We are particularly grateful that the Council could see the point of such research when other funders that we approached (both UK and Scottish) simply could not. Now, suddenly, academic work on the impact of constitutional change in Britain is a serious social science cottage industry. The scales have been lifted from some people's eyes, but in our view, only in part. While some research funders have now grasped the importance of constitutional change, it is still not at all clear that they fully recognise the centrality of communication to this process.

That is where this book comes into the picture. As political sociologists, we have been determined to document and analyse an unrepeatable moment in Scotland during which a new system of political communication has emerged and taken what might prove to be an enduring shape. We believe – and we think we demonstrate it – that the communicative interrelations between media, lobbyists and political institutions are at the very heart of contemporary democratic politics.

The new constitutional settlement of 1999, we thought (and so did many others), might herald a moment of great inventiveness, of innovation, of new solutions to the need for wide engagement in democracy at the Scottish level. We firmly approved of the stated aspirations to create an open political culture, and of the aim of bringing the formal political world closer to the people.

For our part, we would judge that there has indeed been some institutional inventiveness, but that so far it has not produced the open Scotland so much talked about only eighteen months or so ago. What is striking, if our account is accepted, is the extent to which Scotland's system of political communication has been an adaptation of the tried and often mistrusted models of Westminster and Whitehall practice. We have sought to lay bare what has happened in an important corner of national political life so that it can be properly evaluated by others, debated and, if the will and desire are there, changed.

In undertaking this research, we have met with enormous help and great kindness from many individuals. Those we have studied have been passionately interested in our research and its outcomes. We trust they will read this as an honest portrait of a decisive moment, even if they may disagree with some of our interpretations. We have not named all our sources, but they will know who they are. (And, in a small country, many will doubtless think they can put a name to a sentence or two, even if they cannot prove it.) On a few occasions, indicated in the book, we have received more hindrance than help, but those have been the exceptions. Those who are quoted directly are only a small proportion of the more-than-100 people who consented to be interviewed, and reinterviewed, or otherwise pestered. Without their admirable cooperation, we would not have been able to assemble this picture, which we offer as a contribution to the contemporary understanding of post-devolution Scotland, and in due time perhaps it will be seen as a first sketch of very specific history.

Those who have no taste for sociological or political theory should skip the first pages of the introduction and those towards the end of it. Those who are familiar with the contemporary politics of Scotland may skip those in the middle. Of course, those who really wish to understand the context of our analysis will gird their loins and read the lot.

Our formal thanks are due to the ESRC for awards L 126251022 and L 327253003, and to our colleagues at Stirling Media Research Institute for their help and support. Thanks are also due to Sheila Smith for faithfully keeping newspapers for our archive and to Karen Hotchkiss, Louise McKinsley, Gail Clydesdale, Lynne Johnson, Kim Glass, Suzanne Garnham and Laura Smith for transcribing our interviews. Finally, thanks to Annabel Griffin who went through a baptism of fire in the final stages of preparation of this manuscript.

We have completed this work in the month that Donald Dewar, Scotland's first First Minister, met his deeply regretted and untimely end. His presence is certainly felt in these pages, quite fittingly so, as he was the principal architect of a momentous change that has touched us all.

Philip Schlesinger
David Miller
William Dinan

Stirling, November 2000

CHAPTER 1

Introduction

This book analyses the relationships between constitutional change and the reshaping of political and communicative boundaries in the United Kingdom. It does so by exploring what has happened to political reporting, government information strategies, and lobbying in Scotland as the country headed towards – and implemented – political devolution in 1999.

Since the Labour government took power on 1 May 1997, the UK has embarked on a process of constitutional reform, in which Scottish devolution has been accompanied by a transfer of powers to Wales, Northern Ireland and London. The upper chamber of the Westminster Parliament, the House of Lords, has been partially reformed, and debate about some more representative form of government for the English regions is on the political agenda. The European Convention on Human Rights has been incorporated into the UK's legal systems.

Political change has brought significant shifts in patterns of communication in Scotland that have potential implications for the UK as a whole. Relations between the media and the political system have been recast. Devolution in Scotland has offered an exceptional opportunity to study this process at work.

POLITICAL COMMUNICATION AND THE NATION-STATE

Political communication – the purposive communication by political actors about public affairs – conventionally takes the nation-state as its framework. In everyday political life although less and less as devolution takes hold, it is still generally assumed that the UK is a bounded, sovereign polity, with its own national political agenda, communicated by its own national media. This dominant view of the relations between national political space and national communicative space has been theoretically supported by a well-established perspective on nations and nationalism (Schlesinger 2000).

One line of sociological thought has shared a broad concern with how nations speak to themselves, how they mark themselves off as different from others. This argument is to be found in the work of writers such as Karl Deutsch (1966), Ernest Gellner (1983, 1997), Benedict Anderson (1991) and Michael Billig (1995). All share what Deutsch first labelled a 'social communications' perspective whose key premise is that nations are set apart from other collectivities because of the distinctiveness of their internal communications. Consequently, it is held that a given cultural collectivity tends to build up and reproduce a separate national identity over time. While each theorist may point to different factors, it is commonly argued that educational systems, the media, standardised languages or shared cultural practices and symbols are key elements in the historical process of building national culture. Such national cultures and resulting identities are assumed to be both politically underpinned and continually developed by a state.

This underlying assumption has also been shared by the critical theorist Jürgen Habermas (1989) whose influential theory of communication initially took as its framework the nation addressed as a political community. In Habermas' theory, and in the work of the many scholars who have tried to develop it further in recent years (for example, Keane 1991; Mayhew 1997), it is precisely the matter of how to ensure access to communicative power for citizens that has become a central concern.

Much current discussion has centred on the so-called 'public sphere', a term promoted through the English translation of Habermas' work, and now in relatively wide use. This refers to the domain of debate that exists outside the state, but which is centred on the state's activities and engages all who are concerned with matters of public interest. This is the space of 'civil society', where political parties, voluntary associations and organised interests may intervene in the political process. The existence of such a domain – in which the media are also situated – is central to the freedom of expression commonly associated with democracy. Thus conceived, the public sphere presupposes a nation-state in relation to which those who make up civil society can think and organise politically.

The public sphere is therefore commonly seen as co-extensive with nation-statehood. This view affects how we might see the present-day functioning of political communication in the UK, because in reality, the dominant model of the nation-state as a stable, unitary political community in which we speak to ourselves about public affairs is breaking down.

Symptomatic of this reconfiguration is the increasingly voluminous commentary on the difficulties of defining 'Britishness'. An important, and highly visible, part of the New Labour government's politics has been the effort to 'rebrand' the UK. The discourse of modernised Britishness has been the happy hunting-ground of the think-tank intelligentsia (Leonard 1997). Following New Labour's victory, a sequence of events and processes was annexed to the party's aim of effecting a cultural transformation. This included the political appropriation of the sentiments generated by the death of Diana, Princess of Wales, the short-lived selling of 'cool Britannia' as an image of national revitalisation, the quasi-modernisation of the monarchy, and the ill-judged aspirations for an undefined grandeur embodied in the Millennium Dome at Greenwich. All of these have betokened attempts to grapple with a deep-seated problem of collective identity, whose sources arguably lie in the UK's post-imperial drift.

With devolution in Scotland, Wales and Northern Ireland, 'Britain' and 'Britishness' have begun to disaggregate or, at the very least, to be redefined. In the face of the smaller nations' identity claims, and their assertion of distinctiveness through new arenas of representative politics, attempts to characterise 'Englishness' have gathered pace, generating both book-length disquisitions, television series, and increasingly obsessive commentary by newspaper columnists (Paxman 1998; Marr 2000). Along with the reactive concern that devolution has provoked in the English heartlands (at least, among the chattering classes), it seems plain that 'Englishness' will itself be a contested space, with resistance in the north to an exclusively metropolitan, southern definition of the nation. So, whether the first-term programme of New Labour constitutional reform will result in a more united United Kingdom remains to be seen. As a modernising programme, it has certainly been intended to result in a new cohesion of the state, but conceivably it could provoke gradual disintegration.

Views on the likelihood of this are divided. At one end of the spectrum, we find the 'break-up of Britain' thesis, most notably espoused over the past twenty five years by Tom Nairn (1981). In his most recent polemic, Nairn (2000: 76) has argued that the devolution policy of the New Labour government (which took office after eighteen years of Conservative rule) 'is the last ditch at maintaining the United Kingdom' by half-baked constitutional reform. But Nairn is not alone in his assumption that the British state is unlikely to survive in its present form. The historian Norman Davies, in his extensive history of 'the Isles', also argues that the foundations of Britishness are in an advanced state of decay and that break-up may be imminent (Davies 1999: 1053).

Other commentators shy away from the logic of disintegration. The main alternative is the 'recomposition of Britain' line. The political journalist Andrew Marr (2000) has argued that the Scots and Welsh challenge has been provoking a reassertion of Englishness and that this needs to be addressed in order for the Union to survive. Federalism, he believes, offers one solution to the present disarray, a view increasingly shared by others across the political spectrum.

In any case, the complexities of devolution apart, we can less and less sensibly think of the UK as a single political and communicative space. Issues arise, and agendas appear, that derive from the broader political domain of the EU, and these cannot simply be screened out by assertions of British sovereignty. The compelling question of Britain's position on the European single currency, the euro, is the prime illustration of this. The British practice of politics has been steadily 'Europeanised', as Westminster has ceased to be the sole arbiter of decision-making and legislation. Moreover, increasingly, the question of Britain's approach to European integration has the capacity to make and break political parties. After all, longstanding internal divisions over 'Europe' had a decisive role in shattering the Conservatives' long hold over the country both before and during the general election of 1997. And the EU has continued to shape British politics since then.

European integration deeply affects how we think about the nation-state as a locus of political communication, where journalism plays a key role alongside the promotional activities of a range of political actors. As debates about major European policy issues routinely occur in the domestic heartlands of the polity, and are manifestly central to the agenda of British news media, the lines between 'us' (the British) and 'them' (the Continentals) are becoming increasingly blurred.

So, while the EU may be represented by some as external to the British political system, in reality it is increasingly internal to it. The often distance-taking political rhetoric and prevalently negative media coverage obscure this fact (Anderson and Weymouth 1999; Morgan 1999). However, these are surface reactions to a deeper movement. It is hard to see clearly the real, underlying extent of the current change in politico-communicative boundaries, precisely because the way in which the highly complex relationship between the EU and the UK is handled, both politically and in news coverage, varies from moment to moment.

In short, the occupation of British political and communicative space by European matters is undeniable and not just another story. It is integral to the secular melting-down of EU member states' boundaries. The EU has become a key locus for the evolution of a transborder political community centred on its institutions and embodied in a politico-bureaucratic class and its surrounding networks, including elite media and public relations firms (Miller and Schlesinger 2000; Schlesinger 1999). European integration is beginning to have an unevenly distributed impact both on conceptions of citizenship and of collective belonging. After all, since the 1991 Treaty of Union (signed at Maastricht), the category of EU citizenship has existed alongside established national citizenship, and although its precise implications have been a matter of debate, it has introduced a new layer of complexity and of potential loyalty. This may, in time, produce another form of collective identity – 'Europeanness' – for the citizens of member states (Schlesinger 1992).

Political theory is beginning to catch up with the realities on the ground. Habermas (1994; 1997) has written of the EU as itself constituting a complex public sphere, where the historic nation-states articulate with an emergent federal state. This viewpoint neglects the place of 'stateless nations' such as Scotland and Wales, the Basque country and Catalonia. These are regions with a difference: in the words of the sociologist David McCrone (1998: 128), 'territories in which identification with the nation is greater than that with the state of which they are currently a part'. As our research shows, devolution has reinforced and extended a pre-existing Scottish public sphere that both overlaps with that of the UK and is at the same time becoming increasingly distinct within it.

THE UNION

One important factor in understanding Scottish difference within the UK lies in the fact that it is part of a union state. The union of the English and Scottish Crowns was effected in 1603 under the Stuart dynasty of King James VI and I. It was not until a century later, in 1707, that parliamentary union came under Queen Anne's reign: Scotland and England became a single state: the United Kingdom of Great Britain (Colley 1992: 4).

Legal theorists such as Neil MacCormick (1999) have pointed to the divergent constitutional doctrines prevalent in Scotland and England at the time of the union and see these as having continuing significance. Whereas Westminster has adhered to the doctrine of parliamentary sovereignty inherited from the English crown, Scots constitutional reforms have relied on a doctrine of popular sovereignty to legitimise claims for the restoration of parliamentary rule. Given this different conception of the relationship between the people and political power, it may readily be appreciated why – for Scots – the restoration of the Edinburgh parliament in 1999 was an issue of great historical importance, a matter perhaps not adequately understood outside the country.

Scotland has sustained a distinct 'civil society' over three centuries, namely 'the diffuse assemblage of anything and everything which can be located somewhere in between politics and state power on one hand, and the family on the other' in Tom Nairn's disenchanted words (1997: 77). For Nairn, civil society (which holds no mystique) equates to a politically decapitated nation: what is left when the state is removed. It is commonplace in discussion of Scottish civil society to cite the historical importance of the Presbyterian Church of Scotland, of Scots law, of Scottish education – in the form of Scotland's own ancient universities and separate schooling – and to add to this selected elements of a distinctive culture expressed linguistically, musically, and in terms of literature, sport, architecture, painting and much else besides. None of this is to say that Scotland has been closed to influences from south of the border or elsewhere, but it has been different from the rest of the UK. Governmentally, from 1886 until devolution, this distinct civil society had been served by a separate department of state, the Scottish Office. Scotland has long had a distinct voice in the UK Cabinet in the shape of the Secretary of State for Scotland, a post which still survives (although increasingly questioned) in the post-devolution era.

Arguably, if you take the view of the sociologist Lindsay Paterson (1994), Scotland has successfully pursued various forms of autonomy within the British state; devolution is simply the latest form of this. One issue that insistently reappears on the agenda is whether devolution is the prelude to separation. In historical perspective – for instance, that of Norman Davies (1999) – the current crisis of Britishness really began with the partition of Ireland in 1921. From this standpoint, it is no accident today that as Britain devolves power to Scotland, Wales and Northern Ireland, it is also undergoing a transformation of relations with the Irish Republic. The UK's constitutional future is subject to a political experiment, with unforeseeable outcomes.

HOME RULE

'Home rule' for Scotland has been on the political agenda since the mid-nineteenth century. However, the immediate drive towards present-day devolution is rooted in the last third of the twentieth century. It has been the uneven political rise of the Scottish National Party (SNP) that has fuelled present-day concessions to increased political autonomy. In 1967, the SNP won the Hamilton by-election, conventionally acknowledged to be the serious start of the nationalist challenge. The Conservative Party (then in opposition) embraced Home Rule, although it later reversed this policy. In 1974, in the first of two general elections that year, the SNP made a breakthrough as a parliamentary force, gaining 22 per cent of the Scottish vote and winning seven seats at Westminster. The Labour government decided to take up devolution, the new term for home rule. Then, later that year, in the second general election, the SNP took 30 per cent of the vote, winning eleven seats. This rise in support led to the Labour Cabinet producing a White Paper on devolution in the UK in 1975 (Bogdanor 1999: 179).

The historian Tom Devine (1999) has argued that support for nationalism in the 1960s and 1970s was primarily based in a widespread public desire to improve Scotland's position in the Union rather than any desire to break it up. However, Devine has noted the declining appeal of 'Britishness' that accompanied the end of Empire. Like other commentators, he has also observed that the SNP capitalised on anti-nuclear protest and that discontent was focused on the problems of the Labour government's approach to planning and its public expenditure model from the late 1960s on – these being part of the much more widespread crisis of social democracy.

It was the Conservatives' political decline in Scotland that steadily opened a space for the SNP to challenge Labour hegemony. It tends to be forgotten that in 1955 the Conservatives had over 50 per cent of the Scottish vote. From that high ground, they lost support until they were wiped out completely in the 1997 British general election. In 1970, Scotland was still under Conservative rule, although that party held a minority of parliamentary seats in Scotland. The 1970–4 Conservative government shelved its devolution proposals, since it was thought that the nationalist threat had disappeared. But it had not. This was a time of industrial collapse throughout the UK but these problems were especially severe in Scotland. There was also an unpopular incomes policy and anti-trade union legislation. Aside from what were perceived as attacks on Scotland's industrial base and its large working-class population, the ownership and exploitation of the oilfields in Scottish waters became a major issue at a time of oil-production limitations after the Arab-Israeli war of 1973. This combination of issues, both political and economic, pushed devolution to the top of the agenda after the SNP made electoral gains in the two 1974 general elections. For the incoming Labour government, therefore, opting for devolution was premised on stopping nationalism.

However, there were problems for a weak Labour government in securing its devolution proposals and it was forced to hold a referendum as part of its Scotland and Wales Bill. This decision proved fateful as an amendment was passed that stipulated that if less than 40 per cent of the electorate voted 'yes' in the referendum for the Scottish Assembly, the Act would be repealed. The Scotland Act was passed in February 1978 and the referendum held in March 1979. A majority voted for devolution, but because of the low poll, the 40 per cent hurdle was not reached and an assembly was not secured. With the fall of the Labour government shortly thereafter, constitutional issues came off the agenda for some years. The Scotland Act was repealed by the new Conservative government in July 1979 (Denver et al. 2000: 15–25).

The years after 1979 were crucial in building up the momentum to devolution. There was widespread public antipathy to the Conservatives' agenda of monetarism, privatisation, anti-trade unionism, and the restructuring of the welfare state. Scotland's weak economy was especially vulnerable to the new government's policies. There was a major collapse of key industries – shipbuilding, mining, textiles, steel, vehicles and a range of other manufacturing activities. This brought about an increasing shift into financial and public services in the UK in the 1980s and 1990s and Scotland was particularly hard hit by unemployment compared to south of the border.

It was in this context that the SNP began its road to recovery in the 1980s, in which it increasingly defined itself as left of centre. The Conservatives were once again victorious in the general election of 1983, but at this point different patterns of politics in England and Scotland began to be increasingly evident. Labour dominated the parliamentary seats in Scotland, but the Conservatives ruled in London. The constitutional issue was back on the agenda. In the 1987 general election, the Conservatives won only ten seats in Scotland (out of seventy-two), whereas Labour had fifty.

Devine (1999: 606) has commented on this moment as follows:

> Mrs Thatcher disregarded the tradition of the union as a partnership in which Scottish interests had been taken into account and instead seemed to consider there was to be no limit to the absolute sovereignty of the Westminster parliament.

The growing belief that something was wrong with British governance *per se* began to take root in Scotland. In time, this gave rise to a movement for constitutional change and increasing pressure to alter the rules of the game.

After the 1987 election, the Campaign for a Scottish Assembly was formed, drawing together elements of Scottish civil society from the churches, trade unions, universities and business. The underlying aim was to create a Scottish Constitutional Convention. The publication of a *Claim of Right for Scotland* affirmed Scottish distinctiveness within the Union and stressed the need to curb central government power and work on the basis of consent. Its constitutionalist authors rejected any necessary 'tidiness of system' in the UK, accepting that anomalies were inevitable and that these would indeed promote eventual constitutional reform across the board. The convention broadened its base, and was joined by the Labour and Liberal Democrat parties, most local councils, the Scottish Trade Union Congress, the churches, some ethnic minorities, the Green Party, the Communist Party and the Scottish Convention of Women. The SNP stayed outside, as did the Conservatives. In 1990, the Convention recommended the creation of a Scottish Parliament, with proportional representation as an element in its electoral process, thereby making a break with established British practice (Brown et al. 1998: 62–9; Wright 1997: 48–58).

In the 1992 general election, not surprisingly, the constitutional question was once again high on the Scottish election agenda. What were now defined as the 'home rule parties' won 75 per cent of the vote and 85 per cent of the seats. The Conservatives were left with eleven of the seventy-two Scottish seats and faced continuing decline thereafter. In the subsequent general election of 1997, Labour was once again elected and the Conservatives, who had fought on an uncompromising unionist agenda, were completely wiped out north of the border.

The new Labour government's White Paper of July 1997, *Scotland's Parliament*, picked up much of the Constitutional Convention's thinking

(Scottish Office 1997a). A referendum was held in September 1997. In the campaign to win over the Scottish electorate, only the Conservatives opposed the setting-up of the new Parliament. The SNP abandoned its opposition to the creation of a devolved institution and joined the Liberal Democrats and Labour in arguing for it. The voter turn-out was just over 60 per cent: of these, more than 74 per cent voted for the Parliament and over 63 per cent voted for tax-raising powers. The referendum was of profound importance as it redefined Scottish political society as a civic entity: all those resident in Scotland had the vote, irrespective of ethnicity.

The referendum was followed by the Scotland Act of November 1998; which distinguished between 'reserved' and 'devolved' powers. The reserved powers included foreign policy, defence, macro-economics, social security, abortion, and broadcasting (Scotland Act 1998). The devolved powers, however, conceded a major home-rule competence and at present the boundaries of Scottish autonomy are still being explored.

THE SCOTTISH PARLIAMENT

The Scottish parliamentary elections combined the traditional first-past-the-post approach of Westminster with an element of second-preference proportional representation. The turn-out in May 1999 was 58 per cent (significantly lower than the 71 per cent who voted in the 1997 Westminster election). The Parliament has 129 seats, with seventy-three Members of the Scottish Parliament (MSPs) elected for a single-member constituency and fifty-six for eight geographical regions (seven for each region).

The outcome was that Labour fell short of an absolute majority with fifty-six members (fifty-three of whom were elected by first-past-the-post). The SNP was the second party with thirty-five seats (with twenty-eight coming from the regional lists). Proportional representation allowed the Conservatives to stage a come back with eighteen list seats. The Liberal Democrats gained seventeen seats (five on the list) and there were three others. Of especial significance was the fact that 37 per cent of MSPs were women, compared to 20 per cent at Westminster. In this respect, the gender profile of the Scottish Parliament is much closer to the Scandinavian norm than that of the UK. There were no ethnic minority members.

Labour formed a coalition cabinet with the Liberal Democrats, and the SNP became the official opposition. The opening of the Parliament on 1 July 1999 was a very Scottish occasion: the Queen was not enthroned as she would be at Westminster, and compared to the ceremonial in London, the Edinburgh event was relatively low-key. The new body has been quite distinctive – first names are used by members; there is straightforward language; there are no archaic conventions to be drawn on; there is electronic recording of votes and a flexible approach to televising Parliament since electronic media have been welcomed rather than treated with suspicion. The Parliament has a strongly developed education policy as well as a desire to use information technology to connect it to the people.

The thinking behind the Parliament is radical-democratic and was developed by a special all-party body called the Consultative Steering Group (CSG), continuing the civil society tradition of the Constitutional Convention. The CSG was set up in November 1997 by the Secretary of State for Scotland and was tasked with inventing the Parliament's procedures. The underlying philosophy was spelled out in the following principles:

> sharing power with the people and the Executive;
> the accountability of the Executive to Parliament and of Parliament to the people;
> access and participation;
> equal opportunities.

In effect, the CSG's *Shaping Scotland's Parliament* is a kind of informal constitution, a radical departure in the UK, which is a state without a written constitution (CSG 1998b). This constitutionalising process has embodied the aspirations of Scottish civil society, working with the political class and the civil service, to produce something different from Westminster (Paterson 1999).

Arguably, most of the creative thinking about political change was about the Parliament, and hardly any at all concerned the role of the Scottish Executive, which is the seat of governmental and civil-service power in Scotland. This lack of attention has had far-reaching implications for political communication, as we argue below. The creation of a Scottish Parliament and the transformation of the Scottish Office into the Scottish Executive (and the Scotland Office) has provided the key institutional matrix for sociological and political analyses concerned with Scotland as a 'stateless nation'. This study is intended as a contribution to such work.

SCOTLAND'S MEDIA AND NATIONAL IDENTITY

Scotland's media are a crucial element of the country's civil society. They have long been part of the range of institutions constituting the substratum of Scottish distinctiveness within the UK, but seemingly this is so obvious a fact that it has warranted hardly any serious investigation.

In the mainstream sociology and political science of Scotland, the analysis of media has been marginal to say the least. For instance, David McCrone's definitive sociology of Scotland contains one passing mention of the topic

(McCrone 1992: 167), and it is not addressed at all in other important works such as Lindsay Paterson's (1994) study of Scottish autonomy. Even where the question of civil society has been directly considered, as in Jonathan Hearn's (2000: 88–9) analysis of the contemporary nationalist movement, mass media are of tangential interest. Very occasionally, attempts are made within political science to address the significance of media for political change, as in accounts of the referendum campaigns of 1979 and 1997 (Brown 1980; Denver et al. 2000).

In their recent survey of politics and society in Scotland, Alice Brown and her co-authors acknowledge that a 'wider concept' of civil society is needed to accommodate the range of institutions important for preserving Scottish autonomy, over and above the historic ones – the 'holy trinity' as they put it – of the Church of Scotland, Scots law and education. In their list they include 'local government, industry, commerce, the Scottish Office, cultural institutions and the media' (Brown et al. 1998: 3). However, despite this recognition, the media receive a cursory mention rather than any analysis. In its extraordinary disregard for the key role that we would argue the media play in constituting a public sphere, the political sociology of Scotland is of a piece with mainstream theorising on nationalism in general (see Schlesinger 2000). It is as if Scottish media are either so omnipresent as to be invisible, or that their role and impact are simply taken for granted or, again, that they are only worth examining when an exceptional political moment comes along.

Our contention is that mainstream social scientists simply underestimate the routine importance of media in Scottish society. And this is an especially damaging neglect in a small country where elite networks connecting the political class, interest groups, and key media people are manifestly of great importance in shaping the public discourse, determining political careers, and affecting the policy process. Contrary to the prevailing wisdom, we wish to argue that news media in Scotland are, and should now be seen, as quite central to the constitution of the contemporary public sphere and that media more generally should be recognised as a key force within civil society.

In the detailed empirical analysis that follows, we have built upon an existing tradition of work in which a repeated concern has been to demonstrate the distinctiveness of Scotland's media system *vis à vis* that of England and to assert that this is significant for the articulation and maintenance of Scottish national identity, as well as for a range of regional identities in the country (Blain and Hutchison 1993; Hetherington 1989; McInnes 1992, 1993; Meech and Kilborn 1993; Smith 1994). Consistently, it has been argued that media contribute to the Scottish sense of difference within the UK, in short to Scottish national identity.

It has been common to depict the media landscape by enumerating the various newspapers published north of the border and also by describing the television and radio stations operating with a Scottish programming remit

(Lloyd 1987; Linklater 1992). A typical formulation in one standard sociological text goes as follows:

> And the media is ranked by some commentators alongside the original holy trinity as a bulwark of Scottish identity: nine out of every ten newspapers bought on weekdays in Scotland are produced in Scotland for a specifically Scottish market (and seven or eight out of ten on Sundays). This has both reflected a different social and political agenda in Scotland, and also helped to create it.
> (Brown et al. 1998: 3)

From the more detailed accounts written by academic media researchers or produced by journalist commentators, a useful if intermittent history of newspaper circulation and broadcast audience sizes may be derived, all of which serves to underline the distinctive patterns of media production, circulation and consumption in Scotland when compared to the rest of the UK.

Certainly, such work has established a relevant framework for debate. It is plausible to suggest, for instance, that because Scots mainly consume Scottish newspapers, they are daily addressed as Scots by a Scottish agenda and recognise this to be so. It is also reasonable to state that the routine concentration on Scotland as a political, economic and cultural entity by broadcasting north of the border, not least in news and current affairs programmes, also contributes to a self-awareness of Scottish difference within the UK (Kendrick 1990; Brown et al. 1998: 45). Moreover, it has frequently been noted just how much Scottish media concentrate on Scottish affairs compared to those published out of London, a point that underlines the importance of thinking of Scotland as a distinctive communicative space within the wider UK public sphere (Hetherington 1989: 194–5; Kellas 1989: 197–210).

In fact, it is unclear just to what extent the self-conscious identification with Scotland of the Scottish-based press, radio and television promotes a sense of distinctive Scottishness among the public. While some might argue that the media do significantly shape Scottish identity, others have speculated that the distinctiveness of the Scottish media has been shaped by the pre-existing national culture (McInnes 1993). Whatever the precise causal relation, we may assume for present purposes that there is an intimate reciprocal connection between the media consumption patterns of the Scottish public and Scottish national and regional identities. But that does not take us very far along the road of analysing how the Scottish public sphere actually operates.

However, our ignorance does not prevent generalisations from being made about the political role of media in Scotland. Take, for instance, the political scientist James Kellas' remark (1989: 210) that 'There is ample support in the communications media for the operation of an autonomous Scottish political system . . . And the links between the communications networks and the decision-making machinery are close.'

He goes on to write about decision-makers being influenced by press coverage and campaigns, but does not develop any precise analysis of the interactions or processes at work. To the extent that the complex interconnections between the media and the political class have been investigated and described at all, it is by Scottish journalists such as Douglas Fraser (2000b), Murray Ritchie (2000a), Maurice Smith (1994) and Brian Taylor (1999), and not by academics in the social sciences.

Although we agree with those sociologists, political scientists and media researchers who argue that Scotland's press and broadcasting are important actors in the political system, we believe it is now time to go beyond this obvious proposition and begin to analyse what it really means. Thus, to remedy a long-standing neglect, we have undertaken a detailed investigation into how media and journalism interact with both the formal and informal dimensions of the Scottish political system.

COMMUNICATIVE STRATEGIES

The neglect of the media by mainstream political science and sociology has been compounded by a comparable lack of attention paid to the public relations, information, and marketing strategies of government, political parties, and business.[1] If we are interested in such matters we have to turn to the work of journalists, who are much more likely to produce detailed and reflective pieces in the press (or in books) on the activities of spin doctors and others (Ritchie 2000a; Smith 1994).

The neglect of communication in political science is mirrored by media studies' nearly exclusive focus on the media. There is a consequent lack of research on the intersections between media, policy processes, and key organisations such as corporations and pressure groups. Where information management, public relations and news management (or 'spin') have been examined, this has overwhelmingly been from the perspective of journalists. This type of approach, which has shown relatively little empirical interest in the communicative activities of organisations, has been described as 'media-centric' (Schlesinger 1990).

As a counterweight to such media-centrism in research, the present study draws on a relatively new tradition in the sociology of the media: it focuses specifically on the interactions between government, the media, and other organisations in civil society. This approach analyses the communicative and definitional strategies of a variety of political actors: governments, pressure groups, trade unions, corporations (see, for example, Anderson 1993; 1997; Davies 2000a, 2000b; Deacon 1996; Deacon and Golding 1994; L'Etang 1998; Manning 1999; Miller 1993, 1994; Miller et al. 1998; Schlesinger and Tumber 1994).

There is also an increasing volume of research in the US, UK, Australia and New Zealand on the public relations industry and, in particular, its role in corporate power (Beder 1997; Carey 1995; Ewen 1996; Fagin and Lavelle 1999; Fones-Wolf 1994; Hager and Burton 1999; Miller and Dinan 2000; Stauber and Rampton 1995). Research on lobbying is also growing (Miller and Schlesinger 2000; Silverstein 1998).

As yet, however, there is no extensive literature on public relations and government information in Scotland, although the founder of the Scottish documentary movement, John Grierson, played an important role in the origins of public relations in Britain (L'Etang 1999). Our research is intended to start filling that gap. It also aims to add to an understanding of how the communicative strategies of a wide range of political actors affect the formation and transformation of political culture and how power and resources in society are distributed.

We take issue with the still prevalent 'media-centrism' and consequently argue for an empirical examination of the public relations and marketing strategies of political actors. However, at the same time, researchers need to acknowledge the increasing centrality of the media themselves and of communicative action more generally to the constitution, reproduction, and reform of power relations in society.

In short, public relations and promotional strategies are now central concerns of government, business, trade unions, popular movements and even the smallest single-issue protest group. The pursuit of self-promotion parallels, and is intimately intertwined with, the expansion of the role of the media in our society. The need to plan communicative strategies has led to the rise of promotional professionals in advertising, marketing and, especially, public relations, leaving none unaffected by what they produce (Jackall 1994: 7).

THE RISE OF 'PROMOTIONAL CULTURE'

The rise of public relations as an occupation began at the turn of the century in the US and slightly later in the UK. Universal suffrage and other democratic reforms were a key factor in increasing the influence that could be exerted by the people on decision-making. In short, public relations emerged in response to the democratisation that followed increasing social unrest and the rise of organised labour. At the same time, new communication technologies were being developed and it became possible to reach a new mass market.

Public relations work has been at its most intense during moments of crisis. War has been a crucial catalyst. The UK Foreign Office and armed forces first appointed press officers during the First World War (1914–18). The threat of organised labour was another spur to action. In 1919, a covert propaganda agency was set up under Prime Minister Lloyd George to incite hostility against trade unions (Middlemass 1979). Business public relations became important during and after the end of the Second World War (1939–45). An organisation called Aims of Industry was founded by business leaders in 1942–3. This body soon assisted the medical profession in resisting the introduction of the National Health Service and in campaigning against the nationalisation of the sugar and iron and steel industries (Kisch 1964). Since 1945, there has been a significant expansion of information posts in government (Tulloch 1993), both in civil ministries (Crofts 1989) and in colonial counter-insurgency (Carruthers 1995). These developments have led to the rise of the 'public relations state' (Deacon and Golding 1994: 4) and to the emergence of the 'spin doctor' in the political parties (Jones 1995, 1997, 1999). Business PR and PR consultancies have also mushroomed. But it was after the election of Margaret Thatcher's government in 1979 that the PR industry really took off: the PR consultancy sector expanded more than eleven-fold in real terms between 1979 and 1998 (Miller and Dinan 2000).

It was only in the 1970s that organisations such as trade unions started to appoint PR officials and prioritise media relations (Jones 1986). Since the 1970s there has been a change in the character of protest. Mass marches and demonstrations have become less popular and are increasingly seen as ineffective (Engel 1996; Porter 1995). As other avenues for influence or change have closed, the media have become more important as a means for influencing public opinion. Pressure groups and other campaigners have been forced to try to devise media strategies in order to pursue their aims. Radical or countercultural movements increasingly understand the value of focused actions likely to have televisual appeal (Grant 1995; Vidal and Bellos 1996).

In Scotland, the pace of change in government and among corporations has evidently been more sedate than south of the border. However, PR and lobbying activities in Scotland have increased dramatically in the past twenty years, as we show. Those two decades have seen the setting-up of PR and lobbying consultancies and increasing involvement by state and public-sector bodies in PR work alongside the private sector.

POLITICAL COMMUNICATION: A PERSPECTIVE

In this study, we have assumed that Scotland is a distinctive communicative space in its own right, while, at the same time, recognising that Scottish readers, viewers and listeners are also part of the wider British public domain.

By studying a key moment of change – in effect, the far-reaching modification of an existing political system as a result of devolution – we have been able to show how new rules of the game have been invented and, at the same time, to demonstrate how wider constraints have operated in the reshaping of Scottish political communication.

This is the first-ever full-scale, fieldwork-based study of how the media interrelate with government news managers and the world of lobbyists in Scotland. We are therefore breaking new academic ground at precisely the moment that Scotland's political structures have changed so profoundly. Our aim is to shift the focus away from a rather tired and unsubstantiable thesis about the media's role in sustaining national identity (as if there could be some unilinear effect of this kind) to a more precise understanding of how political communication is conducted in a nation that now enjoys enhanced autonomy within a larger state.

NOTES

1. There is research in political science on 'political communication', but this is largely confined to studies of election campaigning and the use of public relations by political parties (Crewe and Gosschalk 1995; Crewe and Harrop 1989; Kavanagh 1995; Maarek 1995 and, in the Scottish context, Denver et al. 2000). A partial exception is Scammell (1995), who includes chapters on government information. There is also a separate subfield of political science on interest and pressure groups (see Grant 1995; Greenaway et al. 1992; and Kellas 1989, on Scotland) and a smaller one specifically on lobbying (Greenwood 1997; Jordan 1991; Moloney 1996). This work has much to teach us about the strategies of political actors in society, but both types of work tend to leave the promotional strategies of government out of the picture and tend not to examine the specifically communicative dimension of strategy. Consequently, the role of public relations and 'spin' normally merits only passing mention, as does communication more generally (Miller 1999).

Part I

Journalists

In the chapters that follow, we offer a portrait of contemporary Scottish political journalism. Our account focuses on the political press and on broadcasting, particularly the BBC. We seek to show how Scotland's indigenous news media have adapted to change, and how that change has itself been shaped by the wider British context, both in terms of professional beliefs about how the job is to be done and the inheritance factor of existing practices and institutions. In that respect, both establishment beliefs about the BBC as a UK-wide institution (Chapter 2) and the practices of Westminster Lobby correspondents (Chapters 3–5) have been particularly important in shaping developments in Scotland.

However, before we enter into the detail, we wish to give a brief description of the most salient aspects of the media landscape. Our study presupposes at least some familiarity with the Scottish scene, but for those readers who do not have this, we provide a thumbnail sketch. This is the background to our analysis of how political communication actually works, but no more than that.

Scotland is characterised by the complex interrelatedness of its politics, lobbying and media, and the smallness of scale of the country's elites. Early in 2000, the *Sunday Herald* produced a 'power map' of these connections, which we reproduce (see Figure 1). As the paper's political editor, Douglas Fraser (2000b: 5), commented:

> Although the media can be reluctant to analyse or even accept that its role is any more than that of an objective observer, its networks are formidable. When Scotland is described as a village, it is politicians and journalists who inhabit its main streets and often together.

Fraser went on to note the role of both major broadcasters – BBC Scotland and Scottish TV – in training politicians and 'as the arena into which former politicians and activists switch'. He also commented on the number of politicians with journalists as partners and the close network of media-

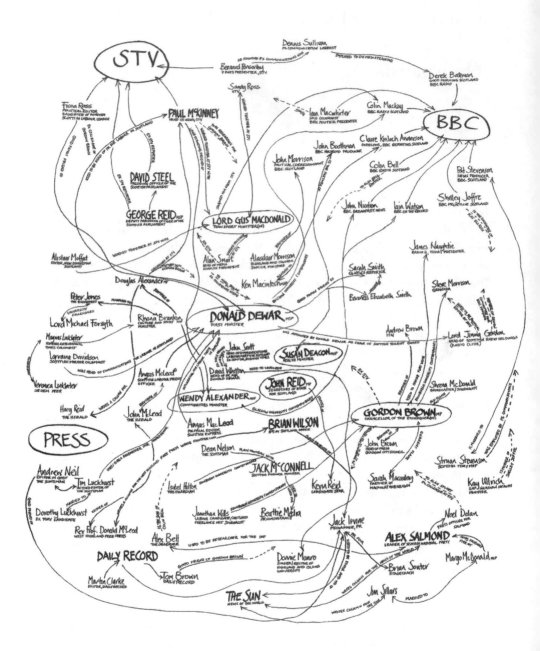

Figure 1 The *Sunday Herald*'s power map shows the close connections between Scotland's political and media elites. The late Donald Dewer was at the centre of this network in 2000. Intriguingly, neither Henry McLeish, his successor as First Minister, nor Peter MacMahon, his official spokesman, are anywhere to be found.

political-lobbyist friendships, stressing the role of the Labour Party as Scotland's political establishment and its dominance within these networks.

A few key media organisations do have a major influence in political life, among which are: BBC Scotland; SMG (formerly Scottish Media Group) which owns Scottish TV, Grampian TV, *The Herald* and *Sunday Herald*; the *Daily Record*, owned by Trinity Mirror; Scotsman Publications, which owns *The Scotsman* and *Scotland on Sunday*. There are also a few key individuals with personal influence who stand or stood at the junction-points of a complex web of interrelations, friendships and obligations. A pivotal figure was Donald Dewar, the late First Minister. Gordon Brown, Chancellor of the Exchequer and Gus Macdonald, UK Transport Minister and formerly chairman and managing director of Scottish TV, remain prominent.

Influential networks do not equate to conspiracies able to 'fix' things. On the contrary, they may – and often do – contain sharp lines of internal division. The point we make is a different one: the key media in Scotland's public sphere and the most active and influential components of its civil society operate on a very small scale. If you inhabit a particular elite political or cultural world in Scotland, you continuously encounter those within it with a frequency and intensity quite different from the interactions that take place in larger countries with major metropolitan centres. Moreover, these worlds are hard to penetrate and have a tendency towards closure and self-protection.

THE PRESS

Scotland presently has the most competitive newspaper market in the UK. Aside from competition between indigenous titles, it has felt the impact of cost-cutting strategies and the pursuit of market share by newspapers from south of the border. The Scottish press comprises long-established Scottish titles as well as the Scottish editions of UK national newspapers headquartered in London. Nationals that do not produce editions specifically for Scotland also circulate in the country. In fact, the use of the term 'national press' is rather complicated: as Meech and Kilborn (1993: 258) have pointed out, in one sense Scotland's national media are located north of the border but 'within a UK framework of ownership control, finance and regulation'.

Newspaper readership and sales figures are crude indicators and tell us little of the meanings attributed to what is read. But they do offer evidence of the distinctiveness of Scottish consumption patterns. The following sketch draws upon data from the Audit Bureau of Circulation (ABC), January to June 2000, and the National Readership Survey (NRS), July 1999 to June 2000.

Scotland has a long-established daily broadsheet press in the shape of *The*

Herald (Glasgow) and *The Scotsman* (Edinburgh). Jointly, these newspapers still dominate the elite opinion-leading market in, respectively, west and east central Scotland, the belt in which most of the population is concentrated. At the time of writing, both newspapers' sales were around 100,000. Between them, the London broadsheets – *The Guardian, The Independent, The Daily Telegraph, The Times* – were selling around 80,000 copies (McGinty, 2000a: 4–5) Thus, more than twice as many Scottish broadsheets circulate than do those from London, with *The Herald* and *The Scotsman* reaching half a million readers, whereas the London papers are read by some 200,000.

These differences underline a general point that applies across the press and broadcasting: there is a distinct news agenda in Scotland that is addressed in detail only by the Scottish media. The country therefore has its own space of political communication although, of course, this is also shaped by the wider flow of news in the UK as a whole, and beyond.

The popular end of the daily newspaper market also diverges from the rest of Britain. It is still led by the tabloid *Daily Record* (Britain's oldest popular daily newspaper). In the six months to September 2000, although circulation had been falling, the paper still sold, on average, almost 620,000 copies (*Press Gazette* 2000: 7) and its readership was over 1.6 million. The *Record* has been losing ground to the *Scottish Sun*, its only serious rival in this market sector. In the same period, the *Sun* was selling about 400,000 copies, with a readership of more than 1.1 million. Against these front-runners, the *Daily Mirror* and the *Daily Star* between them mustered only 100,000 sales and fewer than a quarter of a million readers.

In recent years, the middle market has been increasingly prone to penetration by the Scottish editions of London newspapers. Both the *Scottish Daily Mail* and the *Scottish Daily Express* have significant readerships: the *Mail* a quarter of a million, the *Express* some 220,000. In January–June 2000, their combined sales were in the region of a quarter of a million. Their undeniably significant reach needs to be considered in relation to the continuing 'city state' character of Scotland's press. Mid-market tabloid circulations are almost matched by those of regional broadsheets: Dundee's *Courier* and Aberdeen's *Press and Journal*, each of which sells in its own regional market in numbers comparable to *The Herald* in the west of Scotland, or *The Scotsman* in the east. But *The Courier* and *The Press and Journal* are not regarded as 'national' papers in the same way as those of the central belt.

Popular Sunday newspaper sales are also markedly dominated by Scottish titles. In the period July 1999–June 2000, the *Record's* stable-mate, the *Sunday Mail*, was read by over 1.8 million, and the *Sunday Post* by almost 1.8 million. The only southern popular title to come close was the *News of the World*. The quality end of the market is led by *Scotland on Sunday*, with sales of over 100,000, followed by the *Sunday Times, Scotland*, with the newcomer the *Sunday Herald* gradually building its market share at some 54,000, and an estimated readership of 136,000.

The daily and Sunday Scottish press penetrates everyday life. To succeed in winning market share, papers headquartered in England have had to adapt by producing increased amounts of Scottish content: in effect, to become perceived as Scottish. The campaign for devolution was a good instance of this effect. The topic generated exceptional media interest north of the border, especially so when compared with coverage in the London-based press and broadcasting (Denver et al. 2000). Subsequently, this distinctive pattern of attention was sustained during the reporting of the devolution White Paper, the devolution referendum, the debate over the Scotland Bill, and Scotland's first parliamentary election campaign. The constitutional question has been omnipresent in Scotland's reporting and commentary whereas, understandably, it has occupied comparatively little attention in the London-based media. Moreover, the focus on Scotland has perceptibly increased since 1999, as the Scottish Parliament has assumed a major role in national life. The market still remains attractive for new launches: as this book is being written, *Business a.m.*, financed by the Swedish Bonnier group, has entered the daily quality market.

EDITORS AGAINST THE GRAIN

Two figures were on the margins of the *Sunday Herald*'s 'power map': Andrew Neil, appointed editor-in-chief of Scotsman Publications in October 1996, and Martin Clarke, editor-in-chief of the *Daily Record* and *Sunday Mail* from April 1998 to August 2000. Both were outsiders to the intricate networks described (Fraser 2000: 5).

Neil was brought in to run Scotsman Publications – which groups *The Scotsman, Scotland on Sunday*, and the Edinburgh *Evening News* – by its proprietors, the reclusive millionaires Frederick and David Barclay. His appointment caused a stir, given the long-standing commitment to devolution of *The Scotsman* and *Scotland on Sunday*. His adamant opposition to independence and dismissive views of Scotland's political culture went back to his time at the *Sunday Times* which had consistently attacked devolution in its Scottish edition (Smith 1994: 180, 181). Neil's appointment brought astringent questioning to the devolution project and the new political institutions, and he summed up his mission thus:

> I had laid down that our titles must be broadly in favour of the market economy, defenders of the union between Scotland and England and prepared to tackle head on the many outdated Scottish shibboleths and collectivist attitudes which still dominate politics north of the border. None of this

conflicted with backing Blair . . . [who] . . . himself told me he hoped I might
be able to stir things up.
(Neil 1997: xvii–xviii)

The Scotsman has resorted to a long-running price war to expand its market
share and Neil's tutelage has remained controversial. Martin Clarke was the
editor of *The Scotsman* who first implemented Neil's editorial policies in
1997, before departing for the *Record* and the *Sunday Mail* in April 1998.
Historically, the *Record* had always favoured Labour and the trade unions.
Under Clarke's editorship, the Record campaigned against the Labour Party's
policies on a number of issues, most notably and damagingly over Section
28. The paper also vigorously took the Scottish Parliament to task as is
discussed later. Clarke was finally ousted by the paper's proprietors, Trinity
Mirror, for both commercial and political reasons (Nutt 2000: 12).

DEVOLUTION AND MEDIA OWNERSHIP

In the pre-election year of 1996, Caledonian Newspapers, owner of *The
Herald* and the Glasgow *Evening Times*, was taken over by Scottish Television
(rebranded as Scottish TV in 2000), the ITV central Scotland licensee. Gus
Macdonald, then executive chairman of Scottish Television, played the
Scottish card, arguing that combining the businesses would avoid decision-
making power being sucked down to London.[1] This was a key step in the
formation of the Scottish Media Group (rebranded as SMG in 2000, to
signal its UK-wide holdings). Over a five-year period, SMG has become a
multimedia group, with UK-wide advertising, television and radio interests.
In 1999, the group launched the *Sunday Herald*, which was added to what
are now called Scottish Media Newspapers.

Scottish Television's other growth-point was in television. In June 1997,
just after the UK general election, the Glasgow-based company, holder of the
central Scotland license and Scotland's major commercial broadcaster, bid
successfully for Grampian Television, broadcaster to the north of Scotland.
The takeover, in November 1997, brought 4.7 of the 5.1 million Scottish
ITV viewers within SMG's purview.

As a result, concern was expressed in the north about a concentration of
television ownership, job losses, and the possible loss of a regional
programming identity for Grampian viewers. In May 2000, an inquiry by
the regulator, the Independent Television Commission (ITC), found that
regional services had declined over the past two years and promised to
monitor SMG's activities closely to ensure improved regional output
(Forsyth 2000: 9).

When still at the helm of Scottish Television in 1996, Gus Macdonald argued for 'country' membership of the ITV network – in effect, for a looser, affiliate status. The aim was to reduce Scottish TV's commitment to the network, paying only for the programmes it wanted. Around this time, the company's spokesmen also suggested that it might opt out of network programming to cover the Edinburgh parliament. They floated the idea that a Scottish news at 6pm delivered by the early evening flagship programme, *Scotland Today*, might be combined with UK and international stories in a sixty-minute programme. This proposal challenged the London-based ITN's statutory role in supplying identical UK-wide news to all commercial television contractors. However, as devolution approached, these arguments were quietly shelved by the commercial station and instead became the mission of BBC Scotland, with consequences that we explore below in Chapter 3. In fact a 6pm news came about, not in the expected form, but rather as a result of the knock-on effect of network scheduling changes. When ITN's News At Ten was taken off the schedules in 1999, this affected the 6–7pm hour, in which regional news at 6.30pm had followed ITN's 6pm broadcast. When ITN moved its evening news to 6.30pm, Scottish, Grampian and Border, like other ITV stations, were all forced to move their evening news programmes to 6pm.

SMG has consistently opposed vesting any regulatory powers in Edinburgh, and the BBC, Channel 4 Television and the ITC have taken a similar view. The Scotland Act 1998, which has established the division of powers between London and Edinburgh, treats broadcasting as a matter 'reserved' for Westminster's legislation.

From a UK perspective, the Scottish-Grampian merger was small beer and merely part of a flurry of government-facilitated takeovers in the ITV sector. Since the latter half of the 1990s this has led to the domination of two big players (Granada and Carlton) south of the border. However, in a small country, a unique multi-media concentration has both a good deal of influence and considerable political visibility.

The remaining Scottish ITV audience is catered for by Border Television, whose transmission area straddles the south of Scotland and the very north of England. Border is presently controlled by Granada Media Group, also a major shareholder in SMG. As ownership in ITV becomes increasingly concentrated, the continued independence of SMG remains in question (Reed 2000: 55; Teather 2000a: 34) despite denials to the contrary.

Channel 4, which has a public service remit, has set up its nations and regions headquarters in Glasgow, to encourage the growth of programmes commissioned outwith London. So far as the other UK terrestrial television network, Channel 5, is concerned, devolution has had no discernible impact.

Commercial radio in Scotland is dominated by Scottish Radio Holdings (SRH): its stations Clyde 1 and 2 have a weekly reach of 1.1 million listeners, some 34 per cent of the audience (Reed 2000: 55; RAJAR 2000: 4). SRH also owns Radio Forth, Radio Tay, NorthSound Radio, WestSound Radio, Moray Firth Radio and Radio Borders. Scot FM, owned by the London-based Wireless Group plc, is dwarfed by SRH in Scotland, reaching 437,000 listeners.

It remains to be seen whether the peculiarities of Scotland's media will be addressed by the Communications White Paper 2000 and subsequent legislation. At present, rules designed to regulate media concentration and audience share in the UK-wide market prevail – these were simply not designed to take account of Scotland considered as a political entity.

THE BBC AND THE WEIGHT OF BRITISHNESS

Although broadcasting remains a 'reserved' power, the BBC has undergone extensive public debate about its role in a devolved Scotland. In Chapter 3, we reveal the tenacity of a key institution with an exceptional status in the UK. Not only is the BBC the largest public-service broadcaster, and therefore the inevitable focus for debate about what 'public service' means, it also bears the weight of its unique history as a broadcaster that has always been proximate to the British state. For three-quarters of a century it has been the official bearer of nationhood and therefore seen as having a weighty role in the formation of 'national' – that is, British – identity.

This mission has never been simple and has often been contested. The historians of broadcasting Paddy Scannell and David Cardiff have noted that by the 1930s the BBC had established a pattern of 'national' and 'regional' programmes:

> There was . . . a continuous tension arising from the hegemony of *English* culture and resistance to its imposition in Scotland, Wales and Northern Ireland . . . The term 'regional broadcasting' as applied to Scotland, Wales and Northern Ireland was a misnomer which helped to blur political issues that reached well beyond broadcasting.
> (Scannell and Cardiff 1991: 333)

Centre-periphery relations have remained a sensitive and inherently contentious matter. In the BBC's Scottish headquarters at Queen Margaret Drive in Glasgow, there has been a long-standing history of mistrust of decision-making in London. Alasdair Milne, a former Director-General of the BBC, has recounted various instances of 'suspicions of English manipulation' in the late 1960s and early 1970s, when he spent almost five years as Controller of BBC Scotland. He has written of 'the need to rebuild a mutual trust with London' (Milne 1988: 52) and of concern in both the Conservative and Labour parties that 'there was a strong SNP cell in Queen

Margaret Drive' in 1968, at a time of increasing nationalist aspirations (Milne 1988: 50).

During the failed attempt at devolution in the late 1970s, major problems arose for Alastair Hetherington, then Controller, BBC Scotland. A committed devolutionist, Hetherington waged an unsuccessful campaign to bring about a measure of decentralisation inside the BBC, in line with the expected devolution of political powers. There was fervent opposition to this policy by successive directors-general and the corporation's board of management, who were adherents of the 'One BBC' approach, a nostrum still invoked today. As Michael Leapman (1986: 90), one of the BBC's chroniclers, has noted, 'The traditional corporation standpoint is that the BBC can sustain its legitimacy only by exercising firm control from the centre.' Hetherington's critique of centralism and his proposal for 'mini-devolution' in Scotland led him to fall foul of his superiors in London and to his forced resignation, a cautionary tale still embedded in the folk memory of the BBC's northern outpost (Hetherington 1992).

This history is bound to replay itself because, as Leapman (1986: 95) observes, 'recurrent pressure for regional autonomy is a symbol of a fundamental fault in the BBC's organisational structure'. In the present phase of devolutionary politics in the UK, the difficulties of the 1970s have returned to haunt the BBC, exposing the way in which centralised control continues to be exercised and throwing light once again on its consequences for decision-making in the periphery.

As the date for devolution drew closer, BBC Scotland, and the corporation more generally, had to decide on the appropriate journalistic response to major constitutional change. Even if its management wished to, Glasgow could not easily effect a semi-detached relationship to London. Like its counterparts in Wales and Northern Ireland, BBC Scotland has historically operated as a 'national region' within a unitary corporation. Each 'national region' has had a special Broadcasting Council to act as a policy forum, and its own controller and senior management, with lines of responsibility to London.[2]

Although it is the only pan-Scottish terrestrial news and current-affairs broadcaster, the BBC's Scottish radio and television services differ. BBC Radio Scotland is a general national station – a rarity these days – and has no single direct competitor in Scotland, although it does compete with commercial local radio. The station has had a broad remit since being launched in 1978 in anticipation of a Scottish Assembly. While Radio Scotland's news and current affairs coverage has its detractors, it is nonetheless wide-ranging, and puts a distinctive Scottish slant on the stories and issues covered. Radio Scotland's *Good Morning Scotland* operates as the equivalent of Radio 4's *Today Programme*, attracting more than twice the audience of the networked programme. In ways analogous to the Scottish broadsheet press, Radio Scotland's morning news programme has a major agenda-setting role.

BBC Television Scotland provides a distinct news service and current-affairs programmes, as well as drama, music, comedy and sport. However, by contrast with the comprehensive Scottish national radio service, it takes the bulk of its programming from the two UK-wide BBC networks, opting out with specific programmes for Scottish viewers. It also supplies network programming, notably drama and comedy. While the Scottish ITV stations have specific regional remits within Scotland, the 'national regional' BBC Scotland takes the whole country as its territory in news and current affairs coverage, such as the early evening flagship news programme, *Reporting Scotland*, and the current affairs programme, *Frontline Scotland*.

The BBC's role under a devolved Parliament was summed up thus by the Controller, BBC Scotland, John McCormick: 'Our aim is to ensure that we provide an unrivalled journalistic service that matches the new pattern of governance of the UK' (McCormick 1997: 26). The centrality of journalism both accords with the corporation's public-service mission and the BBC's global strategy of developing its presence as a news and information provider. McCormick made it clear that the corporation was going to retain its unitary structure. At the same time, the BBC recognised that its activities would be properly scrutinised by the Scottish Parliament,[3] but this was not seen as replacing the existing form of accountability through the Board of Governors to the Secretary of State for Culture, Media and Sport.

Devolution has once again forced the corporation to redefine its mission and to specify how it sees 'the nation'. All of that, however, has taken place within a firm commitment to holding the state together. In Chapter 2, we trace the process of planning for devolution and show some of the forces in play inside the BBC, in particular elucidating the tensions between London's centralism and Scotland's push for a certain measure of autonomy.

A SCOTTISH LOBBY?

The Scottish media and broadcasters have been remarkably effective at achieving their aim of shaping the new Scottish system of political communication by dint of lobbying, with no significant publicly-aired dissent or criticism. A political media pack installed itself rapidly on the new Parliament's campus. The rhetoric that preceded this implantation into the heart of the devolved political system was a critical one. Arrangements with both the Executive and the Parliament would be quite different from those prevailing in London, so we were told. This would not be a Lobby, because that was unsuited to the new Scotland. The new Scottish political journalism was being defined more by what it was not than by what it actually was. But now, as we turn to an examination of the details of their practice, is it really the case that Scotland's political journalists have made a break of principle with a British model well over a century old?

The Times's political editor, Peter Riddell, has characterised Lobby correspondents thus:

> Lobby correspondents are, in practice, the main political news reporters of a newspaper . . . Their distinguishing feature is that they cover politics from their offices in the press gallery at Westminster, covering the Prime Minister, the government, the Opposition, the political parties and Parliament. The term, 'the Lobby', refers to the list of accredited correspondents kept by the Serjeant at Arms who are allowed access to the members' lobby and some adjoining areas.
> (Riddell 1999: 26)

The Lobby has been recurrently criticised since the sociologist Jeremy Tunstall (1970) first analysed it in his classic study. Under the governments of Margaret Thatcher (and the tutelage of her press secretary, Bernard Ingham), the Lobby system became a matter of increasing contention. The political communications researcher Bob Franklin has summed up the pre-New Labour state of play:

> First, the Lobby has been transformed from a group of journalists with a disparate set of competitive interests into a *collective*, ready-made press conference, which is briefed *en masse*. Secondly, the Lobby has been appropriated by government as a conduit for information and, in this process metamorphosed from an active and critical observer of political affairs into a passive purveyor of government messages. Finally, the Lobby has witnessed the codification of a set of rules enforcing non-attribution of news sources while simultaneously obliging journalists to rely on a single source, usually the Prime Minister's Press Secretary.
> (Franklin 1994: 86; also see Cockerell et al. 1984)

Whether the Lobby was ever as independent as this sketch suggests is a moot point. At all events, we would not dispute Franklin's (1994: 86) view that it is now 'a cartel for the provision of political information'. With the advent of New Labour and the apotheosis of 'spin doctoring', critics say that political news management through the Lobby has intensified. The Lobby system is centred on the Prime Minister's official spokesman or press secretary. Alastair Campbell, the present incumbent, or his deputy, holds two daily meetings with accredited journalists and broadcasters who are briefed about the government's line on major issues. The main Lobby briefing each week is on Thursdays, following the morning Cabinet meeting. The press secretary also chairs the weekly meeting of information officers who coordinate the presentation of government policy across Whitehall.

The House of Commons has been described by ITN's former political editor, Michael Brunson as:

> a formidably difficult place for new arrivals. The atmosphere of the gentleman's club pervades it, and with it goes the unwritten rule, especially among the journalists who work there, that you are not truly admitted to its workings until you have somehow proved yourself. Information seeps out of the woodwork, and what formal notice there is about what is actually going on, even about such simple things as the calling of briefings or the timing of press conferences, is completely haphazard.
> (Brunson 2000: 136)

Aside from disparaging this clubby and secretive ambience, critics of the Lobby have argued that journalists become complicitous with the system; that they allow themselves to be used by ministers for the kite-flying of policies; and that they become a conduit for misleading information (Franklin 1994: 87–8; McNair 1995: 136–7).

Certainly, not being privy to Lobby briefings can be a disadvantage, as *The Guardian*, *The Independent* and *The Scotsman* found in 1986, when – for a while – they excluded themselves from the process on principle. The sense of deprivation this can induce is captured by Michael Brunson (2000: 138), who says: 'The Lobby system is very easy to criticise, but the plain fact is that, if you are not in the loop at Westminster, you can be at a considerable disadvantage.'

Scottish debate has used Westminster insider culture as its foil. Those journalists who disliked the Lobby described it as the epitome of secrecy, as closed and archaic, and as not at all suited to the brave, new democracy being built in Scotland. But, as we shall see, not all journalists shared this view.

Most public argument about the Westminster system has centred on the briefings emanating from Downing Street. The practice's defenders, such as Margaret Thatcher's press secretary, Bernard Ingham (1991: 158), have argued that off-the-record, unattributable briefings are a good way of opening up government to the media. During Ingham's period, the Prime Minister's spokesman was not directly sourced in reports, but instead referred to obliquely. This obfuscatory style has been criticised as perpetuating Britain's culture of secrecy (Harris 1991) and more specifically of allowing the government to manipulate journalists for its own purposes (Cockerell et al. 1984). Moreover, as *The Guardian*'s David Walker (2000: 237) has observed, journalists have been notably uncritical of their own practice:

> The exercise of 'investigative journalism' rarely extends to the relationships of journalists with each other, with politicians or proprietors. When 'Drapergate' broke in the summer of 1998 (*The Observer* 5 July 1998) coverage of the

suspicious dealings of lobbyists and politicians was sharp and voluminous; but the related ethical position of journalists in their dealings with politicians, special advisers and the corporate sector escaped attention. The irony of 'lobbying' alongside the existence of an institution called the Lobby (the association of newspapers and other media political specialists based at Westminster), was missed, and not for the first time.

Those who aver that the Lobby has changed have concentrated specifically on the New Labour style of news management. A typical statement comes from Michael Brunson:

> All Lobby briefings by Number Ten are now on the record, attributable to the Prime Minister's official spokesman, though they cannot be recorded for use on radio and television. This was one of the first changes Alastair Campbell introduced after Labour's 1997 election victory. It provides, in my view, a useful halfway house between open-to-all briefings and the old, closed, secretive system of the past. It helps to guard against any abuse of the system by the Government, and it means that contact between Government and the press can take place in a more relaxed and business-like manner than if every word uttered was available for radio and television transmission.
> (Brunson 2000: 137)

This is to be easily satisfied with a minor concession. But like most Scottish newspaper journalists that we interviewed, Brunson is an opponent of on-the-record and recorded briefings. He observes, not implausibly in the light of this study and others, and in what is evidently a widespread professional belief, that however open things may seem in public, 'off-the-record briefing for individual journalists would still continue' (Brunson 2000: 137).

Peter Riddell (1999: 27) goes further beneath the surface. He maintains that the masonic characteristics of the Lobby, noted by Tunstall thirty years ago, have now largely disappeared 'under the influence of a younger generation of political editors; a big increase in the size of the Lobby to 230; the increasing domination of broadcasters with their need for more explicit attribution'. He notes, as have many others, the attribution of Downing Street's utterances to the Prime Minister's spokesman, although these briefings are not held on camera. But, in the same vein as Brunson, Riddell goes on to argue that collective briefings are of no great importance (1999: 28). What does remain crucial are the 'close relations, and unattributable conversations, which Lobby journalists often have with politicians and their advisers'. Riddell's key point (1999: 30) is that Parliament is increasingly being bypassed so that,

> the real challenge to the position of Lobby correspondents comes from the shift of power away from Westminster – to the broadcasting studios, to the

courts, to European institutions, to the new devolved assemblies in Scotland and Wales, to new semi-independent regulators.

So far as devolution is concerned, Riddell notes that political journalists in Scotland and Wales are 'consciously looking at new ways of reporting politics – though, so far, the changes in practice have been more modest than the rhetoric about a new open style' (1999: 31). As we detail below, this cautious view seems generally correct.

Although the changing nature of media markets and the constitution have undoubtedly modified how the political Lobby works, there has been no convincing riposte to those who argue that its central principle remains unchanged – namely that of collective, regulated, privileged access to government for a limited number of journalists. As in London, so too in Edinburgh has this prize of proximity been pursued.

NOTES

1. Macdonald was subsequently ennobled by the Labour government following a series of appointments to quangos and a CBE for services to broadcasting. He became Scottish Office Minister for industry some months prior to the Scottish general elections and then Minister for Transport in the UK government. Some observers saw in his political rise the hand of Gordon Brown as sponsor and former colleague at STV (Allardyce and Martin 1998).
2. In a significant move, as devolution approached, the BBC abolished the 'national region' designation and in November 1998 renamed its directorate 'National and Regional Broadcasting', thereby acknowledging the 'national' status of Scotland and Wales (Northern Ireland, of course, remaining a special case). In this, the BBC followed Channel 4's nomenclature. The curiosity now is that England is not seen as a nation but rather as an agglomeration of regions.
3. Although the extent of this scrutiny is limited to the submission of the BBC annual report to the relevant Parliamentary committee and making the controller of BBC Scotland available to appear before it.

CHAPTER 2

Devolution and the BBC

GEARING UP FOR DEVOLUTION

Once the government had published its devolution White Papers on Scotland and Wales in July 1997, the BBC began its planning process. The corporation set up a steering group under the joint aegis of the Chief Executive, Broadcast (Will Wyatt) and the Chief Executive, News (Tony Hall). Membership included Mark Byford (Controller, Regional Broadcasting), John McCormick (Controller, BBC Scotland), and Geraint Talfan Davies (Controller, BBC Wales). The steering group oversaw the activities of four working groups, three of which were chaired by senior members of BBC Scotland's staff. These working groups were to examine: (1) coverage of the Scottish Parliament and Welsh Assembly; (2) daily news coverage; (3) weekly current affairs; and (4) political programmes and news gathering. Each review went into considerable detail. On the basis of the information at our disposal, we analyse the work of the first and second groups.[1] The 'devolution planning process' was accompanied by additional research to evaluate the implications of devolution and, more generally, of the UK government's overall programme of constitutional reform (BBC Research 1998).

This renewed confrontation with devolution, after the lapse of a generation, required the BBC to redefine itself afresh. From the time of its foundation under John Reith, the corporation has seen itself as an 'organisation within the constitution' with a public-service mission based on the unquestioned assumption that there is a national community to be addressed (Schlesinger 1978: 20; Scannell and Cardiff 1991: 15). In the late 1990s, the question was how the BBC would reinterpret its traditional self-conception when dominant ideas of state and nation were being challenged. The singular national community was quite clearly going to become a constitutionally underpinned, plural grouping of national communities. The corporation therefore had to move rather quickly to deal with the changing relationships between state and nation.

In spring 1998, in internal documentation, the top executives of the steering group were using the following formula in their thinking about this issue:

> For the BBC, as a publicly funded UK-wide institution, committed to reflecting regional and cultural diversity and, at the same time, bringing the nation together for the shared experience, devolution has a particular resonance and potential high impact.

But 'bringing the nation together' was rapidly to become an untenable formula. The UK's constitutional uncertainties were agitating the BBC. Only a year later, in 1999, Mark Thompson, Mark Byford's successor, was the bearer of the significantly changed title of Controller, National and Regional Broadcasting. He wrote:

> We're not a unionist organisation in the sense of favouring any one constitutional settlement over another, but we can and should be a clearing house not just for national difference, but the value and heritage that we hold in common. This is a public purpose of the BBC which will grow in importance as devolution develops.
> (Thompson 1999: 5)

This denial of the BBC's 'unionism' was not innocent, given the widespread view among the corporation's Scottish detractors that it was precisely this. Moreover, to speak of 'a clearing house for national difference' is not the same as to envisage a machine for the construction and reproduction of a national culture, encased by Britishness. In Thompson's phraseology, that earlier idea became more abstractly formulated as the bearer of a common 'value and heritage'. But such broad cultural constructs have no necessary national referent, nor indeed do they necessarily entail a defined geographical boundary.

Thompson's reformulation of the BBC's mission was the result of an intense process of internal debate. In late 1997 and early 1998, the BBC's top managers were stressing its integrated UK character, rather than internal devolution, and worried that they might not respond rapidly enough to their commercial competitors' challenge. Like the British state – and at another level – the EU, the BBC had to deal with the contradictions of standing for unity in diversity, as well as of trying to remain the officially-endorsed 'cornerstone of broadcasting throughout the United Kingdom'. The task, then, as devolution approached, was conceived as both 'celebrating' the diversity of the nations and regions and, at the same time, satisfying the UK audience as a whole.

According to our various informants inside the BBC, in December 1997, the first interim report from the Coverage of Parliament/Assembly Group was circulated. The group was chaired by Val Atkinson, deputy head of news and current affairs, BBC Scotland. It also comprised Bill Bush, head of BBC Research, Glyn Mathias, political editor, BBC Wales, Samir Shah of the Regional directorate, and the BBC's chief political adviser, Anne Sloman.

The benchmark for examining how the Scottish Parliament might be covered was the Westminster experience, where televising of the House of Commons had begun in 1989 (Coleman 1999). The BBC has long been committed to covering Parliament and sees itself as undertaking a public service to democracy in its parliamentary and political coverage, keeping its performance under special review (Marsh 1999). Aside from serving the public, the corporation's exceptional amount of coverage (when compared to other broadcasters) is of key importance for the political class and contributes considerably to the corporation's legitimacy and credibility in these quarters.[2] The new bodies, therefore, could simply have been covered within the same framework that had existed since broadcasting first entered the Commons. For the BBC, the devolved bodies were certainly seen as extensions of Westminster, but they also offered a chance to do something different. BBC Research had argued that it was essential to grasp the online opportunities offered by the new bodies and that the corporation was uniquely wellplaced to explain and analyse the new institutions on its parliamentary website. By providing a single 'one-stop guide' to UK political institutions, it was held, this might appeal to young people otherwise uninterested in politics – a good selling-point with the political class as well as a contribution to democracy. But as planning proceeded, online possibilities were understandably overshadowed by the nuts-and-bolts interest in traditional broadcasting.

The prime interest at this early planning stage was to see what kind of system would be acceptable to politicians and civil servants and to establish how 'the feed' – the pictures and sound coming from the floor of the House and committee rooms – would be financed. The working group considered various options and plumped for one in which the Parliament or Assembly would pay for all the capital costs of the hardware and installation while the broadcasters would pay for the feed through a non-profit-making company, as was the case at Westminster.[3]

A particular concern was the ability of broadcasters to exert pressure on the new bodies to keep up with the needs of technological change. BBC Resources were also keen to receive the commission for supplying the capital equipment for provision of the feed.[4] It was intended to ensure that broadcasters' needs would be met in the construction of the new Parliament and Assembly buildings, with studio space, press gallery desk space, sound and picture-editing facilities and 'inject points' for coverage outside the chambers themselves. The BBC also wanted a media centre to be set up that would enable parliamentary coverage in each new body, something not at that time being considered by either Scottish or Welsh Office civil servants.

There was great concern inside BBC Scotland that Scottish Office thinking on media access to the Parliament seemed to be limited to providing desk space for newspaper journalists – an inversion of the press's own anxieties, as we shall see.

BBC Scotland saw itself as the lead broadcaster north of the border, with a mission to argue vociferously for the right standards. Within the BBC, it was felt that both politicians and civil servants needed to be 'educated' about what coverage of the new institutions really entailed. The corporation therefore pressed for the setting-up of a joint working group with civil servants and other broadcasters.

BBC executives felt that coverage of the new bodies should make a fresh start. The broadcasters had long felt hamstrung by the Commons' conservatism and were looking to provide more attractive television in order to arouse more audience interest. The planners wanted no restriction on shots used; they wished to film in corridors and in all committee rooms; and they wanted a broadcast commentator spot overlooking the chamber. Once formal negotiations were concluded in late 1998 and early 1999, prior to the setting-up of the Scottish Parliament, most of this agenda had become accepted wisdom. However, one year earlier, the broadcasters believed that it was going to have to be fought for. They achieved their aims by stages through negotiations with civil servants and by lobbying ministers.

Given agreement inside the Coverage of Parliament/Assembly Group on the broad strategy to be pursued, the BBC next set up two subgroups, one in each country to negotiate separately with the Scottish Office and the Welsh Office.

In Scotland, aside from objecting to the idea of occupying one open-plan room (as did the press), the broadcasters were not happy with the two bookable TV/radio studios proposed for one-to-one interviews. Like the political press, they were aggrieved at the thought that the media would be kept separate from MSPs except where prior permission had been sought. This was seen as undercutting the rhetoric of openness and accessibility with which the Parliament had been sold. The Scottish Office's plans at that point were dismissed as replicating Westminster's arrangements. BBC Scotland's political staff noted the widespread grumbling among journalists and the likely pressures on space. They also observed that the Scottish Office's Devolution Minister, Henry McLeish, was being very responsive to representations made by senior figures at BBC Scotland.[5]

In February 1998, partly in response to the BBC's prompting, along with those of other media interests, the Scottish Office set up a media group to discuss radio, television and press coverage. It rapidly became clear that different issues concerned the press and the broadcasters and it was decided to split the discussions. The broadcasting group consisted of radio and television representatives, and was chaired by Val Atkinson of BBC Scotland.

The Scottish Office side was led by Paul Grice of the Constitution Group, later to become Chief Executive of the Scottish Parliament. The broadcasting group resisted the Scottish Office's suggestions that they should pay for the feed. Together with the newspaper group, all the media representatives also turned down Scottish Office proposals that they should be located in a media centre at some distance from the Parliament. By taking concerted action as a lobby, the media succeeded in securing accommodation on the parliamentary campus in the Lawnmarket Building.

The broadcasters had to fight against some rather entrenched beliefs. Alistair McNeill, Deputy Director of the Scottish Office Information Directorate, wrote to the various broadcasters with whom he had been in discussion (among them the BBC, BSkyB, Border Television, ITN, and Scottish Television), asking them to consider the rules prevalent at Westminster governing the feed and the extent to which they might wish to vary these:

> Given that they appear to have stood the test of time and there appears to be little enthusiasm on the part of Parliament or the broadcasters to alter them in any way, I would hazard the guess that unless there are good reasons to the contrary, Scottish parliamentarians will want to stick substantially with the Westminster rules, subject to any changes at the margin to reflect (say) any configuration peculiarities at the Assembly Hall.
> (Alistair McNeill, letter to Val Atkinson, Mark Smith, Ian Proniewicz, Harry Smith and Jacqui Faulkner, 30 July 1998)

Inside the BBC, two major objections emerged. First, Westminster television coverage was seen as boring, given its limited repertoire of shots. Second, it was felt that Westminster was not a good model for a new, accessible parliament because television had been admitted on sufferance into the Commons rather than being welcomed. Furthermore, senior political advisers at the BBC felt that if Scotland developed a tenable model of good practice, this could be held up as an example that might bring change at Westminster. The new Scottish Parliament (along with the Welsh Assembly) was seen as a more open institution and the corporation wanted to establish the ground rule that broadcasters were there for the audience (rather than for the politicians) and that viewers and listeners should see and hear as much as possible. The BBC argued that the Scottish Parliament should proclaim its modernity and that broadcasting would communicate this. Coverage should be largely left to the good sense of the parliamentary broadcasting service, with a proviso to protect the dignity of the House and that of its members. As a gesture of goodwill, the BBC would follow the Westminster principle of not showing demonstrations in the chamber, cutting to the chair in the event. This was the negotiating position when the rules of coverage were finally discussed in late 1998.

BBC Scotland responded to the Scottish Office in August 1998. It was argued in a paper that if audiences were not offered high standards of camerawork, they would be alienated from the new parliamentary process: particular attention was drawn to Westminster conventions which meant a lack of 'cut-aways' showing reactions in the chamber; the absence of close-ups of facial expressions; the bar on panning shots or zooms; and the failure to show a speaker before an intervention or, indeed, to film from the speaker's point of view. The broadcasters sought to reassure the Scottish Office that a liberal regime would not mean irresponsibility. The result of aping Westminster, it was argued, would simply be to reproduce an old-fashioned grammar of television.

The conditions for the use of the feed, and how this would be paid, were settled at a meeting in January 1999 between the Scottish Office's director of implementation, Paul Grice, and representatives of the BBC, SMG, ITN, BSkyB, Channel 6, Live TV Edinburgh, Channel 4, Border Television, Scot FM and Forth FM (Meeting with Broadcasters: Payment for Feed in the Scottish Parliament, 21 January 1999, Meridian Court Glasgow. Scottish Office Minute SAS 19901.019). BBC Resources had won the contract to televise the Parliament, it was announced. This included operating the sound recording of proceedings for the Parliament's *Official Report* (the equivalent of Westminster's *Hansard*). The cost of the feed over a period of twenty-six months, the Scottish Office said, would be £600,000. It was agreed that the pictures could be used by TV companies and would also be made available to MSPs and their staff.

It was decided that the Scottish Parliament and the broadcasters would not set up a separate company to run parliamentary broadcasting, as at Westminster. However, the same basic system of broadcasters paying a fixed share of costs, and thereby gaining the right to unlimited use of all material, was adopted. The BBC, SMG and Border Television, Sky News, Channel 4 and Channel 6 all agreed to subscribe to the service. Following some debate, the Scottish Office said that the Scottish Parliament would meet 60 per cent of the costs (£360,000 over twenty-six months to the broadcasters' £240,000).

The BBC agreed to take up four shares, whereas SMG, Channel 4, Sky News and Channel 6 each took up one. The BBC evidently thought that SMG ought to take up more than one share but the company argued that it was unlikely to be a big user of the feed. Channel 5 was expected to take up a share, but by March 1999 it had become clear the channel would not sign up to the agreement, so the Scottish Office proposed a new division of costs. The Scottish Parliament would underwrite the newly-available share and the shortfall would be met by retaining the equivalent amount generated by selling the feed. The Scottish Office at one point thought that radio broadcasters should contribute to the costs of coverage, but it became clear that the sound feed would be used mainly by MSPs and to produce the *Official Report.*

Thus, before the Scottish parliamentary elections in May 1999, the new arrangements had created a group of 'core broadcasters' with unlimited rights to the feed (although copyright was held by the Parliament). As part of the package, the core members were also to have office accommodation and technical facilities, to derive income from sales of the archive, to have a place on the Parliament's advisory group on broadcasting along with the Scottish Parliament Corporate Body (the entity that represents the Parliament as an institution).

No Six, please! We're British

The Newsgathering Group, led by BBC Scotland's Colin Cameron and Ken Cargill, reported in January 1998. Its remit was to review the newsgathering capacity in Scotland and Wales and it was driven by the anticipated journalistic needs of these two countries. It was clear that devolution would set up competing demands between news and current affairs reporting in London and the other national capitals. For the BBC in the smaller nations, this was a time to pitch for additional newsgathering resources and posts. At the same time, there was a desire both in Glasgow and Cardiff to plug more firmly into the network news and to make London editors more sensitive to the changing political landscape. Hence, it was argued that Scotland and Wales needed to be incorporated more distinctively into the London newsgathering diaries because of their separate agendas. The heads of news and current affairs in the smaller nations also wanted to ensure that Scotland and Wales could make fuller use of BBC News research facilities.

There was a tremendously strong desire in BBC Scotland for distinctive news coverage. By May 1998 this had taken form as a wish to 'drive' the 6–7pm hour of news and current affairs on BBC1 from Glasgow. The hour consisted of the networked *Six O'Clock News* followed by *Reporting Scotland.* This arrangement had been in place since 1984 and had never been popular in Scotland, either with BBC staff or the audience.[6]

The so-called 'integrated' television news hour proposed as an alternative to the present schedule was seen as the main risk and opportunity inside BBC Scotland at this time. The idea was to make use of the BBC's network resources to edit a customised version of the international, UK and Scottish news from a Scottish point of view. The principle was certainly not new, as BBC Radio Scotland had worked along these lines for many years in its main news and current affairs programmes. Unlike its television counterpart, Radio Scotland is freestanding and does not opt out from the network.

The television news proposal was in tune with the view that programming devolution needed to keep pace with the political process, not least because it was recognised in Queen Margaret Drive that Scottish identity was becoming increasingly important for the audience. In some respects, therefore, this retrod the old ground first visited during the abortive attempt to devolve BBC Scotland in the late 1970s that had led to Alastair Hetherington's sidelining.

The focus on creating an 'integrated' news derived above all from the perceived need to demonstrate to the Scottish public that the BBC in Scotland could serve the audience well, given the BBC's relative lack of popularity in the country. BBC Scotland's leadership had taken note of a private corporate-image survey which indicated that 56 per cent of Scots thought they were not well served by the BBC. This compared unfavourably with other areas of the UK. Moreover, in Scotland commercial television was widely seen as being better. BBC Scotland was concerned that the Scottish Media Group might position itself as the national broadcaster and also worried about the popularity of Channel 4 and Channel 5.

For Queen Margaret Drive, devolution offered an opportunity to rethink BBC Scotland's strategy and to push towards 'market leadership'. The pitch was to be based on the corporation's perceived impartiality and independence in a partisan Scottish media scene. Management clearly recognised that a replacement 'integrated' news hour had to aspire to network standards. In May 1998, an internal assessment of the four devolution review groups was circulated to senior staff. This made astringent criticisms of the BBC's *Reporting Scotland* and Scottish TV's *Scotland Today*, which were both accused of failing to achieve the right balance between genuine significance and parochialism. The strategy paper stressed the need to ensure authoritative standing for BBC Scotland's political reporting team. Journalism was signalled as the strategic ground to occupy.

In short, BBC Scotland wanted to be seen as more Scottish and thought that the news hour was the ideal way to demonstrate this. This explains the amount of attention paid to establishing arrangements in the Parliament compared to Scottish TV. Both public-service ideals and strategic considerations were at work in the desire to launch the new integrated programme before the Scottish parliamentary elections of May 1999. However, this strategy was to be frustrated.

BBC Scotland's top brass publicly maintained that their proposal to replace the networked service on BBC1 had a realistic chance of success. However, as the review process developed inside the corporation during spring and summer 1998, it became increasingly clear that there was serious opposition to the 'integrated' news both inside and outwith the corporation. The workings of the BBC's centralism settled the fate of the *Six O'Clock News* well before the outcome became public knowledge.

The public row over what became known as the 'Scottish Six' finally exploded in autumn 1998, and ran from the start of October to the end of December. It revealed, once again, some fundamental aspects of the relationship between the UK government and the BBC and the limits of strategic autonomy in BBC Scotland.

A major background factor in determining the outcome was the unrelenting political opposition in the highest quarters. Key figures inside the Labour Cabinet were consistently reported by various newspapers (and certainly known inside BBC Scotland's management) to oppose the proposal to have a separate 'Scottish Six'. The UK-wide news was seen as having a symbolic role for the Union, a point picked up on and aired by a number of well-informed metropolitan political commentators (Marr 1998; Preston 1998)

At a time of major constitutional uncertainty, the BBC was increasingly seen inside the government as providing the glue of the body politic. Most of the Cabinet's Scots also evidently feared that a Glasgow-based news broadcast would play to an SNP separatist agenda (Copley and MacMahon 1998: 1; Garavelli 1998: 3). The Prime Minister, Tony Blair, was repeatedly identified as being 'implacably opposed', in a phrase clearly planted for effect. He was joined in that opposition, according to consistent reports that were never denied, by Gordon Brown, the Chancellor of the Exchequer, Lord Irvine, the Lord Chancellor, George Robertson, the Defence Secretary and former Shadow Scottish Secretary, and Alistair Darling, the Social Security Secretary. The Scottish Secretary, Donald Dewar, was commonly described as 'neutral', but had earlier revealed his doubts about a separate Scottish news, and was to do so again once the row was over. Attention was repeatedly drawn by reporters to the close links between Downing Street and the BBC's Director-General, Sir John Birt. The Prime Minister's wish to prevent any fundamental change, it was widely (and plausibly) assumed, was being transmitted to the BBC.

Aside from such political opposition, in autumn 1998 the corporation was especially sensitive to the wishes of the Cabinet. The Davies committee was in the process of being set up to review the BBC's future funding at the height of the row.[7] By then, the decision to limit the changes in news programming had in effect been made, although this was not publicly admitted. Moreover, in Scotland, the BBC's Glasgow chiefs required the BBC governors' support for a much-delayed modernisation drive for state-of-the-art production facilities at Pacific Quay. They certainly had no wish to antagonise London over this key plank in their strategy.

What finally brought the issue to public attention was a row between the Broadcasting Council for Scotland (BCS) and members of the BBC's Executive Committee in London. The BCS is a twelve-member advisory body that normally has a rather shadowy existence. It is officially described as assisting 'in the oversight of the BBC in Scotland' and as helping the BBC's board of governors by effectively championing and representing the distinctive needs and interests of audiences in the country. Similar bodies exist in Wales, Northern Ireland and the English regions (BBC 1997: 5, 7). The BCS is chaired by the National Governor for Scotland, then the Reverend Norman Drummond, an impeccably establishment figure who is a chaplain to the Queen and a former headmaster of Loretto.

The BCS had been engaged in the evolving debate inside the BBC over how programming should respond to devolution. A major paper had come from the BBC's Executive to which the BCS had responded. This report had originally been collated by Mark Byford, Director of Regional Broacasting, and was first circulated in strict confidence to members of the BBC's devolution steering group in March 1998. It covered the whole range of matters addressed by the four working groups. According to sources at BBC Scotland, it was at this moment that the game started to be lost. At Queen Margaret Drive it was believed that John Birt was hostile to BBC Scotland's proposal and that this antipathy determined how the devolution policy would be developed from this key point onwards. True or not, it is clear on any dispassionate reading that BBC Scotland's favoured option had been marginalised.

A revised version of Byford's paper finally went to BCS members (who had repeatedly asked to see it) in late June 1998 with a stern warning from the BBC's chairman, Sir Christopher Bland, about its political and commercial sensitivity. He further wrote: 'The Governors have had an opportunity of reviewing and discussing the paper. Before the Board considers firm recommendations from BBC management, Governors would value the advice of the Broadcasting Councils on the paper' (letter from the chairman of the BBC to Reverend Norman Drummond, 29 June 1998).

The BCS had every reason, on the face of it, to think that they were going to be seriously consulted, but there were some warning signs. The devolution proposals stressed the continuing sovereignty of the UK state and the fact that broadcasting would remain a reserved power. In a sentence that surely left little to the imagination of any unblinkered advocate of the 'Scottish Six', it was stated: 'It will be important to demonstrate an effective response to devolution *but also to retain the strength and unity of an integrated UK-wide BBC*, within a single coherent organisation' (BBC 1998: ii; emphasis added). The document went on to say:

> *The clear starting-point has been that the current pattern of UK-wide network news programmes should remain across the day* – maintaining the strategy that UK-wide network programmes are provided by the UK-wide public service broadcaster, complemented by specific regional services.
> (BBC 1998: xii; emphasis added)

The document went on to offer three options for the *Six O'Clock News* in Scotland: a relaunched UK-wide programme; a relaunched UK-wide programme with an 'integrated' option for Scotland on the BBC Choice digital channel; a new programme to replace the *Six O'Clock News* and *Reporting Scotland* (BBC 1998: xiii). The mere ordering of these possibilities spoke volumes to any alert reader.

The BCS responded to BBC management's analysis with its own document. The starting-point was to stress 'the distinct national identity of Scotland' and to note that independence was not foreclosed by devolution (BCS 1998a: 6). The BCS responded positively to the entire range of programme proposals but focused in detail on the continued hedging of bets over television news. So far as 'the 1800–1900 hour on television was concerned', the BCS was disappointed that the review 'had not yet resulted in a firm recommendation. The Council strongly favours an integrated news programme for Scotland in the early evening' (BCS 1998a: 9). At its July meeting, faced with what it already believed to be an entrenched position in the Executive Committee, the BCS insisted on public-opinion research being commissioned to examine public views about television news in Scotland.

The Executive Committee responded to the BCS after its meeting on 7 September 1998. It reaffirmed its belief in 'the current pattern of broadcasting UK-wide network news' with an integrated news programme to be provided on BBC Choice Scotland, the digital channel (Wyatt and Byford 1998: 2). In a brief response, the BCS argued that its news proposition had 'not been fully considered by the Executive Committee' and expressed 'deep concern about the lack of weight being attached to its views' (BCS 1998b: 1). The BBC's chairman next wrote to Drummond informing him that the governors had considered recommendations from the Executive Committee and the BCS's own paper. He signalled that the board would meet the BCS on 21 October 1998 (letter from Sir Christopher Bland to Reverend Norman Drummond, 28 September 1998).

With its own disillusioned response already on the table, on 2 October 1998 the BCS met Will Wyatt, Chief Executive Broadcast, Mark Byford, Controller of Regional Broadcasting, and his deputy, Michael Stevenson, and Tony Hall, Chief Executive News and Current Affairs. In the course of the discussion, BCS members reiterated their commitment to the proposition of an 'integrated' 'Scottish Six'. Professor Lindsay Paterson, later to resign from the BCS over the BBC's ultimate refusal to budge over the issue, has provided an account of this meeting from his perspective (Paterson 1998: 17). He accused Byford of giving a patronising statement to the BCS and reports that the whole council offered a forensic destruction of London's objections. He wrote that Hall was unable to answer questions as to how the differences north and south of the border would be handled in detail, and further that Wyatt had said that the BBC must not get ahead of constitutional developments, whereas Stevenson had remarked that the BBC was not obliged to be accountable to the Scottish Parliament. By this account, the two and a half hour meeting did not go well and could hardly have left the BCS in any doubt that its case was a lost cause.

The London delegation also used a public opinion survey originally commissioned by the BCS to counter their opponents. The options had been posed in terms that favoured the BBC Executive's position: the status quo; an integrated 'Six' to replace the status quo; the status quo on analogue with the integrated 'Six' on digital. The BCS was told that the last question had been devised in consultation with London, and it would have made little sense to those surveyed. The poll results were never published, but were later used in press briefings – misleadingly – to suggest that there was a majority for the status quo, in short, as ammunition against the BCS's case.

What further infuriated the BCS, and led to a rapidly ramifying row in the press and political circles, and then eventually to the major engagement of public opinion in Scotland, was the failure by the London delegation to mention the planned publication only four days later of their Programme Strategy Review (BBC News 1998). This proposed to revamp the *Six O'Clock News* and also to create a Scottish opt-out from *Newsnight*. The *Six O'Clock News* was to focus on domestic and regional news and to aim at younger viewers. The handover to the 6.30pm regional bulletins was to become 'seamless' (Gibson 1998: 8). BCS members were incensed to find no reflection of the arguments for a 'Scottish Six' in the strategy. On the contrary, the review signalled the 'core of our proposition on BBC1' as '[a] new national news programme at six o'clock reporting the UK in all its diversity to a UK audience' (BBC News 1998: 24, 23). These new plans left BCS members feeling that they had been seriously misled. Both the BCS's vice-chairman, Jim Martin, and member Lindsay Paterson threatened resignation on 7 October if the 'Scottish Six' was not publicly said to be open for further consideration by the governors. The rest of the BCS signalled they would follow suit. Martin sought a further meeting in London the following day with one or other of the BBC's chairman, director-general, or Tony Hall. Both the BBC's chairman and director-general approved this. At a meeting with Hall, also attended by the Controller, BBC Scotland, John McCormick, Martin was assured that no final decision had been made and was able to carry his BCS colleagues with him. Most members of the BCS were in fact doubtful of London's assurances but believed that it was better to maintain a united front in public.

In fact, there was widespread scepticism in Scotland that there was still a game to play, and rightly so as it turned out. Added to the outrage in the BCS, fifty-one of BBC Scotland's journalists came out in open opposition to London's plans, while BBC Scotland's top brass were privately dismayed but maintained the public fable that the battle could still be won (Laing 1998a:

5; Wells 1998: 1). Hall's review was generally interpreted as sounding the death-knell for a Glasgow-based programme and as plainly pre-empting the governors' formal decision on the matter later that month. Without explaining why they had not alerted them the previous week, Tony Hall and Will Wyatt, stressed – disingenuously we can only suppose – in a letter to BCS members that their review 'in no way precludes decisions which the Board of Govenors will take following the current round of consultation with the Broadcasting Councils' (Will Wyatt and Tony Hall, letter to BCS members, 7 October 1998). Ritual honour was saved, but the likely outcome was clear (Fraser 1998a: 3; Kemp and Breen 1998: 4; Laing 1998b: 2).

In a revealing briefing paper to the BBC's governors, BBC Scotland's Secretary, Mark Leishman, set out (1998: 1) how the events looked from the BCS's point of view:

Tuesday, 29 September
BCS members receive the new Executive Committee paper written by Mark Byford which recommends a UK-wide *Six O'Clock News* programme but makes no reference to the Council's view and its preferred option of an integrated partnership news from Glasgow. It becomes clear that the paper was submitted at the same time as the BCS response, therefore the Executive Committee could not have taken the Council's detailed report into consideration at its 7 September meeting. Although there was no constitutional need for ExComm to consult the Council, members were very disappointed at the new document, describing it as 'timid and patronising'.

Friday, 2 October
BCS monthly meeting in Glasgow attended by Will Wyatt, Tony Hall, Mark Byford and Michael Stevenson. A private Council session discusses the Executive paper ahead of the meeting with ExComm representatives and Scottish Management Board. The Council is angry and frustrated at the 'grudging' response set out in the paper. It seeks assurances that its views are being given due weight and that the BBC is retaining an open mind in its approach to the devolution response. There are assurances that 'nothing is ruled out in the future' despite the new paper. There is no mention of the planned announcement on News Programme Strategy Review the following Tuesday.

In the face of a hostile press, Leishman ably persuaded the furious BCS members to 'remain on board' to meet the governors. On 21 October, a meeting of the board of governors and the BCS was held in Glasgow. The BCS, led by Norman Drummond, and BBC Scotland, headed by John McCormick, were reported as strongly urging the board to accept BBC Scotland's proposition (Smith 1998: 2). The governors made it clear that they were unconvinced, but a formal decision was deferred until later in the year (Laing 1998c: 5). In private correspondence to BCS members, Norman

Drummond made it clear that the BBC's Executive Committee 'has been instructed to create a new proposal for the 6pm–7pm slot' (Reverend Drummond, letter to BCS members, 23 October 1988). As it turned out, this was clutching at straws.

On 20 November, the Governors made it clear that they were

> minded to support a new approach to the evening news hour which contains – for the whole of the United Kingdom – a *Six O'Clock News* that gives a comprehensive daily account of developments across the United Kingdom reporting not on one but four democratic institutions, and a full service of international news.

The board further said that the corporation should 'keep in step with but should not run ahead of, the general pace of constitutional change' (BBC Press Office 1998b). The BCS first learned of this decision by way of the press reporting of the announcement (Robins 1998: 5). Drummond publicly expressed the view that the issue was still open to consultation. However, it is doubtful that the board of governors' request for 'further consultation with the Broadcasting Council for Scotland on options for news coverage by the BBC in response to devolution' was anything more than mere pretence (BCS 1998c). Indeed, the BBC's consultation process was described as a sham by the most outspoken member of the BCS, Lindsay Paterson, who chose to resign following the governors' evident rejection.

As the row rumbled on, the 'Six' deveoped from being a broadcasting policy matter to being a key Scottish political story. The issue became the subject of repeated opinion polls and of campaigning journalism. An ICM poll conducted for *The Scotsman*, published on 24 November, showed 48 per cent in favour and a similar number against the 'Six' (Dalton, 1998a: 10). The *Daily Record* took up the cause in what was described by one commentator as a 'virulent, anti-London' campaign, running a story a day in favour of the Scottish Six for a whole month (Fraser 1998b: 17). Support grew in Scotland for the BCS's position. Fuelled by press campaigning, the issue became a major agenda item for the Scottish public. The *Sunday Mail* conducted a poll and announced that 61 per cent of Scots 'demand their own TV news' (Macleod, A. 1998a: 20). In a System Three poll for *The Herald*, some 69 per cent of voters were reported as wanting a Scottish-produced early evening news (Dinwoodie 1998e: 1).

BBC journalists set out their own case against the governors' position, drawing attention to the constant problem of duplication between the *Six O'Clock News* and *Reporting Scotland* (Ritchie 1998c: 3). They disagreed that having devolved news would be running in advance of the political process and reiterated the argument that the programme would offer a Scottish perspective on national and international news rather than being parochial (Wishart 1998: 15). A clampdown on such expressions of dissent by Ken Cargill, Head of News and Current Affairs, rapidly followed at BBC Scotland, where senior executives were worried that this would worsen the climate further (McLean 1998: 1, 4)

Both John McCormick and Cargill went public with their own views. McCormick reaffirmed his preference for the 'Scottish Six', but noted that, whatever the decision, 'London and Scotland will work to deliver the best services available' (McCormick 1998: 4). He was quoted by one newspaper as saying – with realism – that 'if you get into a fight with London, you've already lost' (*Scotland on Sunday* 1998: 17). Cargill noted

> differing views . . . in relation to constitutional change. But we're in complete agreement about the need to ensure that the BBC does not fall behind that change . . . It's important to underline that our proposal has not been ruled out in principle.
> (Cargill 1998: 4–5)

The governors' fudge ensured a further three weeks of furious campaigning by the BCS, BBC Scotland, and most of the Scottish press (Brooks 1998: 1). Finally, after more public rancour, the governors' formal decision was announced on 10 December: a 'Scottish Six' was rejected before the Scottish Parliament had come into existence but was not ruled out for the future. 'In summary,' the governors intoned, 'we are convinced that the BBC can and must provide a news service which serves audiences in all four nations of the UK but which also reflects the four nations to each other as part of the United Kingdom' (BBC Press Office 1998b). Jim Martin, vice-chairman of the BCS, observed after the final negative decision: 'We have been patronised and there has been an attempt to dismiss what we have been saying as nationalism, which it isn't,' (Patton and Starrs 1998: 2). The governors announced that they would invest £10 million in Scottish news and current affairs and fifty new jobs were promised. Integrated programmes were remitted to the digital channels of BBC Choice. The second sop was a twenty-minute opt-out from *Newsnight* on BBC2, leading to the creation of *Newsnight Scotland*. The devolved nations were to be represented at the network level by news editors.

BBC Scotland's Controller, John McCormick, made the most of the situation by stressing the scope of the new investment and saying that this demonstrated the BBC's serious commitment to devolution and the new Scottish Parliament. Disappointed insiders have recounted privately how his attempt to sell this to his staff initially went down like a lead balloon. It was announced that the decision was to come under review. According to our sources, it was indeed reconsidered by the governors in May 2000, who quietly left things as they were. This silence occasioned no public comment.

The Scottish Secretary, Donald Dewar, who had been seen as somewhat equivocal throughout the row, had let it known that he was not opposed to the 'Scottish Six.' After the governors' final decision, Dewar cited the poll requested by the BCS, which he had not seen, but which he maintained showed a majority in favour of the *status quo*, when the figure was apparently well below this. This attracted some flak from Jim Martin, who said it indicated that ministers had been subjected to misinformation by London executives (Hill 1998: 3; *Sunday Mail* 1998: 2). Dewar had earlier codedly aired his doubts in a speech to Scotland's great and good in February 1998. Noting the costs of broadcasting and Scotland's small size, he remarked (1998: 11–12), 'I am not saying, not for a moment, that devolved broadcasting would necessarily mean "kailyard programming", if I can put it that way. But I am saying that it is not evident that separating out a Scottish BBC would be for the best.' Coupled with his stress on UK-wide control of broadcasting, this was a fair indication of low enthusiasm for a 'Scottish Six', without spelling it out.

The matter now resolved, Dewar said that he had not wished to interfere in the BBC's affairs. He was quoted as saying: 'It is vital that BBC Scotland raises its standards and offers proper in-depth coverage of the new Scottish Parliament. It is important we break away from the narrow concept of local news,' (Patton and Starrs 1998: 2). This was widely interpreted as alignment with Tony Blair's 'implacable opposition'.

Otherwise, there had been something approaching a political consensus in Scotland. The SNP had throughout been vocal supporters of the 'Scottish Six': the issue allowed them to ask why broadcasting should be a reserved power. The Liberal Democrats also supported it, holding that the Scottish Parliament could be trusted to exercise power sensibly over broadcasting. And even the Conservatives came round to the idea as polls had shown growing support north of the border (Wells and Hardie 1998: 7).

In the immediate aftermath of the affair, the BBC's Executive Committee acknowledged that there was insufficient sensitivity to the implications of devolution inside the corporation and launched an internal 'awareness campaign'. The public manifestation of the BBC's attempt to raise its staff's devo-consciousness was the editorial style guide, *The Changing UK*, published in March 1999 (BBC 1999), and this was supplemented by internal seminars.

Philip Harding, Controller of Editorial Policy, told us he had intended 'to put across to programme-makers more systematically than before their need to think about the different attitudes and reception by the audiences to whom they were broadcasting'. The BBC's Chief Political Adviser, Anne Sloman, believed that it was no longer possible to cover all of UK politics appealingly UK-wide and that a new balance was needed.

It was during the course of devolution planning that the BBC decided to retitle its 'regional broadcasting' function. Following in the footsteps of Channel 4, which had set up a 'nations and regions' office in Glasgow in 1998, the BBC adopted a similar title for its 'non-metropolitan' activities. According to Michael Stevenson, there was 'growing discomfort' with the term 'national region' to describe Scotland, Wales and Northern Ireland. It was recognised among those most closely associated with the issues that the term 'nation' could not be used unambiguously.

But this incorporation of the devolutionary sensibility into London's thinking did not mean any departure from what is ultimately the centralist view of the BBC. As Harding put it: 'In the end, people voted for a devolved Parliament with tax-raising powers. We didn't vote to have a separate media system. We didn't vote to opt out of the *Six O'Clock News*.' For the BBC in London to acknowledge devolution was, at the same time, to be convinced that audiences on each side of the border needed to know what was going on elsewhere and to reaffirm that the current network news was the best way of providing this.

A CONCLUDING PERSPECTIVE

BBC Scotland won one struggle decisively: it achieved the desired arrangements for parliamentary coverage. In London, the value of a more liberal dispensation in Edinburgh was plain because this might help change the culture of Westminster coverage. From the corporate standpoint, there would be no problem if BBC Scotland served its national audience in this way. It was entirely in keeping with the corporation's historic support for parliamentary institutions. And, ultimately, it was a sideshow.

The real problem arose when the desire to serve the new polity overstepped the mark. Devolved news was a major battleground. London stood to lose power and so the limits of devolution inside the BBC became manifest. There could be no truck with any threat to the conception of 'one BBC'. Against the governors' ultimate determination to back the BBC's Executive Committee, and in a climate of Cabinet pressure to hold the line, the 'Scottish Six' was a hopeless cause.

That said, BBC Scotland's fight was not without results. It put the question of television news and devolution firmly on the public agenda in Scotland and, to a much lesser extent, south of the border. The campaign also forced an increase of the budget for devolution coverage, with undoubted benefits to the service that could be offered. But that was accomplished within the well-established confines of the BBC's continuing centralism. Fundamental questions of principle about how devolution might now affect the corporation's structure have been deferred, once again.

NOTES

1. Much of what follows is based on information given on the strict understanding that it would function as background. We have drawn on several interviews and unpublished documentation. We have respected our undertaking of confidentiality by citing neither specific sources who wished to remain off the record for certain statements nor any of those papers that we have been allowed to read that might compromise those who allowed us to see them.
2. We have only to think of the outcry in the Commons when *Today in Parliament* and *Yesterday in Parliament* were relegated from FM to medium wave in 1998 to recognise that proximity and sensitivity. Politicians' continuing rancour at the axeing of ITN's *News at Ten* in 1999 and their consternation when the BBC moved the *Nine O'Clock News* to fill that slot in 2000 are also cases in point.
3. This company is called PARBUL (Parliamentary Broadcasting Unit Ltd). Televising of the Commons and Lords is carried out by an independent production company, CCT Productions, operating at Millbank. Set-up costs for televising Westminster were some £2 million, split between Parliament and the broadcasters.
4. In the event, the contract was indeed awarded to this part of the BBC's operation.
5. After Donald Dewar's death, Henry McLeish succeeded him as Labour leader and First Minister in October 2000.
6. When Patrick Chalmers, Controller, BBC Scotland, sought to originate his own programme following the news in 1983, he was warned off with the imprecation 'Remember Hetherington' (Leapman 1986: 141).
7. The Independent Review Panel chaired by Gavyn Davies began work in January 1999. Davies was formally appointed by the Secretary of State for Culture, Media and Sport on 30 November 1998, but the government's intentions were known well before this.

CHAPTER 3

The press prepares for Holyrood

WAITING FOR PARLIAMENT

In this chapter we chart how the political press developed into a parliamentary corps from the immediate pre-devolutionary period to the setting-up of the Scottish Parliament. In autumn 1997, when it was clear that the Labour government would indeed legislate for constitutional change, we began asking selected political journalists and editors for their views on devolution and its likely course. At the time, the topic was still relatively low on the UK political agenda but was obviously at the top of the Scottish one.

Devolution was part of the lived experience of everyday coverage and Scottish political journalists felt themselves to be increasingly distinct from their colleagues south of the border. Iain Martin, political editor of *Scotland on Sunday* observed: 'English political journalists, English newspapers, don't even have the language or historical understanding of constitutional changes to get involved in the debate yet.' As Kenny Farquharson, political editor of *The Sunday Times, Scotland,* said, 'The political journalists have been living this Parliament for a number of years. We have a stake in it.' Brian Taylor, BBC Scotland's political editor, similarly noted,

> Certainly the Scottish media have doggedly pursued the constitutional story – but not, I would submit, to the exclusion of other topics. They did so because it was the defining issue in Scotland, underpinning the cross-party debates over education, health, public spending and the rest.
> (Taylor 1999: 23–4)

Farquharson was aware that political journalists might be seen as just 'devo-enthusiasts' intent on creating jobs for themselves. He thought that the press should be seen as holding accountable those in power: 'Some of the business of government is frankly dull. But some of government's internal machinations are fascinating. We're going to be reporting politics red in tooth and claw.' Well before the Scottish Parliament was convened, therefore, there were firm indications that neither the new legislature nor the Scottish Executive would be getting an easy ride. Journalists saw themselves as part of the process of political change, not just as observers.

Martin Clarke, about to leave *The Scotsman* for the *Daily Record*, maintained (in April 1998) that the Labour Party under Donald Dewar had not established a distinctive programme, giving too much room for manoeuvre to the SNP. He pointed at Dewar's failings as a popular politician. His mission for the *Record* was to 'try and stick a rocket up Scottish Labour's arse . . . The *Record* will have to help push a New Labour agenda in Scotland.'

The idea that Labour should be given a hard time was certainly seen as widespread by Kenny Farquharson, at the heart of the political journalists' pack. He noted reporters' satisfaction at putting Tony Blair on the spot over the 1997 devolution referendum, leading Downing Street to berate the Scottish press (see Ritchie 2000: 43). Iain Martin maintained that since Andrew Neil's appointment as editor-in-chief of Scotsman Publications, there had been 'more questioning of the Scottish media consensus, without abandoning the pro-devolution agenda'. He acknowledged that this shift had caused alarm among 'senior home rule activists'.

Our conversations and interviews at this time tapped into a self-image of a political press that was less easily 'spun', less easily influenced, and decidedly pricklier than its Westminster counterpart, which at that time was seen as easily intimidated by the Downing Street press machine. It was believed that the present confrontational, aggressive style of political journalism would not readily disappear, even if the much-vaunted claims of introducing a consensual style of politics were realised. Some journalists made it clear that the SNP would be given careful scrutiny in the May 1999 Scottish elections because they had a chance of sharing power.

Yet, understandably, expectations as to how things might actually change under a devolved political order were both imprecise and rather muted. Kenny Farquharson doubted that there would be a 'new journalism' just because a new form of government was coming along. The apparent willingness to talk about a 'new politics' in the government, he thought, might not produce fundamental change. He did not see the Scottish Parliament as being as important as the 'genuine Scottish government'. Martin Clarke was sceptical that political reporting could avoid the Lobby terms employed in London: 'It might be more transparent than Westminster, but politics is politics. It doesn't matter what kind of formal structure you impose. It always ends up being done behind closed doors.' But he did have hopes for a more open, indiscreet parliament than Westminster.

Kenny Farquharson, Iain Martin and *The Herald's* Scottish political editor, Murray Ritchie, all thought that some kind of Lobby system would emerge, irrespective of how the rules of the game were constructed. A need for off-the-record briefings would remain; official briefings were one thing but there would still be a need for gossip and unattributable talk, they thought. In short, whatever emerged would not be fundamentally different from the system south of the border.

We also asked for views on spin doctors and the Scottish Office Information Directorate (SOID). Clarke said that 'politics these days is all about presentation' and that he would welcome more professionalism in presenting stories by the Scottish Office. Iain Martin described the SOID as 'a shambles' and welcomed the possibility of professional spinning. Ritchie also shared this low opinion of the Scottish Office, which he described as 'a culture of not-speaking'. The clumsy handling of the controversial decision to site the Parliament at Holyrood was taken as a case in point.

Ritchie remarked acerbically of one top civil servant: 'He's always preaching on about openness, more transparency. If you ask a question he won't give you an answer. You can't even speak to him.' In a line of argument that was to assume steadily greater significance after devolution, the finger was pointed directly at the Secretary of State for Scotland, Donald Dewar. As one political editor put it: 'Dewar is not a modern politician,' – a serious failing in his view. In the run-up to devolution, political journalists wanted more professional news management by the Scottish Office.

Several political editors made it clear that spin-doctors gave them no concern. Kenny Farquharson remarked: 'Spin is good because it provides a window into what the politicians are trying to get you to write . . . I'd far rather have spin than silence.' Murray Ritchie expected an Alastair Campbell style of news agenda-setting to emerge in Edinburgh in line with the London model. He believed that the antidote to news management was interpretation by political correspondents. While recognising that journalists would have connections to government, he said: 'What we don't want is an institution-alised process whereby government leaks information to favoured journalists.' As a counterweight to this, The Herald's line (also espoused by the paper's Scottish political correspondent, Robbie Dinwoodie) was to seek attributable, on-the-record material.

Engagement in the pre-devolutionary reporting process had begun to crystallise journalists' beliefs about how political communication would develop in Scotland. Alongside these, we also detected the emerging demands that fuelled a formidably effective lobbying process aimed at gaining access to the political process in the new institutions.

THE PRESS PACK FORMS A NEW CLUB

The perceived lack of engagement in Scottish affairs by journalists in London was more than matched by the intense interest in Scotland in practical arrangements. A small group of established political journalists decided to secure the place of the press pack in the new political order. Robbie Dinwoodie recalled it thus:

> You're looking at a time when *The Herald* had just gone up from having one Scottish political correspondent to having a team of three, gearing up towards the formation of the Parliament. Other papers were in the process of doing the same. So we actually had a small corps of Scottish-based political staffers on newspapers. And that corps was in the process of expanding to meet the new needs of devolution . . . The intention was always to have anyone who was a bona fide working journalist who spent their time covering Scottish politics automatically entitled to join.

A constitution for a Scottish Parliamentary Press Association (SPPA) was first drafted in early 1998 (SPPA 1998a). The group was originally formed late in 1997, principally at the initiative of Kenny Farquharson. It has been difficult to establish an exact figure but about a dozen people became involved at that point, mainly from *The Herald, The Scotsman* and the *Daily Record.* In mid-1999 (by which time it had extended its remit from print journalists to take in broadcasters as well) the new body restyled itself the Scottish Political Journalists' Association (SPJA). In March 2000, the expanded body agreed a new constitution (SPJA 2000). Only in the course of summer 2000 was a first attempt made to establish a firm membership base by collecting a fee of £20. Robbie Dinwoodie became the first convenor. Until then, the organisation had been steered by Kenny Farquharson.

Wittingly or not, the SPPA drew upon the experience of a previous generation of political journalists (some still active) who had anticipated covering a Scottish Assembly. In 1979, during the then Labour government's failed attempt at devolution, an Association of Political Correspondents in Scotland (APCS) was formed. This body produced a 'Memorandum on the Reporting and Information Arrangements of a Scottish Assembly and Executive'. The seven-page document was wide-ranging and embodied familiar aspirations for 'establishing a model of open government and unhindered access to information' and for 'simpler, more straightforward dealings' in the parliamentary chamber (APCS 1979: 2, 7). The language was that of radical democracy. It presumed journalism's place, as of right, in reporting public affairs in the Assembly-to-be. The drafters of the memorandum rejected the idea of Westminster Lobby-style journalism as inappropriate for Scotland and argued instead for wide access for all journalists, as well as for free movement around the spaces of the Assembly: 'Our point is that the existence of such a "corps" should not be taken to confer any special privilege – the flow of information should not be confined to it' (APCS 1979: 4).

The political journalists of the late 1970s also argued that a government spokesman should speak publicly on its behalf (although they thought this would be a minister rather than today's spin doctor). They also proposed an open government approach sharply at variance with the Official Secrets Act, and asked for more media-friendly civil servants.

The rest of the document is more trade-union like, addressing the practicalities of media facilities in the Assembly. But once again, there was an important pre-echo of arguments that preceded the setting-up of the Scottish Parliament in 1999. Two decades ago, the use of closed-circuit television to foster public interest was urged by political correspondents. While the capacities of information and communication technologies have moved on dramatically since then, the same desire to connect with the wider public resurfaced in 1998. However, this did not come from journalists or broadcasters, who were extremely focused on securing their own positions and their access to the Scottish Parliament. Rather, the wider vision came from within the Scottish Office's expert panel on information and communication technologies, where Professor Lesley Beddie of Napier University – later to become Head of Communications at the Scottish Parliament – was, with others, arguing powerfully for connecting the people and the legislature through interactive technologies. This picked up on (and developed) ideas about openness and accessibility already bruited in the government's White Paper, *Scotland's Parliament*, which said:

> The accommodation must allow Scottish Parliamentarians and their staff to work efficiently, harnessing the best of modern technology. People must be able to see and meet their elected representatives and to watch the Scottish Parliament in operation. Provision needs to be made to permit easy reporting and broadcasting of Parliamentary proceedings so that people throughout Scotland can be aware of its work and decisions.
> (Scottish Office 1997a: 31)

There was a striking continuity between the ideas of the previous generation and those being debated in Scotland prior to setting up the Parliament, even if some had been espoused by different players. The professional continuity in the media was certainly obvious as political journalists prepared their case prior to the installation of the Parliament. The SPPA played its hand rather well, showing both a strategic sense of what was wanted, tactical nous in building its credibility, good negotiating skills to achieve its aims, and effective behind-the-scenes pressure on ministers and civil servants when, initially, the organisation was confounded over some matters. Considering how few journalists were being represented, it can be judged to have had a disproportionate impact on events.

The SPPA's formal purpose (as stated in its draft constitution) was 'to represent and promote the interests of political journalists working in Scotland'. The constitution defined eligibility for membership quite narrowly:

> Membership of the SPPA will be open to anyone who meets all of the following criteria:
>
> a. Applicants must have journalism as their primary occupation.
> b. Applicants must work primarily for print media.
> c. Applicants must have political journalism as the primary purpose of their work.
> d. Applicants must be resident in Scotland.
> (SPPA 1998a: 1)

We enquired as to the logic of these rules. The print journalists were afraid that broadcasters might swamp the organisation and define its priorities, although part of the longer-term game-plan was to widen membership to include broadcast journalists once the press's case over media relations and facilities in the new Parliament had been prosecuted to the SPPA's satisfaction. At that later stage, the SPPA wanted to be recognised as the sole political journalists' forum. But that was not the opening gambit. The stress on journalism as the only job was aimed against commercial lobbyists, public relations professionals, and any interest group that had members purporting to be journalists. The aim was to exclude these from access to the Parliament. Finally, the residency qualification was intended to ensure that membership be predominantly composed of those working at Holyrood on a day-to-day basis. It was pointed out that there could be tensions between London and Edinburgh political reporting teams. *The Herald* was cited as an instance of this both inside and outwith that newspaper. In short, the Scottish political press had drawn the wagons round in a rather tight circle.

From the start, the SPPA recognised that it would have to act 'almost like a trade union', in Kenny Farquharson's words. Murray Ritchie described it as 'our vehicle for negotiating with the Scottish Office'. The first objective was to settle the terms of facilities in the Scottish Parliament. The press were particularly concerned not to be elbowed aside by their television rivals. We were told by one political editor, that:

> off the record, there was a feeling that print media and broadcast wanted very different things out of it . . . We have won certain victories. We were always conscious, and still are, that we didn't want to be an add-on to broadcasting.

We didn't want the Scottish Office to think, well, it's all about broadcast media, and then you can find a few rooms at the back to accommodate us.

The political press believed that at Westminster the broadcasters took precedence. Anything that might replicate in Edinburgh the Millbank studio operation therefore caused concern. They were insistent that print journalists had distinctive priorities. On a slightly more elevated note, it was also recognised that the Scottish Parliament was starting with a blank sheet and that some thought could be given as how the job might be done in novel ways. Should some kind of special access to government be sought for political correspondents? The Scottish Secretary, Donald Dewar, had already said of the Scottish Office's policy, that 'We are not likely to wish to recreate the Lobby system,' (Schlesinger 1998: 69). This kind of assurance was certainly not being taken at face value. As Murray Ritchie put it, when explaining why the SPPA had been set up,

> We just wanted a system that in Scotland didn't favour a few, which would be open to the entire Scottish media and anybody else who was interested . . . and we wanted a system where more of the information coming out of government spokesmen would be sourceable.

In the eighteen-month run-up to the installation of the Scottish Parliament, there was time to consider what might be learned from Westminster and other parliaments and to create a system unburdened with precedent. These musings were to emerge more fully into public later in 1998, as we shall see.

The SPPA's first target was the Scottish Office's sixty-six-page *Building User Brief* (Scottish Office 1997b). The political press's perceptions of where the Scottish Office wanted to locate them were rooted in deep suspicion. In Murray Ritchie's words, 'It was a civil servant's solution . . . The whole intention was to screen the politicians from the media.' Aside from their concern about the right to roam the corridors, political journalists were especially incensed by the proposal for a single press room in the new Parliament building. The offending paragraph, describing the proposed 'press room', stated:

> This is a large open-space office with forty desk spaces equipped with a telephone, VDU and printer and writing space. A fax facility is shared among three persons with a four drawer filing cabinet per person. When more than forty spaces are required for special occasions, this should be achieved by the provision of additional temporary IT facilities and desk sharing. The room is also equipped with viewing monitors and earpiece connections to the Parliamentary broadcast channel. It should be possible to divide the room into two equal areas with a sliding, folding, sound-proofed screen.
> (Scottish Office 1997b: 31)

In our interviews with journalists, this was ridiculed. Kenny Farquharson said the civil servants knew nothing of journalists' behaviour. Leave the room for a cup of coffee, or a toilet break, and a rival would be switching on your computer to see what you were working on. Aside from that, you could hardly have a private conversation with the newsroom or sources when thirty-nine pairs of ears were intent on listening in. Sharing space in this way simply did not recognise the realities of the competitive nature of journalism.

It was not just the civil servants' lack of understanding of journalists' working practices that bothered them, as emerged from the SPPA's response to the *Building User Brief* penned by Robbie Dinwoodie in January 1998 (SPPA 1998b). The SPPA questioned whether the Scottish Parliament would indeed be an open and accessible institution. Aside from the restricted office space being offered to the press, it was argued that the proposals indicated limited access to 'the corridors of power', as it was phrased; the proposed Holyrood regime was compared unfavourably to the press's ability to circulate at Westminster. It was noted that larger staff groups would be looking for their own private offices. Particular exception was taken by the SPPA to the failure to plan for the free mingling of the press with MSPs and to the planned exclusion of the press from common dining and bar facilities for Members and political and parliamentary staff. As one political editor observed to us, the civil servants did not grasp 'the mechanisms of newsgathering, especially for print journalists'. They also evidently lacked a sense of how journalism and politics fitted together to produce a culture. Or, as he put it, 'the buzz, the gossip and the social aspect that the press can give to a parliament' would be missing. He believed that the outcomes of plotting and tales of intrigue being spilled to the press were integral to a parliament's life, and went on to remark that politicians actually liked to be close to the press because it was 'an early warning system' for them.

This SPPA agenda was carried forward into the series of meetings between the media and the Scottish Office Constitution Group in the first half of 1998. The journalists were successful in arguing for 'cellular office space' and, through constant pressure, they convinced the Scottish Office that twice the space originally planned for was actually needed. We were told that their arguments were backed up by lobbying from their editors. One broadsheet editor believed that the entire planning process had been dominated by the Scottish Office's 'unimaginative' approach to the question of space. In his view, the press had been seen as more of a nuisance than the electronic media and the civil servants wanted to keep them at a distance. But he did not think the politicians took the same view.

Aside from the use of this kind of lobbying, there were 'chats' with civil servants who also received letters that were 'very direct and to the point', as one journalist source put it. He added: 'We made sure that ministers knew our arguments.' The SPPA was also keen to head off the setting-up of a privately-funded-and-run media centre, an idea floated as ministers became increasingly nervous of the spiralling costs of the Parliament building. The political journalists did not regard themselves as part of a cost-cutting plan to save on space and facilities. On the contrary, they demanded access to a lobby where political correspondents could accost politicians entering and leaving the chamber. If that reflected old-established Westminster practice, then so be it.

The SPPA's agenda of practical demands – like that of the broadcasters – was carried through into the specialist group convened by the Scottish Office to establish arrangements for the media coverage of the Parliament. This first met towards the end of 1998. Although there was some concern about the SPPA becoming 'an administrative arm of the Scottish Office in the press field', as it was put to us, such involvement was seen as essential in order to shape the political journalists' stake in the devolved political order.

THE EXPERT PANEL ON MEDIA ISSUES

The creation of the new, devolved, political order involved a lengthy process of shadow institution-building. The Consultative Steering Group on the Scottish Parliament (CSG) met for the first time in January 1998. Its membership included representatives of the four main Scottish political parties and also of a range of civic groups and other interests. Its remit was:

> To bring together views on and consider the operational needs and working methods of the Scottish Parliament.

> To develop proposals for the rules of procedure and Standing Orders which the Parliament might be invited to adopt.
> (CSG 1998b: 2)

The CSG's report was submitted to the Secretary of State for Scotland in December 1998. Whereas the Scotland Act 1998 set out the formal constitutional position for devolution, the CSG's report may be regarded as embodying an informal constitutional discourse of high aspirations as well as of practical suggestions. The new Parliament was to be open, accessible and accountable. As we have noted, the CSG's thinking was in a direct line of succession from the work of the Scottish Constitutional Convention which had substantially inspired the devolution White Paper of July 1997, *Scotland's Parliament*. The CSG's activities covered a wide range of matters. The activity was administered by civil servants from the Scottish Office Constitution Group, advised by a number of expert panels.

Right at the end of the CSG's reporting period, an Expert Panel on Media

Issues was set up. According to one well-informed source, this was 'cobbled together at the last minute' because the Scottish Office had been so obsessed with ensuring that it sorted out arrangements for who would pay for the costs of broadcast coverage that establishing the rules of the reporting game had been sidelined. The recommendations of the panel were eventually published in May 1999, as a late supplement to the CSG's main report to the Secretary of State. The Expert Panel on Media Issues was a crucial locus for bringing together and systematising the various negotiations earlier undertaken between the Scottish Office, the broadcasters, and the press. It proved a key first step in institutionalising relations between the media and the new Scottish Parliament.

We analyse the steps that led to the Media Issues report, offering unprecedented insights into a hitherto-neglected aspect of the CSG process and a ringside seat at what really happened.

THE VIEW FROM THE SCOTTISH OFFICE

In early 1998, the SOID's Acting Director, Alistair McNeill, was working with the Scottish Office's Constitution Group on its relations with the media. The *Building User Brief* for the Scottish Parliament had been prepared and made available to the media. As we have shown above, its proposals had met with little enthusiasm in those quarters.

By spring 1998, there had been discussions and exchanges of correspondence with a range of media interests: the Scottish Daily Newspaper Society's (SDNS) representatives, James Raeburn and Martin Clarke; Kenny Farquharson for the SPPA; the cable television operators; BBC Scotland, represented by Val Atkinson and Mark Leishman; and Scott Ferguson for SMG. ITN had sent their editor-in-chief, Stuart Purvis, and the Press Association (PA) its chairman, Harry Roche, for discussions with the Devolution Minister, Henry McLeish. Civil servants had been to London to visit the PA, ITN and the Millbank media centre, and also to look at the Westminster parliamentary TV operation, CCT.

At that point, according to civil service sources, the *Building User Brief* was up for discussion, not set in stone. Both the press and the broadcasters had already found the proposed framework for their operations rather alarming. From the Scottish Office's point of view, the 'temporary accommodation' for the Parliament in place at the Church of Scotland's Assembly Rooms on the Mound was a 'delicate matter'.

There was perplexity at what to do with the media, which, according to one insider had 'a desire for a mini-Millbank'. It was recognised that the press and broadcasting had different needs and the civil servants were awaiting documented submissions, which they wished to incorporate into their planning process. The civil service also wanted to take account of media requirements in their plans for the new Parliament building at Holyrood, designed by the late Enric Miralles.

The Devolution Minister, Henry McLeish, believed that there should be a modern, web-based communications infrastructure to facilitate public access to information and make documentation widely available. This was in line with the CSG's aspirations to build an institution different from Westminster. And the media were seen as part of this.

In spring 1998, the Scottish Office was handling media issues purely as a practical matter of creating physical facilities to enable coverage of the Parliament. We were told that the basic debate was over how much it would cost and who would pay. There was certainly no 'principled divergence' over the need for coverage. It was admitted that negotiations had been 'tricky' at times, but they were felt to be 'on track'. The civil servants felt that requests for studio space by broadcasters could not be met. After encountering vociferous opposition they did accept that the initial idea of having an open-plan area with forty desks was not going meet with journalists' approval, not least because it gave them no privacy. It was also clearly recognised that the take-up of space would be of prime interest mainly for the Scottish media. Our impression at this point was that the civil servants felt themselves to be under considerable media pressure. Ministers were taking a strong interest in the negotiations, because they were concerned to avoid adverse publicity and also thinking ahead to the 1999 Scottish general election campaign.

The operation of parliamentary media coverage had not yet been addressed by the Scottish Office. We were told by civil servants that a distinction needed to be made between the Parliament and the Executive. Our sources thought that media relations with the new Executive 'won't be very different' from those prevailing with the Scottish Office. However, it was believed that the Parliament might forge some new connections with the media, perhaps through the coverage of the new, powerful committees.

As summer 1998 approached, the civil servants still felt themselves to be bogged down in less important matters – most notably questions of space for the media and the technicalities of parliamentary broadcasting. They were keen to resolve these issues and move on, as they had yet to start discussions about the rules governing coverage. Thus far, BBC Scotland had figured large in negotiations, and was perceived in the Scottish Office as finding devolution useful for building up its facilities. By contrast, SMG were seen as keeping a low profile in discussions. According to Scottish Office sources, moreover, there were divergent views among press journalists and editors on whether or not a Lobby system should emerge to deal with Parliament and the Executive. This difference of views surfaced later in private discussion and public debate. We detected a wish to bring more voices into the debate to counter the feeling that the larger and more prominent media organisations had been calling the shots. At that time, the Constitution Group was thinking about setting up a group of media experts to ensure that wider soundings could be taken. It was recognised that media questions had been crowded off the CSG's agenda.

FORMALISING CONSENSUS ON MEDIA ISSUES

Discussion between the Scottish Office and media interests had been underway since the devolution referendum but grew in frequency in the course of 1998. These meetings resulted in the gradual, informal shaping of agreements about how the Scottish Parliament might be covered. However, the emergent consensus now needed to be incorporated more formally into the broader process that the Minister for Devolution and his Scottish Office Constitution Group were undertaking through the CSG.

At its 27 July 1998 meeting, the CSG first discussed the establishment of an Expert Panel on Media Issues. That session shaped the eventual terms of reference. The officials reported that meetings had been held with a range of media interests and organisations. Requests for accommodation in the temporary Parliamentary campus on the Mound were to be met by locating the media at Lawnmarket House on the Royal Mile, an annex to the main Parliament's offices on George IV Bridge. The media were also to be allocated space in the Assembly Hall, where the temporary Parliament chamber was to be located. This space consisted of a press gallery and radio and television commentary boxes.

Finally, the question of an Expert Panel was addressed. It was to have media and lay representatives, and cross-membership with the CSG. In a key passage, the CSG Secretariat identified the following issues as defining the relationship between the Parliament and the media:

> Who are to be regarded as media and how will any media accreditation system be policed?
> Where will the line be drawn between areas in which the media has free and unfettered access to MSPs and areas in which MSPs will have a degree of privacy?
> Should there be a code of conduct?
> Where will broadcasters be allowed to film in the Parliamentary complex?
> The relevance of a 'lobby' system'.
> (CSG 1998a)

The CSG's paper was entirely concerned with the Parliament rather than the Executive, and this was of considerable significance, as we shall see. The issues identified all concerned how control over the media might be exercised.

TAKING POSITIONS IN PUBLIC

In between the recommendation to set up an Expert Panel and the panel's first meeting, lobbying by various media interests continued. Some of what had transpired behind the scenes came to the surface at a conference on 'Reporting Holyrood', organised by Napier University in collaboration with the SPPA and held on 8 September 1998. This demonstrated the important role that public fora play in a country the scale of Scotland. They often permit the outcomes of private discussion to emerge in public, before it goes beneath the surface again. Some of the key speakers at the conference were also members of the Expert Panel, namely, Robert Gordon, Head of the Constitution Group, and the conference's chairman, Kenny Farquharson, described at the conference as 'the initiator' of the SPPA.

The SPPA's founders wanted the conference to test the waters among media colleagues whose opinions were unknown. They also wished publicly to draw a line between journalists and lobbyists. The latter were referred to privately by one SPPA activist as 'the brown economy, the bullshit economy'. The SPPA hoped that pressure for regulating lobbyists would build up and prevent them from passing themselves off as journalists. The SPPA's leading lights also wanted to stop journalists writing for lobbying organisations. The conference organisers intended the political parties to make their intentions for news management clear and wished to see if figures such as the Secretary of State's special adviser, David Whitton, might indicate how they intended to work once the Executive was set up.

In the background papers provided for 'Reporting Holyrood', the SPPA described itself thus:

> The organisation has two main aims. The first is to advise the Scottish Office on what kind of accommodation and facilities need to be provided for the press, both at the Parliament's temporary base on the Mound and its permanent home in a new building at Holyrood. The second aim is to stimulate debate on how the political press should operate within this Parliament, given the widespread hope that it will be a model of accountable democracy and open government.

This was a nice statement of the organisation's mix of trade union aims and high principles. It was no accident that these should be coupled. Those at the heart of the SPPA were uncomfortably aware that some of their press colleagues and the broadcasters regarded them as 'rather masonic' and were now seeking a public airing for arguments previously pursued behind closed doors.

The conference's key opening session was on 'briefings and spin'. The question posed – rather guilelessly – was: 'How should the new Scottish

Executive deal with the press – by daily on-the-record and on-camera briefings, or by nods, winks and whispers?' It was addressed by Lorraine Davidson, a short-lived director of communications for the Scottish Labour Party (and later political editor of the *Scottish Mirror*); Michael Russell, Chief Executive of the SNP; Bill Shaw, Head of Media at the Scottish Conservative and Unionist Party; and Willie Rennie, Chief Executive of the Scottish Liberal Democrats.

Lorraine Davidson thought it possible to make a fresh start and that government should be open and not focused on a small media elite. She was against ministerial spokespeople going on camera and expressed concern about security in the Parliament in the event of public demonstrations. Mike Russell argued for open access to information from government and a departure from the 'bad old Westminster ways'. He advocated a minister of information accountable to the government and Parliament. Bill Shaw wondered what would replace the Lobby system and argued that a commitment to openness would not stop off-the-record briefings. Willie Rennie stated a commitment to open structures, with on-the-record briefings for the press and on-camera briefings from government spokespeople and ministers. Thus, the political parties were divided over how the media should be managed.

A question from BBC Scotland's Val Atkinson over the extent to which the Westminster rules governing the coverage of Parliament should change also brought out some differences. Labour and the Conservatives were most inclined towards a restrictive policy. The SNP held that if Parliament were not interesting to watch, the public might be disappointed.

The debate moved on, at the prompting of *The Scotsman*'s Peter MacMahon, to how journalists should be regulated and accredited, an issue later much discussed in the Expert Panel on Media Issues. There was widespread agreement – in a talismanic phrase that was repeated throughout the conference and then during subsequent expert discussion – that even the *Oban Times* had a right to cover the Parliament and the Executive: in short, that there should be no closed shop of political reporters.

An intervention by the SNP's Mike Russell distinguished between the press and lobbyists. Russell said MSPs would draw up the rules for lobbyists whose activities needed statutory regulation. Struan Stevenson (a director of the PS Public Affairs agency and later a Conservative MEP) retorted that lobbyists were drawing up their own code of conduct and that journalists were often apt to push their own proprietors' interests. Murray Ritchie, citing his experience of journalism at Brussels, argued that the EU had difficulty in distinguishing between journalists and lobbyists and that he disapproved of the selling of information in the public domain. The lobbyist Robbie MacDuff of Holyrood Strategy contested that this was an old-fashioned view.

The debate was dominated by the political press. But the broadcasters were also intent on putting down their marker for how Executive briefings should be run. Both Val Atkinson (BBC Scotland) and Mark Smith (Scottish TV) proposed that briefings should be held on camera and underlined the public interest in being able to source statements directly, rather than allowing unattributable leaks to shape public opinion. They could see no difference between press and broadcasting in this regard. Their view received no support from the press.

Robbie Dinwoodie of *The Herald* supported the idea of attribution, arguing that otherwise 'big personalities' such as Alastair Campbell could emerge, invested with mystique. In response, David Whitton, Donald Dewar's special adviser, said daily briefings on government business could be attributable and on the record. He also thought that policy statements by individual ministers could be on camera but would not commit himself to having televised briefings.

Thus, there were differences of view over when spokesmen and ministers might go on, or off, the record, and what should be shown on camera. And, as we shall seen, these played into the private discussions of the Media Issues panel. It was plain, however, that the media people, politicians and news managers present generally recognised that transparency had its limitations: off-the-record briefings and conversations would still take place, whatever the formal rules of the game.

A session on 'the Holyrood Lobby' asked:

> Should any journalist have the right to membership of the Holyrood press pack? What rules, if any, should govern conversations with MSPs in the corridors of the Parliament building? What facilities and access to MSPs will be available at the Mound and at Holyrood? Is there a case for a code of conduct and a register of journalists' interests?

This entire agenda was directly translated into the private deliberations of the Media Issues panel – not surprisingly as the panel's civil service chairman was one of the keynote speakers in the 'Lobby' session. Robert Gordon invoked the Scottish Constitutional Convention's thinking and the White Paper, *Scotland's Parliament*. The philosophy, he said, was to adopt modern working methods, be accessible, encourage participation, and seek views and advice from specialists. The Media Issues panel would advise the CSG on these lines.

In response, Robbie Dinwoodie of *The Herald* and Peter MacMahon of *The Scotsman* both stated that there should be a presumption of access and openness. MSPs and ministers were not to be allowed to hide because correspondents could not freely roam the Parliament buildings; there should be no 'Lobby-basis' conversations. Indeed, off-the-record conversations should be the exception rather than the rule. This line later figured during the panel's deliberations. So did Dinwoodie's argument that only bona fide journalists should be allowed to operate at Holyrood and that lobbyists who practised journalism had the problem of working for another interest. MacMahon was also against restrictions on journalists' right to roam. He picked up another SPPA theme – accreditation – and asked what criteria would be used to define who could report the Parliament. He proposed that a media liaison group be established and that passes be allocated more transparently than at Westminster.

Shaping the agenda

We have argued that the political press became increasingly aware of itself as a collective force as devolution approached. A small group of activists created the SPPA, which then lobbied for its own agenda in reporting the new Scottish political institutions. By being organised, the SPPA shaped the private and public debate that led up to the establishment of the Expert Panel on Media Issues.

Once the arguments began to be aired in public, tensions between lobbyists and journalists were plain for all to see. But there were also differences between press and broadcasters. And just how much access the media would have to the Executive and MSPs – and on what terms – remained an open question. These were now matters for the Expert Panel on Media Issues to resolve.

CHAPTER 4

Writing the rules of the game

THE EXPERT PANEL ON MEDIA ISSUES

The panel met on 8 December 1998 and on 9 February 1999 at St Andrew's House, the Scottish Office headquarters at the foot of Calton Hill in Edinburgh. The Minister of State for Home Affairs, Devolution and Local Government, Henry McLeish, had asked for advice on:

How the Parliament and the media should relate to each other;

How the Parliament should present itself through the media;

How the media should conduct itself while covering the Parliament; and

The terms on which Members of the Scottish Parliament, its staff and the Executive should have contact with and speak to the media.
(CSG 1999: 37)

The remit was framed by the CSG's expectation that the Scottish Parliament should have 'a culture of openness and accessibility'. It was assumed that by informing the citizen the media would enable greater public participation in the parliamentary process. The panel's membership was as follows:

Robert Gordon, chairman	The Scottish Office, Constitution Group
Val Atkinson	Deputy Head of News and Current Affairs, BBC Scotland
Fiona Ballantyne	Director, Network Scotland
Professor Lesley Beddie	Department of Computing, Napier University
Martin Evans	Director, Scottish Consumer Council
Kenny Farquharson	SPPA (Political Editor, *The Sunday Times, Scotland*)
Frances Horsburgh	Political Correspondent, *The Herald*
Harriet Jones	Head of News, Scot FM

Bill Livingstone	Editorial Director, Dunfermline Press Group
John Penman	Assistant Editor, *Daily Record*
George Reid	Consultative Steering Group
John Scott	Editor, *Evening Times*
Mark Smith	Senior Producer, Scottish Television
Ramsay Smith	Editor, *Scottish Daily Mail*
Brian Taylor	Political Editor, BBC Scotland
Derek Tucker	Editor, *Press and Journal*

Secretariat

Paul Grice	The Scottish Office, Constitution Group
Stewart Gilfillan	The Scottish Office, Constitution Group
Ruth Connelly	The Scottish Office, Constitution Group
Roger Williams	Director, Scottish Office Information Directorate

The panel comprised a representative range of media interests from the Scottish daily and Sunday broadsheets, the daily tabloids and evening papers, and radio and television, some lay members, an influential academic member of the CSG's Information Technology panel, and a key member of the CSG itself. Serviced by the Scottish Office's Constitution Group, the membership remained largely stable for both meetings, with the media representatives holding the floor for the most part under the subtly directive chairmanship of Robert Gordon. David Whitton, special adviser, The Scottish Office, was sent the papers and named as a member in the unpublished documentation, but did not attend either meeting.

The group was joined for its second meeting by Bill Livingstone, representing the Guild of Editors, an explicit move to bring in a representative of the weekly press. The attempt to secure a print journalist representative from outwith the central belt failed when the editor of the Aberdeen's *Press and Journal* was unable to attend the second meeting. Scotsman Publications, the panel was informed, had pressured ministers and civil servants to be allowed to attend but were told that they should pursue their grievance about non-representation with the SDNS and the SPPA. Their group's declared opposition to a Lobby system was indeed expressed through the SPPA's representative.

Overall, the panel was unquestionably an influential group. Robert Gordon went on to become Head of Executive Secretariat at the Scottish Executive. George Reid became Deputy Presiding Officer of the Scottish Parliament, Paul Grice its Chief Executive, and Lesley Beddie, Director of Communications there. John Scott became Director of Communications for the Scottish Labour Party.

Panel members were clearly familiar with the CSG's aspirational rhetoric. They spoke in terms of liveliness, openness, moving away from Westminster's Lobby system, and of a desire for access for cameras and journalists. There was a broad consensus on the kind of spirit that ought to inform the creation of the new rules of the game.

The panel was provided with a range of papers for its first meeting in December 1998. These covered its remit and membership; media access at the Mound; Members, ministers, officials and the media; and television rules of coverage. These papers, regarded as confidential, largely set the agenda and framed the discussion. The civil servants certainly believed that they had identified the main issues and that any outstanding matters could be rapidly remedied, given the need to report to the CSG in February 1999.

The papers for the second meeting in February incorporated revisions proposed at the first meeting, and after some internal debate and amendment, these revised papers formed the basis for the report finally issued by the Scottish Office in May 1999, some time after the intended deadline (CSG 1999).

As a result of prior contact with the Scottish Office Constitution Group, one of the authors of this book, Philip Schlesinger, was invited to observe the panel's proceedings for this study.[1] Given the understanding on which this research was carried out, we have respected the concern for confidentiality. We have not identified particular speakers by name, nor directly cited any documents that were not published. We have resumed the panel's recommendations, described the thinking behind these, and recounted in broad, non-attributable terms the process of internal debate that led to the recommendations being made, bringing out key areas of controversy and negotiation.

THE PANEL'S RECOMMENDATIONS

The panel advocated the principle of wide access to the Parliament for the media. However, filmed interviews were to be in defined areas and subject to the interviewee's permission. The panel also established the principle of offering accreditation 'to all reasonable genuine applications' (CSG 1999: 38), subject to these coming from the editors of media organisations on individual journalists' behalf.

There was a clear-cut attempt to prevent the Parliament from becoming colonised by lobbyists 'masquerading' as journalists, in the recommendation that concerned freelances:

Freelance journalists/others should be required to produce evidence that they are engaged in reporting or commenting on events or issues of interest to the

public for news media organisations, broadcasting networks, magazines and periodical publications. They should also be required to declare any interests, paid or unpaid.
(CSG 1999: 38)

The panel recommended the creation of an 'accreditation committee' to advise the Parliament, recognising that temporary accreditation should be extended to visiting or overseas journalists, and that certain events, such as the opening ceremony, might require increased security. It was also further proposed that the media representatives' code of journalistic conduct should be endorsed by the Parliament.

It was recommended that 'formal briefings by the Parliament ought to be attributable and on camera' (CSG 1999: 38). The panel stressed that the Parliament's media relations officer's role would be restricted to factual matters, with any comments on MSPs' conduct excluded from the remit. Parliamentary staff were to be protected from journalistic intrusion.

Finally, in a recommendation that took its distance from ten years' experience at Westminster, the panel proposed that:

The Scottish Parliament should have the minimum of rules for television coverage. The 'gallery-surrogate' model, allowing the viewer to observe any aspect of proceedings at any time, as though he/she were a spectator in the public gallery should be adopted in filming proceedings.
(CSG 1999: 39)

BEHIND THE SCENES

The panel's central concern was with how political journalists would operate in the temporary parliamentary campus. The campus has three main sites that make up the new journalistic beat (see Figure 2). The Assembly Hall, on loan from the Kirk, is the site of the Parliament's debating chamber and located on the Mound. On George IV Bridge are the Council Chambers, where the Parliament's committee rooms are situated, and the former Lothian Regional Headquarters, where MSPs and their staff are accommodated. The media are housed in Lawnmarket House, on the High Street, adjacent to the Regional Headquarters and linked to it via a staircase. The Regional Headquarters is connected to the Council Chambers by a tunnel. The Catalan architect, the late Enric Miralles, had been commissioned to design and build the new Parliament building at Holyrood, so all the discussion related to the 'interim accommodation', as the civil servants called it.

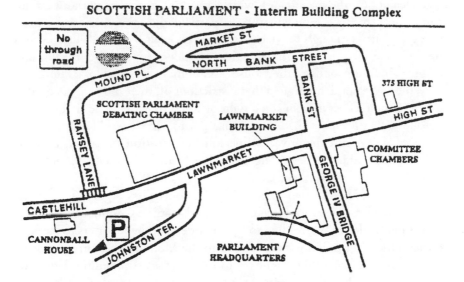

Figure 2 Accommodation on the Mound. This sketch-map was given to political journalists covering the Scottish Parliament. It shows the concentrated form of Scotland's political village on Edinburgh's Mound.

A question of access

> The basic act of journalism is knocking at the door even if all you get is 'No comment'.
> (Political journalist)

> You can't let MSPs be saddled with journalists on their shoulder. It's easier to move from a more to a less restrictive regime over time.
> (Civil servant)

The first issue addressed was media access. The panel's report records that it recognised that the 'interim accommodation' imposed constraints and that it was expected that 'fewer restrictions' would eventually apply at Holyrood. The panel wished 'to ensure that "behind the scenes" access would be properly managed to ensure the right balance between accessibility and such privacy as MSPs might reasonably expect' (CSG 1999: 40). A distinction was made between areas of unrestricted access, those requiring invitation, and those with no access. Restrictions were proposed by the civil servants for a variety of working areas involving the Parliament's Presiding Officer (the equivalent of the Speaker of the House of Commons), the Clerk, ministers, party leaders, staff accommodation and MSPs' offices.

Agreement on the meaning of 'wide access' did not come without a fight from the media representatives, particularly the political press correspondents, although the debate was always even-tempered. In line with the long-standing journalistic practice of 'doorstepping' politicians and hanging about the lobby of the House of Commons in search of a quote or a story, the correspondents argued that restrictions on their movements needed justification, in effect insisting on a right of access to MSPs. The civil servants responded that Members had their own right to private working conditions and needed to ensure the privacy of personal or constituency papers on their desks; they would not be hiding from the media and could be accosted elsewhere than in their offices.

Drawing on Westminster experience, the journalists argued against the proposed restrictions on movement. They said that the Commons lobby was increasingly a 'dead zone' leading to a greater demand by reporters to see MPs in their offices. This 'lesson' was applied to the Mound. The correspondents were concerned that MSPs might try to use strict access conditions to 'hide away', particularly at moments of controversy. The idea of needing an invitation to see an MSP was also disliked.

A compromise resulted: to allow access to corridors and open areas on all floors of the Regional Headquarters where MSPs had their offices, but not to ministerial suites nor to the open-plan areas where MSPs worked (CSG 1999: 49). The journalists were asked to produce a convention on this, which they duly did. The Code of Conduct produced for the Parliament's endorsement notes that '[a]ccredited journalists should observe agreed parliamentary regulations about areas that are out-of-bounds, and other agreed conventions' (CSG 1999: 52). This clash of views set the terms for the rest of the proposals: the civil servants were concerned to protect MSPs, ministers and parliamentary staff from untoward intrusion, whereas the journalists wanted to push out the boundaries as far as they could.

Where to film?

If the Scottish Parliament is to look different, you want to be sure that you make it interesting for the viewer.
(Broadcast journalist)

There's concern about people [MSPs and political correspondents] being frightened away because they could be seen on camera. But it would be Stalinist not to allow cameras in the corridor. We need to find a way around this.
(Civil servant)

Much the same debate occurred over 'areas for filming and sound recording' as over media access. The negotiations this time centred on the pursuit of the visual imperative by the broadcasters which, again, came up against the civil servants' desire to manage space. Interestingly, the broadcasters' need for pictures also raised the hackles of the political correspondents, laying bare the difference of interests that had led to the SPPA restricting its initial membership to the press alone.

The broadcasters wanted to convey the atmosphere of the Scottish Parliament by filming in the equivalent of the House of Commons' lobby, which is out of bounds to cameras. They therefore sought to break new ground by filming in the Black and White Corridor of the Assembly Hall, through which MSPs would enter and leave the debating chamber. The press also wanted to be allowed to take photographs in the chamber, which, once again, is not permitted in the Commons.

Broadcasters came up against two sets of objections. First, political correspondents were concerned that they might be having private conversations with MSPs in the corridor while a broadcast interview was under way with a different Member. The journalists did not want to be inadvertently recorded, thereby compromising a source. The broadcasters rejected the press journalists' suggestion that they be excluded from filming in the corridor. The chairman pushed both sides to devise 'an acceptable convention' to deal with this.

The second objection came from the civil servants and reflected their worries about the formation of media 'scrums' around politicians, endangering safety and security. The officials were also concerned about how many people could fit into the corridor. At the panel's first meeting, it was proposed that the print journalists and the broadcasters jointly work out a solution and a sub-group was set up to address this. The outcome, described in the panel's report as 'a compromise', was the right to film at a set of locations in the Assembly Hall, out-of-the-way areas of the Regional Headquarters building, one location in the Council Chambers and two outside sites (CSG 1999: 51). These areas broadly coincided with those already designated for unrestricted media access and those where access was by invitation only.

The following quotation from the panel's report conveys the attention to detail needed by the civil servants to resolve the dispute between press and broadcasters:

> The Black and White Corridor in the Assembly Hall – Television broadcasters and sound recordists should not be allowed to 'doorstep' MSPs as they exit from the main Chamber. With the agreement of a Member however, interviews may be done on the extreme left-hand side of this particular corridor. (Diagram 1 refers). An inject point will allow interviews to be conducted and pieces to camera recorded or broadcast live into programmes. The convention should be that filming shots would be head and shoulders with a general flavour only of the corridor and atmosphere of the House

behind and at all times within the limits shown in the diagram. Zooming to other Members should *not* be permitted nor should filming beyond the eastern entrance door to the main Chamber from the Black and White Corridor.
(CSG 1999: 51; emphasis in original)

Other locations proved to be much less contentious and there was no separate discussion of sound recording. The 'head and shoulders' convention, avoiding any background activity that might give information about conversations in the vicinity, became the rule for filming throughout the precincts. Still photography, if limited to a particular spot in the Chamber, and if flashes did not disturb Members, was not seen as a problem by the civil servants and occasioned very little discussion.

Who is a journalist?

The Scottish Office's opening position, reflecting the input of the CSG, was that there should be wide accreditation of bona fide journalists. It was also explicitly recognised that any rules should exclude 'single-issue journalists operating as lobbyists', and that the definition of a journalist should exclude those working for publications with restricted circulation lists. This, while generally backed by the panel, nonetheless provoked wide-ranging discussion. Media representatives wanted to know how accreditation would be managed. They asked how many journalists would be admitted, how passes and security clearance would be dealt with, whether there would be a 'Lobby system', whether different categories of journalists would be dealt with differently, and what would be done about accrediting foreign journalists. In short, the media representatives were pre-eminently concerned about how control would be exercised over reporting.

The secretariat held the line on wide access by coupling this with a proposal to regulate accreditation stringently through the Parliament's media relations officer, with advice from a panel of media representatives. The civil servants made it clear that the power to accredit ultimately resided in the Scottish Parliament Corporate Body (the legislature's administration). In response to those journalists who either favoured a Lobby system, or thought that a de facto one might emerge, it was conceded that the latter might indeed happen but that the principle was to try to avoid it. The civil servants argued that the Parliament's strong committees would be covered by specialist correspondents, who would need easy access. Such interest-driven coverage was also likely to apply to the local press. On the media side, it was plainly assumed that regular contact by political correspondents with the Parliament could lead to the emergence of a group of insiders with privileged connections and local knowledge. In the event, this belief proved to be well founded.

The panel's report argued in favour of wide accreditation by stating, first, that neither restrictiveness nor a two-tier system of accreditation was appropriate to a modern Parliament; second, that the specialist committee system would require access for specialist correspondents; and, third, that local papers would wish to develop links with their MSPs (CSG 1999: 42). This largely reflected the civil servants' determination to carry through the CSG's wishes. However, the journalists' desire to exclude lobbyists also found its way into the report through the strict requirement to prove journalistic bona fides, and by endorsing the power of a journalist-dominated accreditation committee.

By the panel's second meeting, 'single-issue journalists operating as lobbyists' had been cast into outer darkness. Editors were now required to vouch for the bona fides of their proposed accredited staff and to show that these were engaged in genuinely unrestricted publication. The media interests represented had also ensured their de facto control of the accreditation process. The Code of Conduct annexed to the report was produced by journalist members of the panel and strongly reflected their hostility to lobbyists:

> Accredited journalists should not act as lobbyists, paid or unpaid, for any individual or organisation that might seek to influence the political process or benefit from inside knowledge of the political process. Accredited journalists should not approach MSPs, civil servants, party officials or parliamentary staff to seek information for such individuals or organisation or to represent their views. (CSG 1999: 52)

However, it was recognised that putting the code into effect would be rather difficult for several reasons, not least because some accredited journalists were believed to act as paid consultants and some political correspondents also considered themselves to be political actors. The panel debated whether or not a declaration of interests could be demanded and ultimately decided that this should be made on the accreditation form, and that editors would ultimately be held responsible for this. This requirement did not find its way into the published Code of Conduct.

On or off the record?

> It's all about common sense. If you're [talking] in the loo, it's off the record. But you'd ask if you could use a quote.
> (Political journalist)

> Being unattributable in the interests of openness! We'll need some very clever drafting here!
> (Civil servant)

One key question addressed by the panel was under what terms exchanges between the media and MSPs should take place. There were no recommendations. The reason was simple: the panel was completely riven over the matter. The panel's report reflects the deep divergence of views, noting that it had:

> identified strong arguments both for and against a presumption that anything said should be attributable or non-attributable. The case for a presumption that conversations between MSPs and journalists were non-attributable – unless it was specifically agreed otherwise – is that it will encourage MSPs to talk to journalists openly without fear that any remark might be quoted. The counterview was that a presumption that anything said by an MSP in the Parliament could be quoted was more consistent with openness and accountability. The panel was unable to reach a unanimous view on this finely balanced issue.
> (CSG 1999: 44–5)

These anodyne phrases veil a divisive episode. In the Scottish Office's original briefing paper and in their interventions, the civil servants followed their interpretation of the CSG's wish: for everything to be on the record, unless otherwise agreed. The panel was advised that everything said by MSPs in the confines of the Parliament should be attributable, unless Members indicated otherwise. This was countered by a strong body of journalistic opinion which argued that openness would be best served if everything said was unattributed, since otherwise MSPs would be continually disclaiming remarks they were reported to have made. It was further argued that MSPs would simply be unwilling to talk to journalists on the record all of the time.

The first panel meeting left the matter surrounded with an air of perplexity and tension. Those arguing for a rule of non-attribution won the case, and indeed that was the minuted position. The Scottish Office was evidently taken aback by the demand to have all conversations off the record. The civil servants emphasised that this position might be publicly perceived as secretive. Most political journalists and newspaper editors present had strong views on what would work best in their relationships with politicians. They prevailed, and a recommendation not to attribute MSPs' conversations with journalists was embodied in the draft report to the CSG.

However, this did not command support from all the political correspondents, and those at *The Herald* and *Sunday Herald* went on record with their dissent. The second meeting of the panel therefore reopened the tricky question of attribution. Evidently not all the SPPA's members went along with its stated hostility to attribution and the organisation's credentials to speak for print journalists were questioned sharply.

The Herald's political staff made it plain that they disagreed with unattributable general conversations on the Parliament's precincts. *The*

Scotsman separately raised more general reservations about off-the-record briefings (Kenny Farquharson, SPPA, letter to Paul Grice, Scottish Office Constitution Group, 5 February 1999). *The Herald* also argued that to restrict press freedom at the outset would go against the aspirations of openness for the Parliament. It was further pointed out that Scottish local authorities did not operate on an unattributable basis. Most journalists and broadcasters on the panel wanted it made clear whether any given conversation was on or off the record.

Those arguing to the contrary said that briefings should be unattributable. If the Parliament allowed wider access, MSPs would be cautious about which journalists they felt they could speak to, since so many would be unknown to them. They would also be more reluctant to fly kites as they would risk public identification. In short, more openness from politicians could be achieved by encouraging greater frankness without running the risk of being reported directly.

The panel was told that the CSG had been shocked at the proposal to go for unattributable briefings as this went against its principle of openness. The result was that the original position – that all conversations should be unattributed – was now reversed. In the draft report sent out to panel members in late February 1999, the convention was reformulated: everything said by MSPs to journalists should now be considered attributable unless it was specifically agreed otherwise.

But this did not make it into the final report. We understand that effective pressure was applied by some editors and political correspondents to prevent attributable conversations becoming the norm. Threats were made to campaign against this. The CSG had no desire for public controversy. Nor, in the run-up to the first Scottish parliamentary election, did the Devolution Minister Henry McLeish wish to make enemies in the media. We were told that the final draft was greeted with some dismay by the CSG in early March 1999. Indeed, we were reliably informed that the delay in publication until May was due to producing the final version cited above. This is not widely known.

What should the Executive do?

The debate about attribution led into another debate about how the new Scottish Executive would deal with the media. The chairman made it clear that the panel's views could have no force, as the Executive's media relations were for it alone to determine. This line was accepted with reluctance by some journalists. Noting that most ministerial briefings were attributable, the panel was invited to consider the three options presented in its final report:

> Daily attributable briefing by a minister which could be either on or off camera.

> Daily attributable briefing by an official spokesman on or off camera on behalf of the Executive.
> Ad hoc briefing on attributable and non-attributable terms by ministers and spokespeople dictated by the timing of planned announcements and statements, or in response to breaking or running news stories.
> (CSG 1999: 47)

Discussion centred on the role of official spokespeople. The civil servants expressed concern about officials becoming media personalities. The media representatives countered by pointing to the public prominence of Prime Minister Tony Blair's official spokesman, Alastair Campbell. A group of broadcasters and print journalists united in the demand that Executive briefings should be on the record. But this was adamantly countered by other print journalists on the ground that they would be bland. This latter group reaffirmed its belief that private briefings would reveal more. In effect, there were two journalistic views: those who believed in the possibility of greater openness and those still thirled to the culture of secrecy. This was cross-cut by the different needs of press and broadcasting as the broadcasters piled in with a demand for attributable on-camera briefings.

Despite a plethora of interventions from media members determined to canvas their various preferences, the panel was steered firmly away from thinking that it should or could have any impact on the Executive's thinking by interventions made on behalf of the CSG and the SOID. The panel was told that this was a highly sensitive issue that could easily become ensnared in the known, divergent party-political views on how the Executive should handle information. The final report once again noted that no consensus could be reached. The panel was compelled to offer the following generalities and to reaffirm the CSG's aspirations:

> We strongly recommend . . . that the incoming administration should adopt an approach which is consistent with CSG's recommendations on openness and accessibility. This should include regular briefings to ensure a steady flow of information and provide the opportunity for the media to question the Executive.
> (CSG 1999: 47)

Televising Parliament

The panel's deliberations began by acknowledging Westminster's restrictive rules on television coverage. These were felt to have distanced the institution from the public. The civil servants proposed a 'gallery-surrogate' model, allowing the viewer to observe any aspect of the proceedings at any time as though viewing these from the visitors' gallery, with a variety of shots that made the coverage more lively. The broadcasters were intent on moving beyond the restrictions on television coverage in force at Westminster. As we have seen, this objective had been pursued by the BBC from the outset of its negotiations with the Scottish Office.

The starting-point for the panel's discussion was existing custom and practice in the House of Commons. Compared to the highly restrictive tone and intent of the Commons' rules, which are above all concerned with the dignity of the House, those for the Scottish Parliament are simple and relatively liberal. That said, they are clearly a variant of the Westminster rules, devised for politicians who actively want television inside the debating chamber, rather than regarding it as an unwelcome interloper. The proposals for rules of coverage eventually tabled at the second panel meeting reflected prior discussions between the broadcasters and civil servants in the Constitution Group. The light-touch approach carried the day through the two meetings, with no significant dissent.

The proposals proved largely uncontentious because so much had been worked out beforehand. Most concern was aired over protecting the 'feed', that is coverage of the proceedings in the chamber, from any abuse. Worries about infringing the dignity of the Parliament were akin to those at Westminster. In a somewhat tongue-in-cheek intervention, one broadcaster asked whether MSPs could be shown asleep in the chamber, as cut-aways from a Member speaking might not always show others manifesting an interest in the proceedings. Broadcasters successfully modified the proposed rule on the use of cut-aways so that it no longer mentioned other Members showing an interest. Westminster's established concerns were reflected in discussion about how disturbances or demonstrations might be reported and in agreeing to limit the use of proceedings in entertainment, satire and advertising.

A CONCLUDING PERSPECTIVE

The panel's report was decisive in setting the framework for how the media interrelate with the Scottish Parliament. In the next chapter, we show how the various systems recommended were installed and how the journalists rapidly turned into a political press corps.

The panel's report was a successful attempt to devise consensual terms of reference for how the Parliament was to be covered, under the banner of the 'new politics'. The rule-makers did not always succeed in making a fresh start. For instance, the proposal for generally attributable conversations between MSPs and journalists was defeated. Moreover, the panel's terms of reference were set up to ensure a procedural vacuum so far as the Executive was concerned. As John Penman, a journalist member of the panel and now editor of *Business am*, subsequently told us:

We were told we weren't able to [discuss this], but we wanted to. I felt the one area that we should really have spent a lot of time and we didn't get a remit for was the Executive briefing . . . We were allowed to make an observation – and that was it.

Brian Taylor, BBC Scotland's political editor and also a panel member, recalled: 'Everyone was aware that while we were actually talking about the parliamentary briefings, what we were really interested in was the Executive.'

An opportunity was lost. While the Parliament's media relations system moved smoothly into place as a result of prior consultation, the Executive's took some months to develop and produced considerable dissatisfaction among many journalists. Arguably, this contributed to the Executive's bumpy ride in the initial institution-building phase of the devolved political order.

NOTES

1. We have no reason to believe that Schlesinger's presence affected the course of the discussion. He was introduced to the panel by the chairman as someone who had been 'incredibly helpful to the Constitution Group' (a generous description as he had merely interviewed people there and not offered any advice). He was known to several of the participants; a number of those who did not know him spoke to him afterwards and some expressed surprise that he had taken his 'observer' remit so seriously and not pitched into the discussion. No-one who was asked for a follow-up interview showed either reluctance or concern; no-one refused to talk. In short, all of this suggests that Schlesinger's presence was perceived as unthreatening, adequately accounted for, and legitimate.

Chapter 5

The 'new' political journalism

Introduction

This chapter describes the first steps taken in constructing a system of political communication around the new, devolved institutions. It also analyses the post-devolution culture of political journalism. The political journalists were installed at Lawnmarket House immediately after the first Scottish parliamentary elections in May 1999. The newly-constructed framework of media relations and parliamentary broadcasting was the direct legacy of the Media Issues panel's recommendations.

The Parliament's Media Relations Office

The Media Relations Office is part of the Scottish Parliament's Communication Directorate, which groups information systems, information technology, research and libraries, and the *Official Report* (the Scottish equivalent of Westminster's *Hansard*). A media relations officer, Andrew Slorance, who came from the Scottish Office Information Directorate, was appointed to the Parliament shortly before the May elections.

The Scottish Parliament issued a Media Welcome Pack on 1 May 1999. Journalists were told about conditions for access, areas for filming and sound recording, the broadcast feed and how to access the Parliament's business. In this way, the rule-making activity of the expert panel was immediately translated into practice.

The Media Relations Office found it difficult to cope with the initial demands placed upon it. By the time the Queen had formally opened the Parliament on 1 July, a second press officer, Eric Macleod, had been appointed, and a third, Nicola Edwards, was in place in 2000. The Parliament's media relations team services the demands of political reporters for committee agendas and papers, news releases, and general information on the legislature's work.

The touchy issue of media accreditation was handled in line with the Media Issues panel's recommendations. Journalists wanting access were required to fill in a form and accept a code of conduct whose key clause states:

> Accredited journalists should not act as lobbyists, paid or unpaid, for any individual or organisation that might seek to influence the political process or benefit from inside knowledge of the political process. Accredited journalists should not approach MSPs, civil servants, party officials or parliamentary staff to seek information for such individuals or organisations or to represent their views. (Scottish Parliament 2000a)

Editors or heads of department are required to endorse applicants' declarations of interests. Each accredited journalist is subjected to a counter-terrorism check.

Almost all accredited journalists have come from the mainstream media, with no indication that this will change. Those accredited have to reconfirm their status annually. In the first wave of accreditations in 1999, some 380 individuals were issued with passes, although many (including some from the London press) never bothered to pick these up. The passes' one-year lifespan allowed the media relations staff to 'weed out' those who simply applied without actually needing or using them. After the first year, all the major news organisations were written to and asked to reapply for accreditation. In the 2000 round of accreditations, the list was reduced to some 200 persons, a large number of whom were technical staff at the BBC. The core users of the passes, as might be expected, were the Scottish political journalists, who numbered between thirty and forty and had mostly been there from the start.

We were told that the code had worked to exclude some who had felt they could not sign up to it. In an unpublicised test case, there was some quiet controversy about the accreditation of Chris Bartter, communications officer of the trade union UNISON. On behalf of the SPJA, Kenny Farquharson protested to Andrew Slorance that Bartter was not a bona fide journalist and that this opened the door to lobbyists. Bartter agreed to keep a low profile and check in with the media relations office before coming to the Parliament, where after protests, he would sit in the public benches rather than use the press gallery. He surrendered his pass during the first year.

The political press had originally envisaged having a formal hand in the process of checking credentials. However, in the rush of business during the opening days, an informal system of vetting was set up with the media relations office using 'channels' to check people out – in effect, resorting either to the Scottish Office or to trusted journalists. This informality has persisted. The political press has seen no reason to change a system that has so far served it well, and where informal protests are effective.

THE PARLIAMENT'S BROADCASTING AND SOUND RECORDING OFFICE

The Parliamentary Broadcasting Unit is staffed and operated by BBC Resources Scotland Ltd which won the contract to televise and produce an audio record of the Scottish Parliament's proceedings. The Unit was set up with a staff of nine. The 'feed' is subscribed to by most of the main broadcasters and transmitted on the Parliament's own in-house television system. The sound feed is used to compile the Parliament's *Official Report*.

The Broadcasting Unit is overseen by the Broadcasting and Sound Recording Office, with a staff of three, headed by Alan Smart, formerly a political programmes producer with Scottish TV. The broadcasting operation is seen as a parliamentary facility and comes under the Corporate Services Directorate, along with such functions as security and finance, and it has separate line management from the Media Relations Office. Smart was appointed some two months before the Scottish elections.

The Head of Broadcasting is supported by an advisory committee on broadcasting composed of the core users. This body meets intermittently. In the debating chamber, broadcasters' commentary boxes are provided by the Parliament and fifty seats are available in the press gallery, with room for an overspill on special occasions.

The chamber is covered by eight cameras. Most decisions about the installation of equipment had been made before the Head of Broadcasting was appointed. Expert circles queried the level of integration of the broadcasting system, whose television, audio and lighting facilities had each been separately installed by different companies. For instance, Fiona Ross, Scottish TV's seasoned political correspondent, dismissively talked to us of 'wedding-type video cameras' being used. The system is analogue, criticised by some broadcasting sources as lacking foresight at a time when digital equipment is commonplace. It is expected that the system will be changed when the move to Holyrood eventually takes place.

Two 'inject points' allow reporting in the Black and White Corridor and also from the steps in the courtyard outside the Assembly Hall. One committee room has four fixed TV cameras while the other four are wired to take sound-only broadcasts. The feed is directed from a control-room in the Assembly Hall's basement. While there might be technical limitations on what can be done, the 'gallery-surrogate' model has been implemented, thereby introducing a less formal style than at Westminster.

Alan Smart said that the tone had been set for him on 13 May 1999 'when [the Independent MSP and Labour rebel] Dennis Canavan famously crossed the floor of the House to shake [First Minister] Donald Dewar's hand – that would simply not be allowed at Westminster'. He gave another example of how he thought the boundaries of coverage had been enlarged:

> Jim Wallace, as the Justice Minister, made a statement in the House. It was a full ministerial statement on legal reform . . . an important statement . . . and what was most noticeable is virtually nobody from the Labour Party was there . . . And I quite consciously instructed the director to pan the full chamber, to show people that they were missing, and I think that's entirely legitimate.

Just as the Media Relations Office had to devise systems to deal with the rhythms of the parliamentary week, so too has the Broadcasting Office. It had to meet demands from the broadcasters for coverage of the committees, which first began to function routinely in September and October 1999. The Broadcasting Office started to identify newsworthy discussions along with the Parliament's clerks and to timetable activity accordingly. Committee convenors have wanted to hold meetings in the sole committee chamber equipped with television cameras. Forward plans for the move to Holyrood anticipate that a second committee room will provide a visual feed.

As 1999 drew to a close, demand for the feed was limited. Most footage was used by BBC Scotland and the Scottish ITV stations, with little going onto the UK networks. From the Broadcasting Office's point of view, the BBC's *Holyrood Live* was the best customer. Research by the media academic and radio critic Ken Garner (1999) has shown that the feed is also little used on Scottish radio stations, which prefer reporting and interviewing to using the proceedings more directly.

The Parliament's hostile press coverage in its first year meant that the quality of broadcasting became a matter of political concern. In April 2000, Christine Grahame, an SNP Member, asked the First Minister to approach broadcasters to ask for improved coverage. She suggested that a dedicated parliamentary public television channel be established. Donald Dewar replied that he thought it would be easier for broadcasters to invest in coverage when the Parliament had moved to Holyrood (Scottish Parliament 2000b).

The Broadcasting Office has been preoccupied with the technical implications of the Parliament's eventual move from its temporary home. Several working parties were set up in 1999: a Holyrood broadcasting and sound recording working group, drawn from across the range of the Parliament's directorates; a media 'end-user' group, bringing together press and broadcasting representatives as well as parliamentary staff to examine the question of media facilities at Holyrood; and a broadcasting and telecommunications working group to study the impact of technological convergence on the Parliament's information services. It remains to be seen what the outcomes will be.

THE JOURNALISTS MOVE IN

When the Labour-Liberal Democrat 'partnership' coalition was formed on 14 May 1999, Scottish political correspondents were still quite openminded as to how the Executive would develop its media relations. It was expected that the new Executive would ensure that a single, common line would come across, rather than allowing displays of policy divergence between First Minister Donald Dewar and his Liberal Democrat deputy, Jim Wallace. This issue was resolved on quite traditional British lines: David Whitton, the official spokesman, would brief on Cabinet proceedings. This followed the longstanding Whitehall convention that 'although formally attached to the Prime Minister, the Press Secretary's briefings of Lobby journalists should be understood as expressing the official position of the entire government, (Franklin 1994: 82). There would be one voice for the Cabinet, UK-style.

From the start, some correspondents expected conversations with those working in the new Executive to be mainly off the record. Journalists wanted to sort out the practicalities of news-gathering from the Parliament and the Executive: to access committee agendas and government reports, to establish the pattern for briefings, and the rules for embargoes and on- and off-the-record statements. Our interviews at this early stage showed that the Westminster model and the existing repertoire of established practice in British journalism had set the framework of expectations.

From the moment that Parliament opened its doors, over twenty full-time political press journalists were based at Lawnmarket House. They came from all sectors of the Scottish press: daily and Sunday, the 'red top' and middle-market tabloids, and the broadsheets. All of the titles were Scottish (or London papers with strong Scottish editions fighting for market share). The broadcasters were also there from the start: BBC Scotland with a bureau of eight political staff, along with Scottish TV's political correspondent. It was immediately apparent that political communication about the devolved institutions would be primarily oriented towards Scotland and the Scots.

THE SELF-IDENTITY OF THE SCOTTISH POLITICAL PRESS

All cultures have their underlying systems of belief and in this respect journalism is no different. In recent years in Scotland, the political press has certainly represented itself as collectively distinct from those who ply the trade south of the border. In particular, Scottish journalists have seen themselves as less credulous, as more capable of seeing through politicians' games, as tougher. This is the journalistic variant of 'Wha's like us?'

The Herald's Scottish political editor, Murray Ritchie, in a commentary on Labour's media relations during the run-up to the May 1999 Scottish parliamentary elections, summed up many Scottish political journalists' perception of Downing Street's approach as follows:

> [Blair] does some one-to-one interviews with television and radio, which he can control. This has become routine. Alastair Campbell, his press secretary, briefs journalists the night before and then Blair delivers the words, taking care to stick reasonably faithfully to the script. This way there can be no awkward questions from the Scottish press which he once famously denounced as 'unreconstructed wankers' . . . Blair remains touchy about the Scottish media, newspapers in particular . . . Whenever he comes to Scotland he gives the impression that he is afraid of putting his foot in it and feeding a gaffe-hungry Scottish media.
> (Ritchie 2000a: 43, 47–8)

In short, Scottish political journalists see themselves treated as a hostile force by London because they are more exigent than the southern poodle press. It is a self-image readily embraced in some quarters as emerged during an interview with two political correspondents:

> *Speaker One:* There is a far less deferential . . . far less easily intimidated thread that runs through our lives here. And we knew that before, when [Conservative Prime Minister, John] Major used to come up. He would bring his people with him and there was a memorable occasion once when the special advisers said, 'It's not like this in the South-East.' We're not abusive, but we just ask them straight questions and don't go away. They don't like that; they really don't like that. Blair in particular.

> *Speaker Two:* People are not going to be intimidated [in Scotland].

This robust stance can have far-reaching consequences. Arguably, one has been the sense of genuine disappointment we detected about the Executive's performance, and indeed, that of the entire Parliament. Angus Macleod, political editor of the *Scottish Daily Express*, reflected on this:

> I think that the journalists expected too much and possibly led the Scottish people to expect too much. There was a kind of energy behind the attainment of the Parliament that led people, journalists and the electorate alike, to expect somehow that it would be all change and that everything would be for the best in the best of possible worlds, and given that background . . . we were guilty of not standing back, of not perhaps reading . . . the small print . . . in that when the . . . whole thing came to fruition we were still not asking critical enough questions as to exactly what the Parliament might do or would be able to do.

For his part, Kenny Farquharson, political editor of *The Sunday Times, Scotland*, also thought that the expectations held about the new devolved politics were 'unreasonable'. However, he believed that the press should not be doing the new institutions 'any favours':

> It's best to see it as a compliment, that people are taking it seriously. People have high demands for the Parliament and the Executive. If they fall short of these, in the short term, that's a fact of life.

Another take on this question played with folk ideas about the national culture and the psychological make-up of the archetypical Scot. Iain Macwhirter, political columnist for *The Herald* and *Sunday Herald*, and presenter of BBC Scotland's *Holyrood Live*, felt that the Parliament was widely regarded as an object of derision by 'Lawnmarket Man':

> I think the Scottish media – and in a sense the Scottish Parliament – have great difficulty taking themselves seriously and thinking this actually is a parliament. And this idea of a 'pretendy parliament' . . . really does niggle at the back of people's minds and they say, 'Maybe this is all pretence and a farce and nonsense, so I'll kick it. So they are all rubbish that cannae be any good. It's just full of Scots.'

This lack of confidence in Scotland's new political class and a rather hard-nosed approach to reporting its activities run like a twin connecting thread through the development of Scottish journalistic culture since devolution.

THE NEW INSTITUTIONAL SPACE

The creation of the Scottish Parliament and Executive meant that all at once Scottish political journalism had a routine institutional focus for its activities in Edinburgh. Hamish Macdonell, political editor of the *Scottish Daily Mail* depicted the new web of relations as follows:

> Since the Parliament started, you now have everything in the one place. You have this small area around the Royal Mile where you have politicians, a lot of the civil servants and the journalists, which means that there is much more interaction between all three parts . . . There's much more access to MSPs, civil servants. You can bump into them in the street. You can go for a coffee with them. Also, having all the journalists together gives it much more of a feel of a Lobby, like there is in Westminster. It's much easier to keep tabs on what other people are doing and what you're doing and you can swap ideas . . . So it's made for much more exciting journalism.

Kenny Farquharson spoke in similar vein, with an underlying appreciation of how the new institutional nexus had improved accessibility: 'I think some of the things are great. Like the walk from Parliamentary headquarters to the Parliament where anybody can collar, say, Donald Dewar, on the way up.'

These descriptions identify some major features of the new political culture: the proximity of journalism to key political and administrative actors; the ability to engage in casual encounters as a matter of routine; the emerging sense of belonging to a group of political reporters with their own norms that enter into exchanges over stories; the general raising of the political temperature as the result of the activities of a media pack.

To a large extent, this account was echoed by Ramsay Jones, political editor of Scot-FM radio, who both reflected the wish for a new beginning and recognised its necessary limitations:

> There is a desire for a different culture [from Westminster], which is a start . . . Because there are only 129 MSPs and a couple of dozen in the press, there is a greater chance of familiarity between those parties . . . I think there is a desire on both sides for it to be fresh and different. I am not sure that the baggage of 300 years of politics can be cast off overnight.

This, too, gives the sense of an emerging new configuration of institutional politics in Edinburgh while drawing attention to its transitional nature and the weight of history in shaping parliamentary traditions. During debates prior to setting up the Parliament, some had argued that the Scotland should avoid a Lobby system, which was decried as closed and secretive (Booth and Penman 1997: 6; Macleod 1997: 6; Penman 1997: 6.) In practice, as both the SPJA, various political correspondents and the Media Relations Office have confirmed, a stable press pack formed in the first months of devolution, with between thirty and forty journalists regularly present on the parliamentary campus, often collectively agreeing on stories, sometimes hunting in pairs. The political reporters are called 'the Lobby' by the media relations officers and also by some MSPs (especially those with Westminster experience).

Although this does not necessarily mean that a classic Westminster-style Lobby system has been installed, with its attendant archaic practices, in effect a kind of closure has occurred. While the most widely-proclaimed view was that Scotland would not reproduce the Lobby, a number of political journalists thought that this had already happened, citing privileged access to briefings as crucial. Others, however, underlined the undeveloped nature of the political culture by comparison with Westminster, citing a lack of spontaneous interaction between journalists and politicians.

It is telling how much the Westminster experience has provided the yardstick for all the judgements encountered about the emergent political culture in Edinburgh. While not surprising, this reflex does put into perspective the aspirations for making a complete break with Westminster's custom and practice. Assessing Edinburgh with London as the benchmark points up the limits of the political imagination in an old-established parliamentary system.

In late 1999, then, being more or less like Westminster was still the inescapable criterion for Scottish political maturity. Certainly, at the level of patterns of interaction, a new culture centred on the devolved institutions had indeed begun to emerge. However, how that culture was evaluated by political journalists, and the terms in which its analysis was even thinkable, were still heavily dependent on the Mother of Parliaments in London.

AN UNTUTORED POLITICAL CLASS

The May 1999 general election created a new group of 129 Scottish parliamentarians. In profile, the MSPs are similar to the Scottish MPs sitting at Westminster. The signal achievement of the election was to deliver forty-nine women to the Scottish Parliament, placing Scotland third in the international table of gender equality, where Westminster is in twenty-sixth place (Hassan and Warhurst 2000: 4).

Despite the familiar social composition of the new political class, journalists interviewed by us considered its parliamentary novitiate status to be significant and a cause of its problems. Tim Luckhurst, then deputy editor of *The Scotsman*, observed:

> The perception from within the government itself is that things have not started well. There are senior members of the Executive who all say quite candidly and honestly, off the record, 'We haven't really thought about this. We've put so much effort into creating a government for Scotland that we haven't thought about how you actually govern.' And it shows.

Another disenchanted opinion came from Angus Macleod, political editor of the *Scottish Daily Express*:

> Quite frankly the performance of MSPs has been so uneven . . . I'm finding myself all the time comparing with Westminster. At Westminster you have your top people, the really great performers, and you have a big wodge of middle-range performers, and you have quite a few non-entities. The problem at Holyrood . . . is that you have . . . an appreciable number, say fifteen to twenty really quite bright, quite talented, quite good political thinkers and performers. But there is no great wadge of people in the middle who are better than average. You know, you tend to go from quite good to pretty damn awful.

These comments touch on an underlying attitude diffused in much political journalism. The poor political handling of a number of controversial issues was directly attributed to the new incumbents' inexperience. Repeatedly cited was the row over 'Lobbygate', which brought allegations of improper connections between lobbyists and a minister into the public domain. Another case was the prolonged furore over the repeal of Clause 2A of the Local Government Act, the legislation banning the 'promotion' of homosexuality in schools. Many of our informants were impatient with the time it was taking for the new institutions to begin to establish themselves. There was a clear link between viewing the political class as untutored and thinking that somehow Scotland had been sold short by those now in power.

But whatever their disappointments at the calibre of the national political class, as the first year of devolution rolled on, all of the political journalists were clear that Scottish politics was becoming more and more centred on Edinburgh. BBC Scotland's political editor, Brian Taylor, had already predicted this reorientation shortly after the first Scottish parliamentary elections, commenting:

> Politicians will be become immersed in Scottish parliamentary politics. Their concerns, their style, their manner of address, and above all, the loyalties which shape their personal futures, will be different from the Westminster pattern, even for those who were previously members of the House of Commons. They will become institutionalised in the Scottish Parliament, owing allegiance to that body.
> (Taylor 1999: 213)

We do not have to accept all of these claims to recognise their broad validity: in short, there has been a significant shift of political gravity. This was well recognised in the Executive, where David Whitton, Donald Dewar's spokesman, told us:

> I very rarely speak to the Westminster-based journalists now . . . As spokesman for the Secretary of State . . . I'd almost have to split my time speaking to the London Lobby and journalists up here in Scotland. Since the Parliament has been established, I could probably count on the fingers of one hand the number of times I have spoken to those who are based in Westminster in the last six months.

This shift in the centre of political gravity was also realised by that other legatee of devolution, the Scotland Office. John Reid, Secretary of State for Scotland, became embroiled in what was widely depicted as a 'turf war' with the First Minister, Donald Dewar. This was interpreted by the media as an attempt to assert the continuing importance of the Scotland Office as against that of the Scottish Executive. The tensions became particularly fierce during the Lobbygate affair, in which Reid's son was involved. By spring 2000, speculative pieces were appearing in the press about the future of the Scotland Office and whether it might disappear into some UK Cabinet post with a remit for constitutional affairs more generally. Doubtless as a counter-measure to such negative reporting, the Scotland Office Minister of State, Brian Wilson, opened up his ministerial box for inspection to show how busy he really was in the dog-days of the August 2000 summer recess (Elliott 2000: 16).

As Westminster has perceptibly receded in importance for Scots – attested to in successive opinion polls (see, for example, Denver et al. 2000: 155–9; Economist 1999) – the new political class has inevitably come more fully into the spotlight of publicity. In a relevant illustration, Paul McKinney, Head of News and Current Affairs at Scottish TV, told us the company had compared their political coverage of October 1998 and October 1999. Whereas in 1998, the year prior to devolution, all the political appearances had involved MPs, by sharp contrast in 1999, the main news programme, *Scotland Today*, had interviewed only MSPs. McKinney knew that politicians watched the station's programmes keenly and said there was now undoubtedly a closer relationship with them than when they had all been solely based at Westminster. Moreover, the news team had found that the Parliament was influencing the entire domestic news agenda. As he put it: 'Our task is easier than the BBC's. So little now comes from Westminster we can concentrate on looking at Edinburgh.' Just as the BBC had needed to issue its style guide, *The Changing UK* (BBC 1999), so too – albeit on a modest scale – had Scottish TV needed to steer its journalists on the language appropriate to a devolved Scotland.

Scottish TV's short guide covered political terms and captions. The news team had debated whether to talk of the 'Scottish Executive' or the 'Scottish government' and had decided to 'fudge the issue' in McKinney's words (Paul McKinney, letter to the authors, 2 July 2000). Both terms – 'Scottish Executive' and 'the government' – were being used and contrasted with 'the UK government' or 'the Westminster government'. So far as the term 'Scottish Executive' was concerned, the news guide noted that '[many] of our viewers are uncertain of its meaning, but people will eventually become used to it,' (Scottish TV 1999: 1).

A few illustrative quotations from interviews with political correspondents towards the end of 1999 give a sense of how far-reaching this reweighting of national politics was felt to be – and just how unexpected, too, for some.

I can't think of the last time that I spoke to an MP. They're just irrelevant. (Andrew Nicoll, political correspondent, *Scottish Sun*)

We have all these Scottish MPs and we never write, we never phone, we never make contact with them. There is no need to. They don't have anything to say. (Brian Taylor, political editor, BBC Scotland)

> I just don't have the names of the UK Cabinet at my finger tips the way I used
> to . . . I don't think anybody thought we would feel quite so disconnected
> quite so quickly. I didn't anticipate it.
> (Sarah Smith, Scotland correspondent, Channel 4 News)

These attitudes bespeak a quite fundamental shift in how Scotland is viewed
as a polity within the UK. Processes of political communication that involve
parliamentarians and government are now seen as largely situated north of
the border, irrespective of the retention of a wide range of 'reserved' powers at
Westminster. This shift of perspective has registered particularly strongly in
the Scotland Office, which remains the broker between Scotland and the rest
of the UK. Not surprisingly, one of the most telling interventions from that
quarter addressed precisely the continuing importance of UK-wide political
communication.

   The BBC's programme *Newsnight Scotland* was fiercely attacked by Brian
Wilson on 9 February 2000. This 20-minute opt-out from the networked
BBC2 programme *Newsnight* was one of the concessions made to BBC
Scotland when the 'Scottish Six' had failed to materialise. By attacking this
new programme, first launched in October 1999, Wilson reignited the
debate in the Scottish press over the whole question of devolved
broadcasting. He was incensed by a *Newsnight Scotland* story on the
diminished role played by Scottish MPs at Westminster post devolution, a
view with which he disagreed. He also denounced *Newsnight Scotland*'s
journalistic standards and BBC Scotland's competence more generally
(Allardyce 2000: 1; Denholm 2000: 7; Harrington 2000: 3). Wilson
broadened his attack to denounce the proposal for a 'Scottish Six'. This
attack made manifest government worries about the role of more devolved
broadcast news and current affairs coverage, a telling measure of how much
constitutional change was provoking anxiety.

THE EXECUTIVE'S MEDIA RELATIONS

Within weeks of the May 1999 parliamentary elections, the SPJA had
presented its wish-list to the Executive. In a memorandum dated 15 June, it
asked for a daily briefing, both on the record and on camera. The document
stated that:

> Senior broadcasters have indicated they would be willing to site cameras
> behind correspondents to stop these briefings becoming media scrums. They
> have also indicated they would be willing to switch off cameras at any time
> when the Executive spokesperson, with the journalists' agreement, felt it
> necessary to go off the record.

Access to ministers, with an on-the-record briefing, was also requested (SPJA 1999). It took until October 1999 to achieve the present thrice-weekly briefing by the First Minister's official spokesman. The on-camera briefing has not been permitted and, in Paul McKinney's words, 'an uneasy truce' has continued to prevail.

One innovative gesture came rapidly, namely permission to name the First Minister's official spokesman. This post was first occupied by David Whitton and his identification was a new convention in British political reporting. This approach stole a march on Downing Street, but it was not an enormous source of satisfaction to the political press. They believed it to be little more than cosmetic in its impact. Their general disenchantment accounts for at least some of the rough ride afforded the Scottish Executive.

Reporters' criticism of the new information system at the Executive centred on a number of themes: First Minister Donald Dewar's hostility to professional news management; his weak hold over ministers' individual briefing strategies; dissatisfaction with the performance of the official spokesman; resentment at the routine favouring of the *Daily Record* in briefings; and continued tensions over whether or not briefings could be televised.

NO HARD SELL

A continuous refrain in our interviews – also widely aired in the press – concerned Donald Dewar's reputedly old-fashioned approach to handling the media. Brian Taylor (1999: 133) has summarised it thus: 'Dewar does not press the flesh with a fixed televisual grin. Indeed, he cordially loathes photocalls, particularly when they force him into an uncomfortable environment.' As we have shown, this approach had already been alluded to by correspondents prior to devolution, and it assumed increased significance. One veteran political editor elaborated, off the record:

> We're in an age when you have to sell something and having got the Parliament, the key thing to do then was to say, 'And here is what it's going to do for you.' But everyone forgot about that. Now, the reason that happened is quite simple: because Donald does not believe in this kind of thing . . . When it came to the selling of the Parliament in 1999, Donald's sort of attitude when Downing Street and Millbank came on to him and said, 'You have got to go with this, you have got to do this, you've got to do that', his attitude, whether Olympian or not, was, 'Oh, no, no. I'm not going to get into spin. That's that. No. no. no.' Now spin may be a modern curse of journalism but it can help get things over.

This opinion was shared by Kenny Farquharson, who noted:

Donald Dewar's own reluctance to get involved in a kind of media politics game, whereas Blair, of course, is a master of how to work with it. Donald really doesn't have a taste for it and therefore he doesn't really sanction anything to do with these kind of things. But I know that that approach causes concern in other parts of the Executive. For example, they would like to see a more pro-active media management style. It makes better stories for us.

Another experienced hand, John Penman, further underlined these views:

I think the problem stems from Donald Dewar because the whole basis on which Labour got into power at UK level was on the basis of being very effective at communicating the message, and that came about from a very streamlined operation they had in terms of dealing with the press . . . It was very successful . . . Virtually every newspaper was not as hostile to Labour as it has been in the past. Then in terms of broadcasting, they developed a very effective method of making it very difficult for broadcasters to operate without thinking about what Alastair Campbell was going to say to their editor.

Scottish TV's political correspondent, Fiona Ross, summed it up like this:

The leader seems to be in a bunker, talking only to the head of the civil service, while the rest of the Cabinet are running around knifing each other . . . Nothing happens in the Scottish Executive. Nobody's telling us what's going on. They don't know what they're doing in media terms. They need a policy, strategy and the determination to carry that out – all three are lacking. And if you report that they're running around knifing each other, they say that's an outrage.
(See also Ross 1999: 38–9)

All of these senior political reporters drew attention to two things. First, the 'unmodernised' approach of the First Minister to media relations by contrast to the media-savvy London style of spin-doctoring: the Executive had not taken the successes of New Labour's news management on board. And second, correspondents emphasised the journalistic disadvantages of Dewar's traditionalism. Not only was the Executive missing out on chances to shape the news agenda, but the media also felt deprived of effective news management against which they could bite.

According to Iain Macwhirter, London-based special advisers had come north of the border in pre-devolution days to help work out the relationship between the Executive and the media:

Part of the advice that they were giving was that the Scottish Executive . . . needed to start thinking about how it could present and coordinate its activities so that it could have a kind of Millbank facility with the media . . . 'Proactive' was a word that kept being used. They needed a much more proactive approach to the media much as Alastair Campbell did in Westminster and in Whitehall by restructuring the Government Information Service and putting the politicians in charge . . . And they were going to try and do that in Scotland . . . [In the end] we're left with Donald Dewar's official spokesman, David Whitton.

As we show in Part II, the radical changes desired by London fell foul of the more general failure to reform the culture of the Scottish civil service. The result was that our journalist interviewees saw Scotland's new government as suffering from relative backwardness and amateurism. The contemporary professional-belief system of the political journalists dictates that they see strategic media management as central to good government. Damagingly, the perceived failure to communicate effectively has fuelled a sense of disillusionment with the management of politics as such inside the media. London's performance was the inevitable comparator. But the much-vaunted New Labour media magic took a battering during summer 2000. In particular, Tony Blair's evident loss of surefootedness, and Alastair Campbell's retreat into the shadows might contribute to a wider revaluation of the relationship between the substance of policy and how it is presented.[1]

Be that as it may, during the period of our research, the perceived lack of overall control over government communications – attributed squarely to Donald Dewar's hands-off approach – was construed as contributing to a weak image of the Executive. It both forced and permitted ministers to paddle their own canoes, as we show later. One veteran political editor referred to 'a very good contact of mine who is a senior minister who has been moaning to me about how Donald [Dewar] was just immovable'. And that 'moaning' occurred just after the May 1999 election. This source went on to note the inexperience of the Cabinet, a variant of the untutored political class perspective:

> Some of the personalities who ended up in government are obviously trying to find their feet. They have not introduced any particularly radical ways of getting their stuff into the public domain. They're all absolutely frightened stiff of being seen as a source of any story. Now the smart ones would not worry about this. If they were really talented politicians who were going to go places, they would be placing things left, right and centre, getting themselves noticed. But they are all so scared of Donald's wrath.

The implication was that a lack of direction in media relations had both forced ministers to try and fill the briefing void, often amateurishly. At the same time, it was said, because 'spin' was so disapproved of at the top, and because (often justifiably) ministers were seen as pursuing their own career interests, they continually denied what they were doing.

His master's voice: the official spokesman

Despite the failure to 'modernise', there were still those who thought Westminster was reproducing itself on the Mound. In the words of the *Mail*'s Hamish Macdonell:

> We've now developed a daily briefing on Tuesday, Wednesday and Thursday by David Whitton, Donald Dewar's adviser, along the lines of the briefings that Alastair Campbell gives twice a day for the Lobby in London . . . The press pack here are sort of evolving into a Lobby as they are down south.

The *Express*'s Angus Macleod agreed: 'I was a Westminster correspondent for some time and I have to tell you that the briefing system, while more of it may be on the record, isn't actually all that much different.'

However, others thought that, although the briefings appeared to be similar to those in London, this impression was rather deceptive, precisely because they were old-hat in style. Kenny Farquharson observed:

> I think a little bit more of the spinning that Campbell does in Downing Street would be welcome here. The daily briefing is all very well, but if people aren't willing to say very much at that briefing, it is not a massive step forward. Whitton does not use the briefings in the same way Campbell does . . . I think we would all like it if Whitton could play politics a little bit more. I think Whitton is unnecessarily coy about his civil service/political role, and more fastidious than he need be about not crossing the boundary into pure politics.

For her part, Sarah Smith, Channel 4 News's Scotland correspondent remarked:

> In terms of getting answers out of it as to what has been truly going on – it's enormously difficult . . . If he [Whitton] says it wasn't discussed in Cabinet, that's an end of it. He's not prepared to talk about it . . . I think David goes in for damage limitation more than he does spin.

These views were echoed by the *Record*'s John Penman, who also enlarged the analysis to ask whether or not there was an underlying political 'project' shared between the head of government and the spokesman. He thought that a common commitment to New Labour had fed into media management in London:

> Blair had a very defined vision of what exactly he wanted. With Alastair Campbell, he had somebody who was a very trusted lieutenant and the two operated beside each other, as part of each other, as one. That never happened in Scotland. Donald Dewar is not from that kind of school of politics. And when David Whitton was appointed, people saw this as an opportunity for somebody to do an Alastair Campbell role . . . I don't think David Whitton has quite the skills or the abilities to be able to do the same.

Whitton's style and demeanour, his straitlaced approach, were diagnosed – predictably, in light of what has already been said – as due to, and a true reflection of, the First Minister's distaste for 'spin'. His master's voice, indeed.

As the public face of the Cabinet, Whitton undoubtedly had to bear both the real and symbolic weight of journalists frustrated because ministers were making themselves too unavailable. Some correspondents spoke of a deep-rooted fear of the media in the Scottish Executive, 'They regard us as the enemy. No doubt about that.' Another added: 'The Executive is paranoid about the media. We laugh sometimes. We run a few stories and they get really upset. I mean seriously upset.' The *Scottish Sun*'s Andrew Nicoll remarked: 'The Executive went into hiding after the coalition was formed . . . And OK, they went into recess . . . So there was a breathing spell, then there was the recess. They've come back from the recess and we still don't see them.' In the view of Kenny Farquharson, the Labour Party were 'not hugely confident of their abilities in talking to the press'.

However, towards the end of 1999, correspondents did note that some of the untutored political class seemed to be learning the ropes. More ministers, we were told, had made announcements in Parliament and then had met reporters to discuss their policies further. Correspondents believed that such informality was the best route to establishing good and credible relations with the press pack.

ON THE RECORD?

As the new system of media briefings became established, the behind-the-scenes dispute between broadcasters and press over how these should be covered was finally resolved. The broadcasters had consistently argued that there should be formal on-camera briefings. Some press journalists and the broadcasters were united in their view that all Executive briefings should be on the record. But a larger school of print reporters believed that this approach would be bland and pointless in news terms. Our interviews revealed that while these positions were still espoused as the briefing system began to be rolled out, all had nonetheless accommodated themselves to the new status quo. Brian Taylor recalled:

> It then came to the establishment of the Executive and we had a stand-off at the very first briefing by David Whitton. It had been put out as a briefing on the record but off camera. I didn't know this. We turned up, and I think STV as well turned up with a camera. The camera was requested to leave, and we agreed because it was the first meeting and we had no opportunity to set the rules and since then the briefing . . . [has been] on the record. And if a newspaper wants to say 'David Whitton, the First Minister's official spokesman, said . . . ', they can do so. What we can't do is record it on camera and use it.

This continued to rankle with the broadcasters. Scottish TV's Fiona Ross strongly maintained that any Cabinet briefings should be on record and on camera. She felt that she was alone in arguing this and that BBC Scotland were not prepared to make an issue of it. She said: 'I would actually turn up with a camera and say "Throw me out!" if the BBC would back me in this.' (See also Ross 1999.) Brian Taylor observed that the BBC had (not very seriously) considered using an artist's impression as in court reporting, or using an actor's voiceover as had occurred when Sinn Fein's voices were banned from the airwaves (Miller 1995). Not surprisingly, Ramsay Jones of Scot-FM shared his fellow broadcasters' views:

> Logic says that if print journalists can give every word verbatim and actually even the source, if they want to print 'David Whitton'. Why not broadcasting? . . . If one medium can do it, selectively or in total, why can't the others?

During 1999, there were skirmishes between the broadcasters and the Executive on the topic of recording briefings. In August that year, Paul McKinney, Head of News and Current Affairs at Scottish TV, wrote to Roger Williams, Director of the Scottish Executive Information Directorate, about a briefing on cancer screening that was on the record but had to be off camera. He protested that this was 'a news conference which we were not allowed to film' and argued that 'if the briefing from a Minister is on the record for the newspapers, it ought to be on the record for broadcasters, which means we should be allowed to film.' McKinney then protested at the regular exclusion of cameras from Scottish Executive briefings, invoking the CSG's principle of accountability and noting that the Media Issues panel had 'recommended that, in general, briefings should be on camera'. He concluded: 'Today's experience and the continued exclusion of cameras from the regular cabinet briefings does seem to fly in the face of the CSG recommendations,' (Paul McKinney, Scottish TV, letter to Roger Williams, Scottish Executive Information Directorate, 25 August 1999).

The following month, in reply, Roger Williams stated that the briefing on cervical cancer had been held under 'very distinct circumstances' and that it contained 'a great deal of technical detail from health board specialists'. 'Our absolute priority was to ensure that reporters were able to gain a true perspective on the call/recall problem and be in a position to define accurately who was affected.' He noted that broadcasters had been able to interview the 'main players' afterwards, and went on to write:

> I do not think you have any grounds to fear that this arrangement – what you describe as 'a proscription on filming' – is part of a wider pattern of exclusion. I would not sanction any change to our standard news conference format in which broadcasters are given free rein to record and film. Your point about whether filming should be permitted at cabinet briefings is an issue being

given careful consideration by David Whitton.
(Roger Williams, Scottish Executive Information Directorate, letter to Paul McKinney, Scottish TV, 15 September 1999)

That latter question was the subject of a special meeting at St Andrew's House on 2 November 1999. We have obtained a minute of this meeting, written by Fiona Ross. Present were Roger Williams (RW), David Whitton (DW), Brian Taylor (BT) and Val Atkinson (VA) for BBC Scotland, and Fiona Ross (FR) for Scottish TV. Ross's account gives the broadcasters' perspective on how the argument was conducted and confirms everything that we were told in our interviews. The minute reads as follows:

There were two separate issues – ministerial briefings and David Whitton's daily briefings.

Ministerial briefings
Initially DW and RW denied this ever happened. They said Susan Deacon's briefing on the Tayside cervical cancer scare was a 'one off' because of the sensitivity of the issue. When confronted with evidence of other such briefings held by Henry McLeish, Jack McConnell, and Jim Wallace, they claimed not to know about these. Both RW and DW insisted that such briefings would continue to be held if the information was of a technical nature. The reason for this being that it was so boring the broadcasters would not wish to transmit it. The broadcasters agreed that this might be the case, but reserved the right to apply independent editorial judgment. Overall RW and DW assured us that cameras would normally be admitted to ministerial briefings. VA asked for a statement of principle that ministerial briefings would always be held on camera, and if that was not the case, a clear explanation would be given. RW agreed to consider this and discuss it with ministers, but the clear impression was given that this was an acceptable procedure.

David Whitton's briefings
DW said it was the First Minister's view that these daily briefings be off camera. The argument being that politicians are elected, and should be public figures, spokesmen are not. *DW said there would be 'sensitivity' among ministers if spokesmen were appearing on TV as the face of the government, as opposed to elected politicians.* He cited Westminster as an example of where the system worked. The broadcasters pointed out that Holyrood is not Westminster. FR suggested the White House model. DW responded that Holyrood is not the White House. The broadcasters raised the illogical position of briefings being on the record for print journalists, but off the record for broadcasters. DW could see no inconsistency. He claimed broadcasters could write down his words, and name him as the spokesman. It was up to us to find suitable pictures to illustrate his words. FR said that under these rules, a newspaper could publish his photograph. He agreed this was possible, but, he thought, unlikely. BT asked why TV couldn't effectively do the same, and why

wouldn't DW go one stage further and permit the cameras. *DW retaliated with the suggestion that it might be more helpful to go one stage back and revert to unattributable off-the-record briefings for everyone.* While both DW and RW eventually gave up trying to argue any logical position, it was clear that they are not inclined to change the current practice. They claim that this is the First Minister's position and see no point in discussing it further with him.
(memorandum from Fiona Ross to Paul McKinney, 5 November 1999; emphases added)

Ross's account, which we have every reason to take at face value, demonstrates the unbudgeable position of the Executive and its information chiefs. By summer 2000, there was still 'an uneasy truce . . . regarding the on-camera briefing question' in Paul McKinney's words (Paul McKinney, Scottish TV, letter to the authors, 7 July 2000). We have drawn attention both to the political concern about a cult of personality developing around the spokesman and also to the clear threat of withdrawing existing privileges if the broadcasters did not back off. Apart from that, the interchange described in Fiona Ross's account also revealed a missed opportunity to put the routines of government information presentation on the record, not just for journalists, but potentially for the whole of the Scottish public. Such briefings, with a different starting point regarding openness, could be broadcast on a specialist channel for those who wish see them along with parliamentary debates and the proceedings of committees.

The hand of Donald Dewar in all of this was confirmed shortly thereafter in a letter to BBC Scotland's Deputy Editor, News and Current Affairs, Val Atkinson, which was copied to other broadcasters. Roger Williams wrote to give the official response:

The First Minister has made it clear that the briefings David Whitton gives as his spokesman on behalf of the Executive should not be on camera. The First Minister and his Executive colleagues have also made it clear that they retain the right to hold briefings off camera. Ministerial briefings are rare because in most cases ministers opt for a full news conference. However, there are occasions when ministers may wish to brief journalists without being on camera, and we discussed the reasons for this last week with you. As you know Ministers usually agree to filmed interviews following a briefing.
(Roger Williams, Scottish Executive Information Division, letter to Val Atkinson, BBC Scotland, 9 November 1999)

Asked about this, David Whitton put the case in neutral terms:

The First Minister takes the view that I am there to pass on information and if we are announcing a new policy or a new programme or whatever, that's what ministers do. We would produce the minister to do that, and the minister would do that to camera.

The broadcasters interpreted the policy as reflecting ministerial insecurities. Paul McKinney, briefly the Scottish Labour Party's communications director, referred to the fear of 'personality creation' and concern that the spokesman's media portrayal 'might undermine the elected politicians'. Certainly, that was the gist of Fiona Ross's minute quoted above. And this was confirmed by Brian Taylor, also a party to the discussions:

> Ministers are suspicious of Whitton becoming a public figure greater than they are . . . David himself is quite reluctant to become a public figure for the reason that he would get it in the neck . . . Ministers say, 'Sorry, ministers speak on behalf of the Executive on camera.' It's the camera bit that gets to them: they can't handle it.

A further reason for the failure to record briefings, according to one broadcaster, was continuing pressure from the press who 'would prefer things to be off the record, discreet . . . I can understand why. Because if everything is on the television news, what have they got for the following day? . . . They feed off the culture of secrecy.'

The SPJA's demand to have briefings on camera evidently disingenuously papered over the cracks between its two constituencies. The broadcasters finally decided they could not win the argument, given continued opposition among most press political correspondents. For instance, Angus Macleod maintained his preference for off-the-record briefings 'because I don't really care how the information comes to me as long as it is out in the public domain'. Kenny Farquharson agreed, distinguishing between going on the record and achieving openness and transparency:

> Openness and transparency is judged on the degree of information about what reaches the public sphere . . . and if that takes some element of off the record and 'senior sources' or whatever, then that is a service to the end of openness and transparency. Transparency of the actual process of government rather than the transparency of the process by which you get it.

The *Mail*'s Hamish Macdonell also adhered to the belief that politicians' and journalists' information-trading relationship was better undertaken in confidence than out in the open:

> I think that there are conflicting interests between the press and the broadcasters on occasion. The broadcasters want to have total access with their cameras, everything on camera and everything on record . . . We would prefer to have everything off record, and no cameras at all, and people to speak when they're not being recorded.

With no unanimity among the political media on which briefings should go on the record or be recorded, by the end of 1999 there was still broad adherence to a set of common practices, and these were largely in keeping with those south of the border.

COVERING PARLIAMENT

Between the general election on 6 May and the state opening on 1 July 1999, the Scottish Parliament had a pasting in the press. Members' reported obsessions with their allowances, seating positions in the chamber, demarcation disputes between list and constituency MSPs, and the proposal to take a long summer recess, all encountered hostile reporting. The state opening, with its popular carnival atmosphere, its relative lack of pomp compared to Westminster (although still pretty regal an affair at that), song, poetry, and a touch of humour, was a counterweight to the relentless barrage of criticism. On that occasion, for the most part, the press waxed lyrical and broadcasting relayed the ceremony, which was also webcast to a worldwide audience. But that was an exceptional moment. In general, the Scottish Parliament got off to a bad start in public relations terms, and as disputes about the cost of the new building at Holyrood have rumbled on, it can justly be said that from the very start of its life the Parliament has had an overall image problem.

To some extent the Scottish Parliament suffered because of a failure in much media reporting to make clear distinctions between it, the Executive, and the Scotland Office. John Penman put it this way:

> The difficulty is that Parliament as a body doesn't exist in people's minds. People see [First Minister] Donald Dewar and they think of the Scottish Parliament. They don't see [the Parliament's Presiding Officer] David Steel, or whoever. And so in terms of defining the Scottish Parliament's identity, I think that has been difficult.

During the first year of devolution, public and media confusion abounded concerning which body should be approached about matters Scottish: even the supposedly well-informed did not distinguish clearly between the Scottish Parliament and those two successor entities of the old Scottish Office, the Scottish Executive and the Scotland Office. As Andrew Slorance of the Parliament's Media Relations Office put it:

> We get a hell of a lot of calls from people, even the political correspondents that should know better, coming on to us and saying . . . 'I want to interview Donald Dewar, or how can we get this document?' . . . And we'll say, 'That's a government issue.' 'But you're the Parliament', they'll say . . . MSPs up in

the chamber sometimes talk about the Parliament and they really mean the government. They're starting to get over that now.

For the Parliament's media relations staff, this lack of identity contributed to being caught up in the controversies surrounding the new Scottish politics. They believed that the Parliament had been assailed in press headlines because the term 'Scottish Executive' meant so little to the public and even to some of the press. This confusion about institutions, even among the political class and media specialists, underlines why those working for the Parliament were particularly committed to establishing its own, distinct image. They wanted the public to understand that the institution was neither to be identified with the MSPs elected to it, nor with the political parties, nor – especially – with the Scottish Executive. Such considerations of Parliamentary credibility and legitimacy were crucial in determining how the Parliament's staff moved to underpin the role of the Standards Committee during the 'Lobbygate' affair of autumn 1999, as we show in Part III.

Kenny Farquharson believed that the Parliament had failed to capture the popular imagination during its first session, not least because of a lack of drama in its political exchanges: 'You don't get the feeling that policy is made and broken on the Parliament's floor . . . No sense that the nation is being governed from the chamber.'

For Hamish Macdonell at the *Mail*, the problem lay elsewhere:

The relationship with the Parliament is more confusing [than with the Executive]. You have the Corporate Body, the Presiding Officer's office, various things that you're not quite clear where their remit is and who to go to. Then again, you don't go to the Parliament so much as you go to the Executive because it's . . . not where the decisions are made.

Some journalists have recognised this confusion and told us that they believed that the work of the Parliament's committees (see Lynch 2000) was seriously undervalued and that the MSPs were actually working rather hard and not receiving enough credit for this (Maxwell 2000: 14; Rosie 2000: 9). The claim that the Parliament's real work has gone unrecognised has persisted in some press coverage, particularly in the fraught debate over Clause 2A when the Parliament was dismissed by the leader of the Scottish Catholic Church, Cardinal Winning, as 'an utter failure', in June 2000 (Kemp 2000a: 35). The devolved institutions have lacked vigorous media protagonists and this is not unrelated to the disappointment they have engendered. Political journalists working for *The Herald* and *Sunday Herald*, both of which have broadly supported the new devolved bodies editorially, were apt in interviews to condemn what they variously described as 'curmudgeonly' or 'rabid' reporting in other quarters of the press. Iain

Macwhirter (2000: 18), a political commentator with both papers, has denounced 'the poisonous coverage to which the Parliament has been subjected by the Scottish tabloids', and has argued more generally that 'Scottish editors and journalists do not really understand the nature of the institution they are reporting' (2000: 21).

Kenny Farquharson suggested that the perceived hostility of newspapers had 'contributed to politicians being wary of the press'. And indeed, concern in the political establishment with this state of affairs was signalled as early as September 1999, when Sir David Steel, Parliament's Presiding Officer, attacked what he deemed to be misrepresentations of the Mound's approach to controlling costs, Members' holidays and their commemorative medallion. He denounced the 'bitch journalism' of the tabloid press, in particular of the *Daily Record*. Complaints referred by Sir David to the Press Complaints Commission were not upheld and, predictably, his strictures led to several papers accusing him of seeking to gag freedom of expression and cover up Parliament's failings. As the *Daily Record* counterattacked, Sir David found himself rather isolated. He became entangled in a political row about whether he was speaking for himself or on behalf of Parliament as an institution.

The *Record*'s view, as expressed by John Penman, was that the Parliament's:

> housekeeping issues . . . should have been looked at beforehand and examined, and rules should have been set . . . Then we had things like giving them a medal . . . You suddenly thought, 'Is there anything else more stupid that they can do?'

This line was far from untypical. We heard it expressed by several other political journalists, almost word for word. It was plainly widely believed that the ineptitude of news management prevalent in the Executive was shared by the Parliament. These public relations problems were commented on widely in the media and undoubtedly shaped most journalists' attitudes towards Scotland's new institutions.

SCOTTISH POLITICAL JOURNALISM

In this chapter, we have described and analysed the rapid development of the relations between political reporting and the devolved political institutions of Edinburgh. Within a few months of the state opening of Parliament, a new system was in operation. Whereas the rules of the game for the Parliament had been established prior to the first Scottish general elections, those for the Executive were negotiated afterwards. The new political nexus on the Mound has begun to develop as a political culture in its own right. It has become the heartland of a Scottish public sphere and communicative space.

However, although it is new and small-scale compared to London, Edinburgh's developing system of political communication remains profoundly British. There have been no radical new departures from established practice at Westminster and Whitehall. In their relationships with the media, both the Scottish Parliament and Executive are heavily marked by practices modelled on those of the mother political system. The Executive's briefings differ in style and efficacy from those at Downing Street, but not in fundamental conception. The uneven take-up of the media modernisers' agenda in the Executive, profoundly shaped by the preferences and dislikes of the First Minister, evidently contributed to difficulties in selling the government's message, and apparently reinforced the often combative outlook of the press. The Parliament differs from the House of Commons in having its own media relations office, which is a sensible recognition of institutional needs in the media age, but little more than that.

Scottish political journalism has now come into its own, with both a Parliament and a government to cover. It has its own beat and is largely centred north of the border. Devolution has increasingly marked out a distinctive Scottish space of political communication within the UK. While there are continuities with the pre-devolution period, Scottish political journalism has begun to develop as a distinctive culture, based at Lawnmarket House. It has had a major impact on the public representation of Scottish political life, for the prevalently negative attitudes of many political journalists towards the political class profoundly coloured the first year's coverage of the new polity. While there is no formal Lobby, London-style, there is, nonetheless, a well-defined corps of political journalists who have acted as an effective interest group that can regulate access to the political class. Now that it has become institutionalised, there is little reason to suppose that Scotland's media-politics nexus is going to change a great deal in the coming years.

NOTE

1. Tony Blair's ill-fated address to the Women's Institute on 7 June 2000 was widely held to epitomise this loss of competence.

Part II

Spin Doctors

The relationship between the political class and the news media is characterised by conflict and cooperation. It is evident that the role of the media has become much more central to the political process in the past twenty years than ever before. One US commentator has referred to this process as 'governing with the news' (Cook 1998). The increased importance of the news media has interacted with the rise of public relations, lobbying and 'spin' in politics so that we now live in an era of 'promotional culture' (Wernick 1991). Many writers in academia, journalism and politics have seen the changes of the past two decades in negative terms. For instance, the political communication researchers Jay Blumler and Michael Gurevitch (1995) have written of a 'crisis of public communication', whereas Bob Franklin (1994; 1997) has argued that the packaging of politics is overwhelming our capacity for serious analysis.

Journalists too (from both left and right) have complained about the increasingly manipulative relationship between politics and the media (Cockerell et al. 1984; Cohen 1998; Jones 1999; Oborne 1999). Some academics and senior figures in multinational media conglomerates see these changes more positively: the public is deemed sophisticated enough to see through news management, and journalistic commentary and reporting are thought to provide the tools for public scepticism (McNair 1998, 2000; Knight 1993).

SPIN, SUBSTANCE AND THE NEW LABOUR 'PROJECT'

The rise of the permanent campaign in British politics, and the emergence of the spin doctor, marked an increase in the importance of the media in political life. The pioneering work of Gordon Reece and Saatchi and Saatchi for the Thatcher administration increasingly brought commercial marketing techniques into politics (Franklin 1994; Kavanagh 1995; Scammell 1995). The Labour response also increased the importance of presentation. The story of Peter Mandelson's recruitment and rise within the party under the Labour leaders Neil Kinnock and later Tony Blair is now well known (Macintyre 2000; Routledge 1999; Scammell 1995). The growing importance of opinion polling and focus groups has also become widely known. Labour's pollster Philip Gould advocated learning from the Tories' presentational skills. He also drew inspiration from the campaign to save the Greater London Council from abolition by Margaret Thatcher's government. As he remarked: 'Sophisticated communication techniques, and in particular advertising, can be used by a radical organisation without compromising either the message or the politics underlying [it]' (Hughes and Wintour 1990: 55).

But the impact of the presentational obsession from 1985 onwards led the Labour Party away from radicalism and systematically compromised its politics in the pursuit of power (Heffernan and Marqusee 1992). Critics and admirers of Thatcher knew her as a 'conviction' politician determined to pursue the interests of those she represented. The Thatcher years certainly did lead to a marked increase in public relations and advertising spending both in government and by the Conservative Party itself. But, spin was used strategically to pursue the 'project' of destroying the post-war consensus, to redistribute wealth from poor to rich, and to disable independent institutions that stood in the way, notably trade unions (Philo and Miller 2000). Thatcher's former press secretary, Bernard Ingham, has been admirably clear on this point: 'Mrs Thatcher came to government with a coherent philosophy and was not one to be driven solely – if at all – by presentation' (Ingham 1991: 235–6).

Labour, by contrast, came to believe that the Tories had won by virtue of spin and presentation and that they needed to do the same. It was recognised that the Conservative Party had won over key elements of the public, but it was also assumed that the Tory 'project' could be replaced with a Labour 'project' that distanced itself from socialist and even social democratic ideas. According to Philip Gould:

> I was determined to help rebuild Labour as a new party, articulating the hopes and aspirations of a new middle class . . . Above all, I wanted to help develop a new progressive majority, holding power not just for one election, but for many. (1998: 232)

Securing and holding power became almost an end in itself. The fundamental orientation of the New Labour project was towards the middle classes and business. And the methods for deciding policy became heavily dependent on tapping the views of the middle classes through focus groups and market research techniques. The policy-making machinery of the Labour Party became obsessed with managing opinion. Spin and presentation became the shaping forces in Labour's platform and whatever the intentions of advisors like Gould, Mandelson and Campbell, their communication strategy tended to drive them away from radical policies, and indeed, from any coherent critique of conservatism (Johnson 1999).

With the election victory of May 1997, the modernisers thought they had acquired the evidence they needed to show that they had been right all along, that power could only be secured by jettisoning all policies that might threaten business interests. They dismissed the view that any competent political party could have defeated the Conservatives at the 1997 election, given the widespread popular resentment at Tory policies and the spectacle of the party imploding over Europe and sleaze. However, the problems of placing trust in spin were to become increasingly felt in British politics. Although 'spin doctoring' emerged under the Conservative administrations of the 1980s and 1990s, it reached its apotheosis under New Labour. The invulnerability of the modernisers was shaken early in the government's term of office by a succession of scandals involving people neatly tagged by the Conservatives as 'Tony's cronies'. But it was not until summer 2000 that Labour began to see themselves as vulnerable. The slow handclapping which greeted Tony Blair's speech to the Women's Institute (WI) in June that year was arguably the moment when spin had had its day. The memos between Blair and his pollster Philip Gould, written during this period (and rapidly leaked), reveal the conservative instincts of both men. In a key passage in a memo written before the WI speech, Gould wrote: 'TB is not believed to be real. He lacks conviction, he is all spin and presentation, he says things to please people, not because he believes them,' (Leppard et al. 2000: 1).

Rather than conclude that policy substance was needed and that the modernisers' headlong rush to abandon Labour's traditional policies had gone too far, Gould's response was precisely the opposite: 'TB's problem is not that he is too much the modernising politician, not that he has changed too much too fast, but rather the opposite. He has changed too little and too slowly' (Leppard et al. 2000: 1).

A government which has not tried to explain to the public what has happened under previous administrations and provided its own gloss on the failures of the past, which has no coherent analysis of taxation and the distribution of resources, will find itself vulnerable to protests supported by business interests and conservative ideologues.

THE GOVERNMENT INFORMATION SERVICE

Throughout the Thatcher years (1979–90) communication and public relations became more important than ever before and the government spent more money on PR and communication advice than any previous administration. This tendency was especially associated with the privatisation of publicly-owned industries and provided a key boost to the PR industry (Miller and Dinan 2000).

Under Thatcher, the Government Information Service (GIS) was centralised under Number Ten's press secretary and the lines between government and party publicity became increasingly blurred. A further development was the commercialisation of the GIS, in line with government civil service reforms such as *Next Steps*. This resulted in 77 per cent of Whitehall staff moving into agencies by 1997 (IPMS 1997). Although the pace of centralisation slowed somewhat during John Major's administration (1990–7), marketisation continued apace.

When Labour took office in May 1997, centralisation and marketisation operated together. The influx of special advisers from outside the civil service indicated this, but more decisive for both tendencies was the removal of almost all the top officials in the renamed Government Information and Communication Service (GICS) (Oborne 1999; Franklin 1999). According to the head of the GICS, Mike Granatt, twenty-one changes took place among the seventeen most senior positions between 1997 and spring 2000 (Haslam 2000). This was far in excess of the changes to the information machine when Thatcher assumed power in 1979. Salaries offered to incoming Directors of Information were significantly increased. The new officials' backgrounds were to an unprecedented extent in commerce, business and journalism.

Centralisation has its most obvious incarnations in Alastair Campbell's operation in Downing Street and in the Millbank media centre. The changes to the GICS were accomplished by means of an internal review – the Mountfield Report (1997) – which imported many of the tactics and techniques of the Labour Party's campaign machine into government, including media monitoring, rapid rebuttal and strategic communications.

The question of whether changes in the conduct of government news management 'politicises' the civil service is a recurrent and seemingly unavoidable question. However, it is not always clear what is meant by being 'political' in this context. It is conventionally assumed that the civil service was at one time 'apolitical', or at least non-party-political following the Northcote-Trevelyan reforms (Hennessy 1989; Richards 1997). In fact, there are accounts which show that the civil service has more often than not impeded democratic reform rather than championed it (Hennessy 1989; Middlemass 1979; Norton-Taylor 1995; Norton-Taylor et al. 1996). Nevertheless, the culture of the civil service has had a strong element of public service. Arguably, the adoption of market reforms under the Thatcher government, which led to the creation of 'next steps' agencies, unelected quangos, and partial privatisation, have replaced key elements of the public-service culture with a more market-oriented approach. It can be argued that the Thatcher government 'politicised' the civil service in a quite specific sense, making it more amenable to the market in its culture as well as in its policy assumptions.

Much of the criticism of the Labour Party and its spin operation has also been conducted with reference to politicisation. Indeed, some have argued that New Labour has gone much further in politicising the civil service than the Conservative administrations. There is certainly evidence for this in the GICS reforms and the employment of large numbers of special advisers. First, officials in the restyled GICS have had to stay 'on-message', or depart. Second, the civil service has further extended the market reforms of the previous administrations, rather than changing their course. Arguably, the culture of public service has been further eroded, leading to less accountability among our public servants. It is this kind of politicisation that has been the result of successive reforms of the civil service by both Conservative and Labour governments.

Government publicity has received less attention than the news management side of operations under New Labour. Government advertising became an important political issue under the Conservatives with Tony Blair (as Shadow Employment Minister) even writing a report about it in 1989. Certainly, the question of politically-partisan campaigns was raised more sharply under the Tories than previously. Commenting on British Telecom's privatisation, John Koski, deputy editor of *Marketing Week*, argued that 'the invisible ink between the lines urging us to share in capitalism's future had become clear enough by the time application for shares needed to be made' (1984: 9). Furthermore, the promotion of other policies such as the poll tax and the 'enterprise initiative' by Lord Young's 'Department for Enterprise' (his restyled Department for Trade and Industry) did use new promotional techniques, which went well beyond mere information provision (Franklin 1994; Scammell 1995). As the Prime Minister's press secretary, Bernard Ingham, noted, 'the art of the publicist had moved so far and so fast that the political impartiality of government publicity was in danger of being compromised' (1991: 374). The change was also noted by the Independent Broadcasting Authority which in the late 1980s 'regularly' required changes to government ads, according to chairman Lord Thomson (Thynne 1988; Brooks and Smart 1988).

Under Labour there has been a significant investment in advertising policy initiatives such as the New Deal. The government has also increasingly brought in external public relations consultancies to do this work in addition to hiring advertising agencies. This trend confirms the marketisation of the publicity side of government operations as does the rebranding of the Central Office of Information as COI Communications (Haslam 2000). In 1996, the new director of the COI, Tony Douglas, a former advertising executive was the first to come from a promotional industry background (Walker 1996). His appointment seems to have set a precedent as his successor, Carol Fisher, was formerly marketing director at Courage, the brewers (Lee 1999). The increasing role of market criteria in advertising campaigns seems set to continue.

CHANGES IN THE POLITICAL SYSTEM

Politics too has changed. There has been an increased presidentialism in Britain – a tendency to sidestep full Cabinet discussions and parliamentary debate – especially under the Blair administration. But underlying this more recent trend is a longer-term process. Over the past half-century, the political system has developed in a direction which limited the power of Parliament and increasingly passed decision-making to ministers and unelected civil servants (Middlemass 1979: 307–6; Sampson 1971: 16). It is this process which also underlies the decline in the media reporting of Parliament. As the real power is exercised outside the House of Commons, journalists gravitate to other sources of knowledge, information and (therefore) power. The decline in Parliament's significance, and the increasing importance of the media in policy-making, have explained the reluctance of spin doctors such as Alastair Campbell in London and David Whitton in Edinburgh, to accept that information should be presented to Parliament first and the media second – a convention increasingly violated since 1997.

SPINNING SCOTLAND

Against the background described above, Part II of this book examines the evolution of government information and the activities of spin doctors in the run up to, and the aftermath of, devolution. Chapter 6 describes the evolution of news management in the Scottish Office and, in particular, the changes wrought by Michael Forsyth and Donald Dewar as Secretaries of State for Scotland. Chapter 7 charts changes in the Scottish Office which accompanied the transition to devolution and especially those occurring in its Information Directorate. The chapter addresses these developments in relation to the question of openness in the field of government information. Chapter 8 evaluates the Scottish Office's voter-education campaign on the new voting system for the first Scottish parliamentary elections. Finally, Chapter 9 examines the news management regime serving the Scottish Cabinet and the Executive more generally in the first year of devolution.

CHAPTER 6

Scottish Office information management: from the Tories to New Labour

The Scottish Office first set up an information service toward the end of the 1930s, when the Secretary of State for Scotland, Walter Elliot (1936–8), enlisted a press officer. The Scottish Information Office (SIO) came into existence at 'the beginning of the war when it also acted as the Ministry of Information in Scotland' (Gibson 1985: 108), during the tenure of Secretary of State, Tom Johnston (1941–5).

The SIO was from the start distinct in its information role in relation to the rest of Whitehall. According to William Ballantine, its first Director (1960: 113):

> The Scottish Information Office differs from the Information Divisions in Whitehall Departments because the Secretary of State for Scotland holds a unique office in government. He is not only a Departmental Minister with a more than usually large number of statutory responsibilities, he is also regarded as 'Scotland's Minister', a situation which involves him daily in troubles which are not in a strict account his business at all. This dualism affects the organisation of the information services in Scotland. Our major statutory responsibility is to provide an information service for the Scottish Departments.

This broad responsibility continued throughout the existence of the Scottish Office and carried over to the Executive when it was formed in 1999. With the exception of the Northern Ireland Office (NIO), created in 1972, no other government department has had information responsibilities of this type. In keeping with its dual role, the SIO also engaged in projecting Scotland overseas by means of newsletters, news stories, and direct contact with Scots expatriate societies around the globe. The Deputy Director of the SIO, Forsyth Hardy, (1947: 219), noted that:

in the year of the Empire Exhibition (1938), the first deliberate attempt was made in Scotland to use film as a medium of national projection. There was acute dissatisfaction with the screen picture of Scotland as drawn by alien hands; and there was also a stirring of national feeling which it was thought should find expression in terms of film.

The SIO also dealt with the full range of publicity material:

> Early in the war the Scottish Office adopted a positive policy in the use of films. There were films of production in the fields and factories, of health plans for the Highlands, and new types of schools in the lowlands, of experiments in preventive medicine, and of enlightened methods with young delinquents. Later there were films of the forward looking projects – the hydro-electric scheme, the new mines with their modern techniques, research in agriculture and fishing.
> (Hardy, 1947: 220–1)

The first Director of the SIO was highly regarded in the civil service. According to the official history of the Scottish Office, 'None was closer to [Secretary of State, Tom] Johnston than the late William Ballantine, the director of the Scottish Information Office whose influence spread far beyond his room on the ground floor of St Andrew's House' (Gibson 1985: 109). A semi-official account by a former civil servant views Ballantine as an 'outstanding' official 'who enjoyed the confidence of Ministers from both parties and the affection of the Scottish press' (Pottinger 1979: 147).

Ballantine remains the longest-serving Director of the Information Office in Scotland, retiring in 1970 after almost thirty years in charge. Since 1979, the press have rarely had as positive an evaluation of the Director, and from 1995 neither have ministers. Ballantine and many of his contemporaries were firmly steeped in the culture of journalism. Both Ballantine and his wartime deputy (Forsyth Hardy) were former journalists and another colleague, Alastair Dunnett, had been a journalist, and after the war returned to journalism editing first the *Daily Record* and then *The Scotsman* (Dunnett 1984). The relationship between the Scottish Office and the press was mutually dependent. According to Alistair McNeill, who became Deputy Director of the SOID in the 1990s, after thirty years' service:

> [The SIO] was an overhang from the government information service in wartime years, it was kept going very much hand to mouth – only announced what had to be announced and keep the editors sweet, because there was something of an old boys' club of editors through the '60s. [Ballantine] considered himself a journalist first and foremost, having worked in one of the Glasgow papers. He and his contemporaries kind of rose through the ranks

and there was this little club that no one could do the dirty on anyone else. And so, comparatively speaking, the government had a good press, if they only knew it, compared to the mischief which is made by modern tabloids.

From the wartime operation as the Scottish 'regional' office of the Ministry of Information, the SIO developed into the regional representative of the post-war Central Office of Information (COI) especially in relation to publicity materials. But during the term of Ballantine's successor, Charles MacGregor, the link with the COI was broken, fostering the sense of Scotland as a separate polity. According to Alistair McNeill,

> In the period when I joined [the late 1960s] publicity material was processed through the Central Office of Information in London, in order to ensure a uniformity of style. But it was as though Whitehall still needed to keep its foot, shall we say, on the neck of the Scottish administration by that means. That tie was loosened and eventually broken under Charles MacGregor. He persuaded them that this was a change which would be to the advantage of the Scottish Office. I think it added to the confidence of [the SIO], in terms of how we presented ourselves to our client departments. It was a quasi-independence from Whitehall which we hadn't enjoyed before. The history of the Scottish Office for so long, until the Scottish Parliament, was that some policy was initiated in Edinburgh, but much of it was a tartanisation of policies developed, processed, in Whitehall. The Scottish Office contributed through the Cabinet structure, so we shouldn't feel too defensive about that, but in some ways . . . you felt like a kind of branch office.

In this early period, the SIO engaged in the standard practices of Whitehall information management, such as distributing press notices, drafting and circulating ministerial speeches, briefing editors and the Lobby, and responding to telephone calls. The SIO seems to have been busy occasionally, according to Ballantine:

> There will be many telephone calls from newspapers anxious to have further information on some subject already announced, the application to Scotland of some decision promulgated in Parliament or questions about some reluctant guest who has escaped from one of Her Majesty's penal establishments. These telephone calls sometimes go on for about eighteen out of the twenty-four hours of the day and no doubt would continue for the whole twenty-four hours if newspapers were published between three and eight o'clock in the morning.
> (1960: 114–15)

Today's press officers would be relieved if the phone calls only came 'sometimes'. It was in the 1970s under MacGregor (at the time of the Heath government) that the service became professionalised, expanding in size and moving away from the 'man and boy' operation of the previous three decades. MacGregor retired in 1980, just after the election of the Thatcher government, and his post was filled by the former journalist and NIO information officer Fred Corbett. According to McNeill,

> Fred's home was in London, so he had the Westminster contacts and that was judged to be most advantageous. Charles MacGregor was a departure from the norm – i.e., not a journalist, he never claimed to be. He called himself the simple soul. But Fred was a return to form as it were. A television journalist, who was as laid back, apparently, as he possibly could be. Whereas Charles MacGregor was very much the old soldier and knew a lot about man-management, and about conflict situations. In fact, he had to handle himself through successive changes of administration which were rapid from Labour to Tory. It was quite a tumultuous time. His style was much more trusting of, respectful of, strengths and weaknesses of staff. Some might say too trusting.

Corbett retired in 1992 and Liz Drummond was appointed as Director. Overall, the period from the late 1960s to the 1990s has seen a decline in the mystique of, and deference towards, the civil service. As Alistair McNeill put it:

> Throughout the period, the most dominant impression as a worker at the coal face was successive administrations expected you to get them a good press. For a long time the civil service proceeded on the basis that these were policies which were good for us and therefore make the most of them . . . The link between presentation and politics was very tenuous and there was amongst policy-makers a kind of arrogance borne of the security of the job . . . The sense of authority which surrounded the civil service at that time was a good deal stronger. [They thought] they had a divine right to govern, in the best interest of all the community and that administrations would come and go, but the policy machine would grind on. Now that got shot to pieces under the Forsyth years and by the incoming [New Labour] administration. They were much much more beholden to the politicians than anything I had seen before.

INSIDE THE SCOTTISH OFFICE

The relationship between information officers and other civil servants in the Scottish Office seems to have followed a similar pattern to other Whitehall departments (Miller 1993; Miller et al. 1998). According to George Pottinger, a Scottish Office administrative official for more than thirty years:

> The PRO [public relations officer] has an uphill task, and he has to face two main hazards. The first is that many, or to be more accurate, most senior civil servants are ingenuous about public relations. Often they are actively hostile to

them. This does not imply furtiveness, or a sinister wish to suppress information. On the contrary, they will maintain that once a government decision has been announced, if there is to be any further exposition the legitimate channel is either through parliamentary questions, or, if public funds are involved, in appearances before the Public Accounts Committee. It follows that on this reckoning the PRO's activities are an unwelcome intrusion on the higher thought.
(Pottinger 1979: 146)

That definition of furtiveness clearly leaves out the reflexive secrecy and paternalism of the official mindset typical of the civil service in this period. The culture of secrecy still retains some hold in the Scottish civil service, as elsewhere. An internal review of the Scottish Office Information Directorate (SOID) in 1997 noted:

We think it is fair to say that Scottish Office staff outwith SOInD are generally unfamiliar about what goes on in the Directorate. It seems that a number of departmental staff may not be fully seized of the importance and interests of the media . . . The face of government has obviously changed recently but so too have the expectations not only of Ministers but also of the media. Departments need to appreciate there is an ever increasing media interest in what we do.
(Middleton et al. 1997: 4, 15)

The decline in importance of Parliament and the introduction of market principles to the civil service, including the GICS, has reoriented the priorities of some parts of the civil service, so that the media are seen as more important. It is not that the civil service has become more open and less secretive, rather that it has invested more in PR and spin techniques.

THE SCOTTISH OFFICE INFORMATION DIRECTORATE

The Scottish Office Information Directorate (SOID) was created out of the Scottish Information Office in 1992, when Liz Drummond was appointed the fourth Director of Information.

One key role of the Information Directorate is to publicise the differences between Scotland and the other Home departments. For instance, the distinction between education or health policy in Scotland and England has not always been well recognised by Whitehall departments. Liz Drummond has explained the problems that may arise:

Departments down south would make an announcement . . . Now, it may or may not apply to Scotland, but they very rarely said specifically in their news releases . . . So we'd get all the Scottish press ringing us up: 'We've seen this announcement. Does it apply to Scotland?' So you ring the [press office of the Whitehall] department to find out, and they don't know, and they have to ask their officials, who are meanwhile asking our officials . . . So, small announcements on parking fines, or some minor thing cause us tremendous problems, because it would made by an English department who wouldn't even bother to tell us.

Such problems are not merely historical but have continued right up to the creation of the Parliament, and beyond.

THE CONSERVATIVE YEARS

Successive Secretaries of State for Scotland (from Malcolm Rifkind and Ian Lang to Michael Forsyth) have adopted differing styles of information control. Jacquie Low worked for five years in the SOID (1987–92) and then for two years (1995–7) as special adviser to Michael Forsyth. According to her account:

Malcolm Rifkind is a very polished, very confident performer and was very relaxed with the media. Ian Lang was less so. When he actually did things with the press he was very good and they liked him because he was very gentlemanly, but I think it was pretty much on the basis that he was doing what he had to do . . . I've seen [Rifkind] making so many speeches, no notes, and delivered a coherent argument, without repeating himself and that is a real skill and he made it look so easy.

According to Low, Michael Forsyth was the most interested of the three in media relations:

Michael Forsyth, I think, had the best understanding of what the media needed and wanted. In terms of personal style, he was much more dynamic. Michael obviously had had a background in public relations.

This view is endorsed by the late Fred Corbett who reportedly 'only really enjoyed working for two politicians': Northern Ireland Secretary Roy Mason and Forsyth (as a junior minister). 'Both', he said, 'knew what they wanted, made fast decisions, and didn't brook much stalling from civil servants' (*The Scotsman* 1995). Forsyth made plain his views on PR when a junior minister at the Scottish Office in the late 1980s. He attempted to steer through an unprecedented corporate redesign. Following the 1987 election, the Scottish Office commissioned a public relations company to redesign its image and raise its profile. Apparently, ministers felt that the government had 'failed to get its message across to voters' and that the Scottish Office was viewed by the Scottish electorate as a 'faceless, bureaucratic and remote institution, playing little or no part in their daily lives'. Surveys reportedly showed that the public had only a 'hazy' image of the Scottish Office (MacAskill 1989). 'Ministers also felt slighted by the high-profile and, in general terms, favourable news coverage enjoyed by organisations such as the Scottish Development Agency, the Scottish Tourist Board and the Highlands and Islands Development Board' which, although government bodies, were not generally perceived as part of government (Douglas 1988).

The PR contract was reportedly worth £90,000, although the Labour Party claimed that a much bigger project had been planned and then scrapped after complaints from Labour about the partisan nature of the proposals (MacAskill 1989). The redesign was carried out by The Corporate Identity Review Group, a design and PR agency operating out of Hall Advertising in Edinburgh. Michael Forsyth was the lead minister on the project, although he withdrew for reasons of propriety when he became chairman of the Scottish Conservative Party in summer 1989.

After Forsyth's withdrawal, other ministerial sources made it clear that the revamp of the Scottish Office would be low-key and carried out 'with dignity'. There would be no new modernistic logo, instead 'the present heraldic symbol, known affectionately inside the Scottish Office as "the barking dog" would be tidied up' (MacAskill 1989). Forsyth carried his ideas over to his own fiefdom of the Health Department 'attempting to gain Scottish Office credit for projects by ensuring, that billboards on building sites and other related projects mention that the cash came from the Scottish Office' (MacAskill 1989).

Staff in the SOID acknowledged that a change in the priority accorded to PR came with the appointment of Michael Forsyth as Secretary of State in 1995. A new entrant to the Information Directorate at the time observed:

> It was absolute bedlam and I had no induction whatsoever. I mean, they had never seen anything like it before and I think it really shook the place up, because Ian Lang, as far as I can tell, was very happy just not to shake things up too much, to go with the flow . . . [He] didn't demand too much in terms of media . . . Looking back on it, and looking at it compared to this lot [New Labour], Forsyth was just dragging the Scottish Office into the 1990s. Forsyth just wanted statements on everything, wanted news releases on everything, wanted to check everything himself and because he was generating that amount of interest, the bids were coming in for him. He basically came in with a mission: he had a year to turn round the Tories.

Forsyth, a key Thatcher loyalist, was defending a marginal constituency as well as the prospects of the electoral survival of the Conservative Party as a whole in Scotland. As Secretary of State, he immediately presented himself as the friend of civic Scotland. As Ian Macwhirter commented:

> No longer the right-wing ideologue, it was a new, improved 'listening' Forsyth who came north in July. His door was open, he insisted, and he wanted to hear from everyone – trades unions, local authorities, industry, the professions . . . Michael Forsyth promised to be Scotland's man in the Cabinet not the Cabinet's man in Scotland. This was the most bizarre ideological inversion of all. Forsyth had long been aligned with those English Conservatives who believed that Scotland was addicted to the 'begging bowl' of state subsidies. The Scottish Office used to be regarded by the Tory right as just the kind of corporatist institution that any good Thatcherite would waste no time in dismantling. But . . . Forsyth let it be known that any reduction in Scotland's spending budget would be 'over his dead body'.
> (1995: 16, 17)

Forsyth's efforts to court Scottish public opinion meant an increased workload for the SOID. As one junior member of the press office at the time saw it:

> At the beginning he went off on a charm offensive . . . I think he wrong-footed the Scottish media . . . It filtered down to us that we were to just start putting more of a Scottish spin on things. You started to pick up, when you are writing for Forsyth, 'You are doing this for Scotland', rather than 'This is Tory Government policy' . . . There was definitely an effort to write in terms of 'Here is Forsyth solving Scotland's problems within the Union.' That was the push.

The remaking of Forsyth was helped by his special adviser, Jacquie Low, and speech writer, Gerald Warner, who we were told, 'spent an awful lot of his time "tartanising" everything he was putting out'. According to former Director of Information, Liz Drummond:

> All we ever got from him was, 'You're not doing this. Why aren't you doing that?' He used to think up gimmicks and we used to have to think up gimmicks to promote him. It all came from him . . . You know, the things he did Ian Lang wouldn't have been seen dead doing – cosying up to Mel Gibson and walking up the High Street in a kilt. It's just not on! Even on the famous Burns night celebration in London, all the Scottish Office Ministers were told to wear their kilts. Lang wore tartan trews, he didn't wear a kilt. He said, 'I haven't got the legs for it!' And Sir Hector Munro was very 'You only wear the kilt in Scotland, you never wear the kilt across the border'. But he turned up in his kilt.

The Director of Information did not get on with Forsyth and, in an unusual move, a relatively junior (although experienced) information officer, Anne

Shevas, was detached to shadow him daily.

Among the most high-profile of Forsyth's actions was the 'return' of the Stone of Scone to Scotland.[1] This was filmed by the Scottish Office Video and Television Unit, bringing what had been an internal training unit of the Scottish Office into PR work for the first time. The PR and logistical planning for this was immense, and the event was seen in the SOID as one of their biggest moments. Indeed, it is commemorated as one of their 'successes' in an internal Scottish Office video (Scottish Office Video Production Unit 1997).

Forsyth's makeover secured headlines but not votes, and staff morale in the SOID became worse. In the two years leading up to the 1997 general election, between fifty and sixty staff members left, a turnover higher than the total number working in the Directorate. Partly, this was due to the long hours and poor pay and conditions, but the screw was turned by increased demands from ministers and increased ministerial criticism. A senior member of the SOID told us:

> It was a story a day. That was his policy. He was an opportunist. He was the despair of many civil servants. One resigned saying that he was 'completely unreasonable'. There's inherent in the machine a flexibility, regardless of who the Secretary of State was, regardless of how outrageous the demands are, to make the policy work. Because that's the deal struck by the service. And so it responded – perhaps in elephantine mode – to Mr Forsyth's chagrin, but they did do their best . . . When Forsyth took over, we are talking about an increase in the effort on his behalf much beyond what had been required of us by previous Secretaries of State. A lot of people felt the pressure and threw in the towel. We had a huge turnover of staff.

The significant turnover was also encouraged by the fact that press officers on around £15,000 (or less) could double their salary in other PR jobs, sometimes in the private sector, but mainly in the public sector, partly as a result of the Conservatives' market reforms of the civil service. This allowed government agencies, quangos and the NHS to pay market rather than public sector rates. Staff turnover also exacerbated the problem of chronic understaffing. As one experienced information officer, Allan Thomson, saw it:

> Not only were the press officers understaffed, but the private offices were understaffed. It was the Calvinistic nature of successive Permanent Secretaries. I mean you had Kerr Fraser who I'm sure wore a hair shirt, basically to prove that the frugalness of the Scots would manifest itself in numbers. Then you had Russell Hillhouse, [and] it didn't change. The frugality of it was if you were seen to be drinking a glass of water instead of having a glass of wine, then you were deemed to be some righteous character. Whereas you might be

selling something to a German industrialist who would feel uncomfortable because you weren't joining him in a glass of wine. And it was a continual battle to get the staffing up and we ran for weeks and months without staff on different desks. Then, just when you thought you had solved it, off somebody else would go, because they had got a job or whatever.

The SOID has generally been directed by Scots (with the exception both of the ex-NIO official, Fred Corbett, and the most recent Director, Roger Williams). The Directorate has undertaken a wide range of relatively consensual activities, such as hosting overseas visitors and producing Scottish public-information films on topics such as immunisation, road safety, health education and domestic violence. Until the mid-1990s, controversies about the SOID were generally at a lower level than those about the GIS in Whitehall. Under the Conservative administrations of the 1980s and 1990s, the Scottish Office cultivated links with the right-wing press and often felt itself under attack from the mainstream of public debate. Under Forsyth, according to SOID sources, 'policy was made by Bill Greig of the *Scottish Daily Express*. There was a hotline between the *Express* and Forsyth's office every day, several times a day.' By contrast, *The Herald* 'won few friends' (Linklater 1992: 132) in the Scottish Office under the Tories.

Under Forsyth, Liz Drummond believed that the *Daily Record* 'turned [Forsyth] into some kind of bogey man and demon from hell. The thing is, the man was bad enough, you didn't need to lie about it to make him look bad.' Forsyth repeatedly and publicly attacked the BBC over its reporting of Scottish politics. In 1985, he complained about a television phone-in which was allegedly 'riddled with unfairness and inaccuracies' (Stead 1985). In 1989, as a junior minister, he complained about alleged political bias in Radio Scotland's *Good Morning Scotland* (Connolly 1989). On that occasion, the BBC defended itself by saying 'the Scottish body politic is out of kilter and that will inevitably be reflected in our programmes', meaning the lack of support for the Conservatives in Scotland was in contradiction with the fact that they formed the UK government (Bateman 1989: 1). The Controller, BBC Scotland, Pat Chalmers, also raised questions about the impartiality of the SIO. A letter to the SIO from the BBC was replied to by Forsyth in his capacity as Chairman of the Scottish Conservative Party (Bateman 1989; Connolly 1989).

Accusations of politicisation of the SOID began to be thrown about by the late 1980s. For example, the Labour Party complained about the planned corporate redesign for the Scottish Office. In 1991, there was concern over a publicity campaign to promote council-house purchase (Reekie 1991). In 1995, just after Forsyth's elevation to Secretary of State, there was concern over a Scottish Office analysis of expenditure and revenue. This allegedly showed that 'Scotland was far better off within the UK' and was published on the first day of the Conservative Party conference (Vaughan 1995; Young 1995). In one celebrated incident, the Director of Information was forced to apologise when a press release included Conservative phrases. On the day he was appointed Secretary of State, Forsyth constructed a press release with Liz Drummond. According to her:

> He wanted to attack the 'non-unionist' proposals of the other parties and he came up with this phrase 'the tartan tax' and he looked at me and said 'Can I use that phrase?' I had never heard the phrase before. It certainly wasn't to my mind a party political slogan. And I said [it] is a very convenient shorthand for the revenue-raising powers of a devolved Scottish assembly.
> (Jacobs 1997b: 5)

The phrase was then used in a number of press releases. But it had been used before as a Conservative party slogan by Ian Lang, as Drummond was subsequently informed. Later, a further Conservative slogan appeared in a press release. This was the Tory anti-devolution slogan 'new jobs to nae jobs,' prominently featured on Tory billboard ads at the time. According to Drummond:

> We'd had the draft speech and we were all set to put it out and then Forsyth changed it. His Private Secretary was ringing the press office at eight o'clock at night saying 'Change this; change that.' And it just went by unnoticed.

The second phrase was removed in a new version of the press release and Drummond had to apologise publicly to Forsyth over the incident for failing to reject the phrase (MacMahon and Mclaughlin 1996). Following a Labour complaint, the Secretary to the Cabinet instructed that neither phrase should be used (Jacobs 1997b). Some long-serving members of the SOID accept that they crossed the line into political activities under Forsyth:

> There were guys that had been around for a long time and seen politicians and institutions come and go. They had that strong independent streak among the civil servants . . . These people had died out and had been succeeded by untrained, inexperienced staff . . . And I think we suffered on account of that foresight or experience having been lost in the service. Some were too anxious to please and they hadn't the background or the stamina to say 'No'.

Given the low morale, high turnover, and their experience of Forsyth, many SOID staff were more than happy when Labour was elected. But the elation of that night in May 1997 was not to last.

NEW LABOUR AND THE PURGE

The incoming Labour government did not improve staff morale, and turnover continued to be high. There was a bedding-in period in which ministers and special advisers adapted to being in government and having civil-service support. There were early confusions about whether the SOID should route all calls and keep a tab on briefings or whether journalists should go straight to special advisers. One Information Officer associated with the devolution team observed, in August 1997:

> I was writing, to begin with, a huge amount of rhetoric about how this is going to be a Parliament for the people in Scotland, business has nothing to worry about – that kind of thing. When these ministers came in, they already had amazing media contacts themselves. The first few months were just getting to the point where they realised the press office is actually a fairly decent thing. To begin with [ministers] such as Brian Wilson were on the phone all the time. Nobody knew what they were saying. Next morning: 'Oh right. That wasn't the special advisers . . . That was just the ministers doing it.'

The transition from opposition to government was also difficult for journalists, after ministers discovered the usefulness of the press office.

> The journalists [were] trying to get used to the fact that you had to speak to the press office. We still get it now. I had somebody who was getting really uppity with me today: 'But I want to speak to Henry.' 'Well you'll have to speak to me.' 'No, I will speak to Henry. Can I speak to his private office?' 'They'll put you back on to me.' 'Well, shall I page him?' 'He will tell me to phone you.' We are coming to the point now, where they [ministers] think, 'Yeah, actually, I think the press office is a fairly useful thing to have.' It kind of weeds out things – although they are all media mad.

The bedding-in period was accompanied by a major change in levels of activity. According to Liz Drummond:

> Basically, the two special advisers [Wendy Alexander and Murray Elder, advisers to Donald Dewar] seemed to have no idea what the press office was for and what their role was. We were getting instructions to . . . organise a press conference tomorrow about such-and-such, without us being asked whether we thought the story was big enough, small enough. There'd been a number of instances of press conferences recently where remarks are coming in the papers as to, why did they have that press conference? I suppose it comes from years of opposition. It was go out and sell this one, go out and sell that one. They were wanting to have a press conference on everything, which to my mind was debasing the currency. There can be dangers in putting the press face-to-face with the politicians, because they might get drawn into saying

things they don't want to say. So there are times when you do it by a news release or a junior minister gives a press conference, or you have a briefing by officials. You wheel out the Secretary of State when you've got a mega announcement.

Drummond gave us one instance, describing the frenetic activity initiated by Dewar's special adviser, Wendy Alexander:

> She talks very loud and very fast – BRRRR! She talks so fast it is hard for your ears to keep up with what they're hearing, let alone for your brain to keep up with what she's thinking. Some of her ideas are off the wall. And she doesn't listen – she never listens.

Another (more junior) information officer had a similar view:

> Wendy Alexander just runs around like a spinning top. I mean, brilliant mind – ideas, ideas, ideas, and then kind of punts them down to us and says, can we do this, can we do that? And some of them we put into action, some of them we don't. She's not a very skilled media person. But she is just there making sure that the messages get through, if you can do that without being a skilled media person.

Alexander taxed the abilities of the SOID so much that a relatively junior civil servant, Owen Kelly, was drafted in specifically to liaise with her.

As both Donald Dewar and Henry McLeish (the Minister for Devolution) became more and more preoccupied with the intricacies of the Scotland Bill, media work appeared to slow down. Liz Drummond recalled:

> My worry throughout was that the public were going to get bored stiff by it, if you kept hammering devolution, devolution, devolution at them all the time. And I'd said to Dewar very early on, 'Look, the press are complaining that there's nothing happening – they're used to a gimmick-a-day story out of Forsyth and they're not getting anything from you.' To which Dewar replied, 'I'll be more interested in what they say after a year in office than after a week in office.' I thought, 'Hooray, a grown-up politician at last!' But his mind was just fixed on devolution – there were other things going on, so we were trying to make sure that we got coverage on all the other things the Scottish Office was doing.

This led to Drummond being caught between the demands of Downing Street and the deliberate low profile of the Scottish Office team. In her words:

> There was nothing to say for a long time. There was nothing you could say, because Dewar was locked into long discussions, first with his own officials

and lawyers, then with other departmental officials and ministers. There was so much you couldn't say. That, I think, is when the press started whingeing – Campbell & co. started worrying that nothing was happening; there was no press coverage.

The worry in Millbank and Downing Street was that the Scottish Office was not doing enough to sell government policy. Drummond's opposition to those worries was one of the things which sealed her fate.

[Campbell] rang me up one Thursday, and said 'What's happening, what are you doing – what are you doing for this weekend's papers?' I said, 'Well, we've got nothing to put out.' 'Well, what would you like to see in this weekend's papers?' And I said I'd like to write nice stories saying that devolution's on course, and ministers are working hard, and all will be revealed in due course. They said, 'Well, go and brief them to that effect.' Well, of course, nobody's going to write that rubbish – it was a non-story.

More fundamentally, Drummond did not get on with Donald Dewar and the same information officer (Anne Shevas) who had shadowed Forsyth became his chief spokesperson in the SOID. Drummond's copy-book was further blotted by a perception among some Labour influentials that she was too close to the Tories, a view hard to maintain in the face of her clash with Michael Forsyth, but not altogether implausible given her admiration for Lang.[2] According to Drummond: 'I'm told that one of the black marks against me was that I'd been appointed by the Tories and I had worked previously for Westminster City Council under Shirley Porter,' (Jacobs 1997a: 4). She also noted press reports that she had gone because of 'ill health' or a 'lacklustre devolution campaign' (Drummond 1997: 16).

A final contributory factor to Drummond's sacking was the decline of morale in the SOID. Two examples are cited by SOID insiders. The first was of a colleague who was so stressed in the job that he literally had to be carried out of the Directorate on a stretcher after he collapsed. The second concerned a colleague removed from his post after it became clear that he was moonlighting in the restaurant business. As Drummond worked out her notice, the Labour hierarchy's dissatisfaction with the SOID's media relations led to an efficiency review.

The review had two main recommendations.[3] First, it advocated the abolition of the Deputy Director's post occupied by Alistair McNeill, in effect dismissing the second most senior member of the Directorate, although he lingered on in a secondment to the CSG for some months. His despatch was not reported by the media. The report suggested a restructuring of the next tier of SOID management by the creation of five Assistant Director posts. The second main recommendation was the creation of a Strategic Communication Unit to coordinate media relations across the

Scottish Office, in collaboration with Whitehall, thus importing Downing Street's priorities into information management in Scotland (Middleton et al. 1997). Internally, the review was seen (like the Mountfield report, the official review of the GIS) as a positive aid in the SOID's battle with the instinctive secrecy of the rest of the civil service.

The new SOID Director was selected from twenty applicants for the job. According to newspaper reports, the favourite was John Brown, brother of the Chancellor of the Exchequer and head of PR at Glasgow City Council. However, Brown pulled out of the race after civil servants made it clear that they thought he was too close to Labour:

> Scottish Office insiders said there was strong opposition to appointing someone from outside the civil service. One source said at the time: 'The appointment should be someone who knows how the Scottish Office works. There would be a lot of opposition if someone was appointed who was seen to be an appointment of the Labour Party.'
> (Swanson 1997: 8)

In the event, the new Director was English-born Roger Williams, director of corporate affairs at the Clydesdale Bank. He was a safer candidate from the Scottish Office's perspective, since he had spent ten years in the GIS (first at the Manpower Services Commission in 1979, then at the Departments of Energy and Trade and Industry) (Scottish Office 1997). For some journalistic observers, the civil service had won:

> One resolutely low-key politician [Dewar] is matched with one scarcely-known chief press officer. The civil service having won its battle, will be pleased. It is no disrespect to Mr Williams to wonder if the corporate affairs of the Clydesdale Bank are a preparation for such a role. Mr Dewar may indeed have hired a man who reflects his own temperament – and that may be the problem.
> (*The Scotsman* 1997)

This was prescient indeed, but not quite in the way that *The Scotsman* intended.

NOTES

1. The symbol of Scottish nationhood on which Scottish monarchs were traditionally crowned. It was reputedly removed by Edward I in the thirteenth century and lodged in Westminster Abbey.
2. She told the *Evening News* after she was sacked that, 'Ian Lang was and is a gent . . . Lang was a man who you feel went into politics because the

circumstances of nature and his life had been good to him and he felt he should give something back,' (Jacobs 1997c: 4).

3. The review was conducted by two Scottish office Officials with the aid of a recently retired member of the GIS. It was shown to the most senior SOID and other staff, but not to the rest of the SOID, causing further anxieties about job security and problems of morale. The review remains a confidential document and we were refused access to it by the SOID Director, an indication of the lack of openness in standard civil-service practice. However, we were able to obtain a copy elsewhere.

Chapter 7

Preparing to devolve in the Scottish Office

Long-term planning?

After the Labour government was elected in May 1997, Scottish Office ministers quickly became heavily involved in planning for devolution. This involved addressing the relationships between the proposed new bodies (Parliament and Executive), the media and the public. Three planning and review processes were initiated: the internal communications review and devolution communication campaign; rethinking the function and role of the SOID; and rule-making in the Media Issues panel of the CSG. The debate on the Parliament's structure and operations was detailed, reflecting the views and input of the civil service, media and political parties. The debate on the Executive, by contrast, took place entirely in private inside the civil service. Consequently, there was little significant reform of either the civil service machinery or the SOID. In this chapter, we argue that in their information efforts the civil service as a whole, and the SOID specifically, have not been significantly reformed. In particular, measured against the normative standard of CSG statements on openness, there was little or no progress. We have not examined civil service structural and functional changes more broadly, but our findings on information and openness are consistent with other research on the civil service transition. For example Parry (2000: 85) writes that the 'default position' was 'replication of the Scottish Office and of Westminster/ Whitehall'. Very much in line with our analysis, Parry (2000: 91) goes on to note that the civil service 'might have saved themselves a lot of trouble by taking the spirit of the CSG on board during 1999 and not holding so jealously . . . to the reproduction of their previous values and structures'.

THE INTERNAL COMMUNICATIONS REVIEW AND THE DEVCOM CAMPAIGN

The approach of devolution necessitated some focused thinking on the administrative support to be given to the new Executive. Once this had been decided, the changes afoot had to be communicated to the staff of the Scottish Office, its related agencies, and non-departmental public bodies. This was done through an unprecedentedly open internal communication campaign. Particularly noteworthy was the role of the head of the Scottish Office, the Permanent Secretary, Muir Russell, who undertook something of a roadshow of appearances and seminars as part of the DevCom initiative from September 1998 to June 1999. Apart from Russell's personal contact with staff, there was a wide-ranging internal communications programme run by a group of nine, followed up by a detailed review of internal communications (McAlpine et al. 1999). The DevCom initiative was intended to 'mark a renewed commitment to communication' by the Scottish Office in its transition to the Scottish Executive (Eames and Watson 1999). But the 'openness' of DevCom was purely internal to the civil service.

The predominant training needs identified by civil servants surveyed for the report related to familiarisation with the work of the Parliament. Of the fifteen seminar modules offered to civil servants as part of the transitional strategy, none included discussion of how the civil service might become more open with the public (Scottish Office DevCom Team 1998).

The aims of the DevCom campaign were:

> To let staff know about the arrangements for the Scottish Parliament and the Scottish Executive;
> To make sure they know how devolution will affect the work of the office and what we need to do in the run up to D–day; and
> To identify the knowledge and skills needed to help us provide an efficient and effective service to the Scottish Executive.
> (Scottish Office DevCom Team 1998: 2)

A review of internal communications followed DevCom and reported in June 1999 (McAlpine et al. 1999). Its remit was:

> To develop proposals for an integrated corporate communications strategy which provides a broad framework within which Departmental Management Boards (or their successors) can operate and which encourages effective three way communication (downwards, upwards and horizontally).
> (McAlpine et al. 1999: 2)

Significantly, there was no requirement to examine communication 'outwards' to the public. Of course, communication with the media is the responsibility of the SOID (discussed below). It is as if the idea of reforming direct communication with the public or with NGOs were simply inconceivable.

The transition process involved no moves in the direction of greater public accountability. Senior civil servants worked to ensure that debate about internal reform was off the policy agenda. Rather, they stressed the benefits of 'creating better trust between managers and between managers and staff through more open and honest communications'. The 'new challenges' of devolution were cited too: 'some of these will be to do with openness, inclusion and accountability' (McAlpine et al. 1999: 14). However, the invocations to openness, inclusivity and accountability were all centred on the civil service's internal hierarchies.

REFORMING THE SCOTTISH OFFICE AND THE CSG

The issue of civil-service openness appears not to have been discussed anywhere by the CSG. Media representatives did raise the issue of the organisation of news management in the Executive in the Media Issues panel. But despite interventions by media members determined to canvas their various preferences, the panel was steered firmly away from thinking that it should have any impact on the Executive's thinking. (As we have noted in Chapter 4, this was a highly sensitive issue.)

The Scottish Office view was that the new Executive should alone decide how to manage its information apparatus. In practice, this meant that there was no discussion about what would happen except within the civil service. The Scottish Office transmuted into the Scottish Executive with very little change in structure, culture or outlook. On the contrary, the Whitehall model was maintained and the senior civil servants saw to it that they remained part of the 'Home civil service'. This was accomplished without too much argument, since Labour ministers, and the Scottish Secretary in particular, were not too interested in such matters, and because the other political parties also seemed unconcerned. The result was an Executive little different from the Scottish Office in structure and culture. This was symbolised in the new corporate design which was almost exactly the same as that of its predecessor (see Figure 3).

CHANGING THE INFORMATION DIRECTORATE

Planning for changes in the SOID did not occur for a considerable while once Labour came into power in London. Our discussions with information officers from late 1997 onwards made it clear that little was being done. Liz

THE SCOTTISH OFFICE

REID HAILS STARTOF DEVOLUTION PARTNERSHIP

Scottish Secretary John Reid was today host at a Gala Dinner to celebrate the formal opening of the Scottish Parliament by Her Majesty The Queen

SCOTTISH EXECUTIVE

Back

Press Release

NHS INTERNAL MARKET AND GP FUNDHOLDING – R.I.P.

Figure 3 The last Scottish Office and first Scottish Executive news releases. These show how minor were the changes in corporate image.

Drummond, former Director, SOID, explained to us:

> The last time that devolution was proposed [1979] there was quite a lot of discussion. This time round, I had been asking people, 'What about the Parliament and how will it work, and where will we [Information Directorate] go?' The impression I got was very much that, 'Yes, we have this in mind, but let's get a bit further down the road before we start doing it.'

Although the planning was not very advanced, the general assumption was that things would go on much as before. A junior member of the press office had gathered as much by August 1997:

> [There's] not been a huge amount of talk about it yet, but I think they think it will basically become two offices: Scottish Office press office and a Parliament press office. And Dover House will be done away with. Now, whether this is [a minister] who would be based in London, full time, and therefore perhaps Dover House would just be his press office, [I don't know]. They have not gone into the details yet.

In the event this is broadly similar to what happened, with Dover House becoming the base of the Scotland Office and being detached from the Executive. We have been unable to identify any attempt to debate making the SOID more open. In August–September 1997, the Scottish Office instituted a review of the SOID, which was carried out by two administrative civil servants from the Personnel and Management Division and a recently retired government information officer. The report was submitted in December. Its terms of reference were principally to examine how the SOID could be reshaped to meet ministerial demands, particularly in light of the approach of devolution:

> The election of a new Government has necessitated a fresh look at the type of service and support the new team of Scottish Office ministers require from the Scottish Office Information Directorate. This will need to take into account changing priorities and emphases, for example the media interest in the new Government's devolution proposals.
> (Middleton et al. 1997: Annex A)

The review was focused principally on the news and press-office side of the SOID, with little attention paid to the publicity operation. This was a source of frustration to staff working in publicity, who felt that they had not been utilised sufficiently by an incoming government seemingly obsessed with news coverage. Staff in the SOID did think through some of the potential implications of devolution and wondered whether, and how, public-service campaigns might help establish the new identity of the devolved government. Some staff lobbied for work on educating the public about the new Scottish Executive and for a corporate redesign to differentiate it from the Scottish Office. One proponent couched the argument in terms of democratic norms:

> There was a very low awareness of what the Scottish Office was. The vast majority of people had never heard of us. Now you could argue that in this era of open government, when we're talking about accessibility and there's been a major structural change in the system, what we should be doing is advertising what we do. The civil service [in Scotland] is conservative with a small 'c'. The Scots have a terrible reputation of being careful with money . . . We affect every aspect of the [public's] life from health to education to roads to farming, and I think they've got a right to know that. But you try persuading people in here that there should be corporate advertising of that kind and they will say to you that they don't think it's our place to do that.

Of course such campaigns can be seen simply as public relations for the incumbent party of government, as in the case of the previous corporate redesign undergone by the Scottish Office in 1992. Our observer saw that as quite different:

> You had a Conservative government who were broadly hated by the populace

and who were seen to be Mrs Thatcher's lapdogs in the North. I think that's different. I think what I am talking about is genuine – I remember when Strathclyde Region had its own newspaper and there was an outcry then about 'selling the Labour Party'. If you serve people, then your job is to work for them. They need to know what you are doing for them and how they can communicate with you. And if you don't tell them, then that's not a very democratic system.

But moving in this 'democratic' direction was not on the agenda of ministers and certainly not on the agenda of senior civil servants.

This problem was exacerbated with the appearance in the Scottish Office of a former Labour Party official, Philip Chalmers. Chalmers began working in St Andrew's House in August 1999, and staff seemed concerned that they did not know what his role was. It later transpired that Chalmers was a special adviser, but his appointment was announced neither in a press release nor in Parliament, and information staff had no clear sense of his role. The failure to announce this post was a clear breach of an undertaking to Parliament given by the First Minister, in May 1999.[1] Chalmers' brief was to coordinate presentation, including publicity. This meant that publicity staff felt that their concerns were being addressed, so morale improved slightly. However, there was no progress on public education about the Executive's work.

The official position of the SOID is that it was not possible to engage in any detailed planning about reform. First, the specific form of government was not known until the First Minister appointed his ministers. Second, the official view was that it was constitutionally improper for the civil service to reorganise except under the direction of ministers. This was a convenient explanation since it was already known that Dewar would leave it to the civil service to determine its own structures. In June 1999, the Director of the SOID outlined the official position to us: 'There was only so much planning you could do in terms of staffing and arrangements. It's relatively easy to adapt arrangements. The number of press officers will have to increase over time as the demands come through.'

PUBLIC RELATIONS AND SCOTTISH GOVERNMENT

The number of information staff working for Scottish government bodies has expanded massively since the beginning of the 1970s. Figure 4 gives figures for the Scottish Office/Executive and other bodies since 1970.

These figures are a clear underestimate for two reasons. First, many Scottish governmental bodies are not listed in the IPO Directory (which lists information and press officers in government departments [COI 2000]) and

Public relations staff in Scottish government 1970–2000

	SOID/ SEID	STB	SSC	SNH	HS	DSS	TOTAL
1970 Jan	15	-	-	-	-	-	15
1971 Jan	18	-	-	-	-	-	18
1972 Jan	16	-	-	-	-	-	16
1973 July	24	-	-	-	-	-	24
1975 July	28	-	-	-	-	-	28
1976 July	32	-	-	-	-	-	32
1978 July	30	-	-	-	-	-	30
1979 Dec	29	3	-	-	-	-	32
1980 July	28	3	-	-	-	-	31
1981 July	25	3	3	-	-	-	31
1982 July	26	2	3	-	-	-	31
1983 Feb	27	2	3	-	-	-	32
1984 Sept	27	2	3	-	-	1	33
1985 Sept	26	2	3	-	-	1	32
1986 Mar	29	2	4	-	1	1	37
1987 Mar	30	2	4	-	1	1	38
1988 Mar	30	1	3	-	1	1	36
1989 Mar	29	1	4	-	1	1	36
1990 Apr	31	1	5	-	1	1	39
1991 Jun	33	3	5	-	1	0	42
1992 Jun	33	3	5	8	1	1	51
1993 Jun	30	3	6	8	2	1	50
1994 Dec	32	7	7	9	4	1	60
1995 Dec	32	6	6	8	2	1	55
1996 Dec	33	9	6	8	2	1	59
1997 Dec	30	11	4	7	3	1	56
1998 Dec	35	10	4	6	4	1	60
1999 Jun	40	10	4	9	5	1	69
2000 Jun	37 (+12)*	14	4	8	5	1	81

*The extra 12 includes 6 at the Scotland Office, 3 at the Parliament, 2 at the new Scottish branch of the Central Office of Information, and one in the new press office of the Employment Service.

Key
- SOID Scottish Office Information Directorate
- SEID Scottish Executive Information Directorate
- STB Scottish Tourist Board
- SSC Scottish Sports Council
- SNH Scottish Natural Heritage
- HS Historic Scotland
- DSS Department of Social Security

Figure 4 shows the dramatic growth of press officers in Scottish governmental bodies over the past thirty years.

the Executive refuses to give information in Parliamentary *Written Answers* using the standard rebuff that such information 'is not held centrally, and could only be obtained at disproportionate cost' (S1W–3222, 18 February 2000). Second, the names in the IPO Directory are mainly professional staff and do not include support staff. Were they to be included we estimate that the numbers here could be some 40 per cent higher.[2]

The number of professional information staff in the Scottish Office and its various agencies have markedly increased in the past thirty years. The professional staff of the Information Directorate in the Scottish Office/Executive increased from fifteen in 1970 to forty in 1999, before devolution took effect. The number of press officers increased by almost 50 per cent between 1970 and 1973 and then stayed relatively constant (between twenty-four and thirty-three) until 1997. On some occasions during this period, numbers dropped significantly, particularly with the setting-up of independent press offices for the Scottish Tourist Board and the Scottish Sports Council. Since 1997, the numbers have increased more rapidly, reaching thirty-five in December 1998, forty in June 1999, and forty-nine in June 2000 (including the staff of the agencies and the Scotland Office). Public relations posts in Scottish government doubled from fifteen in 1970 to thirty-one in 1980, increased by nearly 25 per cent in the Thatcher decade to thirty-nine, and more than doubled in the 1990s. These figures show that the New Labour government has increased its information staff faster than any other government in the past thirty years, and now presides over a PR machine bigger than at any point in Scottish history.

THE NEW ARCHITECTURE OF GOVERNMENT

In the transitional period before the formal transfer of powers to the Scottish Executive and Parliament on 1 July 1999, the SOID worked for both the Scottish Office ministers and those of the new Executive who were already appointed. After 1 July, the Scottish Office ceased to exist and the SOID changed its name to the Scottish Executive Information Directorate (SEID). Information work for the agencies of UK departments was removed from the new Executive.[3]

The rump of the Scottish Office became the Scotland Office, under Scottish Secretary, John Reid, and took over the old London HQ of the Scottish Office at Dover House. Reid's new Principal Private Secretary was an old hand from the SOID, Jayne Colquhoun. She did much of Reid's media work and was supported by another long-standing Dover House press officer, Kirsteen Clark. The Scotland Office conducted its own scoping exercise to see what kind of information support it would need. By mid-2000, the staff had risen to six press officers (COI 2000). There remains an informal agreement for the SEID to use a room in Dover house when Executive ministers travel to London. Reid also appointed a special adviser with responsibility for media work, Mike Elrick, formerly press officer for the late Labour leader, John Smith.

POST-DEVOLUTION CHANGES

The creation of the Parliament was mirrored by the creation of a new body called the Scottish Executive. This encompassed both the twenty-two MSPs who became ministers and the civil service. In London, there is both a civil service and a government, but in Scotland the term 'government' was deliberately avoided. As Roger Williams put it:

> Overnight, we've moved to a governing organisation – not a government – a governing organisation with its own Parliament. We avoid the word 'government'. There is only one government – that's the UK government. This is an Executive with governing functions on devolved issues.

One consequence of this is that there is no easy way to distinguish between ministers and civil servants, since they are both described as 'the Executive'. For some Parliament insiders, this lack of a distinction was troubling:

> What is the 'Scottish Executive'? Is it (a) the Scottish Cabinet or (b) the Scottish Civil Service . . . The answer is that it is both. How convenient: you cannot attack the Scottish civil service (official name 'Scottish Executive') without appearing to attack the government. But who came up with this post-devolution rebranding? The old Scottish Office the organisation the Parliament was set up to police/hold to account. They saw us all coming and the Parliament is now paying the price.

The key change which the new SEID had to address was the increase in ministers from nine to twenty-two. This was said by our sources to be unexpected and involved a rapid redeployment of resources. Roger Williams remarked:

> We knew that certain things would happen – the Parliament would be separate. It advertised in the open market for a press officer. We know him, and he knows how we operate. That was helpful in the early days; that's to our advantage. We knew there would be committees – journalists would now be on our doorstep. We didn't necessarily want to import a Whitehall-style structure. We don't need two briefings a day. The CSG wanted a more open arrangement. We didn't know who would win the election, how many ministers, what would be the precise subject matters. We didn't know how

arts, culture would be organised. Nor if agriculture, fisheries, forestry would be separate, or would they wrap up into rural affairs.

As Williams says, there was genuine uncertainty about how ministerial and departmental briefs would be distributed. There was also, arguably, some uncertainty about who would win the election. But there was no uncertainty about the CSG's wish for openness. Yet there was neither planning nor any reform in the Information Directorate to meet this recommendation. Instead, there were some key changes that attempted to bring the SEID into line with Whitehall practice, or more accurately, that of New Labour. The model, as with many other aspects of devolution, was that of Whitehall/Downing Street. As Roger Williams put it:

> When we came in, we looked at the Number Ten model, which was working very successfully. We took best practice and tried to apply it in Scotland. We have to have a strategic communications unit and also tactical planning for how stories are put over. We need to be aware of when bad news is coming and have to be sure that departments can react. We got the basics of the new system going pre-election. In due course, I imagine there would be people who would be able to write in the First Minister's and others' names, putting across the message of the government rather than being party political. Number Ten do this kind of thing for articles and speeches. We do not want to follow the Number Ten model, because we are smaller and have no financial or foreign affairs, only so much business.

The key differences from Number Ten have been a slightly more open atmosphere, in that David Whitton was named as official spokesman and the televising of Parliament has had fewer restrictions. The difference of scale has also played a role. Whitton concluded that twice-daily briefings were not worthwhile because there was not enough information to justify it. But otherwise, the specifically Scottish dimensions are hard to find.

Following devolution, the SEID underwent four main changes: the creation of the Strategic Communications Unit; the introduction of new methods of media monitoring; the reorganisation of desks to associate press officers more closely with ministers; and the introduction of a new and more proactive cadre of special advisers.

The Strategic Communications Unit

This was set up following the Mountfield report and the 1997 Scottish Office internal review. With Owen Kelly as its head before devolution took place, it worked closely with the special advisers. The unit was said by close observers to work well (although it had a rapid staff turnover in its early months). This is an innovation based on the London model.

News monitoring

This was also an initiative copied from London, and a key concern of Michael Forsyth during his term of office. Forsyth had the press-cuttings service contracted out to a clippings agency so that cuttings would arrive at his London office between 9 and 10am. With the advent of New Labour, Downing Street introduced a media monitoring system to cover press, television and radio twenty-four hours a day, rather than just relying on morning cuttings. But the monitoring did not include Scottish media, and ministers were concerned about the dependence of St Andrew's House on morning news cuttings. Dougie Atkinson, an administrative civil servant from the Personnel and Management Group with a reputation as a 'fixer', was called in and he spent several months working with the press office to resolve perceived problems. According to Atkinson:

> The extent of media monitoring previously with InD seemed to be that the duty press officer basically watched the news or read the papers, either at weekends or in the evening . . . So it wasn't terribly sophisticated, nor did it really pick up on stories as they emerged in the course of a day. For example, *Good Morning Scotland* – at six o'clock – if they were running a particular story about an Executive policy, it wouldn't be until the press officer got out of his bed at half past seven or whatever, and read this, by which time it had been running for two hours. So we were concerned that there was nothing in place to look at that early-morning media monitoring. I was specifically asked to go and introduce early-morning media monitoring arrangements, and devise some system that would satisfy ministers' requirements.

The new system involved civil servants arriving at work at the earlier time of 5.30am to ensure morning media monitoring. This system replicates London's.

Relations with ministers

The other key change was the reorganisation of desks so that press officers became more directly responsible to ministers, in effect acting as their personal press officers. This occurred shortly after the creation of the Executive, when it was found that some ministers were not working as well with what were described internally as 'their' press officers.

This approach had always been resisted by the SOID on the grounds that it identified press officers too closely with given ministers and could be seen as politicisation. The new Executive reshaped press office responsibilities to mirror those of specific ministers, rather than being topic-based. Press officers were described in the official directory of information staff (COI 2000) as covering the 'responsibilities' of minister A or B. As one senior observer put it:

> [The] general culture of understanding [previously] was that if a minister moved, then you stuck with the desk and you were then available to provide the service to the next one. The implication here is that were he to go somewhere else, so would they. Which is more of the personal press officer than previously. On paper it looks like giving way to the theory of the personal press officer, which was something which successive Directors of Information resisted, and resisted vigorously, in the Scottish Office.

Certainly some press officers did feel they were being pushed towards party political activities. According to Dougie Atkinson:

> [Press officers] are there to proactively promote government messages on particular policies. They would do that regardless of which government was in power. So there has been an attempt to get the press office . . . to act in that more proactive way, establish relationships with journalists and political commentators. That's a legitimate activity for the press officer to undertake. But of course some press officers begin to get uncomfortable the closer they get to anywhere near what might be perceived by some as being political. There's always that tension between making sure that press officers don't step beyond, but equally they don't just sit back and in a very neutral fashion give out press releases in the hope that the media will pick up on it.

Among those fearing that a line had been crossed was one of the longest-serving press officers, Tony McLaughlin, who walked out of his job in mid-September 1999, complaining of the stress of the working conditions and of what he saw as creeping politicisation. His departure followed moves to allocate each Scottish cabinet minister his or her own team of press officers. According to *The Sunday Times*:

> These teams will be based in each minister's private office and will be expected to be part of a minister's inner circle, developing a close knowledge of his or her views. Civil-service union leaders are already concerned about press officers being put into situations where it is hard to retain their professional integrity as impartial public servants, especially when they are asked to do 'instant rebuttal' of stories running in the media.
> (Farquharson 1999b)

As well as restructuring news monitoring, Atkinson also examined the relationship between press officers and ministers to see whether further integration between ministers' offices and press desks would work better.

> What became apparent was that some ministers had very close relationships with press officers, and they undertook forward planning on presentation where other ministers didn't enjoy that close relationship. Therefore their responsibilities perhaps weren't being highlighted as much as ministers

thought they perhaps should. So there was this uneven pattern of interface. What we tried to do was look at how some sort of customised arrangement could be introduced to ensure that ministers got the sort of support that they felt they needed. Initially there was piloting with attachments into private offices, partial attachments. Over that period of time it became apparent that we did have to look at that whole bit – it became a bit more complex than we originally thought.

As a result of this complexity, and no doubt partly as a result of the departure of Tony McLaughlin (to say nothing of the press coverage and potential further coverage), the reform which came out of this was a closer formal relationship with ministers by means of regular media planning meetings.

This arrangement is seen as a 'halfway house' between personal press officers and the old system. According to Atkinson:

What we've not done is physically located press officers in private offices. It sounds like quite a logical thing to do, to take the press officer out of the press desk and put him in the private office. But there's a downside to that as well, in the sense that they lose the day-to-day professional contact with their peers. And equally, you put the press officer in the minister's office and the minister will only be there one day a week. So you could end up having the disadvantage of taking a person out of the press office and they'd be sitting alone in some building to no real advantage because the minister is off doing things they don't need a press officer at. Nor are they around to develop this relationship.

The move towards the personal press officer compromises the previous rules designed to keep civil servants away from party politics. However, the result of the review conducted by Atkinson seems to have curbed that tendency, to the relief of traditionalists in the civil service.

Special advisers

The appointment in 1997 of Wendy Alexander and Murray Elder as special advisers to Donald Dewar was followed by the appointment of David Whitton as a third special adviser and Dewar's 'official spokesman'. Whitton was reappointed on the creation of the Executive. This trend was based on the Westminster model and was against the better judgement of Donald Dewar.

The planning for transition and further revisions since devolution have produced significant changes in information practice: specifically, increased media monitoring capacity, more attention to media planning and strategic communications, and closer relations between ministers and press officers. None of these has resulted in any increase in openness.

Pressure on civil servants by ministers has led to a number of lapses that do give rise to justified concern about politicisation. In June 1998, the full text of a speech by Donald Dewar, which contained political attacks on the SNP, was placed on the Scottish Office website. The speech was later removed and the Scottish Office claimed that it was an 'electronic administrative error' (Dinwoodie 1998a: 6). As the election approached, there was a dispute over the official start of the campaign period during which civil servants go into 'purdah' and cease to work for ministers. The election campaign started on 6 April and yet the purdah period commenced a week later. On 7 April, there was 'another spate of announcements, fourteen in all, many of them focusing on good news items such as job creation and NHS improvements' (Dinwoodie 1999: 7). Mike Russell of the SNP complained about a press release announcing a 'significant' inward investment, saying, 'Donald Dewar was extensively puffed in the release about inward investment' and that there was an 'unacceptable blurring of the lines' between party and government publicity (Macdonell 1998: 8). Roger Williams issued a statement declaring that 'The Scottish Office does not write, promote or distribute puff pieces for the ministers. It never has and it never will,' (Macdonell 1998). This is somewhat disingenuous since the Scottish Office had been considering the development of the capacity to have ministerial speeches written by civil servants.

Overall, then, preparations for the transition mainly involved practical considerations. There was no detailed planning about how the Executive might be different in culture or more open in practice than its predecessor. Consistent with this, the SOID was neither more open nor more 'Scottish', but followed the Westminster/New Labour model in its reforms. Its Scottishness came out solely in the caution evinced in the appointment of Roger Williams and, to a lesser extent, that of David Whitton.

MEDIA TRAINING

The Scottish Office media training programme was established around the beginning of Michael Forsyth's tenure as Secretary of State. The SOID approached the Video and Television Production Unit to establish courses specifically for civil servants. Courses last a day and are run about twelve times a year with about five or six people on each course. They are staffed by two trainers (Tim Christie from the Executive and one or other of two Scottish TV reporters, Christina McIntyre and Paddy Christie), backed up, where appropriate, by press-office staff or other journalists.

A variety of senior and sometimes more junior civil servants have been media-trained, including administrative officials from the Scottish Office departments such as the Chief Medical Officer and members of the Chief Scientists' Group, The Employment Service, Benefits Agency, Forestry

Commission and HM Chief Inspector of Schools. The introductory notes for the course run on 9 December 1999 state: 'This intensive one day course is based on three practical sessions during which participants will carry out television and radio interviews in the Scottish Executive Studios in central Edinburgh'. The sessions involve three-minute television and radio interviews down the line and a five-minute television studio interview. The course is introduced by a talk on the role of the Information Directorate of the Executive (or of press offices more generally).

Media training: a conflict of interest?

The Video and Television Production Unit regularly employs journalists as media trainers (and on other paid consultancy work) and has paid well-known Scottish figures to front its training videos (such as BBC Scotland's Jackie Bird and BBC Radio 4's James Naughtie) or to produce them (for example Christina McIntyre). These economic relationships between the Executive and prominent Scottish journalists raise a potential conflict of interest since journalists may be training or working with civil servants and ministers one day and be expected to cross-examine them on the public's behalf the next. The BBC has specific rules on doing work of this kind. In a country as small as Scotland, with such close personal and cultural links between the media and the political elite, it might be argued that adding further economic links raises the potential for a serious conflict of interest.

Training civil servants

According to insiders 'civil service culture is very bureaucratic. People have very fixed ideas about what one should and shouldn't do.' So talking to the media, according to those involved with media training, is 'Oh, no, no, no, that would be something that the minister does.' According to Tim Christie the Head of the Video and Television Production Unit, civil servants often 'come on the course with a fear of the media.' As a result it is only ministers who are subjected to hostile cross-questioning on the courses. As one insider put it: 'Why treat a civil servant Jeremy Paxman style . . . It's just going to make them shit themselves . . . You need to encourage these people to feel that they could actually do an interview.'

Training ministers

During the Conservative years, only civil servants and not ministers attended the media training courses, but since the election of the Labour government ministers have been media-trained in Scottish Office/Executive studios.[4] A number of 'senior' ministers in the incoming 1997 Scottish Office team were media-trained prior to devolution, including, according to our sources

Dewar, McLeish and Wilson. Following the creation of the Executive, all the incoming twenty-two ministers were offered media training. Apparently, all were trained within their first year in post, although there does seem to have been some initial resistance by some ministers. According to David Whitton:

> My own opinion is that every minister should have done it, even those who thought they were good at the media. You can never have too much training for this kind of thing and those who had not done it before found it very useful.

The Executive is trying to open civil servants up to the outside world by means of media training. But the key question is whether the media training encourages openness or evasiveness by ministers and civil servants. The course notes, which we have obtained, indicate the latter may be the case. For example, in a checklist of how to prepare for an interview it is stated that: 'Most essential is the key phrase or message, which should be used in answer to the very first question and hopefully also the last' (Scottish Executive 1999a: 3). If their message is not getting across, civil servants are advised to try 'resetting the agenda': 'If you feel that the interviewer has asked inappropriate questions or is trying to steer you in an unacceptable direction, you can try and change or remove questions' (Scottish Executive 1999a: 3). Tactics to achieve this are given: 'e.g. "that's an interesting question, but our view is (key message)"' (Scottish Executive 1999a: 4).

Participants in the course are advised not to lean too heavily on facts: 'Viewers will be more impressed by sincerity than by a pedantic recital of facts' (Scottish Executive 1999a: 5). There is one point at which the course notes acknowledge that civil servants should answer the questions put to them: 'It is of course, important to give what is asked from you, but also to make the points *you* feel are important' (Scottish Executive 1999a: 5, emphasis in original). But this is undercut by the advice given before and after. Later civil servants are advised to take advantage of multiple questions by answering only 'the bit you want' and by using 'effective' answers, which rather begs the question of whether they are true (Scottish Executive 1999a: 6). The only mention of 'truth' in the document is in a section which advises civil servants to be 'as reassuring as is truthfully possible' which is not perhaps the best advice in the light of the handling of the issue of BSE (Scottish Executive 1999a: 8). There is no mention in this documentation on the importance of public servants being open and truthful or on their democratic responsibility to inform the public. It seems that civil servants are being trained in the techniques of evasion and spin.

CABINET AND PARLIAMENT: PRISONERS OF THE PERMANENT GOVERNMENT?

The transition to the Executive, and the creation of the Parliament, have involved no fundamental reform of the civil service machinery, structure or style. Roger Williams, the Director of Information, put it bluntly when he told us:

> What you have to remember is this: from a civil service point of view nothing has changed. We are part of a unified civil service. That's the glue that holds the thing together. I could be seconded elsewhere. That kind of transfer is still going on.

This is the constitutional position of the civil service but it remains true that there is one unified civil service only in some respects. The senior civil service (grade five and above, namely all civil servants with any formal policy-making power) is part of a unified home civil service. Their terms and conditions are not devolved. However, the rest of the civil service is devolved and it falls under the competence of the Scottish Parliament. The Northern Ireland Civil Service does have separate grades and is a separate organisation – it is not part of the unified home civil service. This separation also affects the Northern Ireland Office's Information Service where few information officers have historically been GICS members. In June 1998, only six out of the sixty or so staff were GICS members, including the Director and his two deputies.[5] The Northern Ireland example was not usually considered in such debates, but the question of whether there should be a separate Scottish GICS or even civil service has been raised by some in the Executive. According to Dougie Atkinson of the Personnel Directorate: 'In a devolved environment there are issues about whether or not you have a separate GICS in Scotland.' But in the transitional period, internal discussion went no further than acknowledging the issue.

Evidently, the official position is that press officers are there to serve ministers. The rhetoric of openness and a new Scotland simply did not apply to the Scottish Office. According to Paul Geoghan, devolution press officer:

> We in the press office and the Scottish Executive are there to serve the ministers who are appointed to the Executive. There's a huge distinction between the Executive and the Scottish Parliament. I never was aware that there was going to be a discussion about how the Scottish Executive press office would change its set up to become any more open than it already is.

Press officers and civil servants see it as their duty to serve ministers and think of this as the equivalent to serving the public. In the words of one senior information specialist:

> They'll not talk about what they do. The caution is that any advice or information gained or obtained in the civil service – you are appointed to advise and inform ministers – that's your only role. It's ministers who are accountable, not you. That's the way it goes. That runs deep through the service. You are not entitled to know that. You are not entitled to know what it is the press office or the Information Directorate know. The minister is. If by openness you mean that the civil service will open up to enquiries of this nature – it won't. It's the culture and ethos of the whole service and I don't think that Scotland's about to break away and open itself to interrogation that a Whitehall department would not, no way.

So any new openness in Scottish politics is unlikely to be replicated in the civil service. The same argument can be applied to the staff of the Scottish Parliament, at least to the extent that they have been drawn from the old Scottish Office, as almost all of the senior staff are. Insiders claim that senior staff have brought the ultra-cautious culture of the Scottish Office with them to the Mound. They also point out that the Scottish Office played a key role in appointing senior staff:

> The Scottish Office selected all the senior staff and has them all on Scottish Office standard term and conditions contracts, with Scottish Office (now Executive) pay grades. Apart from their brief flirtation with Donald Dewar in his brief stint as the Secretary of State, nearly all of them have cut their teeth or enjoyed promotion under the viciously anti-devolution regime of the Tory years. What other new, almost revolutionary (in a Scottish Office context) organisation would let the people they have been set up to police/hold to account run the new institution itself with automatic retransfer rights to that organisation?

In such circumstances, the worry of this observer is that Parliamentary staff owe more loyalty to the civil service than to the Parliament itself:

> This is fundamentally all about the hidden hand of the old Scottish Office And here they are either so incompetent or institutionalised that they should get nowhere near running the Parliament or they are quite content for things to be this way. As career civil servants, their promotion horizons within the 300-strong Scottish Parliament workforce are pretty small, and if you are at the very top, non-existent. The only way you can go up is in the Scottish Executive or the wider UK civil service. But to challenge the impartiality of the civil service, or indeed their suitability to run the Parliament, is sacrilege and no doubt will be dismissed as some devious nationalist plot.

One implication is that the culture of the civil service is likely to impede radical change, or even determined reform, in policy making. Several examples of this have come to light since devolution occurred. One is the removal of all thirty 'key action points' from a report on biodiversity commissioned by the Environment Minister, Sarah Boyack. This was done by civil servants ('to save space') without the minister's knowledge just before it was sent to the printers. One 'leading conservationist close to the process' told the *Sunday Herald*: 'They are still ultracautious. They are burying and blockading the Scottish Parliament. They still want to do things the way they have always been done' (Edwards 2000: 13).

A CONCLUDING PERSPECTIVE

The Scottish civil service has been imperceptibly changed by devolution. The Whitehall model continues to prevail and there has been no serious debate about the opening-up of the civil service to serve the new Scotland. The SOID exhibits similar features as its parents in the Scottish civil service and the GICS in Whitehall. The Whitehall model was followed except where impractical. The organisation of the SOID has been in line with the general tendency of recent years and moved closer to politicisation with the effective creation of personal press officers for ministers. When there has been discussion about alternatives, the fallback position has been the Whitehall/Westminster model. Neither the Parliament nor the Executive has made a major break with the traditions of the past, although devolutionists have seen the need to reform the civil service and the machinery of government as a key reason for creating the Parliament.

There remains a pressing need to reform the civil service machinery. Arguably many (although by no means all) of the problems experienced by the Executive in the first year of devolution can be attributed to the lack of attention which reform of the civil service received in the transition to devolution.

It is to an account of developments in spin and information management that we now turn.

NOTES

1. In a written answer in Parliament, Donald Dewar stated, 'In due course I will announce the appointments of further Special Advisers' (*Written Answers*, 24 June 1999 S1W-4, S1W-5, S1W-8). But many of the other appointments were not announced in Parliament, either through written answers, or in press releases. Instead, word of Chalmers' appointment was slipped out to the *Daily Mail*, *Daily Record* and *The Sunday Times* (*Daily Record* 1999; Farquharson 1999a; Macdonell 1999).
2. For example, *Written Answers* reveal that the Information Directorate of the Executive employed fifty-two staff in February 2000. Eighteen of these are listed

as administrative support staff (S1W-03222, 18 February 2000).

3. A separate press office was set up for the Employment Service, an executive agency of the UK Department for Education and Employment. DfEE had formerly paid the SOID to cover its Scottish interests. The information work of the other UK agencies with Scottish branches the Health and Safety Executive, and the Office of the Gas and Electricity Markets (OFGEM) was taken on by the newly-established Scottish branch of the Central Office of Information, staffed by two information officers (COI 1999).

4. Tory ministers did have media training at a private-sector agency in London. One insider described this as a means of 'pretending they didn't have media training'.

5. Information from data supplied by Charles Skinner, GICS Development Centre, Cabinet Office, 29 June 1998.

CHAPTER 8

'It's a doddle'? The voter education campaign

When the package emerges, if anyone can say it is biased or there is any
political prejudice, I will eat my ballot paper in public.
(Donald Dewar, October 1998, cited in Dinwoodie 1998d: 6)

A SUFFICIENCY OF KNOWLEDGE?

The Secretary of State for Scotland offered the following benign public
account of the aims of the voter education campaign launched by the
Scottish Office:

> I want to make sure that every individual understands the impact of the votes
> he or she casts. Do I think it matters? Yes, I do. I make no apology for it.
> Indeed, every party leader, every newspaper leader writer, every broadcaster,
> every citizen of Scotland should think it matters too. Nothing would more
> damage the credibility of this new Parliament than an election in which people
> did not understand the voting mechanism or misunderstood the significance
> of the votes they cast.
> (Dinwoodie 1998d: 6)

However, in official reports and documents, a rather more conservative, and
apparently easily fulfilled, aim was pursued. In the official evaluation of the
campaign, the aim was to ensure that 'each voter had *sufficient* knowledge of
the new voting system to be able to cast an effective vote on 6 May' (Laird et
al. 2000: 5, emphasis in original). The word 'sufficient' was bandied about in
policy circles as a kind of catch-all defence against any accusations of
incompetence or venality. But, as may be seen from Donald Dewar's words,
that is not how the campaign was presented to the public. Even with the
lower hurdle of sufficient understanding it is debatable whether the
campaign achieved its aims. Furthermore, the notion of 'sufficient'
knowledge ensured that the published official evaluation of the campaign
examined its effectiveness in rather limited terms.[1]

The voter-education campaign was the Scottish Office's major publicity output during the transition to devolution. The campaign was planned by the Constitution Group and run by the Publicity Section of the Information Directorate. Tracking research was carried out by MRS and System Three, opinion and development research by Faulds Advertising, and evaluative focus groups by George Street Research.[2]

Because of the political sensitivity of the campaign, the four biggest political parties were invited to help in its development to allay worries about bias voiced by the opposition parties. Partly as a result of this sensitivity, the campaign ended up emphasising the date of the election and the two votes which electors were to cast. The campaign offered little information on the relationship between the two votes and provided almost no information on how second votes were linked to list seats.

This chapter examines the process whereby the voter education campaign was put together, the research commissioned and used to inform it, and the response from the public. We discuss the political context of the decision-making in the production of the campaign and show how the promise of a voter education campaign based on research evidence was compromised by professional advertising concerns, civil service notions of propriety, and ministerial intervention.

THE CONTENT OF THE CAMPAIGN

The campaign, under the heading 'Have your say in May', was launched at a press conference by Donald Dewar. It consisted of television, radio and press advertising, together with a leaflet drop to every household in Scotland. The campaign was backed up by a freephone number for further advice and information and the leaflet was also available on request in Gaelic, Urdu, Punjabi, Gujarati, Hindi and Cantonese as well as in braille, large print, audio and videotape formats.

In April 1999, the Scottish Office produced a four-page supplement on the election which was inserted into the *Daily Record* and the *Scottish Sun*. This gave guidance on the ballot papers voters should expect. Although the main thrust of the campaign concerned the two votes for the Scottish parliamentary elections, the supplement also included details of a third ballot paper for the local government elections. This additional information was given because the tracking research had shown that the public was largely unaware that there would be three ballot papers, in part at least because the television campaign only referred to two ballot papers (and continued to do so until the date of the election).

The most prominent part of the campaign was the television advertising but 'each aspect of the campaign was designed to complement the others so, for example, the television adverts would prompt interest and greater details of the voting system would be provided by the press adverts and the leaflet' (Laird et al. 2000: 6). There were four television ads: the first focused on the role of the Parliament, the second stated that there would be a new voting system, the third explained 'what the two votes are for' and the fourth explained 'how the ballot papers should be completed' (Scottish Office 1999). All four repeated that the election was on 6 May 1999.

The ads – each lasting thirty seconds – gave limited factual information. They used ordinary voters, each of whom spoke one phrase apiece. The variety of people and settings used suggested a diverse Scottish population. The first ad, which attempted to communicate the powers of the Scottish Parliament, represented a variety of professions associated with the devolved powers, such as fishing, education and health. The final one in the series ran as follows:

> On 6 May we'll all be asked to fill in two ballot papers. On one we put a cross against the name of a candidate and on the other we put a cross against our preferred party or an independent candidate. Sounds simple enough. Nae bother. No problem at all. It's a doddle.

More information was included in the press ads and the leaflet, but there was nothing in these which explained how the seats would be allocated.

The Scottish Office also produced two factsheets. The first was intended to explain the voting system for the Parliament and the second set out the powers of the Parliament and the Executive: 9,600 of each were issued to the media through the *UK Press Gazette*. A further 35,000 in total were sent out in response to requests on the freephone line (although a total of 150,000 of the first and 25,000 of the second were produced). According to Information Directorate sources: 'Colleagues did go out to meetings with the public and copies were distributed then. I am sure many more found their way to schools and public bodies who requested information from Departmental contacts' (personal communication to the authors, 2 March 2000). The lower print run of the second factsheet indicates that informing the public on the powers of the Parliament was accorded a lower priority. According to Information Directorate sources, 'This was an initial run and would have been reprinted had there been a greater demand' (personal communication to the authors, 12 June 2000). At best, around 45,000 copies of the first leaflet were distributed, supplemented by whatever officials personally distributed at public meetings. Somewhere in the Scottish Executive around 120,000 of these leaflets lie gathering dust.

PLANNING THE CAMPAIGN

The campaign planning began with research carried out in October 1998 by System Three. Using their Omnibus Scottish Opinion Survey, and incorporating earlier results of work undertaken for *The Herald,* the researchers found that the bulk of the population (between 73 and 84 per cent) were aware of the basic powers of the Parliament such as education, health and housing. Very few (8 per cent) said – incorrectly – that powers over defence and foreign policy would be devolved. 'Overall then, there would appear to be a reasonable appreciation of the division of responsibility between Holyrood and Westminster in the main issues' (System Three 1998: 5). Awareness that voters would have two votes in the election increased from 22 to 28 per cent between June and September 1998. By October this had reached 41 per cent. However, knowledge of the operation of the voting system was low:

> At best, there was only a slight understanding among just over a third of the sample and the publicity campaign therefore has much work to do to inform the Scottish electorate of the new voting system. The proposed publicity campaign has a major role to play in demystifying the procedures involved in electing the new Scottish parliament and in explaining from first principles the rationale behind these.
> (System Three 1998: 7–8)

Focus group research was carried out by SCPR (partially funded by the Scottish Office) in late summer 1997 in Scotland, Wales, Northern Ireland and London. The researchers commented as follows on their findings:

> There was a clear and fairly consistently expressed desire to understand the operation and implications of the new voting systems before deciding how to vote. To use the new [voting] systems, voters require information that goes beyond the mechanics of casting a ballot. People need to know about the basic operation of the new systems, in particular how votes get translated into seats. Adopting new voting procedures raises questions in people's minds, and they are uncomfortable about being asked to use a system they do not understand.
> (White et al. 1999: 17)

Although this research was only published in March 1999 (after the bulk of the planning work had been completed) the researchers were in contact with Scottish Office officials from the beginning. A Scottish Office civil servant sat in on the Scottish focus groups (conducted in Glasgow) and, according to a senior researcher at SCPR, there was 'interaction throughout the project' with Scottish Office civil servants. The researchers also 'presented key findings at a seminar in London in November 1998, hosted by the European

Parliament' and attended by civil servants. So at least some Scottish Office officials were aware of these findings as the campaign was being planned.

In sum, the available research suggested that people needed relatively little information on the powers of the Parliament, probably because this had already been extensively covered in the Scottish media. On the other hand, extensive information on the voting system was required, from basic information about the two votes, to more sophisticated information about the relationship between the votes, and the roles of constituency and list MSPs. According to the Scottish Office, the campaign strategy developed was 'based on' this research. 'Individual advertising treatments were drawn up and further researched for effectiveness and clarity of meaning,' (Scottish Office 1999). However, when the advertising campaign appeared it aimed to establish the following:

> The date of the election;
> The responsibilities of the new Scottish Parliament;
> The voting system, i.e.
>> It was a new system;
>> There were two votes;
>> One was for a constituency member and the other was for a party or individual candidate;
>> It included a form of proportional representation;
>> It was a fair system;
>> How to fill in the ballot papers.
> (Laird et al. 2000: 6)

Sharp-eyed readers will note that there is nothing in this list about the relationship between the first and second votes, the way in which the seats were to be allocated, or guidance on how to use the first and second votes. This was because 'early research had shown that by and large, the public only wanted basic facts' (Laird et al. 2000: 6). Yet the early research from System Three and SCPR referred to above actually showed that more information was desired by the public. Furthermore, the System Three research was not referred to in the official evaluation of the campaign.

According to our information (from staff at Faulds Advertising and George Street Research), the early research referred to here was carried out by Faulds. The ostensible finding, that the public did not want more than the basic facts, is diametrically opposed to the other research evidence available. Two pieces of Faulds' research were presented to the Scottish Office. The associated documents were not disclosed even to the market researchers who produced the evaluative report on the campaign (Laird et al. 2000) and have not previously been referred to publicly.

We have obtained copies of this research. The first of these (dated 4 November 1998) was carried out around three weeks before the System

Three research referred to above, and was based on twelve focus group discussions carried out across Scotland (in Aberdeen, Dumfries, Edinburgh, Glasgow, Perth and Stirling). However, it did not find anything markedly different from the System Three research. It concluded that:

> Interest in the Scottish parliament will encourage people to want to understand the voting system; evaluation that the new voting system is an improvement is important to head off cynicism; comprehension of the new voting system is essential to effective voting.
> (Faulds Advertising 1998a: 20)

This was a clear signal that proper explanation was required. There was certainly nothing in this report which suggested that voters wanted only 'basic facts'.

The research also found that the public wanted information on the voting system to come from the Scottish Office. As one focus group respondent said, 'It's certainly not the role of the political parties to explain it 'cos then it would come over biased' (Faulds Advertising 1998a: 9). By this stage, however, the planning had progressed to a stage where the communication strategy was described as follows:

The new parliament is coming

⇩

It deals with your issues

⇩

The voting system is better

⇩

There are two votes

⇩

Here's how you vote

⇩

Remember to cast your vote on May 6.
(Faulds Advertising 1998a: 23)

This strategy did not include information about how the voting system worked in terms of members elected. It was limited to the 'mechanics' of how to vote.

The next piece of research done by Faulds involved pre-test mock-ups of potential ads. This work was carried out in November 1998 and presented to the Scottish Office on 1 December. It involved eight focus groups in

Edinburgh, Galashiels, Inverness and Oban. One proposed advertising series, 'Friends and Relations', was rejected by the groups: it was felt to stereotype Scottish people and to recognise insufficiently the multicultural nature of Scotland. The other, named 'Everyone', became the basis for the ads eventually broadcast.

There were indications in this research that too much information was being given in one of the mock-up newspaper ads. We quote this evidence in full:

> 'Too many numbers'; 'Just tell me what the second vote is for, not how it's all added up'; 'I don't like that one. I don't need it'; 'Personally I think it's too confusing. You're getting it all in that, your first one.'
> (Faulds Advertising 1998b: 11–13)

Some of these responses indicated that respondents did not like some of the candidate advertising. So far as we can tell, two suggested that they became confused or overwhelmed by the numbers in the mock-up, not that they only wanted 'basic information'. Two did suggest, however, that information about how the system operated was not wanted.

Other evidence cited in the report gave a different view. A later TV ad was criticised as being too simple and patronising, 'I know how to put a cross in a box,' said one respondent. Another noted that, 'It's not conveying any information to us except it's happening on the 6th of May, we've got two votes and we've got seven regional representatives' (Faulds Advertising 1998b: 17). The consultant's report ended by recommending: 'Different people "switch on" at different places and levels in the process, so all the information needs to be available should they want it at any time' (Faulds Advertising 1998b: 23).

To sum up, four pieces of research were conducted by the end of 1998. Three unambiguously emphasised the importance of information about the voting system in the campaign and found some evidence that there was a strong desire for such information on the part of the public. The fourth contained mixed findings, including evidence of dislike for one of the ads. But at least some of the reservations expressed related more to the content of the ad than to the principle of having more information. This ad may well have put some respondents off by emphasising the arithmetic of the system too heavily. Certainly, there is no strong evidence even in this latter piece of research that the public wanted only 'basic facts' (Laird et al. 2000: 6). Moreover, although the first three pieces of research had been consistent in suggesting a desire for more information, the recommendations put forward by Faulds at the end of their first piece of work (in November 1998) simply ignored the desire of the public (as expressed in the research) for significant explanation of the voting system. This was notably different from the account given by Donald Dewar at the launch of the campaign in February 1999. He stated, 'The shape of the campaign has been influenced by extensive research carried out by the Scottish Office's advertising agency and every step is being taken to ensure the new system is understood' (Scottish Office 1999).

Notwithstanding the evidence to the contrary, the campaign was developed on the basis that the public did not want much information on the voting system. Faulds produced further advertising ideas in January 1999. These concentrated on respondents' familiarity with the proposed ballot paper, and the clarity and ease of understanding of the design, and also tested respondents' reactions to the proposed advertising, asking whether the adverts helped to prepare them to understand the ballot paper (Faulds Advertising 1999). This research fed directly into the actual campaign, which was launched on 14 February 1999. As the campaign developed, it became apparent from the tracking research (Market Research Scotland 1999a; 1999b; 1999c) that the public were becoming confused about the number of votes to be cast on 6 May. The most obvious reason for this was that the TV adverts mentioned only two votes and that the third vote was mentioned only in passing in one of the newspaper ads. As the official evaluation put it: 'Early elements of the information campaign did not put across a clear message about the number of votes to be cast. In separating Parliamentary and local elections in early material, some confusion was caused in relation to the third vote and who it was for' (Laird et al. 2000: 3).

The campaign advertising was supported by a freephone number printed on the press advertisements for members of the public to request further information, either in the form of factsheets or by pursuing specific queries. The latter were referred to Scottish Office officials who were able to explain the system in some detail. The factsheets and the newspaper insert were produced by the SOID (together with officials from the Constitution Group) rather than by Faulds, although the advertising agency did have some input to discussions on their content.

The factsheets were intended to supply enough information on the voting system to allow people to understand it. The second factsheet explained the powers of the Parliament, a task made easy by the fact that most people already had a good idea of what these were. This prior knowledge was reflected in the small print run. Although the first factsheet did go into some depth about the voting system (on six sides of A4: see Figure 5), it was explained in a rather formalistic way, without using lively examples, and was elaborated by a detailed table at the end of the leaflet. Although the table was referred to in the text of the leaflet, it had no heading. In all of the campaign material, the first fact sheet was the only place where the public could glean information to help them to decide how to vote. With a maximum circulation of around 50,000 and an almost unintelligible table, this was

Is this the first time AMS has been used?

No. AMS is already used in a number of other countries. It is also being used for the new Welsh Assembly.

Who can vote?

Anyone registered in the register of local government electors will be eligible to vote - that includes EU nationals, Commonwealth citizens and Peers registered in Scotland.

Who can stand?

Anyone entitled to stand for the House of Commons, including Commonwealth and Irish Republic citizens, plus Peers and ordained members or ministers of any religious denomination. EU citizens must reside in the UK to be eligible.

Who can submit a regional list?

A political party must be registered with the Registrar of Political Parties if it wishes to submit a list. The Registrar may be contacted at:

Companies House
Crown Way
Cardiff
CF4 3UZ
Tel: 01222 380380
Fax: 01222 380149
e-mail: www.party-register.co.uk

	Party 1	Party 2	Party 3	Party 4
Regional votes	61,974	63,362	61,189	37,206
Constituency MSPs	2	4	1	0
1st win - Party 4	÷ 3 = 20,658	÷ 5 = 12,672	÷ 2 = 30,595	÷ 1 = 37,206
2nd win - Party 3	20,658	12,672	30,595	÷ 2 = 18,603
3rd win - Party 1	20,658	12,672	÷ 3 = 20,396	18,603
4th win - Party 3	÷ 4 = 15,494	12,672	20,396	18,603
5th win - Party 4	15,494	12,672	÷ 4 = 15,297	18,603
6th win - Party 1	15,494	12,672	15,297	÷ 3 = 12,402
7th win - Party 3	÷ 5 = 12,395	12,672	15,297	12,402
Additional seats	2	0	3	2
Total representation in region	4	4	4	2

The number of votes cast for each party in the regional ballot is divided by the number of constituency seats gained **plus one** - this allows parties which have not won any constituencies to be included in the rest of the calculation.

After that calculation is done the party with highest resulting figure gains the first additional seat. In this case it is Party 4, which won no constituency seats.

To allocate the second to seventh additional seats the calculation is redone, but each time any additional seats gained are added in - so second time round, the vote for Party 4 is divided by 2, rather than 1.

By the end of the calculation the ratio of votes to seats for each party has been made much more even.

Figure 5 Scottish Office fact-sheet.
The last page of the six-page fact sheet explaining the voting system. The table is the only place to offer an illustration of the relationship between first and second votes. However, as may be seen, and as noted by the evaluation research, the table was hard to decipher.

hardly adequate to the task of adequately informing the Scottish people on how the voting system operated.

So why was the information which System Three, Faulds and SCPR research had identified as important for the campaign not included? And why was only a limited and well-nigh incomprehensible explanation of the voting system provided in the background factsheet? Our information is that this was due to a combination of professional advertising assumptions, civil-service propriety and ministerial intervention. This combination of factors also led to the evaluative research on the campaign being fundamentally flawed.

First, it is necessary to recall that the content of the campaign became a matter of some political controversy in the Scottish media in October 1998, with calls from the SNP for the campaign to be under the control of the all-party CSG and from the Liberal Democrats for it to be run by the Electoral Reform Society (Dinwoodie 1998d: 6). In a bid to head off criticism, representatives of the four biggest parties were invited to have an input into the planning of the campaign. Both the Green Party and the Scottish Socialist Party were excluded from this process, but after the Greens complained, they did have some contact with the civil servants running the campaign.[3]

The Scottish Secretary had clearly given some thought to the campaign by this stage (October 1998) because, according to reports, he 'pointedly gave examples where the SNP could lose out, if its party's supporters wrongly thought, as some electors appear to do, that the second vote had to be used for a different party from the first one' (Dinwoodie 1998d: 6). But as was widely known in the Scottish Office at the time, it was the Labour Party which would be most likely to lose out from electors casting their second votes for a different party. According to Scottish Office officials attached to the campaign, they had calculated that Labour, which was anticipated to gain the greatest number of constituency seats, could lose a significant number of list seats in four of the eight electoral regions, if electors voted differently in the second ballot. Within six weeks of Dewar's comments on the SNP, the ambition to discuss the voting system in detail was dropped from campaign documents.

We will return to the role of ministers in this shortly. Meanwhile, we need to look briefly at the motivation of the advertisers in ignoring their own and others' research findings. By the beginning of December 1998, the campaign strategy had been drawn up and it was confined to giving voters basic information. The advertising strategy was devised in consultation with the Scottish Office Information Directorate.

The only place in the campaign where there was any attempt to explain the allocation of list seats was in the first factsheet. According to our information, the table which explains the allocation of list seats was included on the initiative of a civil servant attached to the Constitution Group. Both the publicity section of the SOID and the advertisers Faulds were sceptical about the inclusion of this information. This was because there was no other explanation of the list calculation in the rest of the campaign. As Lesley Armstrong of Faulds Advertising told us:

> I still felt the leaflet was too much for the general public to take in. But they wanted to put more in the leaflet than was in the ads and more in the factsheet than was in the leaflet. The Constitution Group knew that very little of the material that had been put out to the public at large contained an explanation about the seat allocation and how it was all worked out. I remember this croppling up and both Chris Dempsey [Information Directorate] and myself had said to Lucy Hunter [attached to the Constitution Group] at the time, 'Why are you putting this in because there is nothing of this anywhere else in the advertising or in the strategy?' Questions like seat allocation were put in by the Constitution Group for their own reasons rather than for anything that would affect the success or failure of the campaign.

But the advertisers also objected because they did not believe people could understand the system. According to Lesley Armstrong,

> The complexities of the voting system, and how the seats were allocated, and what happened after the votes were cast, was something that we *just knew* the public couldn't handle - not in any form of complex explanation. Even in the leaflet, it was kept fairly bog standard. The factsheet was designed for the real political junkies who wanted to get to the real hub of everything. (emphasis added)

Certainly, the information in the factsheet was incomprehensible to many respondents. It was found difficult to understand by respondents in the official evaluation of the campaign:

> [The first factsheet] received criticism from a number of respondents for being too complicated. Even some of those respondents who claimed a relatively good understanding of the system found the calculations difficult to understand and explain to other members of the group. The following comment was made by a respondent who felt they had a reasonable understanding of the system and who had taken the time to read an explanatory article produced in *The Herald*:
>
> > The table looks appalling. It would put you right off and yet if you read through it, you probably could work it out. But it's a very complicated way of explaining it. *The Herald* had an article in it which used a pie chart to illustrate how the system would work, and how the seats would be allocated, and it seemed to be much easier to understand than this.

> It's the same information really, but the way they presented it was much simpler (female, 26–45 AB).
> (Laird et al. 2000: 32)

When testing respondents' understanding of the allocation of seats, the official evaluation found that 'There were no instances where any of the group respondents were able to suggest accurately the correct answers or the correct method of arriving at the answer' (Laird et al. 2000: 46). The research concluded that 'few respondents had any idea how additional seats would be distributed. A clearer understanding of how the system worked could influence the way in which individuals voted,' (Laird et al. 2000: 46). The researchers used a much simpler example than that in the factsheet to test whether people could, in principle, understand the system of seat allocation. They found that 'few respondents had any idea how additional seats would be allocated', but that 'when explained to them simply the idea was understandable' (Laird et al. 2000: 46). Furthermore, while an understanding of the voting system:

> was not necessary to allow people to vote, discussion at the groups revealed that more information on these lines may have altered the pattern of voting by encouraging a wider choice of parties between the first and second vote. Some respondents felt that, with hindsight, they had not made best use of their second vote because of a lack of understanding of the relationship between the two votes and the way in which seats would be allocated.
> (Laird et al. 2000: 44)

In other words, the advertisers had underestimated the capacity of the public to understand and consequently failed adequately to convey their desire for information.

A third and extremely significant reason for not including material of this nature was political sensitivity. The advertisers' view was that the information that the public could absorb was extremely limited. The television advertising was confined to informing the public that there were two votes in the elections. Explaining that there was actually a third ballot paper for the local elections was seen by Faulds as just 'too complicated' (according to the agency's Lesley Armstrong). The civil servants in the Constitution Group wanted to include some detailed information and insisted, against the judgement of the advertisers, that the table be included in the leaflet. They, however, would not countenance an examples-based approach, intended to illustrate different potential outcomes and look in detail at how the second vote would influence overall seat allocation. This unwillingness was relayed to the advertisers, as we were told:

> We couldn't mention parties by name or politicians or potential MSPs. It would look as if it was potentially biasing the voter towards that party. You had to do it all very – not quite apples and pears – but keep it all very simplistic.

As one of the Constitution Group officials involved put it:

> To [avoid giving] people the tools to do it [vote tactically] wasn't a decision of a political nature at all. It was a decision purely on whether to advise on how to achieve certain types of outcomes was appropriate for this campaign. And the feeling was that it wasn't. But one reason we were comfortable we didn't do that was that that was exactly the part of the system that the media and the small parties would focus on.

A key assumption, therefore, was that enough information about the second vote would be supplied by political parties and the media. But according to the evaluative research commissioned by the Scottish Office, 'few respondents had any idea how additional seats would be distributed' and 'expectations' that the information would be provided by the media and parties 'were not realised' (Laird et al. 2000: 46–7).

This pursuit of civil service propriety worked to include more information than the advertisers wanted but it limited the intelligibility of that information. There were some worries inside the Scottish Office about potential legal action if the campaign were perceived to be biased. As one official put it 'Big parties have interests too, and what you don't want to do is get stuck in the middle of that fight.' The final nail in the coffin of a fuller explanation, we understand, was the ministerial desire not to have too much conveyed about the second vote in case this might become a 'party political football'. According to one Scottish Office source:

> What you've got to remember as well is that [voters] were being told by the Labour party to vote one and two as well. So this is the influence we don't know about. There were seats where the people – I am thinking particularly Labour voters – and I mention them because I think Labour was probably the big group – would have been far better voting Liberal Democrat on the second vote.

Although the SNP, Lib-Dems and Conservatives were consulted on the campaign, the Labour Party was consulted first, according to our sources, through Scottish Office ministers.

CONCLUSION

On the evidence, the Scottish people did not have 'sufficient' information to cast an 'effective' vote. Certainly, the Scottish Office's own research made it clear that the bulk of the population did not fully 'understand' the voting system and, to some extent at least, were not clear about the significance of the votes they cast.

NOTES

1. The evaluation of the campaign did not directly examine its success in ensuring public understanding of the voting mechanism and the significance of the votes cast. The evaluation report states that the research was conducted 'in order to assess the effectiveness of the Voter Education Campaign'. But this is immediately undercut by the next sentence: 'The research was not intended to assess levels of knowledge and understanding of the new voting system,' (Laird et al. 2000: 8). In other words, the evaluation of the campaign did not focus on assessing whether the campaign met its aims in terms of 'sufficient' knowledge to cast an 'effective' vote. Instead, it focused on research aims which were more likely to show a successful result. For example, assessing levels of awareness and recall of the campaign are of a different order to assessing whether voters understood the information in the campaign. The campaign evaluation objectives were easily met and the campaign declared a success. The publication of the evaluation was delayed by some six months while ministers instructed changes to be made.
2. System Three and George Street are regularly used for contract opinion and market research by the Executive. Together they secured more than half the contracts for market and opinion research which the Executive commissioned in its first six months. The total cost of all market and opinion research in the period was £677,000 (Scottish Parliament, *Written Answers*, 19 January 2000, S1W-03220). Faulds was one of two advertising agencies contracted to the Scottish Office/Executive (the other being Barkers Scotland). In the first six months of its existence, the Executive contracted Faulds to carry out over £500,000 worth of public information advertising, not including the voter-education campaign, which was earlier commissioned by the Scottish Office. The voter-education campaign itself cost £2.5 million in total.
3. The Greens also took the Information Directorate to the Advertising Standards Authority, complaining about the phrase 'everyone's vote counts' in the advertising copy. Their complaint was rejected on the grounds that they themselves had used the phrase in their election literature (www.asa.org.uk/adj/adj3890.htm).

CHAPTER 9

Scotland in a spin

THE MILLBANK TENDENCY

Arguably, the lack of reform of the civil service in general, and the SOID in particular, have cast a long shadow over the development of Scottish politics. This has exacerbated the inevitable tensions attendant on setting up a new administration and those which go with Cabinet government.

In this chapter, we consider the differences in style between the London and Edinburgh regimes. Although spin has been an ever-present topic in the Scottish media since 1997, it is clear that there are significant differences between the Whitehall and Holyrood styles of information management. In part, these are rooted in disputes between 'New' and 'Old' Labour inflected by and entwined with the well-known tensions between the camps of Tony Blair and Gordon Brown (Rawnsley 2000). However, they run deeper than that. The divergences reflect a long-term battle between consensual, paternalistic, and public-service approaches to information management and the PR-based, advertising-friendly, commercially-oriented approach of New Labour.

The traditional culture of the civil service, with its lack of accountability and its instinctive secrecy, has found itself attacked by a proactive impatience for change. This battleground is a microcosm for studying the erosion of a public-service approach to government and its replacement by market criteria. New Labour has commercialised information services and media management at a pace that exceeds previous governments. That said, New Labour has continued the process of commercialisation begun by the Conservatives (particularly under Thatcher) and maintained the stress on information management. It is unlikely that the Conservative Party would reverse any of these reforms, other than to replace key officials with more Tory-friendly staff.

The disputes and conflicts highlighted between Edinburgh and London, 'New' and 'Old' Labour, Blairites and Brownites, Scotland Office and Scottish Executive, Cabinet members in the Executive, special advisers, information staff, administrative civil servants and spin doctors, relate to the personal, professional and political struggles which we describe here. They also derive from contending conceptions of government either as a service for the people or as the executive body of a large corporation.

DOCTORING DEWAR

With the SNP surging in the polls in early 1998, the devolution dream threatened to turn into a nightmare for Scottish Labour. Party modernisers had few doubts about what had gone wrong. The problem was one of presentation and they began to put pressure on Donald Dewar to adopt their own approach. Prior to this, murmurs had been heard in Scotland about Dewar's allegedly out-of-date style of media relations. In August 1997, Tim Luckhurst, a friend of the 'modernisers' reported:

> Mr Dewar's closest admirers fear he has not made the transition to 'the modern media age' . . . his media relations are stuck in the 1970s . . . Staff in Mr Dewar's private office are concerned that he does not accept the need for expert advice on his relations with journalists . . . Mr Dewar's supporters point to his continuing fondness for old-fashioned campaign stunts, like shopping-centre walkabouts as evidence that he is wasting effort on low-impact activity. (Luckhurst 1997: 7)

Dewar did appear reluctant to embrace the Downing Street approach, although he was clearly rattled by media demands and how the press turned against his administration, particularly over the case of Jason Campbell and the refusal to give Sean Connery a knighthood.[1] After Liz Drummond's sacking as Director of Information, Dewar was urged by Downing Street to appoint a Labour Party loyalist to the post. With support from Number Ten, his special adviser Wendy Alexander reportedly tried to persuade Labour's chief spokesman, David Hill, to apply. A Downing Street source told *The Herald* that 'Dave would be just the kind of appointment Donald Dewar needs to turn the Scottish Office press operation into a credible fighting force for delivering the Government's message,' (Campbell 1997: 1). Hill did not apply for the job. But John Brown, head of PR for Glasgow City Council, and brother of the Chancellor of the Exchequer did, and was reported as the preferred candidate. In the event, Brown withdrew, and Dewar followed the civil-service approach by appointing Roger Williams.

Dewar had had long experience of handling the media from his time as Labour's Chief Whip and he certainly did not regard this as unimportant. In mid-1998, he gave a long interview for a fifty-five-minute Scottish Office video for civil servants entitled *Working with Ministers*. Almost half of the video was taken up with discussing civil servants' and press officers' relations with the public and media. Dewar's interview shows his reluctance to adapt to media requirements:

> I turned up in some state of doubt in George Square, Glasgow, not so long ago, on a Sunday, with a small plastic set of figures indicating the number of days to a Scottish Parliament. It was, in my view, a somewhat inadequate prop on which to lean. But it was the right slot, it was the right time, and just because there was a visual impact – even if it was simply holding up 500 days as a somewhat unlikely looking banner with a strange device – it appeared in almost every paper in central Scotland. It did extraordinarily well on television as well. Now, it wasn't a great effort of imagination but someone had just taken the trouble to make it just a little bit different of an angle and get a prop to support it and it did extremely well to make a point.

However, Dewar also revealed his vulnerability to media criticism noting that the 'true' role of press officers is to provide emotional support for their minister:

> It's not just a matter of reminding him to do his hair, walk straight, and try and be coherent. There's a lot of practical help and advice that a good press officer can give. Once the minister is started – well he's on his own, mate. If he goes down in flames, he goes down in flames. There's nothing that the press officer can do there except hold up his little recording machine and groan . . . And it sounds very odd. I mean, it's sometimes just very comforting to have an ally there. If you've had a long day and you're stuck in the dark caverns of the BBC, it's quite nice to have someone to complain to. That's not part of the job really, but it is the truth.

Dewar's approach earned scorn from Blairites north and south of the border and pressure on him continued. The devotion of Blair and Campbell to media management (Oborne 1999) was reinforced by their negative view of the Scottish media as 'unreconstructed wankers'. In March 1998, Blair visited Scotland and made further complaints about the Scottish press. Meanwhile, Campbell reportedly asked assembled Scottish journalists, 'Aren't the Scots just a teensy bit more narrow-minded than their metropolitan counterparts? Don't Scots need to broaden their horizons just a tad?' 'Perhaps,' replied the *Scotland on Sunday* diarist, 'but aren't certain people close to the Prime Minister just a teensy bit patronising to Scots?' (Insider 1998: 12). Some months later, the view from Downing Street was unchanged as the Standards Committee of the Parliament investigated the Lobbygate affair. 'Sources close to Dewar' let it be known that, 'Downing Street is inclined to let devolution work, but only if the Parliament is seen to behave with dignity and competence. Blair is laughing at us. When Alastair

Campbell . . . gets the daily newspaper cuttings about the Scottish Parliament, he simply laughs' (Hardie 1999). Blair and Campbell's visit in March 1998 was accompanied by the revelation that a spin doctor was to be appointed to the Scottish Labour Party's HQ (Nelson and Arlidge 1998: 1). Apparently this was news to Donald Dewar, because the following week it was reported that senior Labour figures were still 'putting Dewar under pressure' to make this appointment (Parker and Penman 1998a: 1). A week after this, Dewar reportedly blocked the appointment of a party press officer:

> Yesterday a senior Labour source claimed that the London leadership are set to overrule Dewar's opposition and insist on an appointment. 'It will take time. But it will happen, however, he may view it at the moment.'
> (Martin 1998:1)

It took time, but not very long. Within a fortnight, it was reported that Tony Blair had approved Dewar's supposed plan to appoint both a party director of communications and a third special adviser to act as a spin doctor. The likely candidate for the first post had already been lined up and was named as Paul McKinney (Parker and Penman 1998b: 6). McKinney, a Scottish Television journalist (and former researcher for Gordon Brown), was close to Downing Street, and shared the Blairites' view that there were serious presentational problems in Scotland.

Within weeks, a third special adviser was appointed at the Scottish Office to act as Dewar's official spokesman: David Whitton was in post by May 1998. A former journalist at the *Daily Record*, *The Scotsman* and Scottish Television, then head of PR for Scottish TV under Gus Macdonald, he spent over a year at the Media House PR consultancy. There, he worked with Jack Irvine and for clients such as Stagecoach and its chief executive Brian Souter, with whom he would shortly do battle over Section 28. His appointment demonstrated again the close-knit nature of Scottish Labour's elite. When Dewar approached him, he says his response was 'But I've never been a member of the Labour Party.' He was told he was 'being hired for his communication skills, not his political allegiance' (McAlpine 1998). Whitton was quoted as saying:

> The Secretary of State isn't a product. I am not paid to express personal views but it would be silly of me to say I don't believe any of it, that I don't support a £1.8 billion increase for the health service in Scotland and £1.3 billion for education. (McAlpine 1998)

The two new spin doctors had been imposed on Dewar by Downing Street with the assistance of special adviser Wendy Alexander and Labour Party adviser, Philip Chalmers. But, as we have seen, Whitton's appointment was in accord with Dewar's own temperament and a cause of later conflict. By contrast, although McKinney was an insider, his appointment led to immediate conflict.

Five days after he was reported as the 'likely' candidate, McKinney was on hand to 'guide' journalists 'through the relaunch of the party in the wake of alarming poll ratings'. Dewar gave a thirty-minute speech under the banner of New Labour in which he stuck 'doggedly' to every printed word. The style was 'alien to the Donald Dewar we have long come to accept as his own, engagingly distinctive man, but it served the PR men's purpose. Even the trademark ums and aws were expunged' (Ritchie 1998b: 7). The reshaping of Dewar met with some scepticism:

> Dewar of course has made errors of judgement . . . Since then, his new spin doctors have been busily repackaging him. We have endless photo-opportunities of Donald planting trees and opening things, of Donald silhouetted against the summer sky. Soon he will be kissing babies.
> (Kemp 1998: 27)

But Dewar proved resistant to reshaping. His spin doctors recognised that his key appeal lay in his image of straightforward trustworthiness, a view widely expressed when he died. According to his official spokesman, David Whitton:

> The key thing about Donald Dewar is that he's unique, I mean he is a well-loved, well-liked, well-respected politician . . . The man who basically drove devolution to the point it's at. If you attempted to change, it wouldn't work for a start, but it would be stupid because the product that you have there is a unique one-off. You give him the bare bones of a speech and he puts all his own self into it and it's much the better as a result, I mean you just could not hand in a speech and say 'read that' and it would come out with New Labour lines and all the rest of it. He knows what the key messages are, 'stronger together and weaker apart,' and all that stuff, but he'll do that in his own way . . . So if you say to me he doesn't like spin, no, he doesn't like that part of spin, where you know there are five mantras that you must say every day in every speech that you make. He won't do that. But what he will do is take those key messages . . . and . . . he will make sure that the message gets across in a different way.

Yet Dewar did accept presentational advice, according to Whitton:

> I think he understands now that that is part of modern politics – although he comes from a slightly different era . . . I think he would probably admit this now, he would underestimate, I think, the way in which the press could take something and use it as a club to beat him with. And part of my job is to make sure that doesn't happen, that the banana skins are identified in advance as much as possible and we take action to prevent that becoming bad news for the government.

Although Dewar became somewhat amenable to presentational pressures, it was the spin doctors who came unstuck when using spin.

LABOUR'S SPIN OPERATION

Although the Scottish Labour Party could long rely on the *Daily Record* and *Sunday Mail*, and it has had close connections with Scottish TV, it has not until recently seen much need for its own public relations. According to Murray Ritchie, a long-time journalistic observer:

> Labour's Scottish press office is the most reticent, which is understandable in these days of sleaze and scandal. Labour has never liked the Scottish press, not least because almost all of it is traditionally rightwing or Labour-sceptic, except for the *Daily Record*, which doubles as a newspaper and Labour Party manifesto. Distrust has bred an attitude in Scottish Labour to the media, which can be summed up as: 'If you're not for us, you're against us.'
> (Ritchie 1998b: 7)

McKinney made a good start in the hot seat as director of communications, so far as the sceptical Scottish press were concerned, not least because of his lack of traditional paranoia about them (Ritchie 1998b: 7). He saw his role as 'introducing Downing Street methods to Scotland'. But he quickly became disillusioned about the job. He was supposed to change the basic press operation and make it more proactive. He was also expected by Downing Street to try to convey the New Labour message more effectively. Once in the job, McKinney found that the resources promised (including a staff of five) were not forthcoming.

> McKinney felt he had been misled by Dewar and Gordon Brown and sidelined with the job of glorified press officer. The appointment of Whitton on a salary double that of McKinney's blocked off much of the access he had enjoyed to the Scottish Secretary. It also meant that he would not rise to be press officer to the First Minister if Dewar did win the election.
> (Martin and Deerin 1998: 13)

Once again, 'senior Labour sources' were on hand to criticise the Scottish Secretary: 'Dewar had made such a fuss about having a spin doctor at all that his position was immediately undermined.' And McKinney's 'little secret' could not have helped his reputation. He reportedly voted SNP in the 1997 election because he 'believed that Blair was taking the party too far to the right and could not be trusted to deliver on devolution' (Martin and Deerin 1998: 13). According to another Labour source:

Can you believe it? They hire this guy in virtual secrecy without widespread consultation in the party or with the Scottish [Labour Party] executive and then Donald forgets to tell Blair that Paul voted Nat until it was too late . . . Then Donald and Gordon Brown cut out their own friend almost by accident . . . If that's the way they treat their friends, what do they do to their enemies? (Martin and Deerin 1998: 13)

After six weeks in post McKinney became unobtainable, finally resigning in the following week. Later the party brought in stopgap spin doctors from London (Adrian McMenamin and Matthew Taylor). Both were reportedly 'shocked' at what they saw in Party HQ. The Glasgow office was 'understaffed and demoralised' (Watson 1999a: 9), but even London's involvement failed to address the problems of morale and resources.

The next incumbent in the job, Lorraine Davidson, was appointed in July 1998, but she fared little better than McKinney (although she did last longer). She took the precaution of speaking personally to Donald Dewar, Tony Blair, Gordon Brown, Charlie Whelan and Alastair Campbell before signing up (Macleod, C. 1998: 6), but still she lost sympathy in some sections of the party. When television cameras were excluded from a speech by Tony Blair in Glasgow, he was reportedly 'clearly irritated' referring to their absence 'three times during his short speech' (Martin and Hill 1998: 3). Meanwhile, Alastair Campbell 'was heard to make acerbic remarks about the skills of the Scottish Labour Party. The words "brewery", "organise", "couldn't" and "piss-up" – not necessarily in that order – were heard to fall from his lips.' An 'animated exchange' between Davidson and David Whitton was also reported, with Whitton telling her 'she should think about taking more time off – perhaps have a short break' (Martin and Hill 1998: 3). Three weeks later, three Sunday papers (*Scotland on Sunday*, the *Sunday Mail* and *The Sunday Times*) reported that Davidson was threatening to quit. A top party source reportedly said:

Lorraine is totally frustrated and deeply depressed. She does not know what she is supposed to be doing . . . She feels there is no direction to the party in Scotland especially on campaigning and that the basics are not being dealt with.
(Macleod, A. 1998b: 5)

Davidson denied the reports, saying 'I think somebody has been actively briefing and I do not know who' (Ramsay 1998: 2). As the Scottish election campaign got underway the following year, further problems arose as Scottish Labour Party officials were marginalised by Millbank.

SPINNING THE ELECTION

For Scottish party modernisers, Millbank was often woefully ignorant of the Scottish political scene and too zealous in controlling what happened. During the referendum campaign, for example, Philip Chalmers worked at Labour Party HQ, acting, in effect, as Scottish Labour's Philip Gould. Yet, party insiders told us, he was 'mistrusted by Millbank, especially by Philip Gould because he could offer his own advice on polling and advertising which they regarded as their expert territory.'

As the election campaign approached, the Scottish Labour Party, according to party sources, 'lacked leadership'. As a consequence, there was nobody to negotiate with London for resources for the campaign. 'Many people in Millbank took the view that if scarce money was going to be used, they would control it.' There was a need to discuss or clear details with Millbank. Some party officials took the view that the 'Scottish party should make decisions – or at least be seen to be conducting a Scottish campaign – since the "Made in London" tag was very damaging.' According to our sources, London was unable to realise that devolution meant devolving power. Consequently, there was a need to 'argue the Scottish corner' at Millbank. This problem was compounded by the political naiveté of senior Millbank officials: 'They didn't know about the elections – "Are they local council elections?" It was necessary to explain the basic politics of Labour and the SNP.'

As the campaign began in earnest, it was the Chancellor's adviser, Ed Miliband, who turned up outside Labour HQ in Glasgow one Monday night in April 1999, rather than Blairite advisers. *The Scotsman*'s headline described the campaign as 'Brown's boys in control at Delta House' (Tait 1999a: 11).

> [Brown] has taken to doing his own media spinning . . . After the SNP's decision to make its 'penny for Scotland' policy the linchpin of its campaign, the Chancellor rang the editors of several Sunday newspapers to solidly put the boot in. The strategy caught Delta House's press operation off guard. But it secured such positive coverage that he tried it again the following Monday and, risking rendering himself a devalued currency, again a few days later. Excerpts of Mr Brown speeches, trailed a few days in advance of them being made, have become a feature of Labour's campaign.
> (Tait 1999a: 11)

As the campaign progressed Dewar and Scottish Labour officials were marginalised. 'Mr Dewar's advisers are privately annoyed at the way they have been forced to tour round Scotland on the election battle bus while all key decisions are made in Glasgow' (Seenan and MacAskill 1999: 10). 'Even Lorraine Davidson . . . was sent to work on Dewar's election bus rather than taking control of the media operation at headquarters as expected' (Martin 1999: 3). Instead, 'bluff Brummie' Ian Austin 'quickly became a key figure. Disliked by journalists, he is seen by Labour insiders as a "professional" who gives no quarter' (Watson 1999a: 9).

In the event, Davidson returned to Scottish Television immediately after the election, subsequently joining the *Scottish Mirror* as political editor. Also, Helen Liddell became persona non grata at headquarters and General Secretary, Alex Rowley, was pushed aside with the arrival of John Rafferty (later credited with a role in sacking Rowley).[2] Philip Chalmers, the pollster with a background in design and marketing, was credited with devising the election slogan 'Divorce is an expensive business.'

As the polls closed, Labour was confident of forming the largest party in the new administration and Dewar's dream of devolution was almost fulfilled. He would be the first First Minister. But the devolution of power did not magically resolve the tensions within the Labour Party. Indeed, they brought new rivalries and problems of organisation and presentation.

A BRIGHT NEW DAWN? THE POST-DEVOLUTION EXPERIENCE

After devolution, internal party divisions were compounded by the sometimes contradictory PR strategies of individual Labour ministers. Some of the more media-conscious among them, such as Henry McLeish, Jack McConnell, Wendy Alexander and Susan Deacon, often bypassed the Executive press office, making it more difficult for the Strategic Communications Unit to coordinate announcements effectively.[3] The profile of ministers and their networks of support within the party are crucial in the battle for career progression either in Scotland or beyond. While their activities did not aim to undermine the coherence of Executive messages, they may have had that effect.

Attaining a profile has clearly been a key concern for the ministers at the newly-formed Scotland Office. Their attempt to achieve this has tended to be reported as part of a 'turf war' with the Scottish Executive. For political correspondents, the Scotland Office has been valuable because it has worked as a foil to the Executive and provided conflict stories. The strong personalities and media savvy of the ministers involved – John Reid and Brian Wilson – and the way in which their spin doctor has approached his work, were seen as quite decisive by reporters. Mike Elrick, the Scotland Office special adviser, would have been a big hitter had his political patron, John Smith, not died. Conflict between Dewar and Reid at the Labour Party conference in 1999 was described by one political editor with relish as 'like speaking to pugilists in their corners'.

The resurrection by John Reid of the Scottish Grand Committee, a House of Commons body closed down by Labour before devolution is one instance of the need to maintain profile (Macwhirter 1999c). The committee performs the useful function of allowing Scotland Office ministers an institutional forum to make policy announcements. An instance was Brian Wilson's statement that international designers would be invited to use Scottish textiles to promote Scottish excellence in fashion shows at the Scotland Office's London headquarters at Dover House (Crichton 2000: 4). Another example was Brian Wilson's appearance as a spokesperson on the EU's 'banana wars' with the USA and their impact on the Scottish cashmere industry. In July 2000, he gave an interview to Arnold Kemp of *The Observer* in which he talked of his 'frustrations' in the job but argued that it would not be in 'Scotland's interests' to abolish the Scotland Office (Kemp 2000b: 13). A couple of weeks later, Wilson secured coverage by opening his allegedly unweeded ministerial red box to a *Scotland on Sunday* journalist, following a precedent set by Jack Straw (Elliot 2000: 16). In autumn 2000, Secretary of State John Reid appeared on television and radio defending the government during the petrol crisis and on the leadership's defeat over pensions at the Labour Party's conference, both topics outside his brief at the Scotland Office. His regular appearances led the journalist Jeremy Paxman to ask rhetorically if he should be described as the 'minister for embarrassments' (*Newsnight*, BBC2, 27 September 2000).

THE FORMATION OF THE EXECUTIVE

With the creation of the Executive, the First Minister appointed John Rafferty as principal special adviser and reappointed David Whitton as official spokesman. But it was only after Rafferty's surprise attendance at the first Scottish Cabinet meeting that his appointment was formally confirmed by David Whitton. 'Four hours later the Scottish Office announced that Mr Rafferty would be chief of staff' (Ritchie 1999: 7). It was reported that all special advisers would report to Rafferty and through him to Dewar. A week later the title 'chief of staff' was dropped and special advisers (including Whitton) were said to report directly to Dewar (Ritchie 1999: 7).

A special order-in-council of April 1999 had allowed Dewar to appoint up to twelve special advisers. The coalition partners, the Liberal Democrats, were allowed two of these. The arrangements meant that no other Cabinet ministers would be allowed special advisers. This was reported as an initiative by Tony Blair, aimed at centralising control of the Scottish Cabinet and avoiding turf wars. In June 1999, it was reported that, 'Younger Cabinet members are pressing for the appointment of staff with strategic communications skills in place of some of the policy officer posts' (Watson 1999b: 9). But the First Minister opposed this. According to David Whitton:

'There has never been a plan to have each Cabinet minister with his own or her own spin doctor. That is something that is resisted by the First Minister – he doesn't think it is necessary.' Dewar's mind seems eventually to have been changed when in summer 2000 other ministers appointed their own special advisers.

DONALD'S SUCCESSOR

An early problem for the new Executive was a rash of stories about the successor to Donald Dewar. This led to one of the early crises of the news management system, when the First Minister defended his official spokesperson in an SEID press release. Within a week of the opening of the Parliament on 1 July 1999 the First Minister was reported as being 'irritated' by ministers and MSPs briefing the media and 'hiding under the cloak of anonymity' (Tait 1999b: 1). Splits with the senior minister (and eventual successor) Henry McLeish and with the Scottish Secretary, John Reid, were referred to. Whitton then briefed the press that:

> unless the first Minister gives you a quote himself, the only other person who
> is authorised to speak for him is me. If it doesn't come from him or me, then
> it is not an authorised quote or an accurate reflection of his views.
> (Massie 1999: 14)

But despite Whitton's and Dewar's best efforts to give out as little as possible to the media (Tait 1999c: 21), the briefings continued. A number of ministers were involved. Jack McConnell was said by journalistic observers to be 'trying not to brief' while Henry McLeish 'just can't help himself'. Meanwhile, Wendy Alexander was also ensuring positive profiles in the press by doing her own briefing.[4]

Matters came to a head at the end of July 1999, when Whitton briefed the press that the speculation about the succession was beside the point because 'there isn't a vacancy' and announced that Dewar was seeking two terms as First Minister. Furthermore, he launched an attack on those doing the briefing, saying, 'Apart from anything else, who is there to take over from him at the moment? A lot of younger ministers who are *still to prove themselves*' (our emphasis). Whitton's remarks were reported under the headline 'Dewar in withering attack on ministers' in *The Scotsman* the next day. The paper claimed that Whitton had described Cabinet hopefuls as 'unproven and unqualified' (Tait 1999d: 1), remarks said to be directed particularly against Henry McLeish (who did have experience as a Scottish Office minister prior to devolution) and to some extent at Jack McConnell. This had certainly identified the key contenders for the succession.

According to the author of the report, Robert Tait, 'One particularly memorable aspect of the conversation is that I twice asked David whether his comments were appropriate descriptions of two specific Cabinet ministers, and he did not take the opportunity to qualify his remarks' (personal correspondence with the authors, 21 August 2000).

The story in *The Scotsman* provoked strong criticism of Whitton in the next day's press. The day after, the Executive issued a press release quoting Dewar in defence of Whitton:

> It is important to set out clearly what we are doing and why, and David Whitton does that job well. He is and will continue to be my press spokesman. He has filled this post with ability for more than a year. He has worked very closely with journalists in every part of Scotland; his professionalism and integrity are unquestioned.
> (Scottish Executive 1999b)

The statement provided both a coded endorsement of Whitton's comments and a slight spin on them, suggesting that all ministers were new to a devolved Scotland: 'I have a ministerial team which combines energy and ability and I value the contribution of every member of it. Whatever our past experience, we are all new players in a new system.'

One aspect of the story provides an intriguing glimpse into the world of the Executive. While not disowning the rest of his words, Whitton denied using the specific phrase 'unproven and unqualified'. In an interview with us in June 2000, he stated:

> I never said that. Robert Tait knows I didn't say that. Robert Tait confessed to me that he did not write that I had said that, but somebody had put that into his copy . . . *The Scotsman* in particular were running their own lines [into the Executive] . . . and they had various links that they thought got them the insight into what the government were doing. Sadly it proved to be incorrect.

Sources close to the late First Minister alleged that the deputy editor of *The Scotsman*, Tim Luckhurst, was the person who inserted the phrase and that the person who had used the words was in fact the special adviser John Rafferty. Presumably, this is the account given to the First Minister before he issued the statement backing Whitton. The first part of this account is endorsed by Tait, but with a significant quibble.

> David never uttered those exact words. I had put quotation marks round the words 'unproven' (which David had said) and used the word 'unqualified' to paraphrase what I believed to be the official assessment of other Cabinet members to take over as First Minister. A middle-ranking newsdesk figure – without my knowledge and somewhat irresponsibly – extended the quotation

marks to cover the word 'unqualified'. I believe the individual concerned . . .
was acting on his own initiative and that the alteration did not have a
corporate stamp on it, so to speak.
(personal correspondence with the authors, 21 August 2000)

According to Tait this person was categorically not Luckhurst, nor was
Rafferty involved in any way. This latter part of the story was emphatically
denied by Tait in an interview with the authors. This is curious because it has
implications for the account given by Whitton to the First Minister. More
interesting, however, is the fact that six months after Rafferty had left the
Executive, senior sources were still willing to give off-the-record briefings
against him. That is to jump ahead but only slightly, since the mounting
tensions between Rafferty and Whitton were, only a few months later, to
become public knowledge.

The difficulties between Rafferty and Whitton had been growing for some
time, partly because Rafferty had become dissatisfied with Whitton's media
management activities, and as a result started briefing the media himself.
This began at least as early as the Lobbygate affair in October 1999. Rafferty
was reportedly responsible for briefing against John Reid after Whitton was
viewed as not being proactive enough. The next month the *Sunday Mail* ran
two stories about Rafferty's background and the drugs problems faced by his
daughter and stepson, both of which had been given to the paper by a Labour
party ex-colleague of Rafferty's (McGarvie 1999; Scott 1999; Fraser and
Watson 1999b).

Rafferty was, by this stage, fast accumulating enemies in various parts of
the Executive and the Labour Party. He was reportedly responsible for a
string of false and misleading stories in the media, including tales that Dewar
wanted to abolish the Standards Committee, that he wished to ban lobbyists,
and that he was about to introduce a graduate tax (Fraser and Watson
1999b). None of these stories had clearance from Dewar. Then, *Scotland on
Sunday* ran two front-page stories about Dewar's 'backing for repealing' the
anti-Catholic Act of Settlement. 'Neither had any truth. Dewar asked
Whitton what was going on. Whitton pointed the finger at Rafferty' (Fraser
and Watson 1999b: 10). Then came the spin too far. On 1 December, health
minister Susan Deacon gave an interview to *The Scotsman* previewing a
speech she was to give the following day and attacking anti-abortion
protestors. Rafferty passed the content of the interview to the *Record* as well,
as part of his strategy of trying to win back its support. The double-exclusive
annoyed Angus Macleod of the *Express* who phoned Rafferty to complain.
'Rafferty promised to make it up to Macleod', and the next day he phoned
Macleod with 'an interesting titbit' (Fraser and Watson 1999b: 10). The
Express duly reported the following day that Deacon had received death
threats and was under Special Branch protection. Neither of these allegations

was true but an Executive source let the *Daily Record* know that Rafferty was in trouble for leaking the story.

From then on, Rafferty, his allies, and his enemies were engaged in a bitter internal struggle which would end with Rafferty being sacked. As the end neared, Dewar phoned and met Rafferty on several occasions, during which time his story changed. Following these meetings, accounts attributed to Rafferty appeared in the tabloids. After this had happened once, Dewar specifically instructed Rafferty not to let it happen again, but it did, and Rafferty's position was fatally undermined.

After a week in which headline writers made good use of the alliterative potential of the word 'dither' and the First Minister's name, Dewar gave an extremely uncertain performance in Parliament. Relying on his instinctive preference for secrecy, he refused to give details to MSPs. Rafferty's downfall was not the end of the Executive's troubles with spin, however. Only weeks later, Rafferty's intervention was to cause more anguish for the First Minister.

THE DEMISE OF PHILIP CHALMERS

Within weeks, a second special adviser was forced out of the Executive. Philip Chalmers, head of the Strategic Communications Unit, resigned after a tabloid exposé of his convictions for drink-driving in Glasgow's red-light area. It was alleged by the police that a woman found in the back of his car with him was a prostitute.

It is clear that Chalmer's drink-driving convictions were known about in the Executive, but only by senior civil servants and not ministers. The question was how had the story leaked? David Whitton claimed that he knew. In a conversation that Whitton claims he thought was off-the-record, he told Andrew Nicoll of the *Scottish Sun* that, 'It's coming from our little friend who was sacked last month [i.e. Rafferty]. It does come with a health warning' (Nicoll et al. 2000: 2). Whitton claims to have been unaware that Nicoll was recording the conversation but his words appeared *verbatim* the next day. Rafferty disputed Whitton's account and threatened to sue. Whitton was then forced to apologise. A chastened Whitton told assembled journalists that he had been 'reprimanded' by Dewar. By other accounts he was 'kicked all over the room' (Dinwoodie and Ritchie 2000: 1). Whitton stated that:

> The First Minister has insisted that I come here and set the record straight. I dealt with a great deal of telephone calls yesterday and had many conversations with journalists. I acknowledge that, in at least one of those conversations, I speculated about the source of the story concerning Philip Chalmers. I should not have speculated in that way. The position is simply this. No-one on the

Scottish Executive has any idea where the story came from. Only the newspaper who first got the story or those who subsequently carried it can answer that question. I deeply regret my remarks. I regret that they have been printed. I withdraw them unreservedly. I think you can take that as an unreserved apology.
(Dinwoodie and Ritchie 2000: 1)

After this, sources close to the First Minister continued to point out (to us and to various journalists) that only three or four people knew about Chalmers' first conviction. Neither the First Minister nor other ministers were aware of it. In other words, someone in the Executive continued to suggest that it was Rafferty who leaked the Chalmers story to the media. Again, this suggests bitter conflict between senior Executive officials.

After the departure of Rafferty and Chalmers, there were no more comparable controversies over spin. To the newspaper-buying public, the problems of spin were replaced by questions about the competence of ministers over issues like Section 28 and the fiasco over Scottish exam qualifications. Nevertheless, beneath the surface there continued to be significant changes in the organisation of the spin operation.

ONE YEAR ON

The irony of Rafferty's dismissal was that he was seen as an ally of some of the 'younger' ministers in the Executive in their battles with the civil service. Rafferty was reported in parts of the media to have been the victim of a 'mandarin plot'. In this version of the story, Rafferty's speech to 200 top civil servants seven days before he was dismissed 'sparked a campaign by mandarins to have him removed' (Allardyce 1999: 2). It seems unlikely that Rafferty was really removed as the result of a plot by senior civil servants uncomfortable with his proposed reforms. That is not just because any plot has been denied by Muir Russell, the Permanent Secretary at the Executive, in a rare newspaper interview (Fraser 1999: 10), but because of the deep divisions in the party itself, and between key officials such as Rafferty and Whitton.

Certainly, Rafferty's views were hostile to the civil service's inherited caution and conservatism. In that controversial speech to senior civil servants, he made some pointed criticisms. He stated that the traditions of the civil service were obstructing the changes pursued by New Labour:

> When I ask the Permanent Secretary [Muir Russell]: 'What's the relationship, Muir, between you and Cabinet?', he cannot tell me . . . The civil service has 100 years of culture. 'You know it when you see it,' is the answer. Frankly that is not good enough. If my job is anything, it is creating the environment for

talented people to build a cauldron of ideas for the benefit of Scotland. Is
Donald Dewar not the chairman of the board of Scotland plc? Is the Cabinet
not the non-executive directors and should the Permanent Secretary not be the
chief executive?
(Rafferty 1999)

Rafferty's agenda was not openness or a revivified public-service ethos.
Rather it was the further commercialisation of the civil service. Given
Rafferty's approach, it is not surprising that some civil servants (including
some in the SEID) breathed a sigh of relief when he went. Rafferty was
regarded in the SEID as something of 'a dark, almost sort of sinister figure',
according to one close observer. Although Rafferty did not have much to do
with the press office, his influence on the Director of Information was said by
some insiders to be significant. So much so that Williams was said to be
'watching his back'. In the event, the departure of Rafferty did not save
Williams, who was sidelined some four months later.

The Information Directorate has had a heightened internal visibility since
Michael Forsyth was Secretary of State. The advent of New Labour and its
reforms of the government information machinery through the Mountfield
report, and the 1997 internal review of the Scottish Office was seen
internally – at least in part – as a victory over the administrative civil service.
As a result, and despite being the appointment of Muir Russell and Donald
Dewar, Williams was able to obtain unprecedented resources for the SEID.

Chalmers' role was said to be to 'stiffen their [SEID staff] backbone'
especially in publicity work. He was seen as being there to ensure that the
Cabinet's key messages were present in all publicity material. He was
described as the 'conscience of the Labour Party'. Press reports describe civil
servants' dislike of Chalmers. Certainly he seems to have tried to cultivate a
particular image with the civil service. One of his misdirected e-mails
suggested that special advisers should not attend a civil service Christmas
party in order 'to maintain an air of mystique' (Fraser 2000a: 15).
Nevertheless, according to one observer, although the press office at St
Andrew's House 'did resent him . . . Chalmers' demise is somewhat regretted
in the publicity section. It gave them a lot of clout with the mainstream civil
servants. The fact was that Chalmers was deemed to have the ear of the First
Minister and could push things through and get things done – break log
jams.'

By March 2000, with the departure of two special advisers, the pressure on
the SEID had abated. The primacy of the information specialists was
reasserted. As one well-placed source put it:

The pressure is off a bit. I think there is a wish to sort of make sure that the gap
left by Philip Chalmers and Rafferty is made good by the GICS. In other
words insofar as the role of the GICS was usurped – Rafferty obviously

believed himself to be as good as any press officer – that is a role which rightly belongs to the information service. I think there has been a tendency of some of the policy divisions to lapse back into not taking as seriously as they should the work of the press office. So I think there has been a bit of a regression.

But the actual developments were not so straightforward. The press office of the Directorate was strengthened, at the expense of the Director of Information. But this was followed by a concerted move to expand the role of special advisers by younger ministers such as Alexander and Deacon. By the end of April 2000, dissatisfaction with the SEID among ministers led to Williams' removal from effective control. Williams' marginalisation was announced by Robert Gordon, the Head of the Executive Secretariat, Scotland's second most senior civil servant, to a startled press office.

The spin doctors could not resist twisting the knife by briefing against Williams to the *Scottish Daily Express* and *The Sunday Times*. The *Express* quoted unnamed Executive insiders as saying:

> Williams didn't know how to spin a top and his team always seemed to be behind the agenda instead of on top of it. He just didn't seem to have a grip and now he has been taken out of the direct line of fire and put into a more neutral role. We just want things done better.
> (*Scottish Daily Express* 2000: 6)

Unnamed 'supporters' were cited as claiming that Williams was a 'scapegoat', which was in turn dismissed by 'others' in the Executive who claimed that he had the nickname 'Roger Rabbit' because of his alleged 'lack of profile'. Williams was dispatched to head internet operations while still keeping the now-nominal title of Director of Information.

> Although he had dragged the press office out of the Dark Ages, ministers had been muttering it still wasn't selling their policies with enough enthusiasm. Williams will still be able to call himself Director of Information but his main job now will be to oversee a new website to rebut media lies about the Executive . . . Old-timers mutter that the traditional civil service ethos is now even more under threat. That sound you can hear is ministers cheering.
> (*The Sunday Times, Scotland* 2000)

One way of looking at these developments is to see them as the reassertion of the New Labour reforms against the weight of civil-service tradition. In particular the appointment of Owen Kelly as the head of news was significant as he was the administrative official drafted in to deal with the demands of Wendy Alexander when she was a special adviser in the Scottish Office. He was also the first head of the Strategic Communication Unit set up as one of the key New Labour reforms, before a brief sojourn in the External Relations division. Williams, on the other hand, was seen internally as the appointee of Muir Russell and of the traditionalist Dewar. Kelly's appointment caused wry smiles among older hands at the SEID, since it re-established a post abolished by New Labour reforms only two years earlier, when Deputy Director Alistair McNeill was, in effect, sacked.

As the summer of 2000 began, and Dewar was safely away from his desk convalescing from a heart operation, two new special advisers were lined up. On 13 June, it emerged that Sharon Ward, a business journalist from the *Sunday Herald* (and formerly Scottish TV), was to be appointed (*Evening News* 2000: 2). It later emerged she would have responsibility for Wendy Alexander, Sam Galbraith and Henry McLeish (Media Watch 2000: 8). On 22 June, a leading Labour-supporting consultant (and adviser to Gordon Brown), Dr Colin Currie, was named as a part-time (policy) adviser to health minister Susan Deacon (Veitch 2000: 15). David Whitton's deputy, Neil Gillam, was also given a new role with specific responsibility for Susan Deacon, Sarah Boyack and Jack McConnell. Dewar's involvement in these appointments is not publicly known. However they did reverse his firm decision that ministers in the Executive would not have their own special advisers, much less their own spin doctors. Until their appointment all special advisers worked directly for Dewar. The argument in favour of this move inside the Executive was partially justified by the exception to the rule that allowed Deputy First Minister Jim Wallace to have two special advisers.

Meanwhile, in the SEID there were two other personnel changes of note. Donald Dewar's chief press officer, Anne Shevas, moved to Downing Street to take over the role of briefing the lobby from Alastair Campbell when he took a lower profile following Blair's Women's Institute speech. Her post was filled by Paul Geoghan, former devolution press officer, and prior to that researcher for a Scottish Labour MP (Media Watch 2000: 8).

It is evident that after only one year of the new Executive being in existence, the Millbank approach was partially victorious and Cabinet ministers other than the First Minister and his Deputy obtained special advisers to act as their own spin doctors. It is an open question, with the death of Donald Dewar, whether the multiplication of advisers will lead to further difficulties in terms of the coordination of information and an increase in the public profile of rivalries in the Cabinet.

OPENNESS

How open is the information regime of the Executive? As we have seen, the practice adopted in Edinburgh strongly echoes the Westminster system. In Scotland, the government website is extremely limited in the information it gives surfers. Nonetheless, as we were reminded by civil servants, it provides more information than can be found in published form:

> Most other GICS offices in the UK run the internet. Here . . . Library Services
> have got it under their control . . . If you take the internet and say 'Right, this
> is what the Scottish Office does', and you then say, 'Well, show me where else
> I can get that information if I don't have the internet', and the answer is
> 'Nowhere', you may say, 'That's a bit bloody strange. Is that not a bit of
> double standards? . . . It's an issue that we haven't addressed, but whether or
> not our new political masters will want to address it I'm not sure.

So far they have not. There could easily be a much more in-depth web site.
The information about the civil service is minimal, including short
biographies of senior figures which give neither real insight into their roles,
functions, style, abilities or competence, nor any means of contacting them.
There is no guide to the structure of the civil service or to the different
divisions, all of which could easily be on the web together with the names of
all branch heads down to grade seven or below.

The biggest potential lever for an increase in openness is the Freedom of
Information bill (Scottish Executive 1999c). This was launched by Deputy
First Minister Jim Wallace, and lauded as more open than its Whitehall
equivalent. To be fair there are some useful provisions in it, such as the
commitment to a 'culture of openness' and a 'presumption of openness' and
the proposal to appoint an Information Commissioner with powers to order
disclosure (Friends of the Earth Scotland 2000; Wilson 1999). But it is
limited in two fundamental ways: there are exemptions for policy advice and
commercial confidentiality, both of which will entitle ministers to withhold
information which could be disclosed without substantial harm. A senior
civil servant told us with a chuckle that 'all the good stuff will be exempted'
by dint of skilful drafting.

In practice, it is likely to remain extremely difficult to find out basic
information about the workings of the civil service and government
machinery more generally. We experienced some relevant problems in trying
to research this book (see Appendix 1 on Methology). The Freedom of
Information consultation paper acknowledges that for the proposals to work,
there needs to be a significant 'culture change' in the civil service (Scottish
Executive 1999c: 57). We would endorse that view and add that there also
needs to be institutional and structural change so that civil servants conceive
of themselves as servants of the public and the Parliament, as well as of
ministers. Senior civil servants need to be re-educated in a new public-service
ethos in which a positive case needs to be made for keeping any information
under the wraps of secrecy.

A CONCLUDING PERSPECTIVE

Two main perspectives on media management contend in the Scottish Executive. The first is rooted in the traditional caution and secrecy of the civil service, which was allied to a traditional Labour dislike of spin as embodied in the person of Donald Dewar. This approach does not favour civil-service openness, but retains significant elements of a public-service ethos, although the market reforms of the Conservative years have taken their toll.

The opposing coalition has been an alliance of Millbank's devotion to spin-doctoring and Scottish modernisers (sometimes Blairite, sometimes Brownite, sometimes critical of Millbank, but modernisers nonetheless). Most of these are younger ministers almost all of whom have a radical past (Macwhirter 1999a). This coalition has been keener on spin, and also on dispensing with concepts such as public service, preferring the market and 'modern' management practice in governance. This tends to mean that they are politically (as well as instinctively and generationally) more at ease with openness. But the openness they tend to prefer works on their terms: they wish to extract more information from the civil service and put it into the public domain as part of the process of selling their policies.

In the Dewar era, Scottish spin remained different from that practised by the Blairites in London, in part because of the First Minister's reluctance and inability to adopt the 'on-message' approach of the Millbank tendency. So while Scotland's reforms have been based on London's models, their style and practice has been different. In addition, Donald Dewar tried to maintain control of the Cabinet: he was once Labour's Chief Whip in the Commons. However, his grip was never complete. The progress of news management in Scotland in the first year of devolution saw the advance of the modernisers and the slow retreat of the First Minister. How things develop under Henry McLeish remains to be seen, but we may suppose – given his known predilection for media relations – that the modernisers will win out, consigning Dewar's old-time fastidiousness to the dustbin.

Thus far, the Executive's problems with news management have echoed those of the London government in relation to the role of special advisers, the rising profile of spin doctors, internal rivalries between ministers and a lack of clarity within the Executive about who has responsibility for putting out information. The problem with spin is that it downgrades the importance of policy debate, ideology and principle, which are sacrificed to presentation. The result is that governments notionally of the left are carried along on whatever tide of opinion appears to engulf society, which are as likely as not to be profoundly conservative. The problem facing the administration in Edinburgh then is the same – if not as acute – as that facing New Labour in London: how to hold onto power in the absence of any clear sense of what it stands for.

Essentially, the battles being fought in the Scottish Executive are about presentation. There is no fundamental point of ideological difference. The modernisers' reforms would clearly shift the culture of the civil service and of governance closer to the market than would the traditionalists' approach. But whichever approach wins, a new open Scotland is not in prospect.

NOTES

1. Campbell was the murderer of a Celtic fan and he requested, and almost achieved, a transfer to the Ulster Volunteer Force wing in the Maze Prison in Northern Ireland although his crime was not 'political'. Dewar was widely believed to have blocked the award of a knighthood to Sean Connery who had put his weight behind the devolution campaign, but as the country's best-known SNP supporter.
2. In spring 1999, Liddell was reportedly cut dead in public by Alastair Campbell as he arrived in Glasgow (Oborne 1999: 155).
3. After Donald Dewar's funeral in October 2000, McLeish and McConnell contended for leadership of Scottish Labour. McLeish won and became the second First Minister.
4. See, for example, the double-page spread of photos in the *Daily Record* which praises Alexander as 'our hardest working MSP' (Gilbride 1999: 40).

Part III

Lobbyists

BACKGROUND

The House of Commons has wrestled with the issue of lobbying and its regulation over the past thirty years. The Select Committee on Members' Interests (SCMI) has considered the matter on four separate occasions in this period: 1969, 1974, 1985, and 1990–1. In the latter case, the committee recommended a mandatory register of professional lobbyists, including details of their businesses and lists of clients, to be enforced by a Resolution of the House. Critics of that proposed register pointed to its limited scope and ambition. With the SCMI apparently lacking investigatory zeal and repeatedly prepared to 'think the best of' fellow MPs (Doig 1998: 39), the debate on the regulation of lobbying in the UK in the past decade has, according to the political scientist Grant Jordan (1998: 524), taken an 'unexpected' turn with its focus on legislators rather than on the lobbyists themselves.

Under successive Thatcher administrations, markets were deregulated and a market-friendly political culture evolved. As a result, the weaknesses of SCMI's policing of the relationship between commercial interests and Parliament became exposed. The 'cash-for-questions' affair was triggered by revelations in *The Guardian* that MPs had been paid in cash and in kind to ask parliamentary questions on behalf of outside commercial interests. The scandal centred on payments made by Mohammed Al-Fayed (via the IGA political lobbying firm) to MPs Neil Hamilton and Tim Smith.

FROM NOLAN TO NEILL

Prime Minister John Major set up the (ad hoc) Committee on Standards in Public Life (CSPL) in October 1994, in direct response to the cash-for-questions affair. Under the chairmanship of Lord Nolan, the committee reported within six months. Despite evidence that confidence in the probity of the political process was being eroded, Nolan decided against the regulation of lobbyists themselves, arguing that the creation of a public register would become a marketing device for them. On this analysis, regulated lobbyists would claim official status, and this in turn would create the impression that to approach MPs and ministers successfully, members of the public or organised outside interests must procure the services of registered public affairs consultants (Nolan 1995a: 36). Thus the emphasis of the Nolan report was to fall upon regulation of legislators.

Nolan recommended that the Register of Interests should be more informative, that the rules governing conflicts of interest should be more explicit, that the rules governing conflicts of interest should be set out in more detail, that a code of conduct for MPs should be drawn up, and that an independent Parliamentary Commissioner for Standards should be appointed. These recommendations were adopted by the House in July 1995 (Doig 1998: 44). Significantly, Nolan also recommended that the Commissioner for Standards should have 'the same ability to make findings and conclusions public as is enjoyed by the Comptroller and Auditor General and the Parliamentary Commissioner for Administration' (Nolan Committee 1995a: 43). This recommendation was not adopted.

The newly-appointed Parliamentary Commissioner for Standards, Sir Gordon Downey, directed a formal inquiry into the cash-for-questions allegations against some twenty-five MPs. His report appeared in July 1997, almost three years after the initial allegations were published in *The Guardian.*[1] Aside from the political impact of the 'sleaze' that characterised the final years of the Major administration, the cash-for-questions episode drew attention to the rather limited nature of Parliamentary self-regulation, even post-Nolan. The powers of the Parliamentary Commissioner for Standards became a matter of contention, as the political autonomy of the office was seen by some (notably *The Guardian*) to be compromised by its dependence on the Select Committee on Standards and Privileges (SCSP).

Being appointed by Standing Order of the House of Commons, the Parliamentary Commissioner has no legislative power. This means that, to see papers or call witnesses, the Commissioner relies on a summons by the SCSP. The Commissioner is also dependent upon the SCSP for resources and, crucially, has no power to publish reports or sanction individuals directly (Woodhouse 1998: 53–5).[2] These last two restrictions are possibly of most concern as they fail to preclude political interference by the CSP, which at any given time is likely to be dominated by the party of government.

The official response of the lobbying industry to 'sleaze' was, in the first instance, to call for government regulation. The Association of Professional Political Consultants (APPC), which represents consultancies whose income is entirely or mainly derived from lobbying, called for statutory controls, arguing that 'official regulation would command far greater respect' (Nolan

1995b: 93) than self-regulation. However, there were reservations regarding the feasibility of the APPC's proposed model for regulating lobbying. Some viewed it as a strategic calculation by the APPC that there was neither the political appetite nor the legislative space to easily implement such legislation. Thus, the APPC could credibly point to its own code of conduct as a next-best alternative. The Public Relations Consultants Association (PRCA), which represents PR consultancies, some of which engage in lobbying, sought 'real self-regulation' (Nolan 1995b: 100) as the optimal guarantee of probity in public affairs. In similar vein, the Institute of Public Relations (IPR), which represents individual PR practitioners, including lobbyists, recommended 'independent regulation of the activities of legislators themselves' (Nolan 1995b: 149). Overall then, the lobbying industry was not keen on statutory regulation.

THE POLITICS OF SLEAZE

Media interest in sleaze continued after the publication of the Nolan report. The ongoing legal action brought by Neil Hamilton and Ian Greer against *The Guardian* (Greer 1997; Leigh and Vulliamy 1997), and the Parliamentary Commissioner for Standards' investigation of allegations of corruption against MPs, kept issues regarding probity in public life on the media and political agenda. Indeed, with a UK general election in the offing, the opposition Labour party were keen to keep the issue of sleaze firmly in the public's mind. New Labour's strategy was to position itself as 'a positive voice in a sea of sleaze and cynicism' (Gould 1998: 350). As the election campaign unfolded, sleaze came to dominate its early weeks, and was a recurrent theme throughout (Gould 1998; Jones 1997; McNair 2000).

The impact of New Labour's landslide election victory on the UK lobbying industry was immediate. Overnight, the caché of advisers to New Labour's front bench rose markedly among commercial lobbying firms whose growth and success had been inextricably linked with successive Conservative administrations (Miller and Dinan 2000). There was a clear demand from government relations consultancies for individuals with contacts in the New Labour Cabinet and party hierarchy, both in terms of the access this would undoubtedly bring, and the ability to interpret New Labour's policy agenda to clients.

Another significant feature of the New Labour lobbying landscape in Westminster and Whitehall was the appointment of a series of special advisers to Labour ministers. Again, many of those appointed to these posts had previously worked for the opposition Labour front bench. Special advisers and former New Labour party advisers-turned-lobbyists were to become embroiled in controversy regarding their ability to gain access to ministers on behalf of commercial interests.

The cash-for-access scandal that became public in July 1998 was the result of a 'sting' operation by *The Observer*. Posing as the representative of a US business interest, journalist Gregory Palast secured offers of access to Cabinet ministers from Derek Draper and Roger Liddle. Both Draper and Liddle had previously been partners in the lobbying firm Prima Europe. At the time, Draper (a former aide to Peter Mandelson) was working as a lobbyist for GPC Market Access (which had taken over Prima Europe), while Liddle was employed as a special adviser in the Number Ten policy unit. Draper resigned from GPC, although Liddle remained in post. Within a few weeks, the government had announced the tightening of rules governing the conduct of special advisers and civil servants (Hencke 1998: 3).

Reviewing developments in regulation and practice one year later, Derek Draper remarked:

> The most worrying thing that is ever sold is information, a little light thrown on how things work . . . I suspect that the close relations which exist between some politicians, advisers and lobbyists (who are often old colleagues) do mean that certain information which should be either public or totally private is passed on. The danger is that one day that information could, literally, be worth a fortune to somebody. Guarding against this danger isn't easy but the intertwined relationships must be disentangled.
> (Draper 1999: 26)

Given the continuing political salience and sensitivity of commercial lobbying under the New Labour goverment, it was fortuitous that the CSPL, now under the chairmanship of Lord Neill of Bladen, should again be considering the issue. Contemporary concerns regarding the relationship between the public and private sectors under the New Labour administration were captured by the term 'cronyism', which suggested that a new elite was emerging in British public life, based almost exclusively on the patronage of Prime Minister Blair and other senior New Labour politicians.

Reinforcing standards

The sixth report of the CSPL was explicitly conceived as a review of the implementation of the original Nolan report, although in the process of gathering evidence it became clear that a 'fresh enquiry' was necessary in relation to the status and regulation of special advisers, rules governing the sponsorship of government activities, and the lobbying of ministers and civil servants (Neill 2000a: 9). The main thrust of the Neill report was to suggest that there had been considerable improvements in the perception and regulation of probity in public life, but that more needed to be done.

The Neill committee's view regarding the regulation of the lobbying industry reaffirmed the orthodoxy established by Nolan. Recommendation 26 of their report states, 'There should be no statutory or compulsory system for the regulation of lobbyists. The current strengthening of self-regulation by lobbyists is to be welcomed,' (Neill 2000a: 4). However, a close inspection of the evidence that underpins this view seems to suggest that the Neill committee have taken a somewhat partial view of this debate.

The six pages of the Neill report (2000a: 84–9) dealing with the regulation of lobbying read confusedly and as an abdication of responsibility. The committee set out both sides of the argument surrounding a statutory register. While acknowledging the importance of this debate, primacy was placed on the principle of openness established by Nolan:

> The democratic right to make representations to government – to have access to the policy making process – is fundamental to the proper conduct of public life and the development of sound policy. The committee is opposed to anything which fetters that right without the very strongest reasons.
> (Neill 2000a: 86)

The committee heard evidence that openness and accountability could actually be enhanced via formal regulation, and that this could be achieved 'cheaply and effectively by electronic information gathering, storage, retrieval, providing easy access to all who wish it' (Neill 2000a: 86), Despite this, the committee arrived at a conclusion which suggests a lack of full engagement with the merits of arguments in favour of regulation.[3] Rather, the committee decided that the principle of openness would be best served by the status quo:

> In the opinion of the Committee, the weight of evidence is against regulation by means of a compulsory register and code of conduct. Lobbyist regulation schemes can help make government more open and accountable, providing useful information about influences on decision-making. But we believe that the amount of information that could be made available through a register would not be proportionate to the extra burden on all concerned of establishing and administering the system. There is also still force in the Committee's original objection, that such a system could give the erroneous impression that only 'registered lobbyists' offer an effective and proper route to MPs and Ministers.
> (Neill 2000a: 89)

Somewhat contradictorily, the Neill committee recommended in its guidance for 'the lobbied' in government that a clear written record of all contacts with all outside interests should be kept: 'We do not think that compliance with a new requirement to the record (sic) would be burdensome for departments, and we believe that it would encourage high and uniform standards,' (Neill 2000a: 91). Regrettably, Neill fails to explain why the onus of compliance should only fall upon the civil service and not the private sector, especially as the benefits in terms of best practice and public confidence are so apparent if there were to be general record-keeping. The committee placed a considerable degree of faith in self-regulation by lobbyists, notwithstanding the evidence submitted by public affairs bodies (notably the APPC and IPR) in favour of statutory regulation. In addition, the Neill committee proposed no solution to concerns regarding those lobbyists who choose not to join self-regulatory schemes and the entrance into the unregulated lobbying market of lawyers, accountants, and management consultants.

NOTES

1. For accounts of the cash-for-questions affair, see Doig 1998, Leigh and Vulliamy 1997, and Greer 1997.
2. Unlike the Comptroller and Auditor General or the Parliamentary Commissioner for Administration (Woodhouse 1998: 54).
3. For example, evidence from the Canadian system was not fully taken into account. See testimony by Professor Michael Rush (Neill 2000b: 41–51).

CHAPTER 10

Preparing for Holyrood

THE GROWTH OF LOBBYING IN SCOTLAND

Lobbyists gravitated towards Edinburgh in anticipation of devolution well before Labour won its landslide election victory in 1997. Shandwick, the largest independent communications consultancy in the UK for the past decade (now part of the Interpublic Group), established offices in Edinburgh in 1979. Despite the postponement of devolution until 1999, Shandwick could attract sufficient PR clients in Scotland (some also using the company for public affairs work) to open and maintain offices in Edinburgh, Glasgow and Aberdeen. The year 1992 saw the launch of Scottish & Westminster, a lobbying venture by Dunseath-Citigate and the Westminster Group, which was premised on a Labour election victory that year (Stokes 1996).

In 1996, Strategy in Scotland and GPC Market Access Scotland, both offshoots of well-established Westminster-based lobbying companies, also set up offices in Edinburgh. According to the managing director of Westminster Strategy, Michael Burrell, they had taken a triple gamble: 'One was that Labour would win the election in May; the second was that the Scottish people would vote "Yes" to devolution; and the third was that the parliament would be given tax-varying powers' (Matthews 1997: 13). All of these paid off and certainly the first two bets were odds-on. Burrell's company was one of only a few to recognise devolution's potentially serious impact on UK commercial public affairs. Michael Craven, managing director of GPC Market Access, believed that for lobbyists working in Edinburgh 'the sky is the limit' (Matthews 1997: 16).

The competitive advantage of establishing lobbying capacity in Edinburgh prior to devolution is evident if one considers the shape of the Scottish public-affairs industry, and how lobbying companies such as Strategy in Scotland and GPC Market Access Scotland sought to market themselves once the Scottish public had given their consent to New Labour's devolution project.

First, while commercial lobbying was virtually non-existent in Scotland before 1996 (as all legislative power over the UK resided either in London or Brussels), the Scottish public relations industry was, and is, relatively well-established (Hogg 1995; Smith 1994; TMA 1989). This can be attributed to a variety of factors, including Scotland's distinctive national news media system (Schlesinger 1998) as well as the strength of the Scottish economy in sectors such as banking, finance and oil. The presence of a mature PR industry in Scotland has been a threat to the specialist lobbying firms seeking to establish a foothold in the Scottish market on the advent of devolution.

Since the Nolan committee's report, there has been a marked differentiation between lobbying and PR. This strategy of distinctiveness has been vigorously pursued by lobbyists who seek to distance their work from that of PR, which they consider inappropriate to the shaping of public policy. Lobbyists believe that communication with audiences such as government and political influentials is entirely different from communication with the media. But, actually, PR work itself often involves communication with specialist audiences. So, the practical distinction between lobbying and PR is often difficult to discern in Scotland, as elsewhere.

The blurred boundaries between PR and lobbying is attributable to the highly-publicised rise of the political spin doctor, who straddles the divide between PR and public policy. As many spin doctors themselves ultimately become political lobbyists and trade in the precious currency of political intelligence, confusion over the credentials of who can legitimately and effectively lobby is hardly surprising.

Being 'in position' before devolution afforded established firms an attractive, if short-lived, marketing tactic, namely the ability to portray late entrants into the market as craven opportunists. As Jane Saren, managing director of GPC Market Access in Scotland, noted:

> There is a real danger that people who wait until 1999 to set up a decent operation will look like opportunists. While it is true that firms up here [in Scotland] do need strategic public affairs, there may well be some understandable resentment up here if that's how the London consultancies go about giving it.
> (Matthews 1997: 15)

In fact, after the devolution referendum was endorsed by the Scottish electorate in September 1997, the migration north from Westminster of lobbying companies was noteworthy. In October that year, Ludgate Communications, then the tenth-largest PR agency in the UK, announced a joint venture with FMS Public Relations, a leading independent PR agency in Scotland, aimed at integrating the public-relations and public-affairs expertise within each company (Atack 1997: 3). In reality, the deal involved the Ludgate group lending public affairs support and expertise to FMS

Public Relations, in addition to any synergies that could be gained from the strictly PR end of the business. The same year also saw the launch of the specialist planning lobbying consultancy PPS Scotland. GJW opened its Scottish branch in 1998.

The growth of the lobbying industry in Scotland is indicated by the trade directory *Hollis*, which provides a fairly comprehensive list of the PR consultancies in the UK. In the 1997–8 edition, thirty-nine consultancies were advertising their expertise in Government Relations in the UK (Hollis 1997). Only three claimed a competence in Scottish Public Affairs: GPC, Strategy in Scotland and Decision Makers. In the 1998–9 edition, forty-six agencies were listed under Government Relations. Of these, four advertised their Scottish lobbying capacity: GPC, Strategy in Scotland, GJW and Public Affairs Europe (Hollis 1998). In the 1999–2000 directory, of the forty-five agencies specialising in Government Relations, six claimed expertise in the Scottish market. The new entries included August. One Public Affairs, whose advertisement offers 'expert advice and guidance on political and policy developments from Westminster, Whitehall and the regions', and the re-appearance of Decision Makers (Hollis 1999: 981).

From 1997, the PR industry in Scotland was beginning to prepare for the Scottish Parliament in ways invisible to the casual observer and not well captured by London-based trade directory compilers. The advent of Holyrood undoubtedly raised the profile of public affairs in Scotland but there is evidence, although difficult to quantify, that Scottish PR firms had engaged in some lobbying work prior to devolution. Tony Meehan Associates (TMA) claimed to have been involved in lobbying the Scottish Office on behalf of clients since the late 1980s. Similarly, Shandwick Scotland have undertaken public affairs work, although they only opened their specialist Scottish parliamentary unit in August 1998. The Scottish branch of The Communications Group engaged in ad hoc lobbying for clients although, until devolution, this was done in conjunction with the London office rather than led from Scotland. Scribe Communications, Carnegie PR, and Proscot PR Consultants have been others in the field for varying periods. At the behest of the former Secretary of State for Scotland, Michael Forsyth, Media House handled the Scottish Office's PR and public affairs campaign to secure the release of two Scottish nurses accused of murder in Saudi Arabia. In 1996, Media House recruited David Whitton from Scottish Television to head its public affairs division. Whitton's later appointment as Donald Dewar's official spokesman was symptomatic of the connectedness of the worlds of media, politics and advocacy in Scotland.

The creation of a Scottish Parliament led to the entrance of new Scottish players into the lobbying market. These comprised established PR consultancies and new lobbying agencies. Companies such as Beattie Media, Barkers Scotland, Neil Baxter Associates, and The Newton Consultancy all began to offer a dedicated public affairs service as part of their portfolio from 1997–8. New consultancies have targeted work related to the Scottish Parliament. PS Communications, founded in 1994, has been one of the more high-profile consultancies. Holyrood Strategy, formed in 1997, has also sought to establish a consultancy business around the Scottish Parliament. In addition, a number of 'one-man-band' consultancies have offered lobbying services.

The commercial interest in devolution was not confined to the public relations or lobbying sectors. Law firms have become involved in public affairs and constitutional consultancy. Westminster Parliamentary agents Dyson Bell Martin began to promote themselves in the Scottish market. In January 1998, the Scottish legal firm Shepherd and Wedderburn WS launched an in-house lobbying service, Saltire Public Affairs. These initiatives were closely followed by the launch of Public Affairs Europe in April 1998, a joint venture between the commercial lawyers Maclay, Murray and Spens and the high-profile, 'streetwise' Scottish PR consultancy Beattie Media. Jack McConnell, the former general secretary of the Scottish Labour Party, was recruited as a director, as was George McKechnie, a former editor of *The Herald*. McConnell's links with Beattie Media were later to become central to the Scottish Parliament Standards Committee's investigation of the Lobbygate affair. Our research indicated considerable unease among commercial and voluntary-sector lobbyists regarding McConnell's involvement. Concern centred on the probity of such an overtly political appointment given the recent history of sleaze at Westminster. Damian Killeen, Director of the Poverty Alliance in Glasgow, wrote to *The Herald* expressing his fears:

> The growth in the number of lobbying companies in Scotland, in advance of the Scottish Parliament, is happening with relatively little critical comment. Some of these companies are staffed by people who recently or currently have occupied prominent political positions. There is little doubt that their access to senior politicians is an important part of these companies' sales pitch. Government in Scotland has, so far, done little to disassociate itself from these developments. What signals does this send out to those who are looking to the new Parliament to provide a level of accessibility and inclusiveness?
> (Killeen 1998: 16)

Lawyers McGrigor Donald also began to offer a public affairs or lobbying service around this time, creating a seven-strong Scottish Parliamentary team. Like the cooperation between Maclay's and Beattie Media, McGrigor Donald teamed up with Shandwick Public Affairs as 'Scottish Parliamentary Healthcheck' to provide information and raise the awareness of corporate clients concerning the likely impact of devolution on their commercial interests.

The in-house public-affairs capacity of companies operating in Scotland has expanded with the establishment of the Scottish Parliament. The 1999 Scottish Corporate Communications Survey suggested that:

> The new Scottish political settlement means that this is a period of uncertainty and opportunity for corporate communicators in industry, commerce, local government and the voluntary sector. Activity is likely to increase as a result of the increased political, diplomatic, research and business presence in Scotland. It is likely that new companies will emerge to provide services, while existing organisations will have to adjust to the new arrangement.
> (Wood and Higgins 1999: 6)

The survey asked respondents (eighty-five in all, of whom fifty-five were working in PLCs) about the plans their organisations were making in preparation for the new legislature. The response to this question was reported as follows:

Preparation for Scottish Parliament	Percentage
Engaged professional lobbyists	2
Increased budget to cover communication in Scotland	9
Expanded existing Scottish communications section	13
Created new communications division	4
Nothing	54
Other	14

(Wood and Higgins 1999: 40)

The authors seemed surprised by the results of their survey, given the anticipated growth in Scottish corporate communications. Nevertheless, their survey did indicate early adjustments to the new political situation in Scotland.

All told, the PR industry in Scotland was not slow to spot the opportunities that devolution presented. The Scottish Parliament was rightly seen as transforming the political landscape, especially how existing bodies such as quangos and statutory agencies would relate to the new seat of power in Edinburgh. PR consultants in Scotland were keen to point out the importance of 'local knowledge' in renegotiating many of these institutional relationships. Writing just days after the Yes-Yes vote in the Scottish devolution referendum, Ken Newton, a partner in a Scottish PR agency, outlined his vision of the role of PR after devolution:

> [Devolution] could create two channels of opportunity for PR and public affairs consultants – firstly, helping these [statutory] bodies position themselves positively with their governmental masters and secondly, relaunching the bodies which undergo reform ... I believe Scottish

devolution can be mirrored by a PR devolution which sees a move towards
campaigns that grant more autonomy to those with local skills, knowledge and
the client base to drive the client's message home.
(Newton 1997: 9)

It is ironic, given this insistence on the advantages of local expertise, that
Newton's erstwhile partner David Budge (of Budge Newton), was later
responsible for a PR disaster while working on an account for Scottish
Enterprise and Scotland the Brand. Charged with producing an information
pack about Scotland's arts, music and film industry to be used promotionally
at the Epcot Millennium conference in Disney, Florida, David Budge
Associates embarrassed themselves and their clients by creating an
information pack riddled with errors or 'McGaffes' concerning contemporary Scottish culture (Wishart 1999).

This incident exposes the hollowness of some of the claims of the Scottish
PR industry. Commercial lobbyists need to be viewed in the same fashion.
The entry of more and more companies into the embryonic commercial
public affairs sector in Scotland has placed incumbent firms in a difficult
position. Formal barriers to entry, as understood in economic theory, do not
apply. The start-up costs of a lobbying consultancy are concentrated in the
personnel who will actually do the lobbying. Thus, it becomes important for
established agencies to protect their existing business by attempting some
form of professional closure. At its crudest, this means trying to discredit new
entrants as mere opportunists. As Chris Lansdell, managing director of
Countrywide Porter Novelli, Scotland, commented, 'At the moment one sees
in the marketplace a number of new public affairs companies springing up,
some of them little more than brass plate operations' (Gray 1998: 14). More
elaborate forms of professional closure and competition were pursued by
leading trade associations, as discussed later.

The expansion of the public affairs sector in Scotland occurred at a time of
unique constitutional and institutional invention. The imminent creation of
a devolved legislature was an extraordinary moment of social and political
change. The period between the devolution referendum in September 1997
and the general election in Scotland in May 1999 was a moment wherein the
rules and conventions that might govern the new polity were available for
public debate and deliberation. As noted, the key arena in which political
construction was centred was the CSG.

LOBBYING AND THE CONSULTATIVE STEERING GROUP

Chaired by Devolution Minister Henry McLeish, the CSG's remit was 'to
bring together views on and consider the operational needs and working

methods of the Scottish Parliament' (CSG 1998b: 3). The CSG would also seek to develop procedures and standing orders that might be used by the Scottish Parliament, and then report to the Secretary of State for Scotland. The CSG's extensive programme of work included an examination of how lobbying might be conducted and regulated post-devolution. Research was commissioned by the Scottish Office in June 1998 on lobbying practice in other parliamentary systems. The study was carried out by the Centre for Scottish Public Policy (CSPP) and initially submitted to the CSG in August 1998, with a final draft in November 1998.

The CSPP report on lobbying practice is a comparative review of the regulation of outside interests across a variety of national parliaments and regional assemblies. The extremely tight timescale for this research meant that depth of analysis had to be sacrificed in order to produce a wide-ranging account of different regulatory regimes. As the authors openly admit, their work 'did not detail in-depth the nature and practice of lobbying parliaments' (Lazarowicz and Jones 1998: 51). The review of European experience was somewhat cursory. The report paid particular attention to regulation in polities with relatively developed commercial lobbying markets, namely Australia, Canada, and the US. Regrettably but perhaps understandably, the study failed to look at the governance of outside interests at the province or state level, save to mention that different systems were in place. That level of analysis might have provided a useful comparison to the Scottish situation in terms of the powers available to the legislatures concerned, and the relative size and scale of economies, civic institutions, and networks.

Much of the received wisdom concerning the issue of regulation of outside interests is reproduced in the report. Its findings are presented almost entirely in terms of the 'problems' created by regulation, with no consideration of the benefits that statutory controls might bring. This is somewhat perplexing, given the CSG's ambition to make the Scottish Parliament an open, accountable and transparent institution. Assessing the current situation in Scotland, the authors of the CSPP report recognised that the home market was in a state of considerable flux. The emergence of the Association for Scottish Public Affairs (ASPA) was noted, as were the various self-regulatory codes of conduct promoted by the commercial lobbyists. The authors seemed to accept the lobbying industry's argument that 'it is the public perception of the growth of lobbying and misconception over its role that tends to lead to recommendations for regulation' (Lazarowicz and Jones 1998: 62).

The CSG did not entirely rely on this commissioned research in reaching conclusions regarding the statutory regulation of lobbying in Scotland. Members of the group told us that the CSPP report was considered rather anodyne and of little use. The CSG also sought evidence from the general public via their open forum meetings in July and August 1998. Annex E of the CSG's report summarises the main points arising from this consultation. Those participating in the open fora recognised the need for business interests to be represented in the Scottish Parliament, yet there was evident public concern at the potential role of lobbyists. Some distinguished between paid commercial lobbyists and those working in-house for charities whose job it was to lobby Parliament. Others wished to see the registration of all lobbying in Scotland. Of the 336 responses to the CSG consultation exercise received by July 1998, there is no evidence of a public contribution (there were six confidential replies) from any of the lobbying or PR industry trade associations, or individual businesses in this sector. This is curious, considering how lobbyists place a premium on early interventions in most policy processes on behalf of their clients. However, ASPA did arrange a meeting with CSG representatives to make their case for self-regulation.

Interest in the political and commercial consequences of devolution extended to the in-house public affairs departments of large corporations headquartered or based in Scotland. A review of corporations responding to the CSG's consultation exercise indicates which businesses were involving themselves in the newly-emerging political system. Major corporations such as the BBC, BP Scotland, Atlantic Telecom, Caledonian Brewing Company Ltd, FirstGroup plc and utilities like Scottish Power, British Energy plc, and BT Scotland contributed to the CSG's opinion-gathering exercise. BT Scotland has been particularly proactive, not only in employing a head of government for Scotland in its parliamentary affairs department, but also in encouraging its own staff to stand for election to the Scottish Parliament by giving them four weeks' leave to campaign, and if elected, guaranteeing their jobs back when their term of office has ended. Furthermore, BT Scotland sponsored the creation of the Centre for Teledemocracy at Napier University, which seeks to explore and develop new forms of democratic participation by utilising the latest information and communications technology. Many of the opinions expressed by these business interests were later to find their way into the CSG's recommendations.

Trade associations and professional bodies are another avenue – besides commercial lobbying – through which the concerns of the business sector can be communicated to the political class in Scotland. Many such bodies took part in the CSG's consultation exercise. Annex A to Appendix D of the CSG report lists thirty-two professional organisations that responded to the CSG. The business interests among these included the Brewers' and Licensed Retailers' Association of Scotland, the Chartered Institute of Building, the Committee of Scottish Clearing Bankers, the Institute of Chartered Accountants of Scotland, the Institute of Directors, the Institute of Management, the Law Society for Scotland, the Malt Distillers' Association, the Scotch Whisky Association, the Offshore Operators' Association Ltd, Scottish Engineering, Scottish Grocers' Association and the Scottish Tourism

Forum. Other umbrella groups and trade associations are listed under business contributors, including the CBI, the Forum of Private Business, the Meat and Livestock Commission, the Scottish Industry Forum, the Scottish Council for Development and Industry, and a range of Chambers of Commerce.

This high level of business involvement in the CSG is noteworthy, given the well-known antipathy of many business leaders to the devolution project. The CBI was probably the most visible example. Prior to the 1997 general election, CBI Scotland opposed devolution, despite considerable lobbying from New Labour in Scotland for its endorsement. In the devolution referendum in September 1997, the CBI remained officially neutral, although prominent members publicly opposed the Yes-Yes campaign run by the cross-party umbrella group, Scotland Forward. The CSG afforded the CBI a chance to play political catch-up by actively engaging with the debate on the standing orders and practices of the new Parliament. As one commentator remarked at the time:

> It is entirely to the credit of Scottish business that more and more people are beginning to think seriously about how to turn the fast-looming Scottish parliament to positive advantage. True, people are discovering potential pitfalls, but amongst those who have the time and inclination to explore the possibilities of this business environment, optimism is starting to emerge. (Jones 1999: 10)

Those most likely to have the resources to engage with the Parliament in this way will have a direct professional concern in the legislature, namely the public affairs directors of business organisations in Scotland.

The CBI's involvement in the CSG led to the creation of a Holyrood watchdog group, aimed at promoting the profile and interests of businesses, and identifying their 'strategic and policy priorities' at Holyrood (Scott 1999b). Since the Parliament has been up and running, the CBI have sought to institutionalise their lobbying access to MSPs of all parties through the creation of a series of economic and industry briefings, a vehicle which CBI Scotland's director of public affairs hoped 'that MSPs would see as a "must see" event, which will provide them with a very useful background for them to make informed decisions,' (Hope 1999: 16).

Reviewing submissions from business to the CSG, Brown and McCrone (1999: 24) reported that 'there was unanimous agreement about the importance of pre-legislative scrutiny, especially in the absence of a second chamber' and that legislative accessibility was a business priority. However, there was less agreement on the precise terms of this access. While most business groups concurred upon the need for a code of conduct and a public register of interests for MSPs, they were split over the regulation of lobbyists and how to balance the interests of resource-poor and resource-rich groups. The Federation of Small Business and the Scottish Council for Development and Industry thought that a code of conduct for MSPs would ensure the proper conduct of interest representation in Holyrood. However, it was recognised that this alone could not prevent possible 'dominance by large, well-funded organisations' and as a corollary 'the subsequent neglect of small and community based businesses' (Brown and McCrone 1999: 21, 22).

The CSG's final recommendations regarding lobbying reflected the contributions made by business interests and the dominant orthodoxy at Westminster established by the Nolan committee. The CSG's Code of Conduct and Lobbying working group proposed nine key principles governing the conduct of MSPs, amounting to a Scottish version of the seven Nolan principles established to promote the highest ethical standards in public life (CSG 1999: 23, 24). The CSG recommended a ban on paid advocacy by MSPs, an onus to declare interests when taking part in parliamentary proceedings, and eleven categories of registrable interests. Failure to comply with the register would be a criminal offence, as would other breaches of the Code of Conduct. Significantly, the CSG did not recommend the regulation of lobbying activity nor the creation of a register of lobbyists. In line with Nolan, the CSG supported the development of voluntary codes by lobbying firms and organisations. The rationale for this decision can be largely attributed to CSG members' belief that their guiding principles and aspirations would obviate the need for Westminster-style lobbying and thereby make redundant the regulation of outside interests.

It is worth restating the CSG's most important principles, as they were to become the template for much of the subsequent debate on models of self-regulation and access to the Parliament:

> The Scottish Parliament should be accessible, open, responsive, and develop procedures which make possible a participative approach to the development, consideration and scrutiny of policy and legislation.
> (CSG 1999: 3)

As we shall see, debate along these lines was concentrated upon the public interventions of, and private discussions by, groups such as the Association for Professional Political Consultants (APPC), the Association for Scottish Public Affairs (ASPA), the Scottish Civic Forum, and the Scottish Council for Voluntary Organisations (SCVO).

CHAPTER 11

Jockeying for position

TRADE ASSOCIATIONS

Since the mid-1990s, professional or trade associations for lobbyists have attempted to occupy an important position within the UK political system. The cash-for-questions scandal at Westminster effectively brought into being the Association of Professional Political Consultants (APPC), the trade association for the larger, Westminster-based, lobbying consultancies. For entry into the APPC, members' fee income must exceed £100,000. This barrier to entry has excluded some smaller 'one-man-band' lobbyists. For the APPC's founding members, it neatly resolved the difficulty of having to represent and regulate what were often seen as the rogue elements in the business, trading on the 'old-boy network' for access and political intelligence.

Nevertheless, Ian Greer Associates (IGA), the lobbying consultancy at the centre of the scandal that prompted the Nolan investigation, was at the time among the largest and most powerful political consultancies in the UK (Leigh and Vulliamy 1997: xvi, 38) and would easily have qualified for membership of the APPC. Moreover, the involvement of GPC, themselves APPC members, in the 1998 cash-for-access scandal exploded the convenient myth that self-regulation is a bulwark against corrupt practice in the lobbying business.

The APPC was created to allow specialist lobbying consultancies to distinguish themselves from other bodies in the governmental affairs and public policy consultancy arena. After the deregulation of financial services in 1986 – the 'big bang' – many accountancy firms began to sell policy advice (Miller and Dinan 2000: 24). Law firms also sought to generate income by advising clients on aspects of parliamentary business. As Andrew Gifford, then APPC chairman, testified to the Nolan committee:

> We have seen increasing competition to our own companies coming from law
> firms in Brussels and in the UK, from a number of merchant banks . . . One

has seen exactly the same thing happening from the accountancy firms . . . We
estimate that the overall market, if one is looking at those people who are
directly involved in lobbying amongst all the different groups, is probably well
in excess of £1 million a year . . . Clearly, with that scale of market there is
pressure among the different groupings to gain access.
(Nolan committee, 1995b: 88)

This 'guesstimate' concerns that part of the lobbying market not already
cornered by specialist lobbying firms. The value of the lobbying industry as a
whole is difficult to quantify. Leigh and Vulliamy (1997: 38) report that by
the end of the 1980s 'it was estimated that the mushrooming lobbyists' firms
. . . were taking £10 million a year from outside commercial bodies for the
sale of political influence'. Indeed, Gifford's own firm, GJW, reported a fee
income for that year (1994) of £3,152,576 (*PR Week*, 28 April 1995: 17).

Plainly, trade associations like the APPC exist to promote and protect the
interests of their members. The APPC's formation may be understood as a
form of professional closure, whereby the incumbents have sought to protect
their market share from new entrants.

THE APPC IN SCOTLAND

While the APPC was created to cater for Westminster-based political
consultancies, the profile of its membership mirrors that of its clients, and is
transnational in character. These lobbyists act for multinational companies
with stakes and interests across borders, and require a presence wherever
clients are located, or wherever policy affecting them is decided. Most APPC
member agencies have offices both in Brussels and London, and many are
affiliated to, or owned by, communications conglomerates with a global
reach. Scotland is merely a local outpost of the global communications
economy.

Eight lobbying companies with offices in Scotland are members of the
APPC. These include the six founder members: Strategy in Scotland (part of
Westminster Strategy, in turn part of the international Grayling group,
owned by the Lopex communication corporation); Shandwick (the Scottish
branch of the Interpublic communication conglomerate); GPC Scotland
(part of the global GPC network, owned by the Omnicom group, which has
other interests in Scotland through Countrywide Porter Novelli); Citigate
Public Affairs (a branch of Citigate Dewe Rogerson, owned by the
communications corporation Incepta); GJW Scotland (the Scottish office of
GJW Government Relations, recently acquired by BSMG Worldwide); and
PPS Communications Scotland (formerly Political Planning Services, now
rebranded as PPS [Local and Regional]), the only one not owned by a

corporation with a global reach. The two members who joined in 2000 were APCO Scotland (part of APCO Worldwide) and August.One.

APPC companies' lobbyists are involved in a highly competitive market. As Fiona Callison, then managing director of Shandwick Public Affairs in Scotland, observed:

> We have got deep pockets. We're hoping that within two years we'll be in the top three of the public-affairs consultancies in Scotland and we would expect in terms of fee income that by year three we're the biggest, or we're dead . . . But that's all part of the Shandwick international destination project . . . They want to become the largest PR and public affairs consultancy in the world.

The lobbying market that developed in Edinburgh directly after the referendum vote in September 1997 was not the exclusive preserve of APPC companies. Indigenous Scottish companies and organisations were also interested in lobbying the Scottish government. The increasing emphasis on self-regulation after Nolan faced all would-be Scottish lobbyists with a dilemma. The APPC membership requirement of fee income of over £100,000 per annum directly generated by each government affairs consultancy was an insurmountable barrier for almost all aspiring commercial lobbyists in Scotland, given the potential size of the Scottish market and the fact that the Scottish Parliament was not to be elected for another eighteen months.

The other self-regulatory options available at the time were somewhat unattractive. The Public Relations Consultants' Association (PRCA) and the Institute for Public Relations (IPR) are the two main trade associations for people working in the PR industry in the UK. The PRCA's membership is open to consultancies, whereas the IPR's membership consists of individual consultants. Both have members who are lobbyists and have largely similar codes of conduct governing the professional activities of their members. Both organisations also have Scottish committees. However, as with the APPC, these associations are seen – by many of their own members as well as outsiders – as having an inherent cultural and political bias toward London. Given this context, and a prevailing climate of opinion in which the political class was promoting a doctrine of Scottish solutions for Scottish problems, the creation of an association for Scottish lobbyists was entirely predictable.

ACCESS, PASSES AND CODES: THE FOUNDATIONS OF OPEN DEMOCRACY IN SCOTLAND?

In an article in *The Herald* on 30 October 1997, Frances Horsburgh exclusively reported that, in an attempt to make the Scottish Parliament a 'sleaze-free zone', the commercial lobbyists PS Public Affairs Consultants were behind moves to set up an association for professional lobbyists in Scotland. The then directors of PS Public Affairs were all mentioned by name (Struan Stevenson, Mike Watson and Denis Sullivan) and by party political affiliation (Conservative, Labour and Liberal Democrat respectively). The report identified issues that the early debate on lobbying in post-referendum Scotland was to cover: the anxiety of Scottish-based lobbyists to avoid 'cash-for-questions scandals' and the related sleaze that had tainted politics and public affairs at Westminster; the SNP's vocal criticism of 'the incestuous relationship' between lobbyists and politicians; and the controversial suggestion that 'only members of the proposed association of public affairs consultants would be allowed to operate within the precincts of the new parliament and could be expelled if they failed to abide by its rules' (Horsburgh 1997: 7). These were to become recurrent themes.

PS Public Affairs Consultants continued to attract publicity for the creation of a trade association for Scottish lobbyists – and for themselves – until the first public meeting to register interest and examine how such a body might be created. On 22 January 1998, *The Herald* reported that 'Pressure grows for Scots curbs on lobbyists'. Denis Sullivan 'confirmed that his firm, which has cross-party personnel, intends to set up an association for lobbyists, complete with a code of conduct and set of penalties for those found guilty of breaching the rules'. The Liberal Democrats were said to favour a register of interests so that politicians knew on whose behalf they were being lobbied. The SNP's initial idea of an outright ban on all lobbyists (Salmond 1996) was said to be being revised in a policy paper that would 'seek to draw a more subtle distinction between different areas' (Dinwoodie 1998a: 6).

The first formal meeting of those interested in setting up a Scottish lobbyists' association took place at the offices of the Convention of Scottish Local Authorities (COSLA) in Edinburgh on 27 February 1998. *The Herald* anticipated more than fifty attendees and suggested that a Scottish lobbying association 'could have a direct input into committees, such as the all-party one chaired by Scottish Devolution Minister, Henry McLeish, which were examining how the new parliament would work' (Horsburgh 1998: 6).

The meeting was attended by over forty individuals representing a variety of interests in Scottish public life. A further thirty-eight interested parties were unable to attend, and another eight invitees declined to come. This latter group were all local councillors, save one, Roger Williams, Director of the SOID. Of those who met to consider the creation of an Association of Scottish Public Affairs Consultants (as it was provisionally titled) three were councillors, two were 'public sector' bodies (COSLA and the European Commission), four represented Scottish quangos, six were delegates from various associations (including PRCA Scotland and IPR's Scottish Local

Government Group), two came from Scottish policy thinktanks, ten represented corporate or business organisations, and thirteen were from public affairs consultancies. Finally, individuals attended on behalf of the voluntary sector (SCVO), the CSG, and the Constitutional Convention. None of the political parties was represented in an official capacity.

The meeting was chaired by Mike Watson, then a director of PS Public Affairs and Labour frontbench peer. In his opening address, Watson stressed that the process of forming an association 'should be inclusive, hence the broad mix of consultants, representatives of the corporate sector, local government, NGOs and quangos. If set up *this body will draw its credibility from representing a broad spectrum of sectors*,' (emphasis added). Watson saw the rationale for the emerging association as a deliberate and explicit effort not to replicate the model of lobbying found at Westminster. The need for a Scottish voice and identity were stressed. Watson argued that any new body should incorporate PR professionals, not simply lobbyists, and suggested that the association's PR element might be reflected in the organisation's name. This pitch reflected the view that the distinction between PR and lobbying is difficult to draw in practice and that many companies in Scotland (including PS Communication Consultants) did both. Lord Watson concluded:

> Inclusivity, not exclusivity, is the ultimate goal. This proposition is not intended to be a public affairs Hadrian's wall . . . Our aim is to create a Scottish organisation, which is seen to be Scottish and practising in Scotland. Any organisation with a base in Scotland is more than welcome to join but they do need to be here on the ground . . . The role of PS Public Affairs is simply to facilitate a discussion forum.
> (ASPA minutes, February 1998)

The debate that followed polarised over how a Scottish lobbyists' representative body should articulate with the political system in Scotland, and to a lesser degree, the UK and Europe. Those who were already members of the APPC and PRCA were keen to defend their existing codes of conduct and emphasised the distinction between commercial lobbyists acting on behalf of a multiplicity of clients and those working in-house for both representative organisations and corporations. Some consultants believed that a Scottish 'sister' organisation to those already in existence might be sufficient to regulate the public affairs industry post-devolution, and that no new body was needed. This idea was strongly resisted by others, who echoed Mike Watson's view that the new politics of devolution demanded a new approach to public affairs in Scotland.

The majority opted for the term 'professional association' to describe the type of organisation they were interested in creating and belonging to. For many, this would necessitate a code of conduct, the form of which was postponed until a further meeting, but not before Canon Kenyon Wright, chair of the executive committee of the Scottish Constitutional Convention, expressed a view at odds with almost all others present. Wright insisted that lobbying was too important an issue for democracy to be left solely to lobbyists and hoped that the Scottish Parliament might regulate and monitor lobbying.

Recollecting the first meeting of what was to become the Association for Scottish Public Affairs (ASPA) Angela Casey, its current (2001) convenor observed:

> There was a very strong feeling at the first meeting of anti the big consultancies, the Strategies in Scotland, GPC, and the bloke who flew up from GJW in London to talk. They all stood up and said, 'This is the wrong thing, we should be going with the APPC,' and were quite anti, which just got a lot of people's backs up . . . There was quite a lot of anti feeling going on and that's carried on, which is a shame.

The starting positions of those engaged in this debate were actually quite enduring. This is not to imply that they are immutable (and there is evidence that any animosity is abating), but rather that different interests limit the kinds of actions voluntarily taken.

Casey believed that the initial trawl 'was too broad and there were a lot of worthies standing up pontificating who didn't really know what they were talking about. But I think what's happened over time is that those have got whittled out.' This is a striking comment given the store that people like Mike Watson and Struan Stevenson attached to attracting as wide as possible a constituency for the association, for reasons of credibility and legitimacy. What Casey candidly conceded was that ASPA aimed to represent the interests of its members. The more varied these were, the more difficult the job became.

The nascent Association for Scottish Public Affairs Consultants (ASPAC) – as it was provisionally called – continued to receive minor press coverage after the exploratory meeting in February. This reporting was mainly confined to the Scottish broadsheets. The most significant intervention came in a column by Struan Stevenson: 'You must be squeaky clean in the lobby' (Stevenson 1998). Stevenson re-emphasised the need for Scottish lobbying to be sleaze-free. The article puffed the February meeting to establish ASPAC, and outlined his vision for the body.

The next stage in ASPA's formation came on 17 April 1998, with a smaller meeting of just over a dozen interested parties to elect a discussion group to take the project forward. Again, this meeting was chaired by Lord Watson. The first item on the agenda was Stevenson's article in *The Herald*. The minutes record that the article simply expressed Stevenson's personal view.

However, Robbie MacDuff, managing director of Strategy in Scotland, who was unable to attend, wrote to Watson as interim chairman, suggesting that such public intervention in the debate on lobbying could not be dismissed so lightly. He complained at 'the continuing public profiling of one particular view about how the debate about regulation of "lobbying" in Scotland is likely to develop' and expressed surprise 'that the article spells out what appear to be the "rules of conduct of members."' He went on to denounce 'heavy handed and unsubtle forcing of hand' and 'using the mechanism of discussions around the issue for company commercial advantage'.

John Downey, research officer for the Federation of Small Business in Scotland, attacked Stevenson's 'insulting and unfair' remarks, accusing him of 'sitting in self-righteous judgement as he pronounced his guilty sentence on Scotland's lobbying organisations' (Downey 1998). Downey's letter to *The Herald* endorsed MacDuff's suspicion that much of what Stevenson said smacked of self-interest and self-promotion.

Downey's intervention distinguished between the commercial lobbyist whose clients may change from one week to the next and the in-house practitioner who represents either a commercial corporation or fixed membership of a trade body. This demarcation has resurfaced repeatedly in the debate on the regulation of lobbying in Scotland. Downey's letter served as a useful reminder that many of those who would be trying to influence Holyrood on behalf of outside interests had a considerable track record, reputation and credibility with Scotland's politicians. Bodies such as the Scottish Council for Development and Industry (SCDI) have a pedigree stretching back to the 1930s. Other membership and trade associations such as the Confederation of British Industry (CBI), the Institute of Directors (IoD), and Federation of Small Business (FSB) and the Forum for Private Business have also been active in Scotland for many years, prompting Downey to assert on their behalf 'we do not need an association to provide "comfort" to the politicians with whom we already have an effective working relationship'.

The meeting on 17 April sought to progress outstanding issues: to consider whether a separate Scottish association was necessary or whether a 'sister' body to one of the UK-wide trade associations would be more appropriate, and to decide on those to be represented by any such organisation. With hindsight, it is clear that the composition of this meeting was significant. No members of the leading prospective sister group – the APPC – were present (both Robbie MacDuff and Jane Saren sent their apologies). The APPC's strategy was evidently to retain a watching brief on how the association developed (receiving minutes of meetings and other communications), thereby reserving the right to re-enter at a later stage. It seems likely that the tone of the initial meeting, and subsequent media coverage of the embryonic ASPAC, encouraged this approach by Scottish APPC members.

The absence of APPC members shaped the course of the ASPAC discussion group's deliberations. The most vocal objectors to the project, seen to be the APPC companies (often referred to as those companies with 'offices south of the border'), were not present and were perceived as excluding, or at least detaching, themselves from those who had made the effort to participate fully in the founding of ASPAC. It was feared that ASPAC could be smeared by other professional lobby groups and that the new association would 'need to face up to the fight and rehearse arguments' (ASPAC minutes, April 1998). The degree of animosity that existed towards APPC was tempered by the recognition that ASPAC might over time develop a working relationship with it and similar organisations such as the IPR and PRCA. Several participants encouraged cordial working links between such organisations, not least because public spats would be damaging to the industry as a whole. As Hamish McPherson, public affairs director of Scottish Gas, noted: 'It is important to take others on board, or recognise why [they] are not on board and work with that.'

Priorities that emerged were: to institute formal contacts with all of Scotland's leading political parties and initiate a dialogue with the CSG; to sell the idea of ASPAC to other groups, both in terms of its inclusive membership and its legitimacy; and to develop a coherent PR strategy to avoid damaging publicity for the association. In the short term, this translated into keeping a low profile and only reacting to publicity should the need arise. The group also began to consider the more mundane practicalities of running a membership organisation, and held a preliminary discussion of membership fees and administrative support. All of these actions were premised on developing a code of conduct for the association. This vital task was to be taken forward by a smaller, self-nominated steering group led by Alan Boyd of McGrigor Donald solicitors, which would report back to the discussion group with a draft code of conduct for consideration. The steering group also included Bill Anderson, FSB; Kate Caskie, Shelter Scotland; Susan Gavaghan, Scottish Arts Council; Kate Higgins, Association of Nationalist Councillors; Hamish McPherson, Scottish Gas; Gemma Swart, PS Public Affairs; and Stephen Young, Stephen Young Associates.

The agenda facing the steering group was sketched out by Alan Boyd, who outlined what he saw as the regulatory options open to the Scottish Parliament:

> We can allow the parliament to regulate our own affairs [or] we get our act together and write a code which will allow us to regulate on our own . . . There is a golden opportunity for us to influence the CSG. We should go for it in a big way and operate as a professional body.
> (ASPA minutes, April 1998)

The code of conduct was seen by the vast majority of participants as being at the core of what ASPAC was about. At this juncture, a previously subterranean issue surfaced: that of access to the Scottish Parliament and what sort of accreditation regime might apply. As Kirsty Regan, then secretary of ASPA, remarked,

> I would say a very small minority, and primarily individual consultants, kept raising the issue of access to the Parliament and would constantly come along to the meetings and raise the question of what's happening with the Parliament giving us [ASPA] passes.

Although the issue became redundant when the Parliament adopted the CSG's key principles (which seek to ensure the Parliament's accessibility) it is worth remembering that in summer 1998 this was not at all resolved. Indeed, the ASPAC steering group proposed that joining the association would entitle members to accreditation passes for the Parliament (assuming the legislature chose to adopt such a system). The steering group minutes of 7 May state boldly that 'the aim is to try and get official accreditation from the [Scottish] Parliament along the lines of the European Parliament'. Any member found to be in breach of ASPAC's code would automatically lose their accreditation rights, again drawing on the European Parliament model. While none of this has come to pass, it lends credence to fears expressed to us during the course of the research that some of the worst aspects of Westminster practice (especially in relation to access and the abuse of press and researcher passes) might be replicated or even institutionalised in Scotland, despite all the public pronouncements by interested parties to the contrary. As we have seen, this was an animating concern of Scotland's political press.

It was agreed that ASPAC should try to get the CSG 'on-side' and work with the Scottish Parliament to promote self-regulation by lobbyists. It was intended to formalise relations with the Scottish Parliament as a necessary first step, and then to expand the code of conduct to cater for local authorities. This has yet to happen. The steering group met again on 20 May. That meeting devised a set of objectives for the association, mapped out how these might be realised in practice, and offered a provisional code of conduct for approval by the discussion group. The objective of the association was:

> To maintain the highest professional standards in all forms of lobbying [later the discussion group added 'and briefing' here] directly affecting members and officials of the Scottish Parliament and groups, companies, organisations and individuals. This will be achieved by accepting members into the association who agree to abide by a Code of Conduct.

The steering group recommended that a series of working groups be formed out of the broader discussion group. These working groups could consider outstanding aspects of the formation of the association. Consequently, the Constitution, Government/Media Relations and Membership working groups were created, and were coordinated by Gemma Swart of PS Public Affairs.

'THERE IS NOTHING MORE PERMANENT THAN THE TEMPORARY'[1]

The nascent association wished to pursue a 'twin-track' strategy aimed at attracting more active support from the political parties, influential political figures, and the CSG, in order to gain credibility. By the end of May 1998, only the Scottish Conservatives had responded to a letter from ASPAC sent to all the political parties. However, the association was encouraged by news that the CSG was willing to accept a late submission on lobbying and that Henry McLeish had expressed 'strong interest' in their efforts and was keen on a formal meeting. Having almost settled on a code of conduct, the emergent association moved on to the next tranche of work to lay the foundations for a formal launch.

These matters were dealt with by the three working groups between June and July 1998. Both the Constitution and Government/Media Relations working groups continued to consider the code of conduct. As the association began to crystallise around the detailed work of these groups, leading members were in buoyant mood. There was a sense that the political tide was running in ASPAC's favour, that the London consultancies and APPC members who had initially been sceptical were now on board, and that the organisation was particularly well placed to make a critical intervention into the debate on the regulation of outside interests in the Scottish Parliament.

The Membership working group set about deciding on practical issues such as at what level to set membership dues, the appropriate categories of membership, and the costs and administrative demands of setting up and running a membership organisation. The steering committee initially recommended four categories of membership with a sliding scale of fees (corporate, £200; small business, £100; quangos, £75; and voluntary/not for profit, £50). The Membership working group rejected this proposal on the grounds that defining each category might prove too difficult, and potential members might not like the category of membership assigned to them. The group finally distinguished between corporate and individual members, which was found to be a flexible and convenient solution, especially for individuals in the public sector whose employers might have reservations about formal links with lobbyists. This distinction was pragmatic, as ASPA sought to maximise its membership and make it as easy as possible for potential members to join. To this end, the association adopted a flat membership levy of £50. The Membership group asked all attendees at the first meeting in February to contribute £50 toward the start-up costs of the association. The creation and maintenance of a database of potential members was agreed, to provide a target audience for any marketing plan.

The Constitution working group, chaired by Alan Boyd, was charged by the steering committee with producing a constitution for the association which would include (among other things) a name for the body, a logo, mechanisms for electing office bearers and a management committee, and a register of members and their clients. As yet, ASPA has to create any such register, and has no plans to do so. The working group was asked to finalise the draft code of conduct which had been tabled at the meeting on 1 June 1998, after feedback from the political parties, the CSG, and Henry McLeish.

It was decided that the name of the association should be the Association for Scottish Public Affairs (ASPA). The objects of the association were quickly established, although a debate emerged over a clause stating that the association would 'establish and keep under review a code of conduct governing members of the association and their staff'. The proposal to make the code apply to corporate entities rather than individuals was hotly disputed. This row re-emerged during the 'Lobbygate' controversy in 1999.

Angela Casey suggested that professional lobbyists would have liked to see the above clause amended to 'governing the lobbying activities of members' but recognised that the voluntary sector would have problems with this. Alan Boyd echoed this concern by indicating that McGrigor Donald tried to avoid using the term 'lobbying'. These semantic sensitivities were to be fully elaborated in the debate on the wording of ASPA's code of conduct. In the end, the group settled on the formulation 'governing the briefing or lobbying activities of members' which seemed to meet the diverse concerns satisfactorily. The main difficulty in drafting the remaining articles of association for ASPA also derived from the difficulty of finding legally-binding wording that could incorporate both business and voluntary-sector interests. The constitution is therefore the product of a largely consensual drafting by those involved. The process was steered by the chair, Alan Boyd, who produced the initial draft, whose legal background informed the working group's deliberations, and whose opinion tended to be respected and deferred to.

The Constitution working group was concerned how the code might be received by politicians and officials and whether it would have any status, given a reported Scottish Office consultation on self-regulating professions. ASPA hoped to utilise Alan Boyd's contacts in the Law Society of Scotland to obtain a 'steer' on current official thinking. It was also widely held that the code as it stood (and still stands) would need considerable refinement in order to operate as a self-regulating instrument. The Constitution working group resolved to exercise extreme caution in their dealings with politicians and civil servants, recognising that it could be counterproductive to seek a definitive policy statement on the regulation of lobbyists from the Scottish Office. It was known that civil servants were particularly sensitive to briefings of their ministers by outside interests. Thus, any contacts with McLeish and his advisers regarding ASPA's code were clearly communicated as provisional. The task of transmitting ASPA's message fell to the Government/Media Relations working group.

Maureen Smith chaired this group. A pressing job was to prepare a submission to the CSG, wherein ASPA would describe its work to date, indicate the probability of the association being formally launched in the near future, and suggest that further contacts might be appropriate. It is likely that this submission did have some impact, as in the CSG's report the formation of ASPA was noted and welcomed. This group also had to execute ASPA's 'twin-track' strategy of promoting the association among the political classes in Scotland. This strategy had three basic goals: to raise awareness of ASPA; to elicit written support for the association from those contacted; and to have ASPA's code of conduct reflected in the respective political parties' manifestos for the Scottish Parliament.

While the steering group sought to arrange a meeting with Henry McLeish, the Government/Media Relations working group began to make overtures to the four main political parties. Individuals who were also party members approached their parties on behalf of ASPA. Councillor Moyra Forrest acted as the intermediary between ASPA and the Scottish Liberal Democrats. Subsequently, Jim Wallace indicated that he was keen to be kept abreast of developments and according, to ASPA minutes, 'become involved'. Stephen Young volunteered to follow up on the Conservatives' reply to ASPA's initial letter. Young felt that ASPA had a good chance of feeding into some of the 'postmortem' internal policy reviews that were underway at the time, following the loss of all the Tories' seats in Scotland at the 1997 general election. Maureen Smith wrote to the general secretary of the Scottish Labour Party, Alex Rowley, seeking a meeting. This formal approach built upon some obvious links between ASPA and the Labour Party. Mike Watson's position as a working peer and leading light in ASPA probably ensured that the association's objectives would be well understood within that party. Watson himself took the lead in approaching the SNP, whose hostility to the idea of commercial lobbying in Edinburgh was a matter of public record. The outcome of the dialogue between ASPA and Mike Russell of the SNP was equivocal. While Russell declined to endorse ASPA publicly, in private he welcomed the work they had done and offered to comment on the code of conduct. In turn, Mike Watson acknowledged that the SNP had made all the political running on this issue in Scotland. It seems little was achieved at this rather polite meeting, yet the ASPA delegation were satisfied that it had been good PR for the organisation to meet the SNP directly and present their case.

The Government/Media Relations group was also responsible for handling the public profile of the association. Initially, this function was to be reactive. In the wake of the acrimony caused by Struan Stevenson's article in *The Herald*, it was felt that the best course of action in the short term was to avoid publicity. However, the group prepared for the possibility of media interest in ASPA's activities, especially in relation to their submission to the CSG. A holding statement was drawn up which set out broad aims and objectives. Thereafter the group focused on preparations for ASPA's official launch, due to take place at the end of August. At the time, this was simply thought to involve drafting a press release for the news media and specialist trade publications. As it transpired, the eruption of the 'cash-for-access' scandal at Westminster (or 'Drapergate' as it also became known) meant that ASPA's media relations function took on added significance.

The fall-out from the 'cash-for-access' scandal at Westminster reached north of the border. Media exposure of yet more political sleaze made it clear that the election of New Labour had not brought about an era of 'new lobbying'. From ASPA's perspective, the timing could hardly have been worse. Although the association had publicly and repeatedly distanced itself from Westminster practice, the 'Drapergate' affair prompted the Scottish media to take a closer look at how the lobbying industry was developing in Scotland. Dave King of the *Daily Record* became a *bête noire* for some ASPA members. King's front-page splash 'Jobs for the same boys' and 'Lobbying their way to power' (King 1998a: 1; 1998b: 6–7) were seen as jeopardising ASPA's 'twin-track' strategy. This publicity provoked a variety of reactions from ASPA members. For some it was simply a fuss that would blow over if they held their nerve. For others, however, the attention of the press in general, and the *Daily Record* in particular, represented a direct threat to their livelihoods and some of their remarks (both formal and informal) evinced a deep sense of persecution. Notwithstanding this uneven distribution of paranoia within ASPA, all were aware that were the *Daily Record* to campaign on this issue, the climate of opinion, particularly among Labour politicians, might rapidly swing in favour of some form of statutory regulation of commercial lobbying in Edinburgh.

Media coverage of the Scottish lobbying industry focused on the number of lobbyists who were prospective parliamentary candidates for Holyrood. Jack McConnell and Mike Watson were the most high-profile of those identified. Struan Stevenson, Michael Kelly, and Charles Brodie, now director of Holyrood Strategy, were also profiled. For ASPA, Watson's position was potentially very damaging. The credibility of ASPA's claims to be establishing a new style of public affairs would be seriously undermined were Watson to continue to act as a lobbying consultant, a working peer, and Holyrood candidate. Watson's important role as a catalyst for the creation of ASPA made this matter particularly delicate. Alan Boyd remarked at one of the working group meetings that he would have no part to play in ASPA if Watson did not resolve the matter before the official launch of the association. A consensus formed that some sort of face-saving public statement should be released, even if behind the scenes Watson might have to be 'invited to stand down', should he not do so voluntarily. For whatever reason, Watson did scale down his involvement in ASPA and declared that he would retire as a lobbyist upon selection as a Labour candidate for the Scottish Parliament.

ASPA adjusted its communication strategy. Bill Anderson had been asked by *The Scotsman* to write an article on lobbying. Originally this was to appear in the business pages and was intended to highlight ASPA's membership drive in advance of the formal launch in August. 'Drapergate' transformed this column from a business to a political story. For Anderson the article would afford ASPA a chance to tell 'our story' and counter the recent spate of negative coverage. The theme of the piece was to be that Scottish lobbying would be different and its objective was to encourage McLeish to record publicly his preference for self-regulation for and by lobbyists in Scotland. Prior to publication, the article was to be circulated to all ASPA's working groups for comments and to ensure that everybody was 'on message'. It was decided that Anderson should not mention his role in the formation of ASPA in the column. In addition, the working group decided to follow up the article with a series of letters supporting the aims and objectives of ASPA. After all this preparation, the piece was never published by *The Scotsman*.

There emerged some concern that ASPA was being driven by events beyond its control. Prior to 'Drapergate' the APPC, PRCA and IPR had instigated reviews of their respective codes. The president of the IPR, Peter Walker, had visited Edinburgh in May 1998 to advocate to the CSG and to the Scottish IPR's AGM, a system of regulating lobbyists akin to that operating in Brussels. Walker was concerned that:

> Consideration has gone into right of access to the new assemblies for the media and politicians, but not lobbyists. The opportunity is there for transparency and sanctions along the lines of the model so successfully operated in the European Union. Individual parliaments should adopt some form of common framework.
> (Barker 1998: 2)

While much of what Walker proposed was adopted by ASPA, his message was not well received by several IPR members in Scotland. Repeated references to the new 'assembly' (rather than Parliament) and misnomers like

'Hamish' McLeish doubtless did little to counter the perception of metropolitan distance from Scottish affairs.

The differences between ASPA and both the PRCA and APPC were more fundamental. While both the APPC and the PRCA insisted that affiliated consultancies could not employ Members of the European, Westminster, and Scottish Parliaments (nor indeed the Welsh and subsequently Northern Irish Assemblies) ASPA were simply proposing a bar on members employing or contracting MSPs and their staff. Although ASPA's code was (and is) a matter for its own members to decide, and thereby within its control, the association was clearly sensitive to the actions of rivals such as the PRCA and APPC. Stephen Young claimed at a Government/Media Relations working group meeting post 'Drapergate' that the London-based trade associations were busy discrediting ASPA. He suggested that ASPA must be seen as the 'responsible members of the industry'.

The Government/Media Relations working group's consideration of ASPA's draft code of conduct paralleled discussion in the Constitution group. All agreed that members must declare the interests they were representing, although the declaration of party-political affiliations, particularly where a member was an office-holder in a political party, was a disputed point. In light of criticism from London-based associations, it was accepted that ASPA's code would have to be at least as stringent as those operated by rival organisations. There were divergent opinions as to how the code might be policed. Bill Anderson suggested that ASPA create a register of members' interests so that it could self-regulate. This suggestion met with almost unanimous opposition. Hamish MacPherson was particularly concerned that any such register might be abused by members who could use it for political intelligence. These points were communicated to the Constitution group to consider as they finalised the code of conduct in the run-up to ASPA's public launch.

The ASPA code of conduct borrows heavily from the Rules of Procedure of the European Parliament (and, to a lesser extent, the IPR code). The similarities between the respective codes lent credence to ASPA's claim that it had produced a code that would be 'recognised throughout Europe'. The code underwent significant redrafting by both the steering and discussion groups before its final adoption. Notwithstanding the reservations of APPC representatives like Robbie MacDuff, the editing and revision of the code was a largely consensual process. Some possible amendments to the code were to be raised in a meeting with Henry McLeish's officials to get an indication of how the Parliament might want to regulate such activities. There was a notable lack of consensus over whether the code should apply simply to its signatories or whether it should be corporate in nature, covering all staff of affiliated companies.

A telling change between the initial code submitted by the steering group, and the final code agreed by the discussion group, was the disappearance of the word 'lobbyist' from the text. The connotations of the word 'lobbyist' in the wake of the series of political sleaze scandals had made its use undesirable in Westminster, and practically anathema in Edinburgh in 1998. The change in the ASPA code from 'lobbyist' to the preferred term 'members of the Association' was more than mere semantics.

An innocent arriving in Edinburgh might be forgiven for thinking that there are no lobbyists active in political affairs in Scotland. Commercial lobbyists reject this label in favour of euphemisms such as 'public affairs consultant', 'government relations adviser', 'public policy analyst', 'political consultant', 'political strategist', or indeed almost any other combination of terms within this lexicon. Lobbyists have made serious efforts to disassociate themselves from the negative connotations of sleaze synonymous with the term lobbyist since the 'cash-for-questions' affair in Westminster. This has been particularly important in the newly-devolved Scottish polity, where the rationale for devolution was often premised on a new politics explicitly defined against Westminster practice. Nevertheless, in our experience, once a ritual denial of lobbying has been issued, it is commonplace for lobbyists to describe themselves as such, and to talk of their professional practice as lobbying.

These sensitivities were keenly felt among many potential ASPA members. In a meeting of the Government/Media Relations working group (ASPA minutes, June 1998), Maureen Smith of the Scottish Tourist Board said that as a quango, her organisation would have 'difficulty in publicly owning the word "lobbyist"'. This sentiment was echoed by another public-sector representative, Susan Gavaghan of the Scottish Arts Council. These concerns actually preceded the 'cash-for-access' affair and the subsequent media interest in Scottish lobbying. Similar anxieties surfaced in the Membership working group where membership status became an issue. Some potential members (from both the public and private sectors) were unsure that their employers would want to associate formally with any lobbying trade organisation. In the best spirit of inclusivity, ASPA offered those whose employers might have reservations about the association the opportunity to join as individual members, rather than having to negotiate corporate membership with their organisation. This arrangement is still in place.

These concerns were particularly acute in the voluntary sector. The participation of the Scottish 'third sector' in ASPA was seen as integral to positioning the organisation in Scottish public life. One of the most potent arguments deployed was that ASPA would be an inclusive and representative organisation. So the involvement of the voluntary sector was felt to be very important. Kate Higgins of the Association of Nationalist Councillors suggested that ASPA should 'play the game and let voluntary sector groups act as the spokesperson[s]'. Moreover, as Kate Caskie of Shelter Scotland pointed out, 'MPs have a door open at all times to the voluntary sector, therefore an association which includes both the private and public sector may increase the credibility of the private sector.' The benefits to the private sector were perhaps more visible than those that might accrue to the voluntary sector. As a consultant for PS Public Affairs, and leading ASPA member at the time remarked to us, the rationale for courting the voluntary sector was straightforward and crude: 'They have the good reputation; we have the money.'

However, other observers were less than convinced that the interests of the voluntary sector and commercial lobbyists could be reconciled and moulded into a functioning formal relationship. Jane Saren from GPC Scotland observed:

> I was a little bit unsure of the basis of that [first ASPA meeting] because what they seemed to be arguing for was some sort of body that would bring together everybody who might want to lobby the Parliament, and I'm not sure that I think that makes sense . . . I think that the challenge is actually trying to get public affairs consultancy recognised as a profession with a code of conduct, and I don't think that it's helpful to try and cast the net as wide as that.

These concerns resonated with many working in the Scottish voluntary sector. As Philippa Jones, the SCVO's parliamentary officer, recalled:

> We were approached by ASPA when it first started up to be on their working party, and we refused because we felt that what we did was so different from them. In an ideal world, we'd really not want them to exist because we would want every person in every organisation to be able to make their own points in their own way to government and the Parliament.

This line of argument is in keeping with the recommendations of the CSG regarding outside interests and access to the political system. A more trenchant variant was expressed by another third force parliamentary officer who distinguished between the voluntary and private sectors, the latter representing commercial lobbyists, or 'hired guns':

> There is a huge difference between what the voluntary sector does in terms of "lobbying" and what the private sector does, in that the key objection is that if you're a private sector lobbyist you'll work one day for the arms trade and the next day for the environment. Whereas we've got ethics about what we do and I think that was the key issue – that these are sort of bad people generally who are unethical and who we shouldn't be associated with . . . There was a feeling that a voluntary sector organisation going and getting involved in ASPA would give more benefit to ASPA than it would to voluntary sector organisations.

Despite such reservations, ASPA remained keen to project itself as an inclusive, representative, and legitimate body. ASPA's code was to be its 'charter mark' of quality assurance and the centrepiece of its claim for recognition in Scottish public life. The presentation problems faced by ASPA at the time were not insignificant. The Government/Media Relations working group anticipated considerable scrutiny from the media at ASPA's formal launch and and planned the event accordingly. There was to be a formal meeting to ratify ASPA's code of conduct and constitution, update members on the activities of the steering and working groups since February, and nominate office-bearers. Thereafter, a press conference would be held. The first issue faced was whether to invite the media to the formal meeting. The group agreed that it would be counterproductive to try and bar the media and decided to err on the side of caution by opting not to invite journalists, but admitting any that turned up. Since none knew about it, none did.

Planning for the press conference betrayed ASPA's fears regarding the sleazy image of lobbying. Members expected to field questions on cronyism and 'Drapergate'. During discussions, Bill Anderson candidly admitted that most lobbying he had ever done was based on personal contacts and networking. Similarly, Hamish McPherson insisted that the cash aspect of 'Drapergate' was fundamental to the scandal, but that the use of contacts per se was not problematic. He drew a parallel with journalism which is also based on contacts and the cultivation of sources, but recognised that it might be unhelpful to air this opinion at the press conference.

The group decided to approach Alan Boyd to see if he would be prepared to act as spokesperson. He was seen as the ideal candidate for several reasons: he was seen as non-political; he had been instrumental in designing the code of conduct and was a legal expert; and, as a past President of the Law Society of Scotland, he could speak authoritively as a leading member of a self-regulating profession. Other factors also suggested that Boyd should front the press conference. In their discussions, the working group admitted that thus far they had been too willing to defer to PS Public Affairs. The ripples from Struan Stevenson's column in *The Herald* a few months earlier had not subsided and it was agreed that he should play no role in ASPA's media relations in future. Moreover, in the wake of recent publicity, PS Public Affairs had indicated that they wished to take a lower profile in ASPA. Boyd became the obvious choice as spokesperson. The final detail in planning the press conference was to ensure that ASPA members were in the 'body of the kirk' to ask helpful questions, counter potential hecklers and, if need be, brief the press afterwards.

BECOMING A PUBLIC AFFAIR: THE LAUNCH OF ASPA

On 31 August 1998, the Association for Scottish Public Affairs was formally launched at the COSLA offices at Rosebery House in Edinburgh. Mike Watson introduced the agenda for the meeting by claiming that the work ASPA had done behind the scenes during the previous six months had demonstrated the need for such an association to come into being.

The first item on the agenda was the presentation of ASPA's constitution and code of conduct by Alan Boyd, chair of the Constitution working group. Boyd stressed two important features of how he envisaged ASPA's self-regulatory regime might work in practice. First, that the code would evolve as the Scottish Parliament evolved. ASPA had received guidance from John Ewing of the CSG, who had been non-committal in his meeting with ASPA's steering committee on 19 August. Ewing indicated that the civil service had taken the view that the regulation of outside interests was a matter for the Parliament to lead on, but that the existence of an organisation such as ASPA might well be of value if and when the Parliament were to consider the issue. The second point Boyd emphasised was that the power of ASPA's code lay in its active enforcement: the ongoing policing of members' conduct had to be an intrinsic part of self-regulation. Boyd claimed that central to the aims and objectives of ASPA was the training of members. As Holyrood offered Scottish lobbyists a fresh start, Boyd expressed the hope that ASPA could be instrumental in developing and disseminating best practice in public affairs.

The composition of the association's membership and ASPA's relationship with the media were again debated. Such debate was of critical importance to external perceptions of the association. This is a widespread concern, as Charles Miller, secretary of the APPC, has noted, 'It's still about looking good rather than doing good' (Garside 1998: 9). For ASPA, issues of presentation and promotion were perhaps more pronounced given the various shifts in political culture and communication in Scotland that devolution was provoking (Schlesinger 1998). Many interventions explicitly addressed this topic. Maureen Ferrier of COSLA welcomed ASPA's inclusivity and insisted, despite concern in certain quarters, that the public sector ought to maintain a presence. Maureen Smith of the Scottish Tourist Board echoed this point, and asked that the voluntary sector should be involved in some way. Opinions expressed about the Scottish media revealed a keenly-felt sense of their potential power. Dick Playfair of Playfair Walker railed at the injustice of it all, questioning why the media should have privileged access to the Parliament (a status clearly both coveted and envied). Others like Iain McConnell and Iain Yuill were exercised by the damage that more negative coverage could do to the nascent lobbying industry in Edinburgh. However, this animosity toward the press in particular was tempered by the realisation that they were an integral part of the Scottish political landscape, and also by the often unremarked fact that some lobbyists were themselves freelance journalists. Furthermore, several of those present, who came from a public relations rather than lobbying background, were also closely connected to media networks in their professional and private lives.

The media coverage of the launch of ASPA was muted, despite the expressed forebodings. *The Herald* was one of the few papers to report the launch (Dinwoodie 1998c: 6), emphasising the spectrum of professional interests represented, and quoting Alan Boyd, ASPA's new convenor, as saying that the association's 'conduct would match the aspirations of the new Parliament'. The report did note the possibility that voluntary organisations were being used by commercial lobbyists to gain acceptance. Denis Sullivan insisted that this was not the intention, although he did disingenuously assert that with such an association 'it's difficult to have a clique if there are a thousand people'. In reality, ASPA had begun with just over 100 interested parties in February 1998 (of which fewer than fifty actually attended in person). By the launch of the association fewer than fifty individuals were actively participating, more clique-like than not.

The official adoption of ASPA's code and constitution were matters for the association's inaugural general meeting, on 2 December 1998. Fewer than thirty individuals turned up. Robbie MacDuff voiced his reservations regarding the scope of the proposed code. These concerns centred on its limitations when compared to the redrafted (post-Drapergate) APPC code. MacDuff was particularly anxious that ASPA was only going to regulate members' contacts with MSPs, and not consider relationships with MPs, peers, MEPs, and indeed members of the devolved assemblies in Wales and Northern Ireland as declarable political interests. Alan Boyd defended the code, arguing that while some of ASPA's professional members would have interests beyond Holyrood, it was not ASPA's job to involve inself in these areas. He drew a parallel with the European Parliament's code, which also does not place restrictions on business relations with members of other parliaments. Julia Clarke of Holyrood Strategy supported Boyd and defended the right of Lord Fraser, a director of her company, to lobby at Holyrood. Boyd reminded those present that ASPA's committee reserved the right to alter the code during the first year. This flexibility was seen as a pragmatic response to the uncertainties of devolved politics.

The comparison with the European Parliament merits closer scrutiny, especially as it seems to serve as the template for the kind of regulation that ASPA favours. This model was also commended by the IPR for its simplicity, 'transparency and sanctions' (Barker 1998: 2). But the vital missing link in ASPA's model for self-regulation is the absence of any official sanction. Whereas breaches of the European Parliament's code (European Parliament 1999) can result in the withdrawal of parliamentary passes, no such provision is enforceable by ASPA. Furthermore, the European Parliament maintains a register of interests of all those issued with a pass, which is available for public scrutiny (although only in person in the European Parliament offices). ASPA decided that it would not create such a register of its own, and its self-regulatory armour is simply the power to 'name and shame' those who breach its code. Whether this is a credible deterrent is a question to which we shall return.

THE LAUNCH OF ASPA

With ASPA's office-bearers (Boyd as convenor, Denis Sullivan as treasurer, and Kirsty Regan as secretary) and its committee now in place, the association was positioned to participate formally in Scottish public life. Alan Boyd was particularly eager to challenge the CSG's Canon Kenyon Wright over his public support for the statutory regulation of outside interests. The media had not been informed about the inaugural general meeting, as it was seen as a purely routine internal matter, and not particularly newsworthy. It was felt that the official launch had gone well and that ASPA could now concentrate on promoting itself through specialist publications such as *PR Week*, *Public Affairs Newsletter*, and a new Stationery Office publication dealing specifically with devolution, *Scotland Forum*. The decision to avoid publicity was understandable given the negative media coverage of lobbying (and ASPA in particular) during 1998, and concerns expressed by members of the Government/Media Relations working group. However, the year ahead would bring an unprecedented level of media interest in the Scottish lobbying industry that simply could not be avoided by any group claiming to be the 'recognised voice' of Scottish public affairs.

NOTES

1. Maria Laptev, speaking at the Scottish Council Foundation 'Corporate Citizenship' seminar, Edinburgh, 2 June 1998.

CHAPTER 12

Lobbygate

I know the Secretary of State very well because he's my father.

THE STING

When Kevin Reid uttered these words in the Balmoral Hotel, Edinburgh, on 31 August 1999, little could he have known the chain of events he would set in train. As a lobbyist for the PR firm Beattie Media, Reid believed that he was involved in a sales pitch to a potential US client. In fact, he was the subject of an undercover investigation by *The Observer* examining links between the lobbying industry in Scotland and the new Parliament and Executive. When the story was published almost a month later, it was quickly dubbed 'Lobbygate' and became one of the most serious crises to face the Scottish Parliament in its first six months. The story of Lobbygate reveals facets of the nature of public life and power in contemporary Scotland and was a defining moment, illustrating the commercialisation of politics in the newly-devolved polity.

Public Affairs Europe was a joint venture in the lobbying business between the PR consultancy Beattie Media and the law firm Maclay, Murray and Spens. Jack McConnell, the former general secretary of the Scottish Labour party, was appointed to establish the company in April 1998. Some questioned the wisdom of McConnell's appointment. One lobbyist argued that such a high-profile public figure would inevitably have political enemies and therefore run the risk of alienating half of those lobbied before even beginning to state a case. There was also a second point:

I can understand that in Scotland, which is a very small network, it potentially could be seen as very clever really because it is trading ... on the old-boy network [in which] it doesn't matter ... what quality of service you are providing, it is all about the people you know. And that of course goes back to the bad old days of Westminster.

LOBBYGATE: MAKING CONNECTIONS

On 26 September 1999, *The Observer* published excerpts from its undercover 'sting'. Ben Laurance, a reporter from the paper's business desk in London, had posed as a representative of fictitious US venture capitalists interested in Private Finance Initiative (PFI) investment opportunities in Scotland. Kevin Reid and Alex Barr of Beattie Media met Laurance to sell their lobbying and political-intelligence expertise. Reid and Barr were asked about their contacts with politicians and what differentiated Beattie Media from the competition. Barr mentioned that his former colleague Jack McConnell was now Minister of Finance in the Scottish Executive. He also pointed out that Beattie Media did 'a lot of [PR] work with the public sector, and with large corporate organisations and we are constantly involving politicians in launches, exhibitions, speeches, presentations, that type of thing,' (*The Observer* transcript, 1999: 3). Barr stressed Beattie Media's links to the business community in Scotland:

> We're in contact on a very regular basis, not only with politicians and the Scottish Office, but also with business journalists, industry journalists, and movers and shakers within local authorities and local enterprise companies . . . So we've got our finger on the pulse of what's happening in business and in construction.
> (*The Observer* transcript 1999: 6)

According to *The Observer*'s transcript, Kevin Reid talked of his own personal contacts in the following terms:

> Three or four of [the Scottish Executive's] special advisers are close personal friends of mine . . . I worked for Jack [McConnell] and for Wendy [Alexander] and for Henry [McLeish] and for Donald [Dewar] on a one-to-one basis [in] the Labour Party media monitoring [team] . . . I know the Secretary of State very well because he's my father, so I know him . . . But I'm not going to promise you access to people because of who I am and who I know. *Certainly as you know, in the business of politics, you have a relationship, it makes things easier.*
> (*The Observer* transcript 1999: 6; emphasis added)

That such access and contacts remain vital to the practice of lobbying goes to the heart of much present-day concern about probity in public life. During our fieldwork, one lobbyist, speaking from experience of both Westminster and Edinburgh before Lobbygate, said that lobbyists trading in access were undermining the industry, while simultaneously conceding that when a potential client wanted to know your connections, it was difficult to refuse to give these:

Of course, one does say, well, you know, over the years I have got to know so-and-so rather well. But I think if you can balance this, perhaps keep the list limited, and balance the small list with those who have got absolutely no interest whatsoever in the particular concern of that client. Then it is about as fair and just, perhaps, to your own sense of not abusing the system as one can be. The media have lost sight of the fact that . . . the check list . . . is driven by the client asking for a display of your credibility.

Although it is tempting to think – much as the CSG did – that the openness and accessibility of the Scottish Parliament would obviate the need for contacts-based lobbying in Scotland, the evidence suggests that this hope has been misplaced.

The Observer's exposé raised questions about Scotland's government and the conduct of lobbying. Ministers in the Scottish Executive were faced with a political sleaze scandal only weeks after the devolution of power from Westminster. The accusations concerned one subset of contacts within the multiple networks that characterise Scottish public life. The implication was that such contacts were corruptible, if not already corrupt. Beattie Media's consultants claimed that they could use ministers Sam Galbraith, Henry McLeish, Jackie Baillie and Jack McConnell to 'make things easier' for their clients. They also maintained that Lord Macdonald, the UK transport minister, had been 'very, very useful' to them.

The allegations about Jack McConnell became the most contentious matter. It was well known that McConnell had professional and personal contacts with Beattie Media dating back to his employment there as a lobbyist. Indeed, his constituency secretary, Christina Marshall, previously worked with both McConnell and Barr at Beattie Media. Marshall was the conduit through which Barr claimed he had been able to influence McConnell's diary and gain preferential access for a client. In one of the more candid and damaging passages in *The Observer*'s evidence, Alex Barr remarked:

We appointed Jack McConnell . . . to head up our public affairs consultancy, in the certain knowledge that Jack would get a safe seat from the Labour Party, and in the hope and expectation that he would also get a Cabinet position within the new administration. So we knew that Jack was going to leave us.
(*The Observer* transcript 1999: 2)

These claims were subjected to considerable scrutiny, but even at face value, they immediately revealed how lobbyists trade on contacts. It is certainly plausible that Beattie Media (and their partners Maclay, Murray and Spens) calculated McConnell's promotional value in their decision to purchase his services. Gordon Beattie's evidence to the Standards Committee later indicated that Public Affairs Europe had failed to attract any clients or generate any income.

The media themselves are party to many of the private networks of Scotland's elites. The instigator of *The Observer's* investigation of lobbying – Scottish political editor, Dean Nelson – played five-a-side football with, among others, Jack McConnell (Hardie and Tait 1999). As one lobbyist noted, with such professional and social proximity,

> it wasn't going to be too long before the [Scottish political] press latched on to the way in which a very small network, and people knowing each other very well over a number of years, had not separated itself off from the proper conduct of professional lobbying.

The proper conduct of public affairs had been a minor news item just before the Scottish Parliament opened for business in September 1999. The *Sunday Herald* had already run a story detailing the emerging lobbying industry in Scotland and alluding to Reid's position (Mackay and Adamson 1999). Part of that publicity was generated by Beattie Media's PR department. Gordon Beattie had written to Donald Dewar appealing for the regulation of lobbying at Holyrood. Alex Barr revealed the company's views:

> There are professional bodies, in inverted commas, the Scottish PRCA, which we've refused to join because we think it's a waste of time. There's also ASPA . . . ASPA have said that you can be a member if you have staff in the House of Lords, MPs – MSPs [Kevin Reid interrupts] – but we don't think that's good enough. Therefore we called for . . . regulation by the Scottish Parliament. That hasn't made us particularly popular with those consultancies which employ MPs, members of the House of Lords as you can imagine.
> (*The Observer* transcript 1999: 10)

Beattie Media's call for the statutory regulation of outside interests was seen almost universally as a publicity stunt. It drew the opprobrium of the convenor of the Scottish Parliament's Standards Committee, Mike Rumbles, who remarked:

> Where I would draw the line is where these organisations . . . suggest that we legislate on this issue to give them what is, to all intents and purpose, a rubber stamp or seal of approval. To me that is anathema. It is exactly the opposite of what we are trying to achieve in the Parliament and, of course, there are vested interests and a lot of money involved. I'm well aware my view with them will not be popular.
> (Dunn 1999: 21)

Rumbles and his colleagues on the Standards Committee had been considering the issue of lobbying as part of their efforts to devise a code of conduct for MSPs. Their deliberations were to be rudely interrupted by Lobbygate.

The Standards Committee of the Scottish Parliament had met four times prior to Lobbygate. It had three Labour members, two SNP, one Conservative, and one Liberal Democrat. At these early meetings, the media were conspicuous by their absence. After two private meetings in June, the first public meeting of the Standards Committee was on 1 September, 1999. In his opening statement, Rumbles alluded to press coverage of the issue of lobbying in Scotland. He stated that he would take great care in handling the committee's media relations and gave his support for the work undertaken by the CSG on lobbying. Thus, at a very early stage, the Nolan/CSG orthodoxy on lobbying was adopted as the default position of the Parliament. Referring to Beattie's letter to Dewar, and to reports that Aberdeen City Council were planning to hire professional lobbyists to monitor the Parliament, Rumbles conceded that events might well move faster than the committee could act. These fears were to be realised far sooner than Rumbles expected.

Item three on the agenda for 1 September was a report from the committee clerks on the initial registration of Members' interests. At this point, the media and public were asked to leave the room. As one senior civil servant at the Parliament remarked to us at the time, the move into private session and then back to public session was ill-advised in terms of public perception. During the recess, the four journalists in attendance immediately went into a huddle to discuss what was newsworthy from the proceedings so far. Apart from speculation about what might be contained in the register of Members' interests, and mild dismay at the procedures of the committee, the focus of the press quickly turned to Aberdeen City Council's proposal to hire lobbyists.[1]

When the committee reconvened in public, discussion turned to the draft code of conduct prepared by the clerks. To the public and press present, these exchanges were bemusing, given that members were referring to paragraphs and lines of text that were publicly unavailable. The proceedings took on a surreal air as Tricia Marwick (SNP, Mid-Scotland and Fife) raised objections to a passage in the draft code. The gallery had to guess that the dispute related to the affirmation or oath of allegiance made by MSPs on election. Marwick later confirmed this to the waiting press and expressed her disbelief that the gallery were effectively in the dark over the discussion and wording of the code. After the meeting closed, Mike Rumbles held the committee's first press briefing. Present were the two clerks and one of the Parliament's press officers, Eric Macleod. Only two members of the media attended. Rumbles explained that his committee's main task was to draft a code of conduct for MSPs. However, the journalists had equally practical and pressing concerns. One complained that the media had little sense of the committee's discussions in the absence of a copy of the draft code and requested formally that these texts be made available to accredited members of the media. Rumbles indicated that he wanted to be as open as possible but was concerned that drafts might not be treated as such in media reporting.

The availability of draft material was the first agenda item for the Standards Committee's meeting on 15 September. Rumbles proposed a compromise, suggesting that all present in the committee room be given copies of drafts under consideration but that these be surrendered at the end of the session. This fudge was challenged by Tricia Marwick who insisted that to withhold such documents flew in the face of the CSG's key principles of openness and accessibility. She was backed by her SNP colleague Adam Ingram and by other members who recognised that the committee should be seen to be operating at the highest possible standards. The committee decided that drafts should indeed be made available to the public, and that their status should be made explicit. Our observation of the Standards Committee's work made it clear that members were sensitive to media reporting. As one committee member revealed to us:

> I am always very conscious, not to say the right thing, but to say it in a way which can't be misrepresented, because people out there do read newspapers, they do watch television and listen to the radio, and if the Standards Committee don't get it right then there's not much hope for the rest of the Parliament.

Our observations indicated that there was no consensus on whether the committee ought to consider the regulation of outside interests. Apart from Lord James Douglas-Hamilton (Conservative, Lothians) who had previous ministerial experience, most committee members were political novices. Their collective inexperience as MSPs meant that the influence of civil servants advising the committee was important. At the initial meetings, Vanessa Glynn, clerk to the committee, was regularly called on by the convenor to explain the technical detail of the drafts under consideration and to some degree steer their public deliberations. The Members of the Standards Committee had only just begun to develop their relations with the media, the public, the civil service and, not least, each other, when they came under intense scrutiny during the Lobbygate scandal.

SPINNING LOBBYGATE

The Observer's front-page splash 'Exposed: Lobbygate comes to Scotland' on Sunday, 26 September (Nelson and Laurance 1999) signalled the start not only of a political saga, but also the beginning of an intense public-relations contest between a variety of interested actors, including the Labour Party, the Executive, the Scottish Parliament, the opposition, and of course Beattie Media. The following version of the Lobbygate story is based on the public utterances and the private views of those involved.

The speed at which Lobbygate became a news event was quite remarkable. Later editions of the Scottish Sundays carried news of *The Observer*'s scoop. By lunchtime that day, *Holyrood*, a Scottish political analysis programme broadcast on BBC2 Scotland, reported Beattie Media's claims of entrapment and deception on the part of *The Observer* and said that the First Minister was backing a full investigation by the Standards Committee. This broadcast also featured an interview with Scottish Executive minister Henry McLeish, himself implicated in the emerging scandal, but also well placed, as chairman of the CSG, to comment on the status of lobbying in Scotland. McLeish affirmed his support (and that of all his ministerial colleagues) for an inquiry into Lobbygate by the Standards Committee, insisting that in the interests of good governance 'the time is now right for a public debate on lobbying'. He added:

> After we have an inquiry by the Parliament, after we look at lobbying, yes, let's make [ministerial actions] as open as possible . . . If it has to become more publicly transparent then so be it . . . I believe that the public interest is best served by open government.

The pace of the Executive's response to the allegations became a disputed matter. McLeish's television appearance to promote the Executive's support for an inquiry into the allegations had been coordinated prior to the story's publication. The Scottish Executive had known about *The Observer*'s allegations since the previous Thursday; so too had John Reid, Secretary of State for Scotland, whose son was at the centre of the controversy. As part of the Executive's response to the allegations, a press release was issued on behalf of McLeish and Sam Galbraith, supporting Jack McConnell's call for a Parliamentary inquiry:

> That is why yesterday the Minister for Finance, with our support, immediately called for the Standards Committee of the Scottish Parliament to investigate claims made by this lobby firm, and to consider any further action required to regulate the activities of such firms.
> (Scottish Executive 1999d)

Stories of political competition – 'turf wars' – between Donald Dewar and John Reid had been running throughout the summer in the Scottish media. These were repeatedly played down by Scottish Executive and Scotland Office ministers, despite the fact that some of the same sources had planted the stories in the first place (Martin and Hill 1999). The Labour Party's centenary conference in Bournemouth, which began on the day that *The Observer* published its allegations, was to have been an opportunity for the Scottish Labour Party hierarchy to demonstrate to their members, and the wider public through the media, that devolution was working and that Edinburgh and London were cooperating to make that happen. Instead, by Sunday evening, 'turf wars' between the Dewar and Reid camps were back in the news. The dramatic combination of sleaze, political rivalry, and personal investment in the story made it uniquely newsworthy. Reports quickly emerged of a 'concerted effort' by Scottish delegates in Bournemouth to 'talk down' Lobbygate, but also to give their version of events. It was revealed that 'friends of Dr Reid' were annoyed at the speed at which it was said that there must be an inquiry, and suggested that the Executive's support for the inquiry had given the story legs (*Good Morning Scotland*, BBC Radio Scotland, 27 September 1999). Gordon Beattie had cut short a holiday abroad to return to manage his very own PR crisis. His first action was to issue a press release which included an 'unreserved public apology' to the ministers named in *The Observer*'s transcript. This apology was seized upon by Executive sources as evidence that ministers had no case to answer (Scottish Executive 1999e).

Lobbygate dominated the headlines in all the Scottish press the following day. The *Daily Record*, splashed the story of a renewed 'turf war' between Dewar and Reid. It reported that 'Senior Labour ministers were at each other's throats last night as the Scottish Parliament was engulfed by sleaze claims' (Mackenna 1999: 1). Dewar and Reid were said to have had 'at least one major bust up yesterday' and that Dewar had pulled back from ordering a full-scale government probe into the affair after pressure from 'senior Labour figures . . . The extraordinary row spilled into the open as Reid's deputy Brian Wilson rubbished the allegations while . . . Henry McLeish contradicted him and said they were extremely serious' (Mackenna 1999: 4). The *Record* backed a full public inquiry into the allegations and, in an editorial, demanded that 'lobbyists must be banned. And even the smell of sleaze must be cleared by public scrutiny.'

In his opinion column, Tom Brown offered the readership an uncompromising view of the place of lobbying in Scottish public life: 'Lobbyists, fixers, go-betweens and influence peddlars are parasites who infect the body politic. They are the scavengers of the corridors of power. They are the pimps who seek to prostitute politics' (Brown 1999: 6). Brown also questioned the probity of the political and commercial networks centred on Beattie Media, and mentioned how these had been the subject of 'caustic comment' by political insiders for some time.

As the political row escalated, both Dewar and Reid appeared on *Good Morning Scotland* on 27 September, BBC Radio Scotland's political 'agenda-setting' news programme, to give their versions of events. Relations between the pair were said to be at an all-time low. Reid defended his son Kevin's personal and professional integrity, claiming he was the victim of 'squalid and contemptible journalism' and subject to 'consistent harassment' on the part of the media. Dewar insisted that the affair must 'quite clearly' go before the

Standards Committee. Pressed on whether he favoured a full investigation of Beattie Media, Dewar indicated a significant shift in the Executive's position:

> No, what I want is a thorough and detailed consideration of the best way of moving forward to try and ensure that there is proper regulation of lobbying in this Parliament. It is not a case of looking into these allegations centrally because we have already had an unreserved apology from the company.

Sources in the Scottish Parliament told us that the Executive had initially been 'hammering' the Parliament to investigate Lobbygate. Opposition spokesmen wanted a different kind of inquiry from Dewar, with the SNP pushing for ministerial diaries to be opened to public scrutiny. Both Tories and the SNP were concerned that the Scottish Parliament's reputation might be tainted as a result of links between the Executive's ministers and lobbying companies. The lobbying fraternity were equally concerned by potential fall-out from the affair, with an ASPA spokesperson quoted as saying that such stories reflected badly on the industry as a whole, and that Beattie Media should be suspended from the precincts of the Scottish Parliament pending a full investigation.

Later, further details became public. On BBC Radio Scotland, Dean Nelson revealed that his paper's investigation had been prompted by a senior Scottish Labour Party source, 'appalled' at the flood of job offers from lobbying consultancies 'who wanted him to basically call in all the favours he was owed on their behalf'.

Revelations that Mike Rumbles also had prior knowledge of *The Observer* story fixed the media's focus firmly on the next meeting of the Standards Committee, set for Wednesday, 29 September. BBC Radio Scotland reported that the Parliament faced the 'thorny issue' of calling ministers before the Standards Committee to give evidence. Rumbles was quoted as saying that he wanted the inquiry to focus on MSPs, and that to ban lobbying from the Scottish Parliament was impracticable.

By 28 September, *The Scotsman* was reporting 'Victory for Dewar in turf war over sleaze' (Carrell et al. 1999: 1) and praised the First Minister in an editorial for pursuing the 'noble principle' that the sleaze allegations must be investigated. Lorraine Davidson, political editor of the *Scottish Mirror*, and a recent director of media relations for the Scottish Labour Party, reported that Dewar and Reid had been involved in two separate rows in public during a reception at the Labour Party conference (*Good Morning Scotland*, 28 September 1999). Indeed, it became known that Downing Street had intervened to quash the row, and that Anji Hunter, the Prime Minister's personal assistant, had been seen remonstrating with Dr Reid in a hotel foyer (Macleod 1999: 1). Fiona Ross described the events in Bournemouth as an 'unedifying public spectacle' and blamed 'the two camps of advisers and so-called friends' for over-reacting to the revelations (*Platform*, Scottish Television, 30 September 1999).

Interest in the fifth meeting of the Standards Committee on Wednesday, 29 September 1999 was intense. The gallery in Committee Room 1 of the Parliament was full. Extra parliamentary staff were in attendance, including the chief executive of the Parliament, Paul Grice; the head of the Scottish Parliament's Information Centre (SPICe), Barry Winetrobe; and senior parliamentary lawyers. One of the Parliament's most senior clerks, Bill Thompson, was drafted onto the committee's support team. Convenor Mike Rumbles made a statement in which he indicated that as he had not received a formal complaint, he was unwilling to discuss the substance of *The Observer*'s story. When this position was challenged by SNP members, the committee moved into private session. The gathered press pack were evidently incredulous at this turn of events. Dean Nelson briefed the media on *The Observer*'s view of how the matter should proceed and rebutted Labour member Des McNulty's attack on the methods used to obtain the story. McNulty later publicly retracted his criticism of *The Observer* (Laurance 1999).

Meanwhile the Standards Committee was in the throes of a crisis behind closed doors. SNP members feared that the Labour Party was trying to block the very inquiry publicly called for over the weekend, and threatened to force a public vote. Labour members wanted time to weigh the evidence provided by *The Observer*. As a member of the committee remarked to us:

> We went to the brink that day . . . We looked over and stepped back . . . Genuinely, we were at the point of the whole thing breaking down. Because it was very new and we'd been through a very tough election for a few months where we were at each other's throats all the time, and this was an issue where . . . I think parties saw an opportunity to make political capital. It would be wrong of people not to think that, but I think that the members of the committee very quickly realised that if the committee was to have any integrity then we couldn't go down that road.

The committee reached a compromise: to go away and think about the terms of reference for an inquiry in the light of evidence received that morning. While recognising that this course of action would be seen as another public relations disaster for the Parliament by the waiting media, one committee member insisted that, 'if we hadn't got to that position, on that day, that committee and that investigation would never have worked'.

When Rumbles announced the committee's decision to meet again in private session on 5 October to consider the terms of reference of an investigation, the media's reaction was even more severe and testing than members expected. Both main televised evening news programmes (*Reporting Scotland*, BBC; *Scotland Today*, Scottish TV) reported a 'day of confusion' at the Scottish Parliament, referring not only to the Standards Committee, but also to news that, after a fractious plenary session, Donald Dewar had announced that he would make a statement to the House the next day. The popular press singled out Rumbles as the culprit, for failing to inform Dewar when he first learned of *The Observer's* story, and for bungling and foot-dragging over the investigation of the allegations (King 1999). *The Scotsman's* reaction was to raise a petition against the Scottish Parliament to force the Standards Committee (and by precedent all other committees) to sit in public. The legal challenge to the Parliament exacerbated an already critical situation, but also demonstrated how the media were becoming ever more deeply embedded in this affair.

For senior staff at the Scottish Parliament, *The Scotsman's* appeal for judicial review could not have come at a worse time. Legal resources were already stretched in coping with the prospect of a public inquiry. A senior civil servant told us how *The Scotsman's* action was viewed:

> It's an attack, and I use the word very deliberately . . . To use a cliché, it's a free country and *The Scotsman* must be free to do what they want to do . . . It's just frankly, in my judgement, a hugely unnecessary and expensive distraction. I don't see what they are going to achieve, other than taking up a good deal of my time [and that of] senior lawyers here. We're having to hire expensive counsel . . . So we will have wasted tens of thousands of pounds of public money.

For the MSPs involved, the legal action was equally disdained. As one asked: 'Who on earth are *The Scotsman* to try to determine what would and what would not happen? It was more about boosting *The Scotsman's* circulation than any regard for the Parliament.' Both parliamentarians and civil servants involved insisted to us that they had every intention of holding their inquiry in public from the outset.

The First Minister's address to the Parliament on Thursday, 30 September, became the source of yet more controversy and spin. Dewar reiterated his confidence in the probity of his ministerial team, and again referred to Beattie Media's apology as 'allowing us to draw a line under this particular part of a very unfortunate business'. Furthermore, he intimated that the Standards Committee ought to now take its work forward by concentrating on finalising a code of conduct for MSPs and considering the general regulation of contacts with outside interests (Scottish Parliament 1999). In the furore that followed Dewar's personal absolution of his ministers, a significant facet of Lobbygate was largely overlooked. Seeking to reassure the public that *The Observer's* claims were baseless, Dewar announced:

> In the light of these events, I have asked my officials to investigate the use of public relations and professional lobbying organisations by all the Scottish

public bodies for which we have responsibility. I want to know the full details of the contacts and contracts involved, and I will want to ensure that there can be no question of any impropriety, conflict of interest or any other grounds for public concern.

The formulation was significant. The First Minister was careful to frame the inquiry to satisfy himself, not Parliament. The official secrecy surrounding this inquiry was to become a recurrent feature of the Executive's response to charges of cronyism. The Executive placed great emphasis on Dewar's personal integrity as a guarantor of probity. David Whitton, the First Minister's official spokesman, suggested to the media that there was now no need for a specific inquiry, claiming, 'I think that the First Minister's word would be good enough for most people in Scotland' (Tait 1999e: 1).[2]

The political reaction to Dewar's revision of the Executive's stance of the previous weekend drew hefty criticism. The *Daily Record* branded his statement a 'whitewash' (Alba 1999). The SNP accused Dewar of a U-turn and then of a cover-up after an early draft of Dewar's statement was leaked to *The Scotsman*. The discrepancies between the leaked and official versions indicate Dewar watered down his rebuttal of *The Observer* story, and that his claim to have learned of the allegations on Friday, 24 September had initially been dated Thursday, September 23. This lent credence to *The Observer's* contention that the Executive had had time to prepare for the looming crisis. It was also apparent that Dewar's advisers anticipated hostile questioning regarding 'the scope of the Standards Committee work you [Mr Dewar] are encouraging today and that requested in Jack McConnell's letter to Mike Rumbles' (Tait 1999e: 1). Challenged on these revisions of the Executive's position, David Whitton rather feebly restated the official line: 'These documents go through many drafts . . . We are not going to comment on leaked documents or drafts – they are what they are' (Tait 1999e: 1).

Meanwhile, the Standards Committee had begun to take a more proactive approach towards the media. Sunday newspapers reported that it would meet briefly in private before moving into public session. Committee sources indicated that the investigation would proceed regardless of the First Minister's statement (Fraser and Watson 1999a; Martin and Hill 1999). By Monday, 4 October, it was becoming evident that the Parliament had managed to assert its authority over the Executive. The Standards Committee meeting on 5 October was a markedly different affair from the débâcle of six days earlier. The transformation was summarised by *Newsnight Scotland*: 'They looked like Inspector Clouseaus last week; now they all looked like aspiring Perry Masons.' The committee had met in private for less than ten minutes before going into public session. Rumbles made a brief statement regarding *The Scotsman's* petition before the committee, and the assembled press and public viewed video evidence supplied by *The Observer*. Thereafter, an immediate investigation was agreed into the matters raised, with the significant proviso (attributed to the SNP) that witnesses would be required to give evidence under oath. The unity and purpose of the committee clearly impressed the assembled media. Reviews of their performance in launching an investigation were glowing: 'Mike Rumbles' committee has created an important constitutional precedent. Parliament rules ok ... It seems Donald's word is NOT "good enough" after all' (Macwhirter 1999b: 7).

The self-assurance that the committee now exuded belied the fact that its investigation was established and sustained by some extraordinary efforts behind the scenes. A committee member confirmed to us that they had taken a conscious decision not to sit in party groups, but to intersperse themselves. The influence of the Parliament's senior staff was crucial, preparing the members and briefing on behalf of the committee (although many committee members also talked to the media throughout the affair). After the committee meeting closed, a briefing by a senior constitutional expert from the legislature took place, which aimed to communicate the status of the Parliament's position. Having observed this briefing, and reviewed the subsequent media coverage, it is evident that the media were convinced by the case put forward on behalf of the Parliament. As one parliamentary source subsequently revealed to us:

> There was a bit of procedurally nimble thinking ... It was wonderful because we found a phrase – we looked in our remit and it talked about 'may investigate members conduct against any code' – and, of course, *any* code in a legalese sense just means any code which happens to be current at the time. We were able to read it as meaning any code including the ministerial code, and it helped that the draft of the ministerial code ... made several references to Parliament – which is very unlike the Westminster code. So, hey-ho. And the government were funny on this.

But the Executive's reaction to these developments lacked humour. In a rather tense and tetchy exchange on *Newsnight Scotland* on 5 October, the Minister for Parliament, Tom McCabe, refused to concede that final jurisdiction lay with the Parliament. When challenged that such an interpretation of events had been rendered obsolete by the Standards Committee, McCabe replied enigmatically, 'I think that the First Minister would disagree with that.' On the same programme, interviewer Gordon Brewer had quizzed Rumbles on the committee's powers to summon. Rumbles emphasised that the committee were 'inviting' rather than compelling witnesses to come. This was part of the Parliament's public-relations strategy, not only to repair the damage inflicted by the press, but also to avoid future embarrassments. Civil servants feared that should any witness refuse to cooperate with the inquiry, the Parliament as an institution would be humbled.

In their efforts to ensure that both the inquiry itself, and its public presentation, ran smoothly, parliamentary clerks, lawyers and advisers began some intensive briefing and preparation of committee members. As one of the civil servants involved recounted, 'I've been there when they [MSPs] needed me, and I've briefed them informally. I speak to them most weekends, for several hours sometimes, because they have found it a terrible experience.' This view was confirmed by a committee member:

> I was very conscious of the support from the legal team and from the clerks, because they provided us with support in a way that folk will never really know. They were there and we knew they were there, and we knew that the advice we were getting was correct and then we could go on and ask the questions because we knew the boundaries we were operating in.

Once the terms of reference, witness list, and running order of the inquiry had been agreed, the news value of Lobbygate abated. As the investigation neared its conclusion, the committee decided that it needed to interview only one minister, Jack McConnell. McConnell was to be the last witness, and on the weekend before his appearance in front of the committee there was a 'fresh outbreak of Lobbygate fever' (Brogan and Dinwoodie 1999). A leak in *Scotland on Sunday* (Hill 1999) suggested that key evidence from McConnell's constituency office had been destroyed. This was said to be a routine office procedure, but the construction placed on the disposal of potentially important evidence (which had also allegedly happened prior to Lobbygate) could have damaged McConnell. Executive sources were reported as 'vigorously defending McConnell' and the possibility of the Executive seeking 'to have members of the Standards Committee take an oath denying responsibility for the leak' (Hill 1999: 1) was mooted. How this would be accomplished under the Parliament's standing orders was never clarified. The unmistakable implication was that an SNP member of the committee had leaked this information.

McConnell accused committee members of 'playing politics' with the truth. A report in *The Scotsman* (Hardie 1999) identified Tricia Marwick as the suspected source of the leak. Dewar was reportedly concerned that the time taken to conclude the inquiry was damaging the reputation of the Parliament with the government at Westminster. One parliamentary source interpreted the leak in the following terms:

> The Executive changed its mind [on the Standards Committee inquiry], and then changed it back again and said we weren't getting on with it quick enough. So they vacillated and, of course, with their great spinning machine they managed to plant some stories which haven't all gone away.

The Standards Committee flatly denied leaking documents to the press. In a media briefing on 25 October, Mike Rumbles insisted he would not be deflected from the inquiry. He stated that he had not questioned his committee members about the leak. In fact, when the committee met informally that morning before their public session, Tricia Marwick had confronted the issue directly. She declared that she had not leaked any information relating to their inquiry. This assurance was accepted by her colleagues. In his briefing, Rumbles asserted the innocence of his committee. Significantly, a parliamentary official who had been observing the briefing interrupted to offer a more robust defence of the committee, stating that the leaked documents had a very narrow circulation and that if it was accepted that the leak did not come from the Parliament, one must inevitably look to McConnell and his office as a probable source. Journalists' reactions varied. A number of younger reporters were sceptical of this spin, whereas to some of the more experienced reporters this scenario was entirely plausible. After the briefing, as the journalists discussed the story among themselves, *The Herald*'s Robbie Dinwoodie admonished a more junior colleague, reminding him that in the black arts of spin 'the leak becomes the story, not the content'.

When Jack McConnell came before the Standards Committee on 27 October, he neatly avoided waiting photographers by using the tunnel between the committee rooms and the Parliament's main offices. In an assured performance, McConnell denied any wrongdoing or impropriety. For some commentators there was a palpable sense of anti-climax. The next day, the *Daily Record* complained in an editorial that the committee's 'kid-gloves handling of McConnell was not so much a grilling as a gentle toasting'. Iain Macwhirter suggested that the minister had been:

> Deeply concerned, anguished even, over this entire enquiry. Before his appearance, he spent hours meticulously rehearsing his testimony with senior Labour officials. He fully realised that his job was on the line, and that his image had already taken a considerable knock because of his connection with the lobbying business.
> (Macwhirter 1999d: 11)

Hours after his appearance before the committee, McConnell, like all the other politicians named in the affair, was fully cleared of any impropriety.

The Standards Committee's official report on Lobbygate refused to adjudicate between the conflicting accounts of Alex Barr and Christina Marshall. Barr told *The Observer* and the committee that he understood he had been able to book a date in McConnell's diary through Christina Marshall. She denied this. The Standards Committee, while expressing its concern over discrepancies in their evidence, (Standards Committee 1999, paragraph 34), stuck to its remit of simply considering the conduct of MSPs.

LOBBYGATE: THE DUST SETTLES?

For many of the political correspondents reviewing the saga, the Scottish Parliament had asserted its authority over the Executive and Dewar had emerged victorious in the 'turf war' with the Scotland Office. However, the precedent established by the Lobbygate inquiry has yet to be tested in constitutional law, and the Executive has reserved its opinion on where ultimate jurisdiction over the conduct of ministers rests. Nevertheless, Lobbygate can already be said to have had an impact on ministerial conduct, not only in Scotland, but also at Westminster, where the Neill committee has stated that:

> We do not think that compliance with a new requirement to record would be burdensome for departments, and we believe that it would encourage high and uniform standards ... The [Lobbygate] case demonstrates the potential for strong public interest in the existence of such contacts and the need for a clear record of meetings.
> (Neill committee 2000a: 91)

The Standards Committee and its staff now see Lobbygate as a beneficial learning experience. It is explicitly cited as informing its deliberations on the Code of Conduct for MSPs (Standards Committee 1999, paragraph 38), and may shape how outside interests are regulated. Some observers have expected legislation in this area (Scott 1999a) but the view from inside Parliament is more cautious. As one civil servant told us:

> This group [the Standards Committee] is very interested. If the inquiry has done one thing, it has strengthened our resolve to look at this issue. What I've said to them is, 'By all means do it, but don't pretend to yourselves or to anyone else that it's easy.'

The Standards Committee has conducted a survey of members to assess their relationships with outside organisations as a first step. The second phase of this inquiry involves a wider consultation with interested parties, especially lobbyists, which is ongoing as this book goes to press.

For the media, central players in the entire Lobbygate affair, the necessity of some form of independent scrutiny of MSPs and ministers is clear. The Scottish media's verdict on the cross-examination of witnesses by the committee has been damning. Privately, some members of the committee have accepted that their questioning could have been more penetrating, but they are not yet minded to sanction the creation of an independent commissioner along Westminster lines (Horsburgh 2000; Nicolson 2000).

Lobbygate was damaging for the nascent lobbying industry in Scotland at the time. Many of those we spoke to reported that clients 'wobbled' and were nervous about public and media interest in lobbying. However, as the scandal has receded it has been business as usual. While the public perception of lobbyists in Scotland since Lobbygate has probably been negative, in many ways this need not matter, as the public are not the focus of such commercial activity. The lobbyists are concerned about their relationships with politicians, civil servants, and other opinion formers. On the evening that McConnell was formally cleared, the 'Politician of the Year' awards, sponsored by *The Herald*, were taking place. One lobbyist who was there told us that she was asked by an MSP (and member of the Standards Committee) not to have a social drink in public with his party afterwards, lest it be misconstrued. Other lobbyists reported that on the same night the Scottish Executive withdrew a number of its ministers from tables booked by lobbyists at the event. While the politicians' sensitivity regarding their contacts with lobbyists is understandable, there is a danger in pretending that such links do not exist. Sweeping these contacts under the carpet does not address the issue. One commercial lobbyist we spoke to summarised the lessons of Lobbygate in the following terms:

> When you have introduced a legislature, when you have introduced a Parliament, when you have introduced professional lobbying, then those [social] relationships have to fall by the wayside and the formality of the relationship has to be established. And what Lobbygate showed us was that when that doesn't happen, when that formality isn't put in place, then all of those accusations and allegations are brought to the fore and the wider community becomes very suspicious, not only of the conduct of professional public affairs consultants, but more importantly, and more worryingly for democracy, of the elected parliamentarians.

Since Lobbygate, professional lobbyists have been wary that the affair might yet have an impact on their practice, were the Standards Committee finally to consider regulating the activities of outside interests.

An issue that received scant critical attention throughout the affair is that of the professional status of lobbying. Both the APPC and ASPA explicitly claim to be 'professional', as opposed to trade, bodies. One of the traditional prerequisites of a profession (such as medicine, accountancy or law) is to have formal qualifications. However, there are no barriers to entering the lobbying 'profession'. During his appearance before the Standards Committee, Kevin Reid struggled badly to explain what qualifications and training he had. Personal contacts were his most obvious asset.

In some respects, the story of Lobbygate reflects the 'limits of spin'. At the time, the Scottish Parliament employed two information officers, as opposed to thirty-four in the Executive's Information Directorate. Yet, confronted with an interpretation of the Scotland Act that granted Parliament the scope to investigate ministers, the Executive's spin machine was ultimately ineffective. While the Parliament's media relations office played a low-key role in the affair – acting strictly as information providers rather than spin doctors – the same cannot be said of senior parliamentary staff. Just what status and latitude such agents of the Parliament's corporate body have in relation to defending and promoting their institution is a moot point. At present, it seems that they are indeed informally licensed to spin.

Lobbygate has shed light on the interpenetration of the worlds of politics, media, and commercial promotion, a persistent facet of Scottish public life. The investigation launched by the First Minister into public-sector PR contracts in Scotland was intended, we were told, to examine the probity of how these were awarded. Regrettably, this inquiry has smacked of expedient spin rather than any real attempt to examine or tackle cronyism in Scottish politics and business.

Published in January 2000, the Scottish Executive's *Report on the Use of Public Relations Organisations by Scottish Public Bodies since 1 July 1999* indicated that of the 112 public bodies concerned, 58 had engaged one or more PR consultancies (Scottish Executive 2000). One hundred and fifteen contracts, worth a total of £3.8 million, were awarded by Scottish public bodies in the period under review, with Scottish Enterprise engaged in sixteen separate contracts valued at £417,000. The value of local enterprise and development agency PR contracts was an additional £972,000. Almost half of the total public spending on PR reported is accounted for by enterprise and development bodies, the very sector in which Beattie Media was most active. The Executive's research revealed sixteen 'ongoing' contracts, or retainers. Considered alongside evidence from *The Observer*, it seems likely that Beattie Media had a number of these. Beattie Media was found to be the firm with most public-sector contracts, accounting for 20 per cent of the total number awarded. However, this figure did not tell us anything about Beattie Media's (or indeed any other consultancy's) share of all public-sector PR contracts by value.

The Executive's report was designed to prevent the reader from identifying which public bodies had hired which PR consultancies, and at what cost. The information published by the Executive has reported that 'the median cost of contracts is under £10,000' (Scottish Executive 2000: 2). Yet the median is but one of three averages that could have been reported, and is arguably the most misleading. The report failed to distinguish between the most economically and politically-important contracts and those which would be of little public concern. On 28 January 2000, an editorial in *PR Week*, the usually supine trade publication of the British public relations industry (Dinan 1999), commented that 'a whitewash and a clean bill of health are not the same thing'. Industry rumour suggested Beattie Media were charging, in some instances, fees up to fifteen times greater than other companies doing comparable work for comparable agencies. Our efforts to establish the truth of such claims have been fended off by invocations of 'commercial confidentiality'. Michael Lugton, the Scottish Executive civil servant charged with producing the report, denied our requests for supplementary information, stating:

> I'm not in a position . . . to release more information because of the general convention [of commercial confidentiality] which applies and the view of ministers that what they released was appropriate in all circumstances . . . The judgement [on what was and wasn't commercially confidential] was made by ministers on the basis of the advice by officials.

A CONCLUDING PERSPECTIVE

It may be concluded that there is no great political appetite to tackle issues of cronyism in Scottish public life. The willingness of Scottish Executive ministers to opt for secrecy is particularly lamentable when the probity and transparency of the new polity are at stake. Lobbygate has not yet been a watershed in Scottish politics. It has dramatically exposed some private aspects of 'public' life and also threw into sharp relief the relationship between the Scottish Parliament and Executive, yet its impact on the regulation of lobbying in Scotland remains uncertain. Any future debate should be premised on openness and transparency. It will inevitably involve issues of commercial confidentiality. Lobbygate may only be acclaimed to have marked a political watershed if and when secrecy is finally abandoned in favour of the public's right to know. As things stand, the default position has been to adopt Westminster practice and stay close to the Nolan/Neill orthodoxy.

NOTES

1. The proposal was later dropped (Innes 1999: 4).
2. We might look at one public reaction to this claim. Defending the spiralling costs of the new parliamentary campus at Holyrood, Henry McLeish asserted on *Question Time* (BBC1, 13 April 2000) that 'no-one in this audience would doubt the integrity of Donald Dewar.' The audience simply laughed out loud. McLeish was visibly taken aback, pleading 'No? Let's be serious.'

CHAPTER 13

The lie of the land: regulating lobbying in Scotland

THE CHANGING LANDSCAPE OF LOBBYING

After the first year of the Scottish Parliament, the lobbying landscape around Holyrood was still taking shape. In the wake of Lobbygate, the Standards Committee of the Parliament began to review relations between elected representatives and outside interests. Their first step in this process has been to undertake a survey of members' experience of contacts with outside organisations. The spectrum of organisations to which this might apply spans community groups, voluntary-sector charities, trade associations, quangos, corporations and commercial lobbyists. Already, there are crossparty groups in the Scottish Parliament, and other established fora, in which lobbyists interact with the political class. Nevertheless, the Standards Committee's inquiry is likely to involve some reluctant participants, including representative bodies like ASPA, the APPC, and the SCVO. For organisations promoting various models of self-regulation which might clash with that recommended by the Standards Committee, these tensions are particularly apparent.

Our research has addressed the role of representative bodies such as ASPA, the APPC, and the SCVO in the debate on the regulation of lobbying in Scotland. By looking at how these organisations position themselves in this debate, and the interests they articulate, we can begin to delineate the field of Scottish public affairs. The investigation by the Standards Committee, and its eventual recommendations, will determine the conditions under which the lobbying industry in Scotland develops.

ASPA AND THE APPC IN SCOTLAND

In many respects, Lobbygate has already proved to be an important moment in the institutionalisation of lobbying in Scotland. As we have shown, there has been competition between the two major representative bodies of the commercial public-affairs sector to be recognised as the 'voice of the industry' in Scotland. The terms of this competition were redrawn after Lobbygate as the industry began to anticipate scrutiny by Parliament.

The founding of ASPA was a bid by would-be lobbyists at Holyrood to establish and advocate their own system of self-regulation. By promoting a distinct code of conduct, ASPA was vying for political legitimacy with the established representative body for lobbyists in the UK, the APPC. After ASPA's official launch, and the bedding-down of the new Parliament, relations between the two associations began to normalise. The concerns of commercial lobbyists turned away from issues of regulatory competence and focused instead on boosting their business now that devolution had arrived. However, once the Lobbygate affair had revived regulatory issues, the underlying tensions between the two bodies re-emerged.

The official view from within ASPA is outlined in the following terms by Angela Casey, convenor for 2000–1:

> ASPA is looking at how lobbying is happening at the Scottish Parliament. Anyone who has any form of interest in lobbying the Scottish Parliament can sign up [to ASPA's code] and it's looking at helping, educating people, bringing people together to learn about how an industry is growing. Whereas the APPC is purely about, 'If you're going to do lobbying, sign up to this code.' They are two different things and I can't see why somebody couldn't be a member of one and the other at the same time.

Leaving aside the requirement for APPC members to generate an annual fee income in excess of £100,000, political considerations also tend to make the two organisations mutually exclusive. Robbie MacDuff, managing director of Strategy in Scotland, was a member of both groups during 1999 but declined to renew his membership of ASPA in 2000. MacDuff believed that the regulatory regime operated by the APPC was more rigorous than that of ASPA. The media picked up on this divergence during Lobbygate, although the headline 'Lobbyists plan breakaway group' (Adamson 1999: 6) did annoy MacDuff, given that only Strategy in Scotland were members of both associations. Instead, MacDuff preferred to emphasise the 'natural constituency and natural agenda' that applied to APPC members in Scotland, while also implying that the same could not be said for ASPA.

The reaction of ASPA members to these developments at its AGM in late November 1999 was mixed: some regretted losing a member, while others, echoing the mood of early ASPA meetings, were glad to be rid of such an unwilling, 'elitist' participant. This vignette reveals the persistent efforts of commercial lobbyists in Scotland to define the terms of their professional practice to suit themselves best. The overriding concern for affiliates of the APPC has been to distinguish between their preferred self-description as 'professional political consultants' and the activities of what might be termed dilettante lobbyists, those who have recently begun to offer commercial lobbying services as part of a wider business portfolio. George Edwards, chairman of GPC Scotland and an APPC committee member, commented:

> I have been very careful in conversation over thirty years now to try to explain to people what public affairs actually means, because most people will assume it's public relations. There's a distinction between the two ... I didn't like being described as being in the public relations field and I still don't ... We're not members of ASPA, and that's not by accident. I mean ASPA is entitled to do what ASPA wants to do and I appreciate this role is different, but our position is that we are professional political consultants. The code of conduct for the APPC is ... more stringent than the ASPA code.

Edwards' differentiation between the worlds of public affairs and public relations is not entirely shared by other lobbyists, even among members of the APPC in Scotland. The overlap between lobbying and public relations in Scotland is probably a defining feature of the industry at present. Fiona Callison, of August.One (formerly of Shandwick), remarked:

> I think the [Scottish lobbying] market is very immature ... A client comes with a mix of problems, and actually to say what is originally a PR issue, and what is actually public affairs, that is something for accountants to get excited about back at base. It's not actually a meaningful distinction in the way that you might find in London or in Washington or in Brussels, where there is a much more mature market.

It would appear that the category 'professional political consultant' is not as exclusive in Scotland as elsewhere. For Angela Casey, managing director of Countrywide Porter Novelli in Scotland, ultimately owned by the same multinational group as GPC, the issue reduces to a question of emphasis in practice:

> We're both [Countrywide Porter Novelli and GPC] doing the same thing in a sense, but we're coming at it from different directions. So there's quite a large overlap between what we do. We tend to be doing media programmes that have government relations elements to them ... and they [GPC] do it the other way round: they do government relations programmes and they also do the media.

The debate in Scotland may best be understood by reference to the constituencies from which the associations draw their memberships, and the main differences in their respective codes of conduct.

The APPC in Scotland currently has eight member consultancies. Of the six founding members, two (Shandwick and Citigate) are essentially PR firms with specialist lobbying divisions. Moreover, other members such as GPC and Strategy in Scotland, offer PR services in addition to their core business of commercial lobbying. The number of APPC members in Scotland may increase as more firms from London reshape their business to cater for client demand for lobbying in Edinburgh. The arrival of APCO Scotland and August.One on the Scottish lobbying scene in 2000 suggests the market is still expanding. The response of the APPC to devolution has been somewhat uneven. The six original member consultancies in Scotland met informally throughout 1999. A sense emerged that these consultancies needed to speak with a Scottish voice rather than rely upon the London-based secretary of their association to act as their spokesperson. The decision to formalise a Scottish character was aimed at adapting the APPC itself to the realities of devolution. As Edwards explains:

> We felt that even within the APPC there wasn't sufficient understanding in London of the Scottish situation . . . There was quite a lively discussion whether it should be called APPC Scotland or the Scottish APPC and it was pretty universally decided that . . . the best way to refer to it is the APPC in Scotland.

The 'lively discussion' centred on whether the Scottish members of the APPC should operate as a fully devolved association in their own right, or remain within the APPC and seek to negotiate whatever autonomy they felt necessary. They opted for a gradualist rather than radical alternative.

The APPC in Scotland therefore remains bound to negotiate with its London-dominated management committee. The membership requirement that firms earn an annual fee income of £100,000 remains in effect, and any change in this policy would have to be sanctioned by a committee in London:

> It is not a problem for us or for any of the other companies who are members [of the APPC in Scotland], but for any new company coming in it would be difficult. So we're trying to find a way round this because there are one or two good personal operators in Scotland who are experienced, who are willing to work to the standards that the APPC require, but who will never get a fee income of £100,000. So we're trying to find a mechanism for these people to join.

The income barrier to APPC membership contrasts with ASPA's claim to be an inclusive and accessible organisation, in the spirit of devolution. One consultant from an APPC member firm complained that the earnings threshold meant that opening up a consultancy was effectively impossible unless it operated outwith the APPC code. One ASPA official suggested, should the need arise, publicising these restrictions to the Standards Committee. The APPC, of course, operates another barrier to entry, namely its code of conduct, which is more likely to be important in any future debate on the regulation of outside interests in Scotland.

There are some significant differences between the respective codes of the APPC and ASPA, with the former tending to be more prescriptive. It prohibits the employment of politicians such as MPs, MEPs, peers, and others. The APPC keeps a register of clients and indicates whether contracts relate to specific projects or involve retainers, and the code constitutes part of each individual lobbyist's contract of employment. As noted, the ban on employing peers was problematic for both PS Communications (Lord Watson) and Holyrood Strategy (Lord Semphill and Lord Fraser), and underlined the disparities between the two models of self-regulation. Whether ASPA can bolster its own code of conduct to match that of the APPC is very much an open question, given the membership profile of the group and the fact that membership can be either corporate or individual.

In 1999, its first year, ASPA had over forty members. Most were from commercial communications consultancies, but there were also in-house practitioners, lobbyists from legal firms, and a few members with a background in the public sector. Obviously, the range of interests represented by ASPA is less homogenous than the APPC's 'natural constituency'. ASPA sees this inclusiveness in positive terms, allowing the association to speak on behalf of a greater range of interests. However, this initial advantage has been dissipated in ASPA's second year, as the membership of the organisation has roughly halved. There are currently some twenty members of the association, and their profile reveals a continuing dominance by commercial lobbyists. The decline in membership confirms doubts originally expressed regarding ASPA's direction and purpose. Several members initially joined in order to stay abreast of developments in the industry and to pick up political intelligence at ASPA seminars and events. Within a year, those sources were questioning the value and efficacy of ASPA, whether as a collective lobbying voice or as a forum for information and debate. Nevertheless, other members were glad of the networking opportunities afforded by ASPA, and keen to participate.

After a period of suspicion and (at times) hostility between both trade bodies, by summer 2000 relations had improved to the point of an *entente cordiale* between ASPA and the APPC. Angela Casey and George Edwards met 'informally' to discuss matters of mutual interest, not least the Standards Committee's review of lobbying. Both associations came to recognise the merits of presenting a united front to any official inquiry. Common ground is shared by both bodies in their support for the principle of self-regulation. Nonetheless, in private, each body harbours mixed opinions of the other, with some lobbyists at ease with the notion of cohabitation while others remain firmly wedded to the idea that there can only be one voice of the industry.

As the public affairs industry becomes more established, the relationship between the main trade associations is likely to evolve. Much of the posturing that characterised the early days of ASPA has receded, with references to the southern or English character of the APPC becoming less commonplace. It can now be acknowledged that the local expertise heavily emphasised by early ASPA members was somewhat hyped. As Angela Casey explained: 'The bigger consultancies, because they've moved people up here from London, they know what they're doing and everyone else is finding their feet really.'

This recognition of the importance of Westminster practice as an early – and possibly enduring – benchmark for lobbying practice in Edinburgh is significant. The local knowledge that Beattie Media (and others) traded upon has been discredited in the eyes of the Parliament.

Commercial lobbyists might still be invited to reflect on this experience by the Parliament's Standards Committee. If the committee does decide to hold a public investigation (or 'go down the silly route', as more than one lobbyist has described it), it will be approached with extreme caution by the professional public affairs industry in Edinburgh. During our research, it was difficult to identify any commercial lobbyist who respected the Parliament's Standards Committee. There was, instead, a widely-shared belief among lobbyists that the Standards Committee did not understand how lobbying is actually accomplished. But these self-same lobbyists have not sought to correct the Parliament's 'misconceptions'. This reluctance to engage with the Standards Committee is consistent with most lobbyists' acute anxiety about publicity for their industry and their expectation of negative media coverage. Hence, ASPA's position since Lobbygate has been to offer co-operation by making its code and constitution available to the Parliament, while at the same time shying away from the direct gaze of both parliamentarians and the media. Angela Casey reasoned that, 'if giving evidence means that we are going to be shot down [then] it's not necessarily a very sensible move. I think it could just be damaging. I think it would be slightly foolish.' So far lobbyists have chosen to remain in the shadows rather than stating their case in the open.

THE SCOTTISH VOLUNTARY SECTOR

The voluntary sector – or 'third force' – is an important but often neglected actor in Scottish public life. There are an estimated 44,000 voluntary organisations in Scotland, including 21,000 recognised charities. Approximately 100,000 people are employed in this sector, supported by a further 300,000 volunteers, who generate a combined income of nearly £2 billion in the Scottish 'social economy' (SCVO 1999). The Scottish Council of Voluntary Organisations (SCVO), as the national umbrella body for the third sector, is responsible for lobbying on behalf of this panoply of interests and causes. Arguably, the powers devolved from Westminster, and the Executive's early legislative programme, have to date impacted most upon the voluntary sector. This is unsurprising as the campaign for devolution was shaped and promoted by the interests of Scottish civil society. These interests engaged in the work of the CSG and participated in many of the consultation exercises that informed the creation of the new Parliament. The CSG's 'accessibility' principle, which has significantly shaped the operation of the Scottish Parliament, owes much to the sustained interventions of the Scottish voluntary sector.

Ironically, given the sector's enthusiasm for the principle of devolution, the SCVO's response to its practicalities was somewhat uncertain. In 1999, the SCVO created a Parliamentary Information and Advisory Service to assist small, resource-poor organisations 'to respond to developments in the Scottish Parliament and exploit the opportunities presented to the full' (SCVO 1999: 30). The main form of assistance on offer involves the provision of information through general briefings, the pooling of information and resources across policy networks, and a 'bespoke' service to member organisations which provides updates in particular policy areas. This work is seen as the realisation of the logic of devolution:

> The voluntary sector will be of great worth to the Scottish Parliament. The new MSPs will need expert advice on a range of issues and voluntary organisations are well placed to fill this role. Research and information produced by voluntary organisations will be a useful resource for decision-makers, offering them sensitive, well-sourced information from groups and individuals affected by their deliberations.
> (SCVO 1999: 4)

The SCVO has a dual mandate: it seeks to promote an inclusive Parliament by enabling voluntary bodies to lobby for themselves, while simultaneously lobbying on generic issues.

The lobbying capacity of the voluntary sector has been increased by the creation of a third force policy officers' network. It currently comprises some forty people, employed either as dedicated full-time policy and parliamentary officers, or as part-timers. These lobbyists interact with the Parliament mainly through the work of the committees and some of the crossparty groups that have been established.

The novelty of the committee system at Holyrood and the extent of the committees' workload have meant that some of the ideals suggested to the CSG have yet to fully materialise, and that abstract principles are sacrificed to pragmatism. As Philippa Jones, Parliamentary Officer for the SCVO, recounts,

> We keep coming up against stuff that people haven't really thought about, and I don't think there's any big agenda behind it, it's just they . . . suddenly realise they've got all this work to do, and not enough time, and hey, they do it this way in Westminster.

The recourse to established British practice is, of course, both expedient and fairly predictable, yet it does raise some fundamental questions about the limits of innovation in the political culture. Nevertheless, the voluntary sector has had some opportunities to invent new practices in its public-affairs activities. The policy officers' network is possibly the best example of this to date. In the words of Elspeth Alexander, it provides for its participants 'a good way of sharing resources . . . a good forum for sharing tactics, sharing knowledge'.

Lobbygate has had a marked impact on how the voluntary sector thinks about its role in Scottish public life. There is an anxiety that the voluntary sector and the commercial sector will be treated in the same fashion by political decision-makers if, and when, they come to regulate contacts with outside interests. Arguably, Lobbygate has jeopardised the openness and accessibility of the Parliament that the voluntary sector fought so hard to establish:

> Understandably parliamentarians wish to distance themselves and their new institution from the practices associated with the 'sleaze' scandals of previous years at Westminster, but the upshot was that far from seeking to identify ways of promoting the sensible participation of external bodies, the discussion focused on ways to exclude, such as a requirement for formal registration of all forms of organisations approaching the Parliament. Inevitably it is a delicate distinction to make, but there is a clear difference between the activities of for-profit companies hired to influence parliamentary debate, and representatives of the myriad of voluntary organisations and community groups speaking directly on behalf of communities. Both have their place in the system, but the activities of one should not by implication limit the scope of the other. (McTernan 2000: 141)

Some voluntary-sector lobbyists are uneasy about the regulation of their activities. One policy officer wished to avoid the Standards Committee inquiry into lobbying so as not to be tarred with the same regulatory brush as commercial lobbyists. The voluntary sector, like the commercial one, perceived giving evidence as a potential threat rather than as an obligation or an opportunity. There is something to lose as the third sector is probably more engaged with work on Executive consultations than commercial lobbyists (although the latter are interested in these initiatives and some clients have reportedly found them useful exercises). This may partially explain a widespread view of voluntary-sector lobbyists. Philippa Jones has pointed to:

> an interesting difference between what the Executive say in terms of involving the voluntary sector, and consultation, and so on, and what the Standards Committee say about lobbyists. I don't think they [the Standards Committee] recognise that voluntary organisations often have a duty to represent the interests of their members or users, because nobody else can do it. And they have the expertise and experience and on-the-ground knowledge which is extremely useful . . . I've spent ages trying to avoid the word 'lobbying' at all because I think it's got negative connotations which we don't need, but all of those groups ought to be able to access the Parliament . . . I think there is a radical difference between that and the people who are paid to represent different organisations all of the time.

The participation of the third sector in such consultation is not only focused on the work of the SCVO. The creation of the Scottish Civic Forum has been designed precisely to involve civil society in policy debate. The Civic Forum is funded by the Scottish Executive (for the first three years' start-up phase at least) and its remit is to facilitate, or channel, the participation of civic bodies in Scottish public life.

By summer 2000, the Civic Forum had appointed a new director, Donald Reid, charged with raising its profile, elected a new council and board, and identified a work programme centred on promoting legislative participation and civic priorities, and auditing democratic participation by 'looking at both the Parliament and the People and the information interface between the two' (Scottish Civic Forum 2000: 2). Because the Forum is a membership body, and represents a diverse range of interests, it does not see itself as a lobbying organisation, and is therefore wary of offering a corporate view on specific policy proposals or political issues. However, the Civic Forum is certainly seen as a site for lobbying. In its early days, commercial lobbyists such as Holyrood Strategy tried to join but were refused membership, which is not open to profit-making companies. For those members with the resources to participate in the policy debates organised by the Civic Forum, the opportunity to lobby lead officials and others from the Scottish Executive who actually draft bills is more than welcome, especially as many voluntary-sector lobbyists have begun to question the efficacy of responding to Executive consultation exercises.

Many policy officers expressed their frustration at the short timescales in which to reply to consultations, a lack of feedback on the impact (if any) of their submissions, and a perception among voluntary-sector actors of complacency on the part of the Scottish Executive. Some observers fear the

Executive now feels that consultation is a success simply by virtue of the fact that it is reaching a larger range of bodies than before. Unhappily, the quality of the participation is not always given precedence over legislative timetables. As Debbie Wilkie of the Civic Forum noted: 'They [ministers and the civil service] need to realise that it's the beginning of a journey, not the end.'

An oft-cited example of best consultative practice was the Cubie inquiry. According to the SCVO's Lucy McTernan (2000: 142):

> the early appointment of the Independent Committee of Inquiry into Student Funding (1999) may have been conceived as a political fix, but it developed into a good model of extensive consultation on a complex matter.

The chairman of that inquiry, Andrew Cubie, pointed out to the Civic Forum in Edinburgh (on 10 June 2000), that one major factor in the success of the consultation process had been the substantial PR budget allocated by the Executive. Such PR resources publicised and disseminated information about the committee's work and effectively enabled meaningful participation in the consultation process. As McTernan (2000: 143) concedes:

> Of course the most effective way to open up public debate remains attracting the interest of the established media . . . Unfortunately, despite efforts to encourage journalists to broaden the analytical coverage of social issues, civic bodies continue to find it difficult to voice opinion on policy unless it can be interpreted as an attack on an individual politician or party.

This rather depressing scenario contrasts sharply with the aspirations that the CSG harboured for the role of the media in the newly-devolved polity, where they would ideally act as an information service for civil society and actively encourage and foster democratic participation (CSG 1999: 7). The media's disinclination to do this on a major scale is a serious shortcoming. The launch of the Civic Forum in March 1999 failed to attract a single journalist. That such an initiative, drawing together over 500 civic organisations throughout Scotland, should be ignored by the media is certainly a cause for concern. In terms of the lobbying strategies of the voluntary sector, it is evident that the media are still accorded special status: 'building a relationship with journalists is every bit as important as working with the politicians' (SCVO 1999: 25). Yet serious doubts must remain about the capacity of the Scottish media to air the concerns of civic Scotland.

REGULATING INTERESTS?

The Standards Committee has repeatedly identified the activities of 'hired-gun' commercial lobbyists as central to their deliberations. Members appear to harbour most concern for how relations with outside interests could be compromised through their contacts with commercial lobbyists' clients. Both the APPC and ASPA codes require lobbyists to declare the interest they represent in dealings with elected members and officials, and this now appears to be standard practice throughout the industry. However, there remains an anxiety that as commercial lobbyists trade in political intelligence that may be used to the material advantage of any of their clients, their relations with MSPs are inherently compromised. This suspicion is not easily dispelled, and the policing of such matters at present rests with lobbyists themselves. The requirement upon APPC members to publish their client list is in part designed to meet such fears. The Standards Committee's examination of lobbying practice is intended to review events in the first year of the Parliament. The survey distributed to MSPs by the committee before the summer recess 2000, focused on members' experience of contacts and relations with lobbyists, seeking to establish some baseline data to guide their inquiries. Such data may capture formal relations with outside interests, but not informal, unnoticed, or hidden relations. In other words, the survey addressed the go-betweens rather than the behind-the-scenes.

Before the Scottish Parliament was installed, fears were expressed within the emergent public affairs industry of a likely over-supply of lobbying capacity in Scotland. It is still difficult to predict how much the market will grow, but it seems (if recruitment advertising is taken as a crude benchmark) rather healthy. The Parliament is radically reshaping the Scottish public affairs arena, with new spaces opening up for lobbyists to interact with politicians and officials. The formation of crossparty groups in the Parliament is one such instance, and other recognised fora are establishing themselves, including regular conferences and seminars organised by bodies such as the Hansard Society, COSLA, ASPA, SCDI seminars under Chatham House rules, and the usual policy debates sponsored by think-tanks like the Scottish Centre for Public Policy and the Scottish Council Foundation. These sites afford lobbyists an opportunity to engage with Scotland's political elite in informal or social settings, and are by their very nature difficult to regulate or scrutinise.

Of course, not all lobbying is hidden or covert, as the case of Section 28 illustrates. The decision of the Scottish Executive to repeal Section 28 (properly titled Clause 2a of the Local Government Act) was a fairly minor political story until the multimillionaire businessman Brian Souter financed a campaign (to the tune of over £2 million) opposing the Executive's policy: thus, the 'Keep the Clause' campaign was born. One of the signal features of Section 28 was the role played by Media House in promoting the Keep the Clause campaign in the Scottish press. Media House, like Beattie Media, was originally a PR consultancy which expanded into public affairs and lobbying with the advent of the Scottish Parliament. With such a background, Jack

Irvine of Media House outlined his views on the developing public affairs industry in Scotland:

> A lot of English firms came up and set up shop, but I think where they have struggled is that they didn't know the politicians personally, even on a superficial level, but what they couldn't get into was the media. Because the media is a very, very closed shop up here and [Media House] are fortunate or unfortunate enough to have been involved in it for all our lives, and you cannot do one without the other. I mean you could present the most brilliant public affairs case you want, but if you can't get the editors convinced of it, you'll lose it . . . I go into clients now and say we come at it from two levels, the political/intellectual level and we have the guys who go in with the boots on and kick politicians' brains out.

The targeting of editors, rather than key ministers or civil servants, runs counter to conventional wisdom at Westminster (John 1998; Miller 2000). Without the active support of the *Daily Record*, the Keep the Clause campaign could never have had the impact it did on Scottish politics nor achieved any significant concessions from the Executive on policy, a fact readily accepted by Media House. The resources Souter made available to fund the campaign were a necessary but insufficient factor: what distinguished the campaign was the political clout of the *Daily Record*. Section 28 again reminds us of the interpenetration of the worlds of media, politics and promotional culture in Scotland.

The shaping of public policy by outside interests has brought only the activities of lobbyists into sharp relief. It is curious that in the sporadic official debate in the UK (Nolan, the CSG, Neill) the regulatory gaze has yet to fix on the role of clients and their proper conduct. In the Scottish context, clients have been conspicuous by their absence from this dialogue, a fact only partially explained by the location of many clients south of the border. So, while bodies like the APPC in Scotland and ASPA become focal points for the debate on lobbying at Holyrood, their clients and beneficiaries remain neglected.

The Standards Committee published the results of its survey of Members' experience of contacts with outside interests in September 2000. Forty-seven MSPs (36 per cent) responded to the questionnaire. Of this sample, 77 per cent had been lobbied more than twenty times, 98 per cent had been lobbied by voluntary bodies and charities, and 49 per cent had been lobbied by commercial lobbyists. MSPs were also lobbied by professional bodies (87 per cent), trade unions (87 per cent), religious groups (85 per cent), and business associations (79 per cent) (Standards Committee 2000: 2).

The most divisive matter in the survey relates to how MSPs view commercial lobbyists. While the exact figures are not reported, the implication is that there is a range of opinion on this topic, with the majority satisfied with current practice:

On the basis of the members' responses to the questionnaire on lobbying there is little support for the regulation of lobbyists. While a few respondents indicated that they would support the regulation of lobbying companies most were content that the system is open and transparent. At the same time there were also some members who felt that professional lobbying companies should be banned from the Parliament altogether.
(Standards Committee 2000: 7)

The Committee's report rehearses all the truisms about commercial lobbying that characterise Nolan, Neill and the CSG report: that regulation is impractical; that it cannot be defined properly; and that it enhances the status of professional lobbyists (Standards Committee 2000: 5–7). Lobbying at Holyrood is merely business as usual. Public affairs remain essentially unchanged in conception post-devolution.

But this cosy picture can be challenged. As already indicated, the regulatory orthodoxy established at Westminster through the Nolan and Neill committees has been largely shaped by political insiders with a vested interest in the status quo. Evidence about successful regulatory regimes has yet to be accorded its proper weight. The definitional problem is solved if all outside interests are regulated. The Standards Committee report does not allow for the vaunted 'openness and transparency' of the Scottish Parliament being secured and enhanced through a register of lobbyists. Instead, the template developed at Westminster is being uncritically replicated at Holyrood.

The report concludes that 'lobbying by professional companies is not as widespread as that by voluntary organisations and charities' (Standards Committee 2000: 8). This is an astonishing conclusion, given that we estimate there to be three times as many full-time commercial lobbyists in Scotland as there are voluntary sector lobbyists. What the Members' survey measured was their contacts with outside interests, not the volume of lobbying-related work done by such groups. Several lobbyists have remarked that their work tends to go on behind the scenes. The hand-holding and advocacy that characterised lobbying a decade ago is now passé. The message of the client is simply more credible if the client, rather than the lobbyist, delivers it personally. Lobbyists are now very much focused on research, analysis and gathering political intelligence. Thus, private networks and contacts are integral to their work. The value of such channels of information should not be underestimated (Draper 1999). As one lobbyist remarked:

There are rings within rings within Scottish politics, of who's not speaking to who, and cliques and little networks that go on which you have got to be sensitive to because it can impact on your client quite badly.

Such contacts are vital for lobbyists. Another lobbyist confessed to feeling somewhat compromised when 'told things or offered things because of the people that I know' but recognised this as a feature of Scottish political culture. Furthermore it is plain that the bulk of lobbying targets the Executive rather than the Parliament. Contacts at this level have been neglected. How such contacts can be regulated is a serious issue if the CSG's aspirations for an open and transparent polity are to be meaningful. Undoubtedly, such practice exposes the limits of self-regulation by lobbying umbrella groups. During our research post-Lobbygate, we were told of supposedly regulated lobbyists still promising access to ministers. Bodies like the APPC and ASPA arguably cannot police such practice. Their aversion to bad publicity reinforces the likelihood that any malpractice will remain private and unpunished. The question of lobbyists operating outwith the recognised trade associations also merits attention. The history of lobbying in the UK suggests that investigative journalism is the means by which corruption is likely to be exposed.

WHAT NEXT FOR LOBBYING?

What can be done to safeguard the probity of Scottish public affairs? In the absence of a statutory register the self-regulatory codes operated by the APPC and ASPA are to be welcomed, but in our view they do not go far enough. The need for an official register is pressing. This should include a mandatory code of conduct that draws on best practice from other regulatory regimes, and should record the clients on whose behalf lobbyists act, and the fees and resources that they devote to their efforts to influence the political process. Crucially, the relations between lobbyists and the Executive need similar regulation. It may be objected that the Parliament has no power in this area, but we can point to the example of Westminster where the Neill committee recommended that ministers record all contacts with lobbyists. Such a demand could be replicated in Scotland and extended to cover civil servants. Such information would make a telling contribution to openness and transparency in the new Scotland.

CHAPTER 14

Conclusion: Open Scotland?

This book has charted the impact of devolution on the framework and practice of political communication in Scotland. When we began our task, the air was filled with the rhetoric of opening up the political system and the importance of engaging the citizen in a brave new constitutional experiment. Fine ideals may shape new institutions, or, in the face of resistance, fail to do so. We have provided some of the necessary material to allow an informed judgement to be made about just how far some key elements of Scotland's political culture have changed in line with the new constitutional arrangements. These are early days, and whether what is now in place is also substantially the shape of things to come is open to conjecture.

Those who seek to transform the world are all the servants of their imaginations. If these are well stocked, replete with alternatives drawn from a range of models, then what can be accomplished in attempting change may well be the richer. If the limits of our inventiveness are indeed shaped by the ideas at our disposal, and by how our conceptions interact with the relatively intractable legacy of history, then the more limited the range of what can be imagined, the more inevitable-seeming certain off-the-shelf solutions will be. In this study, we have been interested in how the opportunity to shape a new political culture has been addressed by some of those with the power to do so. To discover these processes at work, we have lifted the veil on a discrete but crucial aspect of Scotland's new order: the space in which politics is communicated. We have traced the key forces at work, and some of the decisive moments in the crucial first year of the making of Scotland's new political communicative space.

It cannot be denied that in the proposed transformation of the relationship between civil society and the state in Scotland, the news media and political reporting have been of prime importance. If civil society in one of its aspects consists of the people armed with the capacity to knowledgeably affect policy-making and to intervene in political debate, then 'lobbying' as a prime form of organised action is also deservedly at the centre of the stage. Conceived quite generally, to talk of lobbying is another way of addressing the exercise of power and influence by organised bodies in the political sphere. Its key interest for the analyst lies in who has the capacity and resources to lobby the political institutions effectively.

From the political sociologist's point of view, the implementation of the devolution settlement has been akin to an experiment. Of course, it is much more than that: it is a transfer of power that affects the lives of millions and still has the potential to reshape the British state quite fundamentally. But from the analyst's perspective, it has offered a unique occasion to study the precise impact of major constitutional change, and in the UK such opportunities come but rarely. While we would be the first to accept the limits of our research, what we have uncovered is likely to be typical of the scope and limitations of the devolution process in its initial phase.

JOURNALISTS

Devolution has unquestionably raised questions about what is meant by 'Britishness'. It has fed into wider debate about this topic, most notably of late in the dispute occasioned in October 2000 by the Runnymede Trust's report on the future of multiethnic Britain (www.runnymedetrust.org.uk/meb/TheReport.htm). The Runnymede report raised the question of whether the UK could become a 'community of citizens and communities' or whether different regions and communities would instead become inward-looking. This formulation has not proved uncontentious, as it presumes the continuation of the UK state, refounded on an explicit recognition of diversity with a political culture that takes account of this. Of course, the central question posed relates to the signal divide in contemporary Scottish politics, although not all would frame it in the same way. For the foreseeable future, Scotland's political life will be dominated by the question of whether devolution offers a stable settlement for Scots within the UK (the vision of the late Donald Dewar), or whether independence for Scotland will lead to the end of Great Britain and the foundation of a separate Scottish state within the wider framework of the EU.

Inevitably, this structural dilemma has profound effects on the conception and conduct of political communication. After all, such communication is fundamentally about how a political community speaks to itself. If the Great British structures are anywhere under pressure, one of the first places to look for signs of this would be the BBC, undoubtedly the single most important pan-UK cultural institution, for which journalism is a key activity. It has hardly been a secret to anyone interested in political life, not just in Scotland, but in the UK more generally, that the BBC's journalistic role has been a matter of deep contention north of the border.

We have added some further depth to the tales that have been in public circulation. We have shown how the BBC sought to embrace the new Scottish Parliament in ways long established at Westminster, for the corporation has had to cohabit intimately with the political class. If that class reproduces itself in a new place, then corporate logic dictates that its demands must be satisfied. Of course, there is more to it than that, because the BBC is constitutionally committed to supporting parliamentary democracy, and has been since its inception. Holyrood has offered the corporation an opportunity to undertake a different kind of parliamentary reporting from that which prevails at Westminster, and the uncluttered style of the new legislature has been better served by minimising the formality of the rules of coverage. Whether Scottish lessons will make the journey south to the Mother of Parliaments is another question. In our view, they certainly ought to, as that body could do with a revitalised public image.

We do not minimise the importance of this attempt to make the Scottish Parliament more accessible to the public, although such coverage does attract small audiences and is far from being popular. Much more far-reaching in its consequences – and these still remain unresolved – has been the question of news coverage of the new Scottish polity. We have shown in more detail than has elsewhere been published the trail that led to the killing of aspirations for a 'Scottish Six'. No doubt, those who argue that digitisation will solve the problem of a Scottish national and international news are right in principle. But that is a medium-term solution, at the earliest, and the resources will have to be there to support it. We would maintain that the absence of a main news broadcast framed by Scottish priorities (it does not have to be at 6 pm, after all, although that has assumed talismanic status), has left the new polity underserved. As a result, it is very much prone to the unchecked influence of the press, especially at the tabloid end of the market. Arguably, this has been a significant factor in the low-key campaign for the Scottish parliamentary election and in the low voter turnout.

The BBC has always been buffeted by the political winds, and the row over the 'Six' has been no exception. Labour's hierarchy both in London and Edinburgh have feared the nationalistic potential of a Scottish national news. Within the BBC, the prevailing wing of the governors and the corporation's top management went for the more cautious option of sticking with the existing schedule, sheltered by the doctrine of 'One BBC'. There is unquestionably a case for the UK – as a polity – to be addressed by a common network news. That is the normal currency of political debate and the proper entitlement of citizens. But these high principles are more tractable and expedient than we have been led to believe. The BBC's sudden leap into the slot vacated by ITN's *News at Ten* in October 2000 showed unmistakably that the high ground of news has become part of the ratings battleground of television. Addressing the widest possible public with the best possible news was the ostensible motive for this shift in the schedules. But besting the opposition and retaining audience share was the real reason. By making the main national news into so malleable a commodity, the BBC has lost the high ground of the argument for defending the existing schedule. Economic argument prevailed over political argument when convenient. This has made it rather harder for the corporation to move back to political ground. The debate about what kind of television news is needed to serve a devolved Scotland should be revisited now that the constitutional changes have bedded down, and the BBC will find it harder to defend the status quo.

In our analysis, the BBC has figured large, because it has been such a key point of connection between Scotland and the rest of the UK. Turning inwards, as it were, we have charted the largely unknown story of how the press went after its place in the sun. In short, we tell the tale of how the growing political press pack sought to achieve insider status for itself in the new parliamentary system. Those who have noted the major investment of Scotland's media in the devolution project (even if only to criticise it) have not been wrong. We have shown how key journalists organised themselves into an exceedingly effective lobby – although, ironically, they disdain lobbyists and lobbying with no little fervour – and how they drew upon Westminster and Whitehall experience to imagine their relationships with the new political class. While the rhetoric of high politics was often employed in their quest, it was the nuts and bolts of low politics (securing space and facilities and the right to roam the corridors of power) that was the prize. Scotland's political press is certainly not identical to the London Lobby. It has no venerable encrustation of custom and practice. It does not formally lock the door on new entrants. But in practice, it has drawn deeply on Great British models of conduct, because that has been the common experience of most key members. And when the press interacts with politicians, it does so in relation to government information practices and political modes of behaviour which derive from the mother parliamentary and governmental cultures. There are obvious dangers of undue media dependency on the political class in this model.

It is rare to have a ringside seat at how the deal is cut between media and political institutions. We have provided the reader with a detailed account of the processes that led up to formation of the Expert Panel on Media Issues, the rule-generating body for media coverage. We have analysed the private debating process and have shown its outcomes. Without effective lobbying of the civil service and politicians before the event, the eventual rule-making process would certainly have been much more tortuous, and the stability that it has engendered for parliamentary coverage may be judged a considerable success. Of course, that is not to say that it secured favourable coverage for the Scottish Parliament, nor should that have been the presumption. How the rules were created can be read as a case study of elites speaking to one another and finding solutions to their problems, and is one insight into what occurred inside the Consultative Steering Group, the story of which still remains to be told. One problem to which no solution was found – and that was inscribed in the very process – was that of how the new Executive should be covered. We have argued that the lack of debate about this impeded the immediate development of stable understandings between the press and Scotland's government. This hardly helped the fledgling Dewar administration, or indeed the Parliament, which both had a bad press in their first year. The political media were raring to report the new politics and found themselves frustrated by the time it took to let them become insiders.

Although in many respects the framework for political communication in Scotland is that of London writ small, with rather minor adaptations, that is not the end of the story. We have shown the great rapidity with which a novel political culture grew up around politicians, civil servants, and media in Edinburgh. However much this has derived from the master patterns of London, its focus is unquestionably Scottish. There is now a Scottish space of political communication in ways that simply was not the case before devolution. There is a great element of continuity given Scotland's pre-existing indigenous media system, but since devolution more journalists have been reporting Scottish politics than ever before. Moreover, there has been a major shift in how Scottish political reporters now think about what it is worth communicating about political life. We have shown how much of the style of government information management was perceived as being shaped by the late Donald Dewar's preferences. With Dewar's untimely passing, we may expect this to change under his successor Henry McLeish. But most fundamentally, as a result of devolution, the centre of political gravity has moved north of the border, understandably fuelling the concern of Westminster politicians about the cohesion of the state. What happens in London remains decisive for the wider business of government, but for the Scottish media UK politics has been substantially relocated.

SPIN DOCTORS

We have provided a first sketch of the history of Scottish Office information management, which has been a curiously neglected aspect in studies of Scottish politics and government. The SOID was affected by the centralisation of the Thatcher years and also by a creeping politicisation. We have provided evidence from Scottish Office insiders that they themselves felt the pressure to politicise and did not always resist it. This was especially the case under Secretary of State Michael Forsyth, whose enthusiasm for public relations was a shock to the Scottish Office system. In a way Forsyth prepared the SOID for the greater shock of New Labour in 1997. Certainly, the

Labour government brought with it a range of new techniques and demands, but this was no decisive break with the past. In fact, it can be argued that the tendencies towards centralisation, commercialisation and politicisation under Labour have their origins in the reforms of the Conservative years. What was different was the extent of the purge of information chiefs throughout Whitehall. In Scotland, the two most senior officials were removed, the Director Liz Drummond in part because of a lack of personal chemistry with the new Scottish Secretary Donald Dewar. But Dewar's personal style was more low-key than Number Ten and Millbank would have liked. He resisted the importation of New Labour methods from south of the border, even when his closest advisers thought differently. Dewar's mind was eventually changed and his spokeman, David Whitton, appointed.

The transformation of the civil service with devolution was, by any standards, quite minimal. We have shown how the communicative dimensions of this focused on internal openness – namely, on communication up, down and across the civil service. Notably, there was little in the internal documentation we obtained which discussed communication outwards to the media and the public. In the shift from the Scottish Office to the Scottish Executive Information Directorate, there were changes in practice, but in almost every case we were told that the changes were in line with those developed in Millbank and Downing Street. The lack of reform of civil service openness is particularly worrying in the face of the findings of the BSE inquiry, where the Whitehall 'culture of secrecy' has been identified as a key shortcoming (www.bseinquiry.gov.uk).

We are not suggesting that the secrecy of the civil service, or latterly its commercialisation, render it unreformable. In fact, significant elements of public-service ethos do remain. People do not go into the civil service for the high salaries. We interviewed a number of civil servants who were clearly concerned about the public-service responsibilities of their jobs. But if their responsibilities are to be exercised and supported, there are real issues to face about openness.

Our examination of the voter education campaign highlighted this starkly. It is crucial that government information campaigns about voting be seen as politically impartial. All political parties need to be fully consulted about such information campaigns. The importance of this point is that it is precisely the smaller parties that may suffer as a result of the inadequacies in a voter education campaign. In particular, the role of commercial research and advertising companies in public information work might be re-evaluated. There is a need for public information campaigns to inform the public, based clearly and carefully on research evidence, rather than conforming to professional or political judgements of what the public needs or can take. Research organisations need to be independent and to operate explicitly in the public interest. We did find some disturbing anomalies in the conduct and evaluation of the voter education campaign. Most fundamentally, the official evaluation of the campaign makes it clear that few people fully understood the new voting system. This suggests the need for a more explicit campaign before the next Scottish general election.

The resistance of First Minister Donald Dewar to spin was well rehearsed in media reporting. The ongoing battle between the forces of spin and the forces of tradition was a key factor in many of the Executive's problems in its first year. The lack of CSG-type discussion of structural and cultural change meant that the machinery of news management had to be invented on the hoof and was subject to little democratic oversight. It was for ministers to decide. Certainly, the battle over special advisers, and who should have them, would have been less likely had there been inclusive debate on the form the Executive would take. Inclusive debate would also have been a bulwark for the Scottish Labour Party against Millbank and Numbers Ten and Eleven Downing Street.

So far as the civil service is concerned, there is some scope in the Freedom of Information legislation for serious pressure to be exerted to reform its culture by installing a strong information commissioner. Indeed, this is one of the explicit functions of this post. It is correct to see this – as the consultation document, *An Open Scotland* (Scottish Executive 1999c), does – as a matter of significant cultural change. But to achieve this change through the individual efforts of an information commissioner is a tall order.

The confusion in the public debate between the Parliament and the Executive has masked the real seat of power in the Executive. Our research suggests that it is the Executive that stands most in need of reform if we are to move toward an open Scotland. If the Parliament remains too subordinate to the Executive, then it may forfeit the confidence of the Scottish people.

The practice of government information in Scotland has always been slightly (if variably) different to that of Whitehall. Direct communication with Scots overseas, an opt-out from London control of publicity campaigns, and an alignment with key elements of Scottish society marked the SOID out from the media operations of its Whitehall cousins. The irony of devolution is that there has been a more determined attempt to impose Whitehall norms on Scotland than in any other period. The adoption of the spin techniques pioneered in London is not likely to lead to greater openness in Scottish politics. If anything, the experience of Scottish devolution points up the problems of spin. Arguably, it has been at the heart of the major problems of governance in post-devolution Scotland.

LOBBYISTS

The proper place of commercial lobbyists in contemporary British politics has been a matter of renewed dispute and controversy ever since the 'cash-for-questions' and 'cash-for-access' scandals at Westminster. In the wake of such political sleaze, the role played by the professional lobbyists' trade associations, particularly the APPC, has been significant. In the absence of statutory regulation of lobbyists, the political system relies upon self-policing by the lobbying industry for the maintenance of standards in public life.

The recent history of lobbying scandals in the UK demonstrates this situation to be unsatisfactory: investigative journalism rather than self-regulation has exposed corrupt practice on the part of some lobbyists. It would appear that representative bodies for lobbyists are profoundly ill-equipped to govern and monitor their own members' activities. The desirability of self-regulation is also questionable: issues such as natural justice, commercial competition and, indeed, the reputation of the industry as a whole, could all potentially disrupt or corrupt the efficacy of self-regulation. In fact, the framework for how outside interests should articulate with the political system requires urgent reappraisal if Scotland is to be truly open and transparent.

Devolution opened up a debate in Scotland on how, in practice, democracy might be brought closer to the people. Part of this official debate, under the auspices of the CSG, focused on the role of commercial lobbyists. As we have shown, these lobbyists were not slow to mobilise, and sought to shape the early debate on lobbying in a devolved Scotland. Our research has also identified the cleavages within the public affairs business in Edinburgh. Aside from the obvious distinction between commercial and voluntary-sector lobbyists, which framed much of the Parliament's Standards Committee's initial consideration of the issue, there were differences within Edinburgh's commercial lobbying sector. The shifting relations between the two main trade associations for commercial lobbyists (ASPA and the APPC in Scotland) that we have described are symptomatic of the divergent interests of their respective memberships. Of course, it remains the case that both organisations share many common concerns.

The principles of openness and accessibility established by the CSG on behalf of the Scottish Parliament were intended as a template for practice rather than as a rhetorical refrain. Yet the logistics for realising the CSG model for lobbying at Holyrood are not in place. The idealism of the CSG is now confronted, through the Standards Committee inquiry, with the routine practice of a Scottish lobbying market which is part and parcel of the UK public affairs industry.

The commercial lobbying sector is an established multimillion pound business in the UK. Reliable estimates of the size of the public affairs industry in Edinburgh have yet to be calculated, or at least be made public. Nevertheless, lobbying at Holyrood and Westminster share key characteristics, not least their ability to trade on privileged access to decision-makers. Despite several reports by Parliamentary watchdogs at Westminster, no satisfactory system has emerged which would regulate lobbyists' activities. Furthermore, the activities and influence of lobbyists are almost entirely hidden from public view (outwith periodic media-led scandals) and beyond the mechanisms of democratic scrutiny. Whether Scotland diverges from this British model is an open question, as this book goes to print.

The Standards Committee's review of lobbying practice at Holyrood has now entered a second phase. Following its research on MSPs' experience of lobbying in the first year of Parliament, over a year after the Lobbygate affair, the Standards Committee has sought the views of outside interests. The resources for this consultation are limited. The consultation document was sent to thirty umbrella and representative organisations across Scottish public life. The Parliament's media relations office publicised the consultation with a press release, which failed to attract any media attention. The profile of opinion canvassed, and the relatively short time allocated to prepare submissions, suggest the inquiry will focus on the views of commercial lobbyists themselves, voiced through their representative trade organisations. Whether commercial lobbyists' opinions are accorded the weight, or privileged status, they are at Westminster has yet to be seen. At present, just as was the case in Westminster with the Nolan and Neill inquiries, it is difficult to envisage political outsiders shifting the terms of the debate on statutory regulation of lobbying in Scotland.

Public confidence in the probity of those involved in public affairs has been eroded with a series of sleaze scandals at Westminster. Lobbygate became the first Scottish entry into the political sleaze catalogue, and was probably most damaging in terms of public perceptions precisely because it came so soon after the devolution of power to Edinburgh. The way the allegations and issues were investigated, by both the Standards Committee and the Scottish Executive, was ultimately, unconvincing. The secrecy that characterised the Executive's inquiry into the awarding of PR contracts throughout the Scottish public sector exposed the emptiness of political slogans proclaiming a 'new' politics.

Regulating cronyism in Scottish public life will not be easy. As we have repeatedly pointed out, the proximity of politicians, lobbyists, and many of the journalists the public rely upon to hold these actors to account, is potentially unhealthy for Scottish democracy. The dense social and professional networks that comprise Scottish public life are conducive to the information flows between politicians, lobbyists and journalists. We have illustrated how this criss-crossing of interpersonal networks impacted on public policy in the extraordinary case of the 'Keep the Clause' campaign. It is obvious that the interplay of private understandings in Scotland's public domain needs to be more fully incorporated into future analyses of Scottish political culture.

The openness and transparency of the Scottish polity envisaged by the CSG as an antidote to the discredited politics of Westminster will only be realised through consistent effort on behalf of decision-makers by bodies such as the Standards Committee. A statutory register of those seeking to influence policy at Holyrood appears to us an urgent and necessary step. The logic of devolution suggests that the delegation of power permits different solutions to emerge. The regulation of outside interests is an area ripe for innovative political thinking. Whether the imagination, courage, and resources to depart from Westminster orthodoxy exist at Holyrood remains to be seen.

A FINAL WORD

When we began this research, we were entirely open-minded about how the political system might develop. We took the rhetoric of new politics and an open Scotland seriously. We did not expect to find what we did and in many respects we have been sobered by our analysis. This book has been written in the spirit of the new Scotland. It is not intended to undermine the devolution project or to be critical of particular individuals. Instead, we hope that those who read it will see our study as a contribution to the broadening and deepening of Scottish democracy.

Afterword

In the three months since this book first went to press, the scene that we have depicted has evolved in line with our analysis. The key developments are documented below.

THE MEDIA-POLITICAL VILLAGE

> Scotland is so small, and we are so clannish, that there are bound to be links and friendships across public life. Politicians and journalists work in what is vitually a closed environment, and there are inevitably close social contacts. Indeed there is often cross-fertilisation – and yes, I do mean in the biological sense.
> (Tom Brown, political commentator, *Daily Record* (2000c: 36))

Controversy about the new First Minister's media connections arose almost from the moment that Henry McLeish was installed as Donald Dewar's successor. His reported intention to 'dump the crap' in Dewar's legislative programme, and make changes in ministers' portfolios, was revealed to the public at large by Tom Brown of the *Daily Record*, first in his own paper, and then in the *New Statesman* on 30 October (Brown 2000b). Brown, it was alleged, would be McLeish's special adviser and speech-writer, and remain at the *Record* (Fraser 2000c). Brown (2000c: 36) denied this 'foul calumny' writing: 'I have spoken exactly four words to McLeish since he became First Minister'.

The official opposition SNP came into the frame when David Kerr, editor of the BBC's *Newsnight Scotland*, resigned to stand as a candidate for Westminister. Kerr had been criticised for prioritising an interview with John Swinney, the SNP leader, when Donald Dewar was still fighting for his life in hospital. 'Senior insiders' at the BBC were reportedly concered that the BBC's impartiality would look compromised. Brian Wilson, Scotland Office Minister of State, a robust critic of *Newsnight Scotland*, complained of being quoted out of context on the programme that week (Hardie 2000; McGinty 2000b). The BBC attempted to distance Kerr from the decision to screen Swinney's interview. The Conservatives and Liberal Democrats weighed in with accusations of political bias (Madeley 2000).

The row refocused attention on the extensive political affiliations and personal relationships of key media players involved in political reporting. The two-way traffic between the news media and the Labour Party, and also that involving the SNP, was extensively documented by the press (Luckhurst 2000; McGinty 2000c; Mackenna 2001).

McLeish immediately sacked Donald Dewar's spin doctor, David Whitton, replacing him with Peter MacMahon, said to be close to Tony Blair's official spokesman, Alastair Campbell, and to have a direct line into Downing Street. Before his appointment he was political editor of the *Daily Mirror* in London and is a former political editor of *The Scotsman* (Allardyce and Macleod 2000). McLeish was reported to be 'appalled' at the lack of direction in Dewar's private office, and is known to be especially keen himself on managing the media (Ritchie and Dinwoodie 2000), which Dewar famously disdained, as we have shown.

McLeish also right away dismissed Dewar's head of policy, Brian Fitzpatrick, and two other special advisers responsible for media work. In his resignation letter, Fitzpatrick thanked colleagues 'across Britain' who had helped 'Team Dewar' (Fitzpatrick 2000). One Labour MSP described the letter as 'bittersweet – sweet about Donald and bitter about Henry' (Ritchie and Dinwoodie 2000). Junior spin doctors Neil Gillam and Sharon Ward were also sacked, being identified as too close to 'Team Dewar'. David Whitton reportedly thought the treatment of junior staff to be 'unnecessary and brutal'. He let it be known that he was considering writing a memoir of the Executive's first year (Mackenna 2000). Team McLeish might well worry about Whitton's revelations, given his briefing against McLeish on Dewar's behalf (see pp. 175–7).

In McLeish's first three months, further special advisers were appointed. John McTernan became head of strategy, a policy post now filled by the former Carlton Productions media professional, who was once a special adviser at the Department of Social Security (Ritchie 2000b). Two advisers on media relations were appointed: Andy Rowe, previously a Millbank operative for the Labour Party, brought in as an 'events manager'; and Bill Heaney, an ex-local newspaper executive, tasked to push the Executive's message with local newspaper editors (Alba 2001).

THE SILENT ECLIPSE OF THE SEID

The SEID has been quietly abolished, to be relabelled the Scottish Executive Media and Communications Group. The new name is supposed better to reflect information officers' work. But the rebranding smacks more of a commercial PR outfit than of a public service. The name change was entirely unreported by the media and evidently has been kept quiet. It occurred after the sidelining of the SEID's Director, Roger Williams. Then, it was said (see p. 181) that Williams would still be called Director of Information. However, with the creation of the Media and Communications Group the title was quietly dropped.

SCOTLAND'S MEDIA MARKET

In September 2000, *Business a.m.* was launched into the UK's most competitive newspaper market. A pink tabloid intended to have pan-Scottish appeal, it is aimed at the business, financial and political classes. The Swedish media conglomerate, the Bonnier Group, are said to be backing *Business a.m.* with £15m over the next five years. Eventual sales of 15,000 are intended (Doward 2000). *Business a.m.*'s launch was welcomed by the often-beleaguered Scottish Executive.

Apart from competition with Scottish titles, *Business a.m.* also has to contend with *The Financial Times*, which sells 10,000 copies in Scotland. The Bonnier project came under fire from *The Scotsman*, whose publisher and editor-in-chief, Andrew Neil, decided to launch his own pink business section on 1 September in an apparent 'spoiler' (*The Drum* 2000: 3). Some commentators regard *Business a.m.* as a 'Scotsman in exile', given its significant recruitment of journalists from the Edinburgh broadsheet.

The other major development in the Scottish media market concerned SRH (Scottish Radio Holdings), which was at the centre of buy-out speculation after SMG had bought a 20.8 per cent stake early in December 2000. The possibility of further concentration of ownership in Scotland raised the hackles of the SNP. However, under current legislation, SMG would be debarred from owning radio stations in the same regions as its ITV licenses. At this time of writing, the bidding war for SRH has remained unresolved. It undoubtedly reflects market moves in anticipation of new communications legislation that will change the present points ceiling for radio station acquisitions (O'Connor 2000; Stokes 2000; Teather 2000b).

THE UK COMMUNICATIONS ENVIRONMENT

Although Scotland has become an increasingly distinctive media-political space since devolution, it remains profoundly shaped by the wider UK media environment, as is underlined by recent developments. These include decisions about the scheduling of network news; the impact of UK political coverage on a Scottish by-election; and the emerging framework of UK communications regulation.

As we have noted (see pp. 262–3), the BBC decided to move its flagship *Nine O'clock News* into the 10 p.m. slot vacated by its rivals ITN. The *Ten O'clock News* was launched on 16 October 2000, putting ITN on the defensive. The ITV network decided to restore a version of *News at Ten* on 22 January 2001.

The new *Ten O'clock News* has been followed by a six-and-a-half minute Scottish news bulletin. BBC Scotland has presented this replacement of the old *Reporting Scotland* late edition as a more than doubling of late news output. However, some rethinking of the BBC's journalism north of the border is surely needed as the new UK schedule competes with BBC Scotland's nightly half-hour digital news programme on BBC Choice at 10 p.m., and also tail-ends into *Newsnight* (Williams 2000). The BBC's director-general, Greg Dyke, has indicated that the corporation will maintain the status quo for news (Dyke 2000: 31) although it seems that *Newsnight Scotland* may be extended to half an hour. This would not satisfy proponents of a peak-time Scottish news.

UK-wide scheduling decisions have also impacted on Scotland's political communications in another respect. On 12 December 2000, the ITV network screened *Ask the Prime Minister*, a one-hour peak-time programme in which Tony Blair answered questions from a studio audience. The opposition parties in Scotland complained that this UK-wide broadcast gave Labour an unfair advantage in the last days of the Falkirk West by-election, which was held on 21 December. After complaints by the SNP and the Conservatives, the ITC determined that the Prime Minister's appearance had direct party-political relevance in Scotland. Consequently, to achieve balance and impartiality it directed Scottish TV to provide political coverage of Labour's opponents in peak time before the by-election. The views of the leaderships of Scotland's other parties (SNP, Conservatives, Liberal Democrats and Scottish Socialists) were broadcast in a Scottish TV political programme, *Platform Special*, with a studio audience, on 18 December in peak time (Cusick and Fraser 2000; Miller and Farquharson 2000).

The ITC's intervention showed how the complexities of Scottish politics may still defeat broadcasters who take UK-wide scheduling decisions. But the situation was also misread by Scottish TV, although there was a precedent in this case: in 1995, after a legal challenge by the SNP, the BBC was forced to stop the transmission north of the border of a *Panorama* interview with Prime Minister John Major, three days before Scottish local government elections. Memories are evidently short.

As the ITC showed, the UK broadcast regulatory framework remains decisive for Scotland. The government's Communications White Paper has indicated this is now being rethought (DTI-DCMS 2000). So far as Scotland is concerned, two proposals are of especial importance. The first is the intended smoothing of the path to one ITV, which has weighty implications for the country's largest media company, SMG. Will further concentration of ITV ownership soon extend north of the border and, if so, what will be the consequences? The second is the White Paper's continuing stress on the importance of the regional dimension. This has two aspects: the provision of regional content and the location of production in the regions. Both face new challenges and there can be little doubt that any commitment to 'regionality' will be modified in the face of tendencies towards the increased concentration of ownership and as digitisation brings more channels on stream.

LOBBYISTS AND THE STANDARDS COMMITTEE

The Standards Committee's review of lobbying at Holyrood is under way as we go to press. The committee embarked upon a consultation with interested parties in October 2000, the purposes of which were twofold:

> To gather information on the manner in which lobbying groups organise themselves and operate in relation to the Parliament [and] to invite those groups to provide comments on their own experience of lobbying in the first year of the Parliament.
> (Scottish Parliament 2000c: 1)

The committee intended the exercise to be brief and to cover major issues, the most contentious of which was the statutory regulation of lobbying. Among the organisations targeted were the representative associations of commercial and voluntary-sector lobbyists. The voluntary sector was less prepared for a consultation and its submissions less detailed and co-ordinated than the responses of the commercial bodies. The SCVO policy officers' network debated and finalised their collective response only the day before their submission was due. Of twenty or so policy officers attending a meeting on 4 December 2000, only two had already completed individual responses on behalf of their own organisations.

ASPA had kept a watching brief on the Standards Committee's proceedings throughout 2000, liaising with APPC Scotland about a joint strategy. When the consultation exercise was announced, ASPA quickly organised a round-table discussion to consider its response. ASPA's submission was finalised in November 2000 after a draft had been discussed with the APPC, IPR and PRCA.

The commercial lobbyists' bodies coordinated their responses to the Standards Committee and the sector argued against the statutory regulation of lobbying because it is ultimately concerned that this will be bad for business. The SCVO, on the other hand, remains keen to distinguish its work from that of commercial consultants and is still worried about being officially tagged as a 'lobbyist'. Compared with its position under previous Tory administrations, however, the voluntary sector in Scotland enjoys enhanced access to the political process.

Yet, the current level of voluntary-sector participation in consultations and cross-party groups places severe demands upon scarce resources. Preparing a voluntary-sector response for the Standards Committee's consultation was not easy, given policy officers' mushrooming workloads.

However, the pace of political change has also been felt by the Standards Committee, which has limited resources and a considerable workload. As noted above (see pp. 242–5), in the aftermath of Lobbygate there was parliamentary concern that the complexities of regulating lobbying might require exceptional time, resources, and political appetite. Moreover, the matter of whether ministers and civil servants are actually accountable to the Standards Committee was not settled by the Lobbygate inquiry.

The committee considered an initial report on responses to its consultation on 19 December 2000. Its discussion shows a major drift from the principles of the CSG and the inquiry seems to be following the well-worn Westminster lines already laid down by the Neill Committee (see pp. 189–94).

That committee's rejection of the statutory registration of lobbyists was inevitable, according to one well-placed source, because a majority had already espoused this view before evidence was taken. Those submitting evidence were largely political 'insiders' who do not necessarily represent the public interest. Thus, it was no big surprise that the Neill committee would endorse the view already taken in 1995 by its predecessor, the Nolan committee. As it was in London, so it is in Edinburgh: the profile of those responding to the Standards Committee's consultation is similarly dominated by insiders. The public has effectively disappeared from the debate.

As the committee's clerks prepare a report to be considered early in 2001, the committee has signalled the limited scope of its deliberations and likely recommendations. The sole focus will be the interaction between MSPs and lobbyists. Evidently, unlike during Lobbygate, ministers (and civil servants) will not now be accountable to the committee for their relations with outside interests. Thus, whatever conclusions the Standards Committee reaches, how the Executive should deal with lobbyists still remains an open question.

THERE SHALL BE A SCOTTISH GOVERNMENT . . .

The debate on what can be done about the low public recognition of the Scottish Executive (from which the Scottish Office also suffered) has moved on. As noted (on pp. 135–6), some civil servants had been raising this issue since the early 1990s. Progress came indirectly through internal debates about the public image of the NHS and whether its activities were properly understood by the public. As part of the process of setting up a Scottish version of NHS Direct, the Faulds advertising agency was commissioned to research public perceptions of the health service. The resulting new logo for the NHS in Scotland was used when launching the strategy document, *Our National Health*.

The rethink inside the civil service was part and parcel of the process which led to ministers and civil servants reconsidering the name and image of the Executive itself. According to our sources, the question of whether the Executive should be formally renamed a 'government' first came up in internal meetings of the Executive at which the new image for the NHS was discussed.

We have already pointed to the sensitivities surrounding the terminology for Scotland's new government (see p. 129). The title 'Executive' was preferred, under the terms negotiated by Donald Dewar, to indicate that there was only one government, that of the UK. Anything else, it seemed, would be to demote the supremacy of Downing Street and Westminster. The thought that a devolved administration might be titled a government, without threatening the Union and lending succour to the nationalists, was apparently positively off-limits.

When the subversive call for a name-change came, it was from the heart of Scotland's Cabinet. Although deniable tactics were used, the voice was that of Henry McLeish, Scotland's second First Minister. Within twenty-four hours, amid a deluge of opprobrium from assorted Labour MPs and a definitive put-down by Tony Blair's spokesman, Alastair Campbell, McLeish and his rebranders in the Scottish Cabinet was forced to eat the g-word. Or only half-eat it: McLeish told the Scottish Parliament on 11 January that although there would be no name-change the Executive was, nonetheless, a government. During the furore, the spin from official spokesman Peter MacMahon was that the minister for parliament, Tom McCabe, had simply made an 'off-the-cuff' response to reporters' questions (Atticus 2001). This does not square with what we have been told. Although the political communication was undoubtedly inept, the need to redescribe Scotland's institutional map, and to distinguish the politicians from the civil servants in the Executive, was unquestionably right. Rather like the ballad of the 'Scottish Six', this sang will be sung again, and again.

Appendix 1: Methodology

Our research was carried out using a variety of methods, sources and strategies. These included:

(1) systematic monitoring of the relevant press and broadcast media, as well as selected specialist publications
(2) semi-structured interviews with those involved in the processes under investigation
(3) documentary and archival research
(4) ethnographic fieldwork in both public and private fora.

Our media monitoring enabled us to track the Scottish political news agenda from before the elections to the Scottish Parliament up to the completion of this study. Our sample included the Scottish broadsheet and tabloid press, broadcast media, and specialist publications such as *PR Week*, *The Drum*, and *Holyrood*. This media archive became a vital source of primary data which allowed us to develop a comprehensive picture of public political communication in post-devolution Scotland. This archive also served as an important resource in our preparations for interviews with selected informants.

RESEARCHING THE NEW SCOTLAND

Elite interviewing was central to the research. We encountered few problems of access. The one area of real difficulty has been in obtaining information from the SEID. Roger Williams (SEID's Director) refused to let us see a copy of the 1997 review of the Information Directorate on the grounds that it 'is not only way out of date for current comparisons but was also an internal, confidential document'. We later obtained a copy of the document from another official source outside the Executive, suggesting that the new system in Scotland is in some respects less open than the old Whitehall system.

Furthermore, Williams would not tell us how many staff worked in the SEID on the grounds that it was in flux. He wrote: 'I cannot help you at the moment regarding your request for information about the Information Directorate as we have yet to finalise plans for the Strategic Communications Unit and how we run the press office in an expanded ministerial scenario' (letter to the authors, 8 September 1999). Provisional figures could have been provided. When we approached an MSP to ask written questions, word came back from his party's spin doctors that these were regarded by the Executive as 'unhelpful'.

When we tried to investigate the media training programme run by the Executive, an attempt was made to stop us finding out about ministerial media training. According to internal documents, which we have seen, one of the Executive's chief press officers, Susan Stewart, instructed the Video and Television Production Unit not to divulge any information about ministerial media training to us, because 'that is always liable to misrepresentation' (December 1999). We have not misrepresented the activities of the media trainers, surely a matter of public interest, but our efforts to give an account have not been helped by the hindrance put in our way. We were told that we would have to go to Susan Stewart for information about ministerial training. But she refused to talk to us about it, saying only that 'a number' of ministers had taken the training course and that the system of media training was the same as that operated under the previous government, with current ministers making no greater proportional use of it. This latter point was incorrect since Conservative ministers had evidently not been through the media training programme. Later, when we rang journalists involved in media training, civil servants emailed us in an attempt to insist we ask their permission to have such conversations. When we persisted, one of the journalists – Paddy Christie – refused to speak to us.

Another area where we encountered difficulty was in establishing the facts about media passes to the Scottish Parliament. The Parliament's media relations office were happy to supply us with details of their accreditation procedures and code of conduct governing journalists' activities on the parliamentary campus. However, they refused to allow us access to a list of names (this was not a matter of providing contact details or any other personal information) of those with passes, claiming that such information was for internal administrative purposes only. Andrew Slorance, the senior media relations officer, said he 'thought that it was the understanding of journalists that their names would not be circulated' outwith Parliamentary staff. That such basic information should be private strikes us as a remarkable perversion of the openness and transparency of the Parliament's guiding principles.

Otherwise, the picture was much happier. Civil servants outwith the SEID were very helpful indeed and we were refused no interviews. Where specifically requested, these were treated as off-the-record or as confidential. There was both interest in the study among interviewees and a widespread desire to contribute to it. Interviews were conducted across the political communications spectrum in Scotland as well as with some key people in London. Interviewees comprised broadcasters, journalists, media executives, commercial and voluntary sector lobbyists, civil servants in the Scottish Parliament and Scottish Executive, and MSPs. Key informants have been very willing to repeatedly cooperate with the project team in sharing information and ideas. In total we interviewed 105 individuals (thirty-three broadcasters and journalists, thirty lobbyists, twenty-nine civil servants, and thirteen others including politicians, experts and interested parties. We conducted at least one follow-up interview with thirteen interviewees. This cooperation and user engagement is the legacy of previous research undertaken at the Stirling Media Research Institute and has given the present study a timeframe that has added considerable value.

We also collected documentation in the public domain relating to the various strands of the project. These documents comprise early drafts of the code of conduct for MSPs, research papers produced by the Scottish Parliament Information Centre (SPICe), research undertaken by the Scottish Executive when evaluating its public information campaign prior to polling in the Scottish general election, and promotional literature produced by lobbying organisations.

Our credibility as researchers has afforded us access to meetings, events and internal documentation from several sources. Notably, we have had access to those drafting the rules of media coverage for the Parliament and several committee and working group meetings of the Association for Scottish Public Affairs (ASPA). In the course of these contacts, Will Dinan became membership secretary for ASPA in 2000. This involved maintaining ASPA's membership database, but we did not provide any consultancy or advice to that organisation. Our access to ASPA meetings was entirely and openly premised on our status as social scientists studying a moment of extraordinary constitutional and institutional change of which ASPA was a part. We formally interviewed several members of ASPA during our fieldwork. Our participation in ASPA was based – and understood to be – on strictly academic grounds. We were also privy to highly confidential BBC material, to detailed accounts of the lobbying conducted by the SPPA, to internal minutes of ASPA meetings, and to internal documents on external and internal communication in the Scottish Office/Scottish Executive. Our observational fieldwork included attending all the public sessions of the Scottish Parliament's Standards Committee during the Parliament's first session, which considered the code of conduct for MSPs, and also the inquiry hearings of that committee into the 'Lobbygate' affair. It also included the meetings of the Expert Panel on Media Issues established by the CSG. The research team also attended numerous conferences and seminars where issues relating to public affairs and political communication in Scotland were discussed. From our point of view, the ethnography of the private meeting is entirely continuous with the ethnography of the public conference and has allowed a cross-check on our various sources of information.

Bibliography

Adamson, L. (1999), 'Lobbyists plan breakaway group', *Sunday Herald*, 17 October, p. 6.

Alba, C. (1999), 'A whitewash', *Daily Record*, 1 October, p. 2.

Alba, C. (2001), 'McLeish calls in makeover experts', *Sunday Times, Scotland*, 14 January, p. 2.

Allardyce, J. (1999), 'Edinburgh Blairite "was victim of mandarin plot"', *The Times*, 15 December, p. 2, http://www.thetimes.co.uk/news/pages/tim/1999/12/15/timpolpol01013.html

Allardyce, J. (2000), 'Fury as minister denounces "crass" Scots *Newsnight*', *The Times*, 10 February, p. 1.

Allardyce, J. and I. Martin (1998), 'How Brown opened the door for Lord Gus', *Scotland on Sunday*, 9 August, p. 10.

Anderson, A. (1993), 'Source-media relations, the production of the environmental agenda', in A. Hansen (ed.) *The Mass Media and Environmental Issues*, Leicester: Leicester University Press.

Anderson, A. (1997), *Media, Culture and Environment*, London: UCL Press.

Anderson, B. (1991), *Imagined Communities: Reflections on the Origin and Spread of Nationalism*, 2nd edn, London: Verso Editions.

Anderson, P. J. and A. Weymouth (1999), *Insulting the Public? The British Press and the European Union*, London: Longman.

APCS (1979), Association of Political Correspondents in Scotland, Memorandum on the Reporting and Information Arrangements of a Scottish Assembly and Executive.

APPC (2000), APPC in Scotland: Response to *Lobbying in the Scottish Parliament: Standards Committee Consultation Paper*, December.

Arlidge, J. and D. Nelson (1998), 'Labour equality pledge under threat', *Observer in Scotland*, 15 March, p. 1.

Atack, S. (1997), 'FMS-Ludgate form alliance in Scotland', *Public Affairs Newsletter*, vol. 4, no. 2, October, p. 3.

Atticus (2001), 'Margo is right behind McLeish – that's what worries him', *Sunday Times, Scotland*, 14 January, p. 21.

Ballantine, W. M. (1960), 'The case for Scotland', *Public Administration*, vol. 38, pp. 111–18.

Barker, S. (1998), 'National assemblies urged to follow Euro lobbying code', *PR Week*, 5 June, p. 2.

Bateman, D. (1989), 'Leak escalated BBC-Forsyth saga', *Scotland on Sunday*, 17 December, p. 1.

BBC (1997), *Governing today's BBC: broadcasting, the public interest and accountability*, December, London: BBC.

BBC (1998), *Devolution: A BBC Programme Response*, Strictly Confidential, 29 June.

BBC (1999), *The Changing UK*, London: BBC.

BBC News (1998), *BBC News, The Future: Public Service News in the Digital Age*, 6 October, London: BBC News.

BBC Press Office (1998), Statement by the BBC Board of Governors, 10 December, London: BBC.

BBC Research (1998), *Constitutional Reform*, London: BBC.

BCS (1998a), The Broadcasting Council for Scotland, *Devolution: A BBC Programme Response*. The Council's Proposals, Glasgow: BBC Scotland.

BCS (1998b), Summary of BCS Responses to the Executive Committee Papers on the Programme Response to Devolution and Enhancing Accountability.

BCS (1998c), A BBC Programme Response to Devolution, Statement from Broadcasting Council for Scotland, 20 November.

Beder, S. (1997), *Global Spin: The Corporate Assault on Environmentalism*, Totnes, Devon: Green Books.

Billig, M. (1995), *Banal Nationalism*, London: Sage.

Blain, N. and D. Hutchison (1993), 'The limits of Union, broadcasting in Scotland', in S. Harvey and K. Robins (eds), *The Regions, the Nations and the BBC*, London: BFI Publishing, pp. 49–58.

Blair, T. (1989), *Privatisation Advertising: The Selling of Water and Electricity*, London: Labour Party.

Blumler, J. and M. Gurevitch, (1995), *The Crisis of Public Communication*, London: Routledge.

Bogdanor, V. (1999), *Devolution in the United Kingdom*, Oxford: Oxford University Press.

Booth, P. and J. Penman (1997), 'Journalists want Washington's way, not Westminster's', *The Scotsman*, 22 October, p. 6.

Brogan, B. and R. Dinwoodie (1999), 'Minister denies Lobbygate cover-up', *The Herald*, 25 October, p. 1.

Brooks, R. (1998), 'BBC accused of dumping Scots news', *The Observer*, 22 November, p. 1.

Brooks, R. and V. Smart (1988), 'Tories "breaking TV ads code"', *The Observer*, 24 April, p. 1.

Brown, A. and D. McCrone (1999), 'Business and the Scottish Parliament Project, Report', March, Edinburgh: Governance of Scotland Forum.

Brown, A., D. McCrone and L. Paterson (1998), *Politics and Society in Scotland*, Basingstoke and London: Macmillan.

Brown, M. (1980), 'The Scottish morning press and the devolution referendum of 1979', in H. M. Drucker and N. L. Drucker (eds), *Scottish Government Yearbook 1980*, Edinburgh: Paul Harris Publishing.

Brown, T. (1999), 'The peddlars of power', *Daily Record*, 27 September, pp. 6–7.

Brown, T. (2000a), 'McLeish hits the ground running', *New Statesman*, 30 October, p. 36.

Brown, T. (2000b), 'Populist and incorrect? I plead guilty', *New Statesman*, 4 December, p. 36.

Brunson, M. (2000), *A Ringside Seat: The Autobiography*, London: Hodder & Stoughton.

Campbell, D. (1997), 'Spin doctor's emergency call', *The Herald*, 4 October, p. 1.

Carey, A. (1995), *Taking the Risk out of Democracy: Corporate Propaganda versus Freedom and Liberty*, ed. Andrew Lohrey, Sydney: University of New South Wales Press.

Cargill, K. (1998), 'The future of broadcast news in Scotland', speech to the Voice of the Listener and Viewer Conference, 28 November.

Carrell, S., R. Tait and A. Hardie (1999), 'Victory for Dewar in turf war over sleaze', *The Scotsman*, 28 September, p. 1.

Carruthers, S. (1995), *Winning Hearts and Minds: British Governments, the Media and Colonial Counter-Insurgency 1944–1960*, Leicester: Leicester University Press.

Cockerell, M., P. Hennessey. and D. Walker (1984), *Sources Close to the Prime Minister: Inside the Hidden World of the News Manipulators*, London: Macmillan.

Cohen, N. (1998), 'The death of news', *New Statesman*, 22 May, pp. 18–20.

COI (1999), *The IPO Directory: Information and Press Officers in Government Departments and Public Corporations*, December, London: COI.

COI (2000), *The IPO Directory: Information and Press Officers in Government Departments and Public Corporations*, June, London: COI.

Coleman, S. (1999), *Electronic Media, Parliament and the People: Making Democracy Visible*, London: The Hansard Society for Parliamentary Government.

Colley, L. (1992), *Britons: Forging the Nation 1707–1837*, London: Pimlico.

Connolly, T. (1989), 'Forsyth letter provokes protest', *The Observer Scotland*, 17 December, p. 3.

Cook, T. (1998), *Governing with the News: The News Media as a Political Institution*, Chicago, IL, University of Chicago Press.

Copley, J. and P. MacMahon (1998) 'Cabinet tells BBC, Say no to Scots News at Six', *The Scotsman*, 11 November, p. 1.

Crewe, I. and M. Harrop (eds) (1989), *Political Communications: The General Election Campaign of 1987*, Cambridge: Cambridge University Press.

Crewe, I. and B. Gosschalk (eds) (1995), *Political Communications: The General Election Campaign of 1992*, Cambridge: Cambridge University Press.

Crichton, T. (2000), 'Scotland Office calls in Versace', *Sunday Herald*, 11 June, p. 4.

Crofts, W. (1989), *Coercion or Persuasion? Propaganda in Britain after 1945*, London: Routledge.

CSG (1998a), The Scottish Office, Consultative Steering Group Information Paper, Media Issues. CSG Secretariat, September. Paper no. 98.

CSG (1998b), Report of the Consultative Steering Group on the Scottish Parliament, 'Shaping Scotland's Parliament', Edinburgh: The Scottish Office. http://www.scotland.gov.uk/library/documents-ww5/rcsg-02.htm.

CSG (1999), The Scottish Office, Consultative Steering Group, Supplementary Report, Edinburgh: The Stationery Office.

Cusick, J. and D. Fraser (2000), 'Sheridan misses out on TV debate', *Sunday Herald*, 17 December, p. 2.

Daily Record (1999), 'Labour line up new Holyrood spin doctor', 2 August, p. 2.

Dalton, A. (1998), 'Viewers split over 6pm Scots news', *The Scotsman*, 24 November, p. 1.

Davies, A. (2000a), 'Public-relations campaigning and news production, the case of the "new unionism" in Britain', in J. Curran (ed.), *Media Organisations and Society*, London: Arnold.

Davies, A. (2000b) 'Public relations, news production and changing patterns of source access in the British national media', *Media, Culture and Society*, vol. 22, pp. 39–59.

Davies, N. (1999), *The Isles: A History*, London: Macmillan.

Deacon, D. (1996), 'The voluntary sector in a changing communication environment, a case-study of non-official news sources', *European Journal of Communication*, vol. 11, no. 2, pp. 173–99.

Deacon, D. and P. Golding (1994), *Taxation and Representation*, London: John Libbey.

Denholm, A. (2000), 'BBC Scotland on defensive as Wilson comes out fighting', *The Scotsman*, 10 February, p. 7.

Denver, D., J. Mitchell, C. Pattie, and H. Bochel (2000), *Scotland Decides: The Devolution Issue and the Scottish Referendum*, London: Frank Cass.

Deutsch, K. W. (1966), *Nationalism and Social Communication: An Inquiry into the Foundations of Nationalism*, 2nd edn, Cambridge, MA and London: MIT Press.

Devine, T. (1999), *The Scottish Nation 1700–2000*, London: Allen Lane, The Penguin Press.

Dewar, D. (1998), 'Broadcasting and Devolution', speech to the Broadcasting Council for Scotland's Symposium in Glasgow, 27 February.

Dinan, W. (1999) 'Love and loathing: the British public relations industry and its trade press', *Media Education Journal*, issue 27, Winter, pp. 25–8.

Dinwoodie, R. (1998a), 'Pressure grows for Scots curbs on lobbyists', *The Herald*, 22 January, p. 6.

Dinwoodie, R. (1998b), 'Propaganda claims over Dewar speech on internet', *The Herald*, 3 June, p. 6.

Dinwoodie, R. (1998c), 'Lobbyists pledge to match openness', *The Herald*, 1 September, p. 6.

Dinwoodie, R. (1998d), 'Ballot campaign row rages on', *The Herald*, 13 October, p. 6.

Dinwoodie, R. (1998e), 'Scottish Six gains top poll ratings', *The Herald*, 4 December, p. 1.

Dinwoodie, R. (1999), 'Rivals unite to claim foul on use of information staff', *The Herald*, 8 April, p 7.

Dinwoodie, R. and M. Ritchie (2000), 'Three spin doctors and an apology', *The Herald*, 27 January, p. 1.

Doig, A (1998), '"Cash for Questions", Parliament's response to the offence that dare not speak its name', *Parliamentary Affairs*, vol. 51, no. 1, pp. 36–50.

Douglas, D. (1988), 'Scottish Office to announce choice for its image-maker', *Glasgow Herald*, 22 December.

Doward, J. (2000), 'Looking for a tartan army', *The Observer*, 10 September, p. 7.

Downey, J. (1998), 'The virtuous side of lobbying', *The Herald*, 22 April, p. 16.

Draper, D. (1999), 'You were right, I was wrong', *The Observer*, 4 July, p. 26.

The Drum (2000), 'Scotsman bosses plan new 16-page pink business section to thwart Bam', *The Drum*, 4 August, p. 3.

Drummond, L. (1997), 'Stop shooting the messenger, Tony', *The Scotsman*, 13 December, p. 16.

DTI-DCMS (2000), *A New Future for Communications: Communications White Paper*, http://www.communicationswhitepaper.gov.uk, 12 December.

Duncan, G. (1996), 'Outrage over "propaganda offensive"', *The Scotsman*, 22 February, p. 6.

Dunn, C. (1999), 'Setting the scene for the Scottish Lobby', *Holyrood*, 13 September, pp. 20–1.

Dyke, G. (2000), 'Devolution means giving BBC Scotland the power to improve', *Business a.m.*, 16 November, p. 31.

Dunnett, A. (1984), *Amongst Friends*, London: Century Publishing.

Dyke, G. (2000), 'Devolution means giving BBC Scotland the power to improve', *Business a.m.*, 16 November, p. 31.

Eames, B. and A. Watson (1999), 'Milestone on the road of change marks renewed commitment to communication', *Scoop* (Scottish Office internal magazine) June/July, pp. 7–14.

Economist (1999), 'Undoing Britain?' *Survey Supplement*, 6 November, pp. 1–18.

Edwards, R. (2000), 'It was supposed to be a vital weapon to save Scotland's wildlife. So who pulled the teeth on Sarah Boyack's plan of action?', *Sunday Herald*, 6 August, p. 13.

Elliott, F. (2000), 'Mission impossible', *Scotland on Sunday*, Spectrum, 6 August, p. 16.

Engel, Matthew (1996), 'Protest locale that can't square the circle', *The Guardian*, 25 March, p. 2.

European Parliament (1999), 'Rules of Procedure of the European Parliament, Provisions governing the application of Rule 9(2) – Lobbying the Parliament', June, Brussels: European Parliament.

Evening News (2000), 'New adviser for Scots coalition', 13 June, p. 2.

Ewen, S. (1996), *PR! A Social History of Spin*, New York, NY: Basic Books.

Fagin, D., M. Lavelle and the Center for Public Integrity (1999), *Toxic Deception: How the Chemical Industry Manipulates Science, Bends the Law and Endangers Your Health*, Monroe, ME: Common Courage Press.

Farquharson, K. (1999a), 'Holyrood adviser snub for Dewar's spin doctor', *Sunday Times*, 1 August, p. 2.

Farquharson, K. (1999b), 'Press officer in bias row', *Sunday Times, Scotland*, 26 September, http://www.sunday-times.co.uk/news/pages/sti/99/09/26/stiscosco01008.html.

Faulds Advertising (1998a), 'The Scottish Parliament: The Communications Strategy', 4 November, research report.

Faulds Advertising (1998b), 'The Scottish Parliament: Communications Development Research', 1 December, research report.

Faulds Advertising (1999), 'Scottish Parliament: Hall Test Results (Top Line Findings)', 22 January, research report.

Fitzpatrick, B. (2000), 'Final message from the outgoing policy chief', *The Herald*, 27 October, p. 12.

Fones-Wolf, E. (1994), *Selling Free Enterprise: The Business Assault on Labor and Liberalism*, 1945–60, Urbana, IL: University of Illinois Press.

Forsyth, I. (2000), 'ITC launches second attack on Grampian', *Aberdeen Press and Journal*, 25 May, p. 9.

Franklin, B. (1994), *Packaging Politics*, London: Edward Arnold.

Franklin, B. (1997), *Newszak and News Media*, London: Edward Arnold.

Franklin, B. (1999), *Tough on Soundbites, Tough on the Causes of Soundbites*, London: Catalyst Trust.

Fraser, D. (1998a), 'BBC warned of revolt over Scottish news', *The Observer*, 25 October, p. 3.

Fraser, D. (1998b), 'Here is the news. It's war', *The Observer*, 6 December, p. 17.

Fraser, D. (1999), 'Yes, First Minister', *Sunday Herald*, 19 December, p. 10.

Fraser, D. (2000a), 'How it all works', *Sunday Herald*, 30 January, p. 15.

Fraser, D. (2000b), 'Politics gets personal', *Sunday Herald*, 27 February, p. 5.

Fraser, D. (2000c), 'McLeish dumps Dewar's lagacy', *Sunday Herald*, 29 October, p. 1.

Fraser, D. and I. Watson (1999a), 'Reid called to face sleaze inquiry; Watchdog moves for public hearing', *Sunday Herald*, 3 October, p. 1.

Fraser, D. and I. Watson (1999b), 'Less spin . . . more grip', *Sunday Herald*, 12 December, pp. 10–11.

Friends of the Earth Scotland (2000), *Access All Areas: New Freedom of Information Proposals for Scotland*, briefing, Edinburgh: Friends of the Earth Scotland.

Garavelli, D. (1998), 'Compromise plan to screen Scottish Six', *Scotland on Sunday*, 6 December, p. 3.

Garner, K. (1999), 'Muted Proceedings: Scottish Radio Broadcasting's Response to the New Scottish Parliament', paper presented at 'RADIOCRACY, Radio, Democracy and Development', international conference, School of Journalism, Media and Cultural Studies, Cardiff University, 26–28 November.

Garside, J. (1998), 'Lobbyists get serious about new standards', *PR Week*, 5 July, p. 9.

Gellner, E. (1983), *Nations and Nationalism*, Oxford: Basil Blackwell.

Gellner, E. (1997), *Nationalism*, London: Weidenfeld & Nicolson.

Gibson, J. (1998), 'BBC to "tell us why news matters"', *The Guardian*, 7 October, p. 8.

Gibson, John S. (1985), *The Thistle and the Crown: A History of the Scottish Office*, Edinburgh: HMSO.

Gilbride, P. (1999), 'Who is Whirlwind Wendy?', *Daily Record*, 9 December, pp. 40–1.

Gould, P. (1998), *The Unfinished Revolution: How the Modernisers Saved the Labour Party*, London: Abacus.

Grant, Linda (1995), 'Just say no', *Guardian Weekend*, 3 June, pp. 12–22.

Grant, Wyn (1995), *Pressure Groups, Politics and Democracy in Britain*, 2nd edn, Hemel Hempstead: Harvester Wheatsheaf.

Gray, R. (1998), 'Taking the hi-tech road', *PR Week*, 20 February, pp. 13–14.

Greenaway, J., S. Smith and J. Street (1992), *Deciding Factors in British*

Politics: A Case Studies Approach, London: Routledge.

Greenwood, J. (1997), *Representing Interests in the European Union*, Basingstoke: Macmillan.

Greer, I. (1997), *One Man's World: The Untold Story of the Cash-for-questions Affair*, London: Andre Deutsch.

Habermas, J. (1989), *The Structural Transformation of the Public Sphere: An Inquiry into a Category of Bourgeois Society*, Cambridge: Polity Press.

Habermas, J. (1994), 'Citizenship and national identity', in B. van Steenbergen (ed.), *The Condition of Citizenship*, London: Sage Publications, pp. 20–35.

Habermas, J. (1997), *Between Facts and Norms*, Cambridge: Polity Press.

Hager, N. and B. Burton (1999), *Secrets and Lies: The Anatomy of an Anti-environmental PR Campaign*, Nelson, NZ: Craig Potton Publishing.

Hardie, A. (1999), 'Bungling MSPs are damaging devolution', *The Scotsman*, 25 October, p. 1.

Hardie, A. (2000), 'Newsnight editor outs himself as SNP runner', *The Scotsman*, 18 October, p. 1.

Hardie, A. and R. Tait, (1999), 'Shambles', *The Scotsman*, 2 October, pp. 11, 13

Hardy, F. (1947), 'The Cinema', in Henry W. Meikle (ed.), *Scotland: A Description of Scotland and Scottish Life*, London: Thomas Nelson and Sons Ltd.

Harrington, A. (2000), 'Wilson apology demanded over BBC attack', *The Herald*, 10 February, p. 3.

Harris, R. (1991), *Good and Faithful Servant*, London: Faber and Faber.

Haslam, F. (2000), Modernising government: Have public relations practices changed under New Labour?, Unpublished dissertation, MSc, Public Relations, Stirling: University of Stirling.

Hassan, G. and Warhurst, C. (2000), 'A new politics?' in G. Hassan and C. Warhurst (eds) The New Scottish Politics, *The First Year of the Scottish Parliament and Beyond*, Edinburgh: The Stationery Office, pp. 1–14.

Hearn, J. (2000), *Claiming Scotland: National Identity and Liberal Culture*, Edinburgh: Polygon at Edinburgh.

Heffernan, R. and M. Marqusee (1992), *Defeat from the Jaws of Victory: Inside Kinnock's Labour Party*, London: Verso.

Hencke, D. (1998), 'Tough new code on lobbyists', *The Guardian*: 28 July, p. 3.

Hennessy, P. (1989), *Whitehall*, London: Faber and Faber.

Hetherington, A. (1989), *News in the Regions: Plymouth Sound to Moray Firth*, Basingstoke and London: Macmillan.

Hetherington, A. (1992), *Inside BBC Scotland 1975–1980: A Personal View*, Aberdeen: Whitewater Press.

Hill, A. (2000), 'Media maw is fed another sacrificial victim', *The Observer in Scotland*, 3 September, p. 12.

Hill, L. (1998), 'Dewar denies Scots want Six news bulletin', *Scotland on Sunday*, 13 December, p. 3.

Hill, L. (1999), 'Key Lobbygate evidence destroyed', *Scotland on Sunday*, 24 October, p. 1.

Hogg, G. (1995), *Service Quality in Public Relations in Scotland: Research Summary*, Research Papers in Marketing, Occasional Paper 95/001, Stirling: Department of Marketing, University of Stirling.

Hollingsworth, M. (1991), *MPs for Hire: The Secret World of Political Lobbying*, London: Bloomsbury.

Hollis (1997), *Hollis UK Press & Public Relations Annual*, 28th edn, Middlesex: Hollis Directories Ltd.

Hollis (1998), *Hollis UK Press & Public Relations Annual*, 29th edn, Middlesex: Hollis Directories Ltd.

Hollis (1999), *Hollis UK Press & Public Relations Annual*, 30th edn, Middlesex: Hollis Directories Ltd.

Hope, C. (1999), 'Briefings aim to give MSPs "easily digestible" overview', *The Scotsman*, 20 September, p. 16.

Horsburgh, F. (1997), 'Lobbyists attempt to clean up their image', *The Herald*, 30 October, p. 7.

Horsburgh, F. (1998), 'Lobbyists to agree code', *The Herald*, 27 February, p. 6.

Horsburgh, F. (2000), 'Standards Committee wary of having Scots watchdog', *The Herald*, 27 January, p. 6.

Hughes, C. and P. Wintour (1990), *Labour Rebuilt*, London: Fourth Estate.

Ingham, B. (1991), *Kill the Messenger*, London: Harper Collins.

Innes, J. (1999), 'Lobbyist ruled out by Council', *The Scotsman*, 11 November, p. 4

Insider, The (1998), 'Off message', *Scotland on Sunday*, 8 March, p. 12.

IPMS (1997), '77% of all civil servants now in Next Steps agencies', *IPMS Bulletin*, June, p. 7.

Jackall, R. (1994) 'The magic lantern: The world of public relations', in R. Jackall (ed.), *Propaganda*, Basingstoke: Macmillan, pp. 351–99.

Jacobs, B. (1997a), 'Inside Scotland's new labour empire where "facts are no longer sacred"', *Evening News*, 29 December, pp. 4–5.

Jacobs, B. (1997b), 'Tartan tax is not Tory propaganda', *Evening News*, 30 December, p 5.

Jacobs, B. (1997c), 'Lang fought like a tiger for Rosyth. He lost . . .', *Evening News*, 31 December, p. 4.

John, S. (1998), 'Survey of Public Affairs', London: Public Affairs Newsletter.

Johnson, J. (1999), 'Spinner fakes all', *Red Pepper*, May, pp. 20–1.

Jones, N. (1986), *Strikes and the Media*, London: Blackwell.

Jones, N. (1995), *Soundbites and Spin Doctors*, London: Cassell.

Jones, N. (1997), *Campaign 1997: How the General Election Was Won and Lost*, London: Indigo.

Jones, N. (1999), *Sultans of Spin: the Media and the New Labour Government*, London: Victor Gollancz.

Jones, P. (1999), 'Eye for detail', *Scottish Business Insider*, January, pp. 10–11.

Jordan, G. (ed.) (1991), *The Commercial Lobbyists*, Aberdeen: Aberdeen University Press.

Jordan, G. (1998), 'Towards regulation in the UK, From "general good sense" to "formalised rules"', *Parliamentary Affairs*, vol. 51 no. 4, pp. 524–37.

Kavanagh, D. (1995), *Election Campaigning*, Oxford: Blackwell.

Keane, J. (1991), *The Media and Democracy*, Cambridge: Polity Press.

Kellas, J. G. (1989), *The Scottish Political System* (4th edn), Cambridge: Cambridge University Press.

Kemp, A. (1998), 'Donald Dewar's spin doctors have been busily repackaging him. Soon he will be kissing babies', *The Observer in Scotland*, 24 May, p. 27.

Kemp, A. (2000a), 'Winning on a loser', *The Observer in Scotland*, 4 June, p. 35.

Kemp, A. (2000b), 'I'm frustrated says "Colditz" inmate Wilson', *The Observer in Scotland*, 23 July, p. 13.

Kemp, K. and S. Breen (1998), 'BBC chiefs face quiz on news plans', *The Scotsman*, 8 October, p. 4.

Kendrick, S. (1990), 'Scotland, change and politics', in D. McCrone, S. Kendrick and P. Straw (eds), *The Making of Scotland: Nation, Culture and Social Change*, Edinburgh: Edinburgh University Press, pp. 71–90.

Killeen, D. (1998), 'Short shrift for paid lobbyists', *The Herald*, 15 July, p. 16.

King, D. (1998a), 'Jobs for the same boys', *Daily Record*, 8 July 1998, p. 1.

King, D. (1998b), 'Lobbying their way into power', *Daily Record*, 8 July, pp. 6–7.

King, D. (1999), 'Major Gaffe', *Daily Record*, 30 September, pp. 1–2.

Kisch, R. (1964), *PR: The Private Life of Public Relations*, London: MacGibbon and Kee.

Knight, A. (1993), 'A British Success Story – An Examination of Prospects for the UK Media', Speech to the Institute of Directors Annual Convention, 27 April.

Koski, J. (1984), 'For the campaign was then selling not just BT shares but a political philosophy', *The Guardian*, 10 December, p. 9.

Laing, A. (1998a), 'BBC's radical shake-up may hinder Scottish news opt-out', *The Herald*, 7 October, p. 5.

Laing, A. (1998b), 'BBC plans for news spark major row in Scotland', *The Herald*, 8 October, p. 2.

Laing, A. (1998c), 'Here is the news from BBC Scotland', *The Herald*, 22 October, p. 5.

Laird, A., S. Granville and J. Fawcett (2000), *Assessment of the Voter Education Campaign for the Scottish Parliament Elections*, report by George Street Research for the Scottish Executive Central Research Unit, Edinburgh: Scotland Office.

Laurance, B. (1999), 'McNulty to withdraw attack on Observer', *The Observer*, 3 October, www.guardianlimited.co.uk/Scotland/Story/0,2763,200989,00.html.

Lazarowicz, M. and A. Jones (1998), Parliamentary Practices in Devolved Parliaments, Edinburgh: The Scottish Office.

Leapman, M. (1986), *The Last Days of the Beeb*, London: George Allen & Unwin.

Lee, J. (1999), 'Cheers to the beers', *The Guardian*, Money, 5 June, p. 25.

Leigh, D. and E. Vulliamy (1997), *Sleaze: The Corruption of Parliament*, London: Fourth Estate.

Leishman, M. (1998), Briefing note for all governors in advance of meeting with BCS, 21 October.

Leppard, D., P. Nuki and G. Walsh (2000) 'Secret memo says Blair is out of touch', *Sunday Times*, 21 June, p. 1.

Leonard, M. (1997), *Britain TM: Renewing Our Identity*, London: Demos.

L'Etang, J. (1998), 'State propaganda and bureaucratic intelligence: the creation of public relations in 20th century Britain', *Public Relations Review*, vol. 24, no. 4, pp. 413–41.

L'Etang, J. (1999), 'John Grierson and the public relations industry in Britain', *Screening the Past: An International Electronic Journal of Visual Media History*, July, http://www.latrobe.edu.au/www/screeningthepast.

Linklater, M. (1992), 'The media' in M. Linklater and R. Denniston (eds), *Chambers' Anatomy of Scotland*, Edinburgh: Chambers, pp. 126–44

Lloyd, J. (1987), 'Media – whose message is it anyway?' in K. Cargill (ed.), *Scotland 2000: Eight Views on the State of the Nation*, Glasgow: BBC, pp. 135–58.

Luckhurst, T. (1997), 'Thinking man's politician wary of soundbite age', *The Scotsman*, 30 August, p. 7.

Luckhurst, T. (2000), 'Cold blast of integrity needed', *The Herald*, 30 October, pp. 6–7.

Lynch, P. (2000), 'The committee system of the Scottish Parliament', in G. Hassan and C. Warhurst (eds), *The New Scottish Politics: The First Year of the Scottish Parliament and Beyond*, Edinburgh: The Stationery Office, pp. 66–74.

Maarek, P. (1995), *Political Marketing and Communication*, London: John Libbey.

McAlpine, A., A. Watson,. G. Herbert, P. Watson and G. Scullion (1999), *Review of Internal Communications in the Scottish Office*, June.

McAlpine, J. (1998), 'Short step from news to spin', *Sunday Times, Scotland,* 19 July, p. 4.

MacAskill, E. (1989), 'Low-key revamp for Scottish Office', *The Scotsman,* 26 December, p. 2.

McCormick, J. (1997), 'The BBC and the Changing Broadcasting Environment', Town and Gown Lecture, University of Strathclyde, 4 November.

McCormick, J. (1998), 'We have to work together to make the BBC the best', *Daily Record,* 2 December, p. 4.

MacCormick, N. (1999), *Questioning Sovereignty: Law, State and Nation in the European Commonwealth,* Oxford: Oxford University Press.

McCrone, D. (1992), *Understanding Scotland: The Sociology of a Stateless Nation,* London and New York: Routledge.

McCrone, D. (1998), *The Sociology of Nationalism: Tomorrow's Ancestors,* London and New York: Routledge.

Macdonell, H. (1998), 'Rebuke for SNP over attack on civil service', *Daily Mail,* 8 April, p. 8.

Macdonell, H. (1999), 'Dewar's army of bureaucrats send Holyrood costs soaring', *Daily Mail,* 2 August, p. 4.

McGarvie, L. (1999), 'Despair of girl junkie', *Sunday Mail,* 14 November, p. 8.

McGinty, S. (2000a), 'Bad news on Home Front', *The Scotsman,* S2 Supplement, 29 September, pp. 4–5.

McGinty, S. (2000b), 'Whitewash or colour television?', *The Scotsman,* 19 October, p. 9.

McGinty, S. (2000c), 'Who's sleeping with the enemy?', *The Scotsman,* 19 November, p. 9.

McInnes, J. (1992), 'The press in Scotland', *Scottish Affairs,* no. 1, Autumn, pp. 137–49.

McInnes, J. (1993), 'The broadcast media in Scotland', *Scottish Affairs,* no. 2, pp. 84–98.

Macintyre, D. (2000), *Mandelson and the Making of New Labour,* London: Harper Collins.

Mackay, N. and L. Adamson (1999), 'Fears over Scots Secretary lobby links', *Sunday Herald,* 15 August, p. 5.

Mackenna, R. (1999), 'Dewar's sleaze probe blocked', *Daily Record,* 27 September, pp. 1, 4.

Mackenna, R. (2000), 'Threat of sacked aide telling all in book', *The Scotsman,* 31 October, p. 8

Mackenna, R. (2001), 'Friends in high places', *The Scotsman,* S2, 15 January, pp. 6–7.

McLean, G. (1998), 'Gagged; Beeb "advises" staff to keep quiet in fight for Scots news', *Daily Record,* 2 December, pp. 1, 4.

Macleod, A. (1998a), '61% . . . of all Scots demand their own TV news', *Sunday Mail*, 29 November, p. 20.

Macleod, A. (1998b), 'Labour's Lorraine in a spin', *Sunday Mail*, 6 December, p. 5.

Macleod, C. (1997), 'Press secretaries in a spin as Labour acts to change off-the-record lobby system', *The Herald*, 22 November, p. 6.

Macleod, C. (1998), 'BBC correspondent turns her hand to spin doctoring', *The Herald*, 10 July, p. 6.

Macleod, C. (1999), 'Peace breaks out for Dewar and Reid', *The Herald*, 29 September, pp. 1, 8.

MacMahon, P. and McLaughlin, C. (1995), 'Inquiry into Tory propaganda claims', *The Scotsman*, 19 January, p. 6.

McNair, B. (1995), *An Introduction to Political Communication*, London and New York: Routledge.

McNair, B. (1998), *The Sociology of Journalism*, London: Edward Arnold.

McNair, B. (2000), *Journalism and Democracy*, London: Routledge.

McTernan, L. (2000), 'Beyond the blethering classes; consulting and involving wider society', in G. Hassan and C. Warhurst (eds), *The New Scottish Politics: The First Year of the Scottish Parliament and Beyond*, Edinburgh: The Stationery Office. pp. 138–44.

Macwhirter, I. (1995), 'Doomsday two, the return of Forsyth', *Scottish Affairs*, no. 13, Autumn, pp. 15–26.

Macwhirter, I. (1999a), 'A secret network', *Sunday Herald*, 12 September, p. 11.

Macwhirter, I. (1999b), 'The day Parliament asserted its authority', *The Herald*, 6 October, p. 7.

Macwhirter, I. (1999c), 'Would you trust these men?', *Sunday Herald*, 24 October, p. 12.

Macwhirter, I. (1999d), 'Trial and errors', *Sunday Herald*, 31 October, p. 11.

Macwhirter, I. (2000), 'Scotland Year Zero: the first year at Holyrood', in G. Hassan and C. Warhurst (eds), *The New Scottish Politics: The First Year of the Scottish Parliament and Beyond*, Edinburgh: The Stationery Office, pp. 16–23.

Madeley, G. (2000), 'Bias at the BEEB', *Daily Mail*, 19 October, p. 17.

Manning, P. (1998), *Spinning for Labour: Trade Unions and the New Media Environment*, Aldershot: Ashgate.

Market Research Scotland (1999a), Monitor of Public Perceptions Related to Scottish Parliament Elections: Graphic Report of Findings (Wave 1), February.

Market Research Scotland (1999b), Monitor of Public Perceptions Related to Scottish Parliament Elections: Graphic Report of Findings (Wave 1), March.

Market Research Scotland (1999c), Monitor of Public Perceptions Related to

Scottish Parliament Elections: Graphic Report of Findings (Wave 3), April.

Marr, A. (1998), "And finally . . .", *The Observer*, 13 December, p. 28.

Marr, A. (2000), *The Day Britain Died*, London: Profile Books.

Marsh, K. (1999), *Confidential Report of the Independent Advice Panel on Parliamentary Programmes*, May, London: BBC Production.

Martin, I. (1998), 'Labour in crisis as Dewar blocks new spin-doctor post', *Scotland on Sunday*, 22 March, p. 1.

Martin, I. (1999), 'So which of these two men is really running Scotland?', *Scotland on Sunday*, 23 May, p. 13.

Martin, I. and C. Deerin (1998), 'Man in a spin', *Scotland on Sunday*, 31 May, p. 13.

Martin, I. and L. Hill (1998), 'What could have made Lorraine burst into tears?', *Scotland on Sunday*, 15 November, p. 3.

Martin, I. and L. Hill (1999), 'Is time running out for Dr Reid?', *Scotland on Sunday*, 3 October, p. 14.

Massie, A. (1999), 'So who is to speak the mind of Donald?', *Daily Mail*, 7 July, p. 14.

Matthews, V. (1997), 'Setting up new house rules', *PR Week*, 31 October, pp. 13–16.

Maxwell, F. (2000), 'Says, give our parliament a chance', *The Scotsman*, 24 March, p. 14.

Mayhew, L. (1997), *The New Public: Professional Communication and the Means of Social Influence*, Cambridge: Cambridge University Press.

Media Watch (2000), 'Mare Scotsman horseplay and shuffle for spinners', *Sunday Herald*, Business, 13 August, p. 8.

Meech, P. and R. Kilborn (1993), 'Media and identity in a stateless nation: the case of Scotland', *Media, Culture and Society*, vol. 14, no. 2, pp. 245–59.

Middleton, D., S. Brown and J. Gee (1997), *Review of the Scottish Office Information Directorate*, report prepared for the Principal Establishment Officer, The Scottish Office, December.

Middlemass, K. (1979), *Politics in Industrial Society: The Experience of the British System since 1911*, London: André Deutsch.

Miller, C. (2000), *Politico's Guide to Political Lobbying*, London: Politico's Publishing.

Miller, D. (1993), 'Official sources and primary definition, the case of Northern Ireland', *Media, Culture and Society*, vol. 15, no. 3, July, pp. 385–406.

Miller, D. (1994), *Don't Mention the War: Northern Ireland, Propaganda and the Media*, London: Pluto.

Miller, D. (1995), 'The media and Northern Ireland: censorship, information management and the broadcasting ban', in G. Philo (ed.),

The Glasgow Media Group Reader, Volume II, London: Routledge.

Miller, D. (1999), 'Risk, science and policy: BSE, definitional struggles, information management and the media', *Social Science and Medicine* special edition 'Science speaks to policy', vol. 49, pp. 1239–55.

Miller, D. and W. Dinan (2000), 'The rise of the PR industry in Britain, 1979–98', *European Journal of Communication*, vol. 15, no. 1, pp. 5–35.

Miller, D. and P. Schlesinger (2000), 'The changing shape of public relations in the European Union', in R. L. Heath and G. M. Vasquez (eds), *The Handbook of Public Relations*, London, Thousand Oaks, CA, New Delhi: Sage Publications, pp. 675–83.

Miller, D., J. Kitzinger, K. Williams and P. Beharrell (1998), *The Circuit of Mass Communication: Media Strategies, Representation and Audience Reception in the AIDS Crisis.* London: Sage.

Miller, P. and Farquharson, K. (2000), 'The politics gameshow', *Sunday Times, Scotland*, 17 December.

Milne, A. (1988), *DG: Memoirs of a British Broadcaster*, London: Hodder and Stoughton.

Moloney, K. (1996), *Lobbyists for Hire*, Aldershot: Dartmouth.

Morgan, D. (1999), *The European Parliament, Mass Media and the Search for Power and Influence*, Aldershot: Ashgate.

Mountfield, R. (1997), *Report of the Working Group on the Government Information Service*, November, London: Cabinet Office.

Nairn, T. (1981), *The Break-up of Britain*, (2nd edn), London: Verso Editions.

Nairn, T. (1997), *Faces of Nationalism: Janus Revisited*, London and New York: Verso.

Nairn, T. (2000), *After Britain: New Labour and the Return of Scotland*, London: Granta Books.

Neil, A. (1997), *Full Disclosure*, London: Macmillan.

Neill Committee (2000a), *Reinforcing Standards: Review of the First Report of the Committee on Standards in Public Life*, vol. I, Cm 4557-I, London: The Stationery Office.

Neill Committee (2000b), *Reinforcing Standards: Review of the First Report of the Committee on Standards in Public Life – Evidence*, vol. II, Cm 4557-II, London: The Stationery Office.

Nelson, D. and J. Arlidge (1998), 'Labour turns to spin after a black week', *The Observer in Scotland*, 8 March, p. 1.

Nelson, D. and B. Laurance (1999), 'Exposed: Lobbygate comes to Scotland', *The Observer in Scotland*, 26 September, p. 1.

Newton, K. (1997), 'A brave new world for those with heart', *PR Week*, 19 September, p. 9.

Nicholson, S. (2000), 'MSPs go cool on move for anti-sleaze watchdog', *The Scotsman*, 27 January, p. 11.

Nicoll, A., A. Muir and A. Carson (2000), 'Midnight, a red light area . . . and Dewar has lost his second aide: Chalmers' downfall', *Scottish Sun*, 26 January, pp. 2–3.

Nolan Committee (1995a), *Standards in Public Life*: vol. I, Cm 2850-I, London: HMSO.

Nolan Committee (1995b), *Standards in Public Life: Transcripts of Oral Evidence*, vol. II, Cm 2850-II, London: HMSO.

Norton-Taylor, R. (1995), *Truth is a Difficult Concept: Inside the Scott Inquiry*, London: Fourth Estate.

Norton-Taylor, R., M. Lloyd and S. Cook (1996), *Knee deep in Dishonour*, London: Victor Gollancz.

Nutt, K. (2000), 'Off the record', *Sunday Herald*, 3 September 2000, p. 12.

Oborne, P. (1999), *Alastair Campbell: New Labour and the Rise of the Media Class*, London: Aurum.

Observer transcript (1999), Evidence to Standards Committee of the Scottish Parliament: transcripts of meeting with Alex Barr and Kevin Reid, Beattie Media, Balmoral Hotel, 31 August 1999, Edinburgh. www.scottish.parliament.uk/official-report/cttee/stan99-00/append2-pdf.

O'Connor, A. (2000), 'SMG puts SRH on the block', *The Financial Times*, Companies and Finance UK, 20 December, p. 29.

Parker, A. and J. Penman (1998a), 'Dewar pressed to get media minder', *The Scotsman*, 12 March, p. 1.

Parker, A. and J. Penman (1998b), 'Dewar's reinforcements on the way', *The Scotsman*, 3 April, p. 6.

Parry, R. (2000), 'The civil service and the Scottish Executive's structure and style', in G. Hassan and C. Warhurst (eds), *The New Scottish Politics: The First Year of the Scottish Parliament and Beyond*, Edinburgh: The Stationery Office, pp. 85–91.

Paterson, L. (1994), *The Autonomy of Modern Scotland*, Edinburgh: Edinburgh University Press.

Paterson, L. (1998), 'The true story of the Scottish Six', *The Scotsman*, 24 November, p. 17.

Paterson, L. (1999), 'Why should we respect civic Scotland?', in G. Hassan and C. Warhurst (eds), *A Different Future: A Modernisers' Guide to Scotland*, Edinburgh and Glasgow: The Centre for Scottish Public Policy and The Big Issue in Scotland, pp. 34–42.

Patton, L. and C. Starrs (1998), 'Scots news bid hit for six', *The Herald*, 11 December, p. 2.

Paxman, J. (1998), *The English: A Portrait of a People*, London: Michael Joseph.

Penman, J. (1997), 'Should Scots Parliament have a lobby system?', *The Scotsman*, 22 October, p. 6.

Philo, G. and D. Miller (2000), *Market Killing: What the Free Market does and what Social Scientists can do about it*, London: Longman.

Porter, Henry (1995), 'Crowd control', *The Guardian G2*, 12 October, pp. 2–3.

Pottinger, G. (1979), *The Secretaries of State for Scotland, 1926–76*, Edinburgh: Scottish Academic Press.

Preston, P. (1998), 'Breaking news', *The Guardian*, 7 September, p. 14.

Press Gazette (2000), 'National newspaper ABC circulations, September 2000', 20 October, p. 6.

PR Week (1995), 'Top 150 PR Consultancies', *PR Week* Supplement, 28 April, p. 17.

PR Week, (2000), 'Scottish lobbying isn't cleared yet', 28 January, p. 10.

Rafferty, J. (1999), 'Startling blueprint that led to the sack', *The Times*, 15 December, p. 11.

RAJAR (2000), *Quarterly Summary*, June 2000. www.rajar.co.uk/summar/002/summarytable.cfm.

Ramsay, H. (1998), 'Spin Doc "No Quit Plans"', *The Mirror*, 7 December, p. 2.

Rawnsley, A. (2000), *Servants of the People: The Inside Story of New Labour*, London: Hamish Hamilton.

Reed, D. (2000), 'Highland race', *Marketing Week*, 11 May, p. 55.

Reekie, C. (1991), 'Concern over Scottish Office publicity costs', *Glasgow Herald*, 2 March, p. 9.

Richards, D. (1997), *The Civil Service under the Conservatives 1979–1997: Whitehall's Political Poodles?*, Brighton: Sussex Academic Press.

Riddell, P. (1999), 'A shift of power and influence', *British Journalism Review*, vol. 10, no. 3, pp. 26–33.

Ritchie, M. (1998a), 'Comment', *The Herald*, 13 February, p. 6.

Ritchie, M. (1998b), 'A promising glimpse into the future', *The Herald*, 9 April, p. 7.

Ritchie, M. (1998c), 'Split on devolved news', *The Herald*, 16 October, p. 3.

Ritchie, M. (1999), 'New man at policy unit as chief of staff title axed', *The Herald*, 28 May, p. 7.

Ritchie, M. (2000a), *Scotland Reclaimed: The Inside Story of Scotland's First Democratic Parliamentary Election*, Edinburgh: The Saltire Society.

Ritchie, M. (2000b), 'McLeish makes strategic choice', *The Herald*, 16 December, p. 3.

Ritchie, M. and R. Dinwoodie (2000), 'McLeish draws first blood among old guard', *The Herald*, 26 October, p. 1.

Robins, J. (1998), 'Scotland denied own BBC news', *The Independent*, 21 November, p. 5.

Rosie, G. (2000), 'Holyrood can hold its own against the London rowdies', *Sunday Herald*, 13 August, p. 9.

Ross, F. (1999), 'Where the cameras can't go', *New Statesman*, 18 October, pp. 38–9.

Routledge, P. (1999), *Mandy: The Unauthorised Biography of Peter Mandelson*, London: Pocket Books.

Salmond, A. (1996), 'Lobbyists must be banned from Parliament now', *The Herald*, 9 October, p. 16.

Sampson, A. (1971), *The New Anatomy of Britain*, London: Hodder and Stoughton.

Scammell, M. (1995), *Designer Politics: How Elections are Won*, Basingstoke: Macmillan.

Scannell P. and D. Cardiff (1991), *A Social History of British Broadcasting*, vol. 1, 'Serving the Nation, 1922–1939', Oxford: Basil Blackwell.

Schlesinger, P. (1978), *Putting 'Reality' Together: BBC News*, London: Constable.

Schlesinger, P. (1990), 'Rethinking the sociology of journalism, source strategies and the limits of media-centrism', in M. Ferguson (ed.) *Public Communication: The New Imperatives*, London: Sage.

Schlesinger, P. (1992), 'Europeanness – A New Cultural Battlefield?', *Innovation in Social Sciences Research*, vol. 5, no. 2, pp. 11–23.

Schlesinger, P. and H. Tumber (1994), *Reporting Crime*, Oxford: Clarendon.

Schlesinger, P. (1998), 'Scottish devolution and the media' in J. Seaton (ed.) *Politics and the Media: Harlots and Prerogatives at the Turn of the Millennium*, Oxford: Blackwell, pp. 55–74.

Schlesinger, P. (1999), 'Changing spaces of political communication: the case of the European Union', *Political Communication*, vol.16, no. 3, pp. 263–79.

Schlesinger, P. (2000), 'The nation and communicative space' in H. Tumber (ed.), *Media Power, Professionals and Policies*, London and New York: Routledge, pp. 99–115.

Scotland Act 1998, Chapter 46, London: The Stationery Office.

Scotland on Sunday (1998), 'Profile: John McCormick: Will his calm approach do the trick?', *Scotland on Sunday*, 29 November, p. 17.

Scotsman (1995), 'The Forsyth Saga', *The Scotsman*, 6 July, p. 14.

Scotsman (1997), 'His master's voice', *The Scotsman*, 3 December, p. 16.

Scott, D. (1999a), 'Holyrood standards committee looks at lobby firm regulation', *The Scotsman*, 9 November, p. 4.

Scott, D. (1999b), 'CBI Scotland sets up Holyrood parliament watchdog', *The Scotsman*, 20 May, p. 25.

Scott, D. (2000), 'Executive to set up high-tech response to media "distortion"', *The Scotsman*, 29 April, p. 5.

Scott, M. (1999), 'Dewar aide's stepson is on the run after drugs charge; fugitive fled to sun', *Sunday Mail*, 21 November, p. 5.

Scottish Civic Forum (2000), Summer Plenary, Information Pack, 10 June.

SCVO (1999), *Guide to the Scottish Parliament*, Edinburgh: SCVO.

Scottish Daily Express (2000), '"Scapegoat" claims as MSP image-maker is moved', 11 May, p. 6.

Scottish Executive (1999a), *Facing the Media, Course Notes,* internal document.

Scottish Executive (1999b), 'First Minister backs spokesman', News Release, SE0178/99, 28 July. http://www.scotland.gov.uk/news/releas99_7/se0178.htm.

Scottish Executive (1999c), *An Open Scotland,* Edinburgh: Scottish Executive. http://www.scotland.gov.uk/library2/doc07/opsc-01.htm.

Scottish Executive (1999d), 'Ministers join call for lobby firm probe', News Release, SE0715/99, 26 September. http://www.scotland.gov.uk/news/releas99_9/se0715.htm.

Scottish Executive (1999e), 'Statement from Donald Dewar', News Release, SE0716/99, 26 September. http://www.scotland.gov.uk/news/releas99_9/se0716.htm.

Scottish Executive (2000), *Report on Use of Public Relations Organisations by Scottish Public Bodies since 1 July 1999,* report lodged in the Scottish Parliament Information Centre (SPICe) 19 January.

Scottish Office (1997a), *Scotland's Parliament,* presented to Parliament by the Secretary of State for Scotland by Command of Her Majesty, July, Cm 3658, Edinburgh: The Stationery Office.

Scottish Office (1997b), *Scottish Parliament, Building User Brief,* TCR03001.018.

Scottish Office (1997c), 'Roger Williams appointed Director of Information', *News Release,* 1904/97, 2 December.

Scottish Office (1999), 'Dewar urge voters "Have Your Say in May"', News Release, 0319/99, 14 February. www.scotland.gov.uk/news/release99_2/pr0319.htm.

Scottish Office DevCom Team (1998), *The Scottish Office Devolution Communications Strategy,* version 2, 9 October.

Scottish Office Video Production Unit (1997), *To-day the Scottish Office Announced . . .,* Edinburgh: The Scottish Office.

Scottish Parliament (1999), *Official Report,* vol. 2, no. 10, cols 939–43, 30 September.

Scottish Parliament (2000a), *Journalists at the Scottish Parliament: Code of Conduct,* Edinburgh: Parliament Media Relations Office.

Scottish Parliament (2000b), *Official Report,* 27 vol. 6, no. 2, cols. 160–1, 27 April.

Scottish Parliament (2000c), *Lobbying in the Scottish Parliament: Standards Committee Consultation Paper,* SP Paper 200, October pp. 1–8. www.scottish.parliament.uk/official_report/cttee/stan-00/st-consult.htm.

Scottish TV (1999), 'Politics Style', Fross/dec.99/ministers/captions, December.

Seenan, G. and E. MacAskill (1999), 'Labour risks turmoil when spin doctors go', *The Guardian,* 5 May, p. 10.

Silverstein, K. (1998), *Washington on $10 Million a Day: How Lobbyists*

Plunder the Nation, Monroe, ME: Common Courage Press.

Smith, I. (1998), 'BBC delays its final decision on Scots-based news plan', *The Scotsman*, 22 October, p. 2.

Smith, M. (1994), *Paper Lions: The Scottish Press and National Identity*, Edinburgh: Polygon.

SPJA (1999), Scottish Parliamentary Journalists' Association, 'Media Access to Scottish Executive', 15 June.

SPJA (2000), Constitution of the Scottish Parliamentary Journalists' Association, 28 March.

SPPA (1998a), Draft Constitution of the Scottish Parliamentary Press Association.

SPPA (1998b), *Scottish Parliament, Building User Brief.* A Response by the Scottish Parliamentary Press Association, January.

Standards Committee (1999), *Report of an inquiry into matters brought to the attention of the Committee by* The Observer *newspaper*, first report, SP paper 27, ST/99/RI, 19 November.

Standards Committee (2000), Papers for meeting 13, 12 September, Lobbying ST/00/13/1, http://www.scottish.parliament.uk/official_report/cttee/stan-00/stp00-13.pdf

Stauber, J. and S. Rampton (1995), *Toxic Sludge is Good for You: Lies, Damn Lies and the Public Relations Industry*, Monroe, ME: Common Courage Press.

Stead, J. (1985), 'BBC accused of bias by Scottish Tories', *The Guardian*, 7 May, p. 30.

Stevenson, S. (1998), 'You must be squeaky clean in the lobby', *The Herald*, 14 April, p. 11.

Stokes, R. (1996), 'PR firms bank on home rule', *Scotland on Sunday*, 19 May, p. 4.

Stokes, R. (2000), 'Russell fires warning shot over SMG plans for radio', *The Scotsman*, Business Section, p. 1.

Sunday Mail, (1998), 'Dewar's Scottish Six claim slammed', *Sunday Mail*, 13 December, p. 2.

Sunday Times (2000), 'Roger Williams', 30 April, p. 21.

Swanson, I. (1997), 'Roger's new spin on government', *Evening News*, 3 December, p. 8.

System Three (1998), Election for the Scottish Parliament: Awareness and Attitude Tracking, Wave 1, October, prepared for the Scottish Office Central Research Unit, 4 November.

Tait, R. (1999a), 'Brown's boys in control at Delta House', *The Scotsman*, 19 April, p. 11.

Tait, R. (1999b), 'Dewar to stamp on leaks by ministers', *The Scotsman*, 6 July, p. 1.

Tait, R. (1999c), 'Open government? Oh no it isn't', *The Scotsman*, 9 July, p. 21.

Tait, R. (1999d), 'Dewar in withering attack on ministers', *The Scotsman*, 27 July, p. 1.

Tait, R. (1999e), 'Lobbygate crisis deepens', *The Scotsman*, 1 October, p. 1.

Taylor, B. (1999), *The Scottish Parliament*, Edinburgh: Polygon at Edinburgh.

Teather, D. (2000a), 'Interview, Andrew Flanagan, chief executive, SMG: the media tycoon Soho forgot', *The Guardian*, 26 August, p. 34.

Teather, D. (2000b), 'Scottish radio signals start of takeover trend', *The Guardian*, 21 December, p. 25.

Thompson, M. (1999), 'This country of nations', *Media Guardian*, 17 May, p. 5.

Thynne, J. (1988), 'Government adverts "regularly ruled as not acceptable"', *Daily Telegraph*, 20 April, p. 11.

TMA (1989), *Summary of a Survey of Public Relations in Scotland*, June, Glasgow: Tony Meehan Associates.

Tulloch, J. (1993), 'Policing the public sphere: the British machinery of news management', *Media, Culture and Society*, vol. 15, no. 3, pp. 363–84.

Tunstall, J. (1970), *The Westminster Lobby Correspondents*, London: RKP.

Vaughan, M. (1995), 'Neutrality that means saying "No, Minister"', *The Herald*, 11 October, p. 13.

Veitch, J. (2000), 'Doctor who will spin for Deacon', *Evening News*, 22 June, p. 15.

Vidal, J. and Bellos, A. (1996), 'Protest lobbies unite to guard rights', *The Guardian*, 27 August, p. 5.

Walker, D. (1996), 'Under the public eye', *Independent*, 10 September, p. 20.

Walker, D. (2000), 'Newspaper power, a practitioner's account', in H. Tumber (ed.), *Media, Power, Professionals and Policies*, London and New York: Routledge, pp. 236–46.

Watson, I. (1999a), 'Salmond v the killing machine', *Sunday Herald*, 25 April, p. 9.

Watson, I. (1999b), 'Young guns to put new spin on Scots Cabinet', *Sunday Herald*, 20 June, p. 2.

Wells, M. (1998), 'BBC kills hopes for Scottish evening news slot', *The Scotsman*, 7 October, p. 1.

Wells, M. and A. Hardie (1998), 'BBC chiefs resigned to defeat over Scottish Six', *The Scotsman*, 10 December, p. 7.

Wernick, A. (1991), *Promotional Culture: Advertising, Ideology and Symbolic Expression*, London: Sage.

White, C., A. Hedges. and B. Seyd (1999), *New Electoral Systems: What Voters Need to Know*, March 1999, London: SCPR/Constitution Unit.

Williams, C. (2000), 'Knock-on effects BBC moves news', *Business a.m.*, 4 October, www.businessam.co.uk.TodaysPaper.

Wilson, S. (1999), *Proposals for a Freedom of Information Act for Scotland*, June, Glasgow: Scottish Human Rights Centre.

Wishart, R. (1998), 'New approach needed to broadcasting', Letters, *The Scotsman*, 28 November, p. 15.

Wishart, R. (1999), 'Scots guide has McGaffes galore', *The Herald*, 27 August, pp. 1–2.

Wood, E. and M. Higgins (1999), *Scottish Corporate Communications Survey 1999, Internal Communications Trends*, Edinburgh: Carter Rae Communications.

Woodhouse, D. (1998), 'The Parliamentary Commissioner for Standards: lessons from the "Cash for Questions" Inquiry', *Parliamentary Affairs*, vol. 51, no. 1, pp. 51–61.

Wright, K. (1997), *The People Say Yes: The Making of Scotland's Parliament*, Glendaruel: Argyll Publishing.

Wyatt, W. and M. Byford (1998), Commentary on the Broadcasting Council for Scotland and Broadcasting Council for Wales Reports.

Young, A. (1995), 'When arithmetic gets in the way of rhetoric', *The Herald*, 10 October, p. 23.

Index